CITIES OF THE 21ST CENTURY

NEW TECHNOLOGIES AND SPATIAL SYSTEMS

Edited by
John Brotchie, Michael Batty, Peter Hall & Peter Newton

Longman Cheshire

HALSTED
PRESS

An imprint of John Wiley & Sons, Inc., New York

Published in Australia by
Longman Cheshire Pty Limited
Longman House, Kings Gardens
95 Coventry Street
Melbourne 3205 Australia

Offices in Sydney, Brisbane, Adelaide and Perth. Associated companies,
branches and representatives throughout the world.

Published in the United Kingdom by
Longman Group UK Ltd
Longman House, Burnt Mill, Harlow
Essex CM20 2JE

Published in the United States of America by
Halsted Press: An imprint of John Wiley & Sons, Inc.,
605 Third Avenue, New York, NY 10158-0012

Copyright © Longman Cheshire 1991
First published 1991

National Library of Australia
Cataloguing-in-Publication data

Cities of the 21st Century.
Bibliography.
Includes index.
ISBN 0 582 87126 3

1. City planning. I. Brotchie, J.F. (John F.).
307.76

Library of Congress Cataloguing-in-Publication Data

Cities of the 21st century, new technologies and spatial systems
John Brotchie ... [et al].
p. cm.
Includes bibliographical references and index.
ISBN 0-470-21742-1
1. Cities and towns– –Effect of technological innovations on–
–Congresses. 2. Cities and towns– –Forecasting– –Congresses.
3. Technological innovations– -Economic aspects– –Congresses.
4. Space and economics– –Congresses. I. Brotchie, J.F.II. Title:
Cities of the 21st century.
HT107.C44 1991
307.76– –dc20

British Library Cataloguing in Publication data
A cataloguing in Publication record for this book is available from the British Library.

CONTENTS

EDITORS AND CONTRIBUTORS

Editors

Dr John F. Brotchie

Chief Research Scientist
Commonwealth Scientific & Industrial
Research Organisation, Melbourne

Prof. Michael Batty

Associate Director
National Center for Geographic Information &
Analysis, State University of New York,
Buffalo

Prof. Peter Hall

Director
Institute of Urban & Regional Development,
University of California, Berkeley

Dr Peter W. Newton

Senior Principal Research Scientist
Commonwealth Scientific & Industrial
Research Organisation, Melbourne

Contributors

Prof. Kozo Amano

Department of Transportation Engineering,
Kyoto University, Kyoto

Prof. Edward Blakely

Department of City & Regional Planning,
University of California, Berkeley

Mr Philip Cooke

Department of City & Regional Planning,
University of Wales, Cardiff

Prof. Peter Daniels

Department of Geography,
Portsmouth Polytechnic, Portsmouth

Dr Mark Dodgson

Science Policy Research Unit,
University of Sussex, Brighton

Prof. Marshall Feldman

Department of Community Planning,
University of Rhode Island, Kingston

Dr Joanne Fox-Przeworski   Urban Affairs Division, OECD, Paris

Prof. John Goddard   Centre for Urban & Regional Development Studies, University of Newcastle-Upon-Tyne, Newcastle-Upon-Tyne

Mr Andrew Gillespie   Centre for Urban & Regional Development Studies, University of Newcastle-Upon-Tyne, Newcastle-Upon-Tyne

Prof. Britton Harris   Department of City & Regional Planning, University of Pennsylvania, Philadelphia

Dr Mark Hepworth   Centre for Urban & Regional Development Studies, University of Newcastle-Upon-Tyne, Newcastle-Upon-Tyne

Prof. Denis Maillat   IRER, University of Neuchatel, Neuchatel

Dr Thomas Mandeville   Department of Economics, University of Queensland, Brisbane

Prof. Richard Meier   College of Environmental Design, University of California, Berkeley

Prof. William Melody   Centre for International Research on Communication & Information Technologies, Melbourne

Mr Ian Miles   Science Policy Research Unit, University of Sussex, Brighton

Prof. Mitchell Moss   Wagner Graduate School of Public Service, New York University, New York

Dr Dai Nakagawa   Department of Transportation Engineering, Kyoto University, Kyoto

Dr Keith Newton   Economic Council of Canada, Ottawa

Prof. Peter Nijkamp   Faculty of Economics, Free University, Amsterdam

Dr Adriaan Perrels

Economic & Social Institute,
Free University, Amsterdam

Prof. Peter Rimmer

Department of Human Geography Research,
School of Pacific Studies, Australian National
University, Canberra

Mr Kevin Robins

Centre for Urban & Regional Development
Studies, University of Newcastle-Upon-Tyne,
Newcastle-Upon-Tyne

Prof. Roy Rothwell

Science Policy Research Unit,
University of Sussex, Brighton

Mr John Taylor

Department of Organisation, Management &
Employment Relations, University of Strathclyde,
Glasgow

Prof. Tsunekazu Toda

Institute of Regional Economics,
Hiroshima University, Hiroshima

Prof. AnnaLee Saxenian

Department of City & Regional Planning,
University of California, Berkeley

Dr Peter Wells

Cardiff Business School,
University of Wales College of Cardiff, Cardiff

Prof. Howard Williams

Management Science Department,
University of Strathclyde, Glasgow

PREFACE

Early in the twenty-first century, economy and society will complete their rapid transition to the information age. The industrial city of the late nineteenth and early twentieth centuries will rapidly become an artifact from the past, to be visited in the form of an open-air museum like New York's South Street Seaport or The Rocks district of Sydney, while our lives become increasingly dependent upon information technologies. Already the majority of us work at pursuits which involve the processing of information; and, as manufacturing industries become ever more automated, our society will be driven no longer (as in the past industrial age) by energy, but by media based directly upon information technologies.

Neither information technology nor communications technology is new; the telegraph was an invention of 1837, an effective office typewriter was available by 1873. But what is new, in the late twentieth century, is a massive convergence in information and communication technologies which have hitherto been quite separate. The convergence of computers and telecommunications; the emergence of new forms of physical communications, as, for example, in the new transport technologies associated with fast rail; new forms of building, in which information is being used to enable 'intelligent' responses to physical change. These are but some of the trends which are changing the face of our society. Moreover, another convergence – the synthesis of technologies based on energy with information through automatic control and computer-aided design and manufacturing – continues to have a profound impact on the structure of employment and the provision of services.

The most obvious impacts of these changes are on the physical form of our cities. The traditional pattern of urban land use, in which residential activity is clustered around nodes of employment which maximise accessibility, has been breaking down now for well over fifty years as the widespread proliferation of the automobile has provided a new dimension in personal transport. These changes, combined with more rapid and cheaper forms of telecommunications, have increasingly made cities dependent upon economies which transcend the nation state, thus enabling local-to-global communications which had hitherto been unimagined. But not only do these technologies enable existing processes and practices to be executed more efficiently and often at less cost, they also generate new opportunities, which in turn lead to new patterns of behaviour, new practices and new institutions. Far from simply enabling old technologies to be substituted for new, the emergence of the information society has heralded new ways of communicating which allow a much wider section of the urban population to interact purposefully.

Yet the impact of this new-found freedom on our cities is constrained by the parallel emergence of new forms of organisation and control, which are often difficult to identify. The development of an on-line economy, which finds its most dramatic expression in the world's stock exchanges and the emergence of a market in information, is only the most spectacular example of forces constraining these new freedoms. Moreover, these are also serving to segment society into new classes, such as those who are increasingly information-rich in contrast to those who are becoming information-poor. Many of these trends are difficult to trace: they have an 'invisibility' to sustained research, never found in the earlier industrial age when urban life was 'simpler' and seemingly more transparent. With the development of new political alliances in Europe and the Pacific Rim, and the deregulation of markets such as telecommunications which were traditionally under the remit of the state, research into the impact of these new information technologies on cities is complicated further still.

In this book, we will attempt to explore these diverse themes, and to provide some insights into the way new technologies are beginning to have an impact on the structure and form of cities. The book forms the third in a series developed to evaluate the spatial and urban impacts of new technologies, a project sponsored and financed for the International Council for Building Research by the CIB Working Commission 72. The first, edited by Brotchie, Newton, Hall and Nijkamp, and published in 1985, outlined the development of transport, communication and information technologies and their industrial and urban impacts. The second, edited by Brotchie, Hall and Newton, and published in 1987, examined the nature of new high-tech industries and their incubation, spatial distribution and location needs, in the wider context of the transition from an industrial to an information economy. This third volume considers the expected impacts of these information, communication and transport technologies on the information society in general and the information city in particular. The chapters which follow will address the ways in which technology is providing new forms of communication, both in terms of physical networks and in the way people, goods and information are likely to interact and communicate. We will emphasise how these networks are enriching existing activities and enabling new opportunities, how local and global urban economies are changing, and how new industrial structures and work practices are having an impact on patterns of urban employment.

We have organised the contributions into four parts. First we concentrate on the nature of the new transport technologies and on their spatial impact; secondly, in parallel, we consider the new information and communication technologies. The third part of the book introduces contemporary thinking on new forms of technology-based settlement; while in the fourth and final part, the authors address the spatial impact of high-tech industries and the emergence of policies to enable them to be most effectively developed.

We begin with new transport technologies for the high-speed movement of people and information. These include the fast-rail systems already operating in Japan and Europe, the experimental MAGnetic LEVitation-linear motor (maglev) systems and the vacuum tunnels being proposed in various countries. The fast-rail systems are both complementary to, and competitive with, air transport and high-speed inter-city roads, and are increasing in operating speed and network size. Over 20 000 kilometres of new and upgraded lines are planned for Europe alone. The TGV Atlantique, for example, is currently operating at 300 kilometres per hour and design speeds of up to 350 kilometres per hour are planned on new routes, while maximum speeds in test runs already exceed 500 kilometres per hour.

New forms of guided transport beyond fast rail are being considered for the most congested routes. Maglev is proposed for higher speeds in the Tokyo–Osaka corridor, allowing greatly reduced travel times as compared with the existing Shinkansen, and providing further levels of integration and development for the cities en route. The proposed vacuum tunnel system, with potential for even higher speeds, involves the concept of intercity travel in air-evacuated tunnels or tubes. It is in effect a form of (inner) space travel through lowered atmospheric densities – similar to those of outer space, and allowing equivalent potential speeds. Its guidance and propulsion could be maglev. It is considered primarily for travel within Europe where surface travel is made difficult by existing urban development and environmental considerations. However, greater distances such as London to New York could be possible on such a system in the next century, as automation reduces tunnelling costs and times, and as international barriers to travel continue to diminish.

These transport modes are complemented by – but are also in competition with – global telecommunications systems such as electronic mail (email), facsimile transmission (fax), and fast, broadband digital networks; systems which are competing with each other. User-friendliness and network compatibility are proving as important as speed and technical sophistication within these media. Thus fax is presently in much wider use than email, and fast wheel-on-rail networks are spreading in Europe and Japan, thereby reducing the opportunities for the introduction of maglev. Telecommunications traffic is clearly increasing at a much faster rate than passenger travel, but both are continuing to increase rapidly, indicating that they may be more complementary than competitive. Optical fibres, satellites, and fast packet switching, as well as a wide range of interactive facilities such as intelligent terminals, are increasing the scope and capacity of telecommunications. These systems, together with fast transport, are facilitating an increasing coordination of information-based industries and their management, support and distribution systems.

The cities at the hubs of these networks are generally the first to be connected through new technologies. They thereby gain a clear advantage as global and regional nodes for the exchange of information and knowledge. Other nodes on these networks appear to be affected differently, depending on their mix of industries and services and on the nature of their network connections. These issues are important in assessing the impact of the new technologies. For example, in Japan, a distinction is made between fast rail, fast road and a combination of the two. Fast rail in Japan is an exclusively passenger-carrying mode, and has been found to stimulate the growth of information-based industries. Freeways or a combination of fast rail and road also facilitate the movement of materials and goods, and thus facilitate the growth of manufacturing industries. The impacts in Europe, where fast rail has had a shorter history, are less well defined. In contrast, the proposal to link a system of major cities in the Tokyo–Osaka corridor by maglev is likely to bring these cities much closer together, thus forming an integrated regional daily system relating business, urban living and recreational activities; in short, it will help form an articulated supercity extending from Tokyo to Osaka.

The international impact of these new technologies is also of some importance. Global networks are being extended to embrace an ever wider set of nodal cities, while the emergence of the idea of a high-tech city somewhat independent of its parent system is currently finding favour. For example, the proposed Australian 'multi-function polis' is being marketed by the Japanese as a living and working environment similar to their indigenous 'technopolis concept' which is based upon precompetitive high-technology R&D and on an integrated recreational and living environment. Plans for such developments include a number of sites in South-East Asia and in Australia. This concept of an international high-tech city will only be viable if new attitudes regarding the cooperative development of new technologies emerge. The changing nature of interactions between firms in high-tech industries, both at local and global levels, is another critical theme in adoption of the new technologies; it is accompanied by the development of alliances across these levels for information and knowledge sharing, as the sophistication and integration of these technologies grows. The multi-function polis would appear to provide a further venue for the sharing of information and new technologies at both the local and international levels.

The increasing speeds and capacities of global travel and communications bring an increasing awareness of the finite nature of our planet and its limited capacity to digest our wastes, whether on land, in water or in the air. The limits to growth in the 1990s and beyond are not likely to be so much resource-bound, as we feared in the 1970s, but receptor-bound. The impact of these capacity constraints may well shift the balance between various trans-port modes even further, with the emergence of more energy- and emission-efficient forms like fast rail. The substitution of telecommunications for travel, knowledge and information for labour and energy-intensive capital, as well as the evolution of more sustainable and emission-controlled energy forms, will all change the patterns and ways by which we communicate, as the traditional locations of land uses and activities become more footloose.

Cities in the twenty-first century will be linked by better communications and travel, as the new information technologies help to dissolve international barriers and hasten new forms of political alliance and cooperation. New trade routes will emerge on the continental and world scales, as global patterns of accessibility are changed by these new networks. The fortunes of these world cities, and those that depend on them at lower levels in their local hierarchy, will clearly be determined by both their traditional and new roles as hubs or central nodes shaping the trunk lines of these networks, as well as by their natural resources and attributes, energy sources and urban amenities. Cities themselves will become increasingly multi-centred around information-based industries, and the development of local centres will help to shorten travel generally and commuting distances in particular. And recreational facilities may be expected to be increasingly important components in (and between) these centres, as the quality of life increases in importance in the hierarchy of human need.

These profound changes require the development of entirely new policies at national and international level. Until now, urban and regional planning policies have been developed in response to the industrial age that is ending. During the 1980s, a number of countries have made major shifts in their information and communications policies – most notably, the partial deregu-lation of telecommunications and of broadcasting – apparently without any consideration for their impact on the competitive fate of cities and regions. As a number of our contributors independently stress, these impacts are already large and are likely to become larger. In particular, they may well give a massive advantage to the largest and most central urban areas at the expense of smaller cities and peripheral regions – thus often flying in the face of traditional regional policies. Further, especially in the mosaic of nation states which make up Europe, the impacts are felt right across national frontiers. Here, our contributors' research results in a direct challenge to national governments and supernational agencies, which they will ignore at their peril.

1

MOVING INFORMATION:
A TALE OF FOUR TECHNOLOGIES

Peter Hall

INTRODUCTION

This is the age of the informational economy. Information-handling industries and activities represent the fastest growing sectors in so-called advanced industrial economies, and may soon account for most employment in them. During the period 1973–83, while the United States lost over a million manufacturing jobs, it gained nearly five million goods-handling service jobs but no less than eleven million new information-processing jobs; the United Kingdom, which lost over two million manufacturing jobs and no less than 2.6 million overall in goods-handling industries, recorded a gain in information services of less than 1.4 million. Thus, in Britain, the growth of information jobs was only 53 per cent of the decline in industry and goods-handling services combined; while the American economy generated growth in both goods handling and information handling, though the latter was far greater (Hall 1987a, p. 97).

Longer-term analysis of a wider spectrum of countries (Nijkamp & Giaoutzi 1988; Figure 1) shows the same trend. By 1980, informational jobs constituted 50 per cent of all employment in the United States (Nijkamp 1988, p. 26). A large-scale 1981 study by OECD indicated that in France, Germany and the United Kingdom there had been a 2.8 per cent increase in share of information workers every five years; this has been updated for the early 1980s at 2.3 per cent (Howells 1988, p. 24). As Howells (1988, p. 175) puts it, 'Information services have become a key element in the growth and development of the European economy'.

The growth of the informational economy is closely related to (though not precisely equivalent to) the growth in producer service employment, which – depending on definition – included between 4.5 and 5 million jobs or 22 to 24 per cent of total employment in Britain by the mid-1980s. The share is

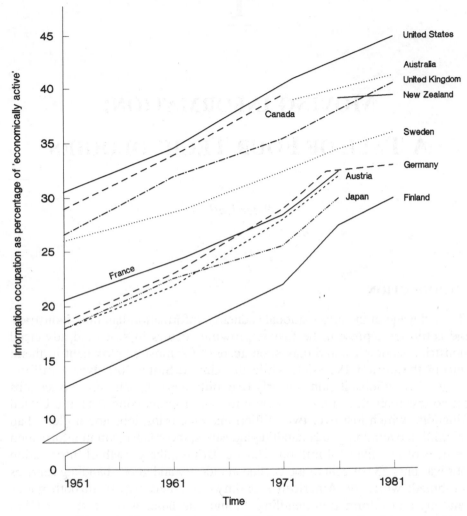

*Figure 1 Changes in the share of 'information occupations' in
all 'economically active' countries since 1950.*

growing, for two possible reasons: first, an increasing level of intermediate
service inputs for any level of output; second, lower productivity growth in the
office-based service sectors than in other sectors of the economy (Marshall
et al. 1988, pp. 27, 41). Similar results are reported for Germany (Ochel &
Wegner 1987, pp. 72–6).

THE LOCATIONAL DILEMMA: CONCENTRATION VERSUS DISPERSAL

Traditionally, service industries have been supposed to follow the distribution
of the population and thus, implicitly, the distribution of goods-producing and
goods-handling industry. But, though consumer services are thus distributed,
producer services are as highly concentrated as manufacturing. In Britain,
they are traditionally concentrated in and around London and the other major

cities, and this has continued: in banking, insurance and financial services, 49 per cent of growth in the 1970s went to the south-east region. It also appears that the higher-level services are concentrated in the south-east everywhere, though there is very marked deconcentration from larger centres to smaller places around them. On present trends, by the early 1990s there will be more commercial office floorspace in the rest of the south-east (i.e. outside central London) than in central London itself (Daniels 1986, pp. 300, 306; Marshall *et al*. 1988, pp. 63, 73, 177, 198; Gillespie & Green 1987, p. 404).

So researchers in this field are still groping for an adequate locational theory. It will probably come, as it is coming elsewhere, from a reinterpretation of traditional neoclassical theory with insights drawn from the political economy tradition. In Britain, recent work concludes that the observed patterns and trends cannot be explained simply in terms of rents or communications costs; rather, the shape of the corporate hierarchy is crucial, with national head-quarters and many administrative research and technical functions in the south and east, and branch offices carrying out production activities or serving local markets elsewhere (Marshall *et al*. 1988, p. 198). Banking and insurance have decentralised away from London but gone to smaller labour markets in the south-east and in the secondary financial market of the north-west; but the growth of international trade in financial, engineering, oil and consultancy services has encouraged growth in and close to London, because of its unique international airports and other communications links, as well as its special-ised labour pool and services (Daniels 1986, p. 310; Marshall *et al*. 1988, pp. 199–200).

The conclusion therefore is that structural changes – above all, the increasing globalisation of capital and scale of producer service firms – massively reinforce traditional neoclassical location economies. There is a kind of Weberian triangle for the information industries, depending on the costs of information transfer, whether in the form of packages, or electronic impulses, or the physical movement of brains and the rather weightier bodies that unfortunately have to travel with them. There is also an equivalent for Weber's agglomeration principle: it consists not only in the traditional economies stemming from a range of specialised services, markets and pools of labour, but also in a process of constant innovation in what the late Philipe Aydalot (1986a; 1986b; 1988; Aydalot & Keeble 1988a; 1988b) called an innovative milieu. The concept goes quite beyond the static framework of neoclassical economics: it hinges on the processes first identified by Joseph Schumpeter (1911), in a work ironically published exactly two years after Weber's (1909), and then deepened by him in his best-known works of the 1930s and 1940s (Schumpeter 1939; 1942).

There is an apt academic example. A researcher studying a new topic has a range of choices. He or she may start in the local university library. The density of such information has a very steep spatial gradient, which descends very rapidly from information-rich places like London and Greater Boston down to smaller and more isolated university cities: in Britain there is one

Matterhorn peak in London–Oxford–Cambridge (Figure 2), in the United
States a whole series of smaller summits (Hall 1987b). A researcher not
resident in one of these agglomerative centres will need either to travel there
or, alternatively, conduct an expensive computer search and obtain materials
by inter-library loan. But this will of course miss the 'unprogrammed' information that comes from browsing on library shelves, or from colleagues met
outside the library.

This homely example suggests two rules of information transfer:
1 Movement of information is a substitute for movement of people.
2 It is not a perfect substitute: the information thus obtained may be poorer
  in quantity, quality or both.

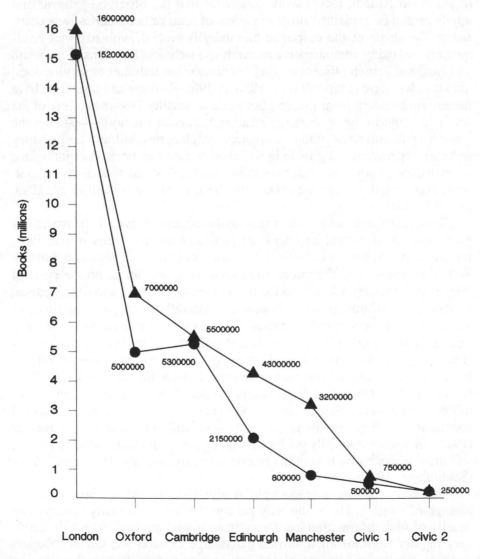

Figure 2 Holdings in selected British libraries.

Thus big centres offer great agglomeration economies in acquisition of information, though they clearly demonstrate the usual negative externalities also. And it is the kind of information obtained in this way that is most likely to lead to fundamental innovations. Conferences are temporary innovative milieus, but great intellectual cities are permanent ones (Andersson 1985a; 1985b; Andersson & Strömquist 1988; Aydalot 1986a; 1986b; Aydalot & Keeble 1988a; 1988b).

This suggests that the growth of the informational economy ought to be accompanied by a growth of the economies of the highest-order centres. And, if these are redefined to include the subsidiary centres around them – as in the case of London – empirical evidence suggests that in some cases this is true. Yet other evidence, from America (Noyelle & Stanback 1984; Stanback 1985) and more recently from Europe (Cheshire & Hay 1988), seems to suggest that intermediate-level service centres – the regional nodal centres in the Noyelle–Stanback terminology, the small national capitals and major regional cities in the Cheshire–Hay analysis – are performing best in the transition to the informational-service economy. And this is supported also by deductive speculation that technological change, in the form of rapid adoption of New Information Technology (NIT) will release much informational activity from its dependence on high accessibility centres, as well as greater speed and lower costs of personal movement.

This paper makes no general attempt to resolve this bundle of issues. Instead, it tries to make a partial contribution by looking at some specific recent areas where technological substitution seems to be occurring, and may be about to occur even more rapidly, in information transfer between people. Particularly, it looks at:

- two technologies for the movement of people: air versus the high-speed train (HST). Under the latter head, it looks at alternative HST technologies: steel wheel on rail versus maglev (magnetic levitation);
- two technologies for the movement of information: specialist postal services versus electronic mail. And again, under the latter head, it looks at alternatives: 'pure' email versus fax.

The paper will argue two points. First, that in both cases, the outcome of technological competition is odd and even perverse, but that there are good reasons for this. Secondly, that the locational outcome may be actually to reinforce existing patterns.

VARIANTS OF THE HIGH SPEED TRAIN

Though the HST is now much in the news, especially in Europe, the first essential is to understand that there is no such thing; instead, there is a whole array of variants. At one extreme is the upgraded classical railway with improved curves and signalling, but with mixed traffic. Where the original infrastructure is capable of this treatment, as with the western region and east coast mainline of British Rail, it can support dense interval services at 200 and even 225 kilometres per hour. But Britain is unusual in this respect; most European railways were built to far lower standards, so that in Germany speed is restricted to 50 kilometres per hour on 22 per cent of the network, to 70 kilometres per hour on another 40 per cent, and to 80 kilometres per hour on a further 25 per cent (Raschbilder and Wackers 1987, p. 147).

Next is the dedicated new line built for high-speed running, and invariably reserved for HSTs; this model is represented by Japan National Railways' Tokaido Shinkansen, opened as long ago as 1964 between Tokyo and Osaka, and by the later Japanese extensions of the system (Kamada 1980, pp. 52–5; Horiuchi 1989, p. 487). The Shinkansen operates an extremely dense service at 200 kilometres per hour, but considerably higher speeds are now possible on such formation because of improvements in friction technology; the dedicated part of the French TGV-SE operates at 275 kilometres per hour and the TGV-A, which opened late in 1989, achieves 300 kilometres per hour.

The TGV, however, represents an intermediate form, since the dedicated track (the TGV proper) is employed only over densely trafficked corridors, the train then reverting to HST or even lower speeds for the remainder of the journey. It is this intermediate or mixed mode that is almost certain to be used on the future high-speed European network, with a mixture of new and upgraded track. Such a model is already being followed by Deutsche Bundesbahn (DB) in their new north-south corridor between Hamburg and Würzburg, and will certainly also be the case for the proposed Paris–Brussels–Köln link. The 1985 National Transportation Plan, DB intends to build only 783 kilometres of new lines against 1550 kilometres of upgrading (Raschbilder & Wackers, 1987, p. 148). Indeed, one crucial feature of all conventional steel-wheel rail technologies is their ability to use classical track on sections on which new construction is either technically or economically ruled out – as, for instance, TGV-SE uses on the approaches to the Paris and Lyon termini.

At the far end of the spectrum are the magnetic levitation technologies. The German TRANSRAPID uses an attraction system, the Japanese a repulsion system based on lightweight superconducting magnets, or cyrogenic levitation. Both have been the result of long and exhaustive development work, the Japanese since as long ago as 1962, the Germans since 1969 (Rhodes & Mulhall 1981, pp. 70–4; Raschbilder & Wackers 1987, p. 148). TRANSRAPID, which has completed over 35 000 kilometres on its test track in the Emsland, reached a world speed record of 412 kilometres per hour in 1987 and is expected eventually to achieve 500 kilometres per hour in regular service, though its track was closed due to breakdown at the end of 1988. Essentially, however, both require a dedicated track designed on quite different principles from conventional rail technology, with a central magnetic field above which the train levitates.

A critical question therefore is whether it might be possible to create a bivalent system in which maglev trains could descend on to classical track. The German promoters of TRANSRAPID claimed that this would be possible, but there is no evidence of substantiation (Raschbilder & Wackers 1987,

p. 152; Alexy 1987, p. 198); nor, so far, has one come from the Japanese. If not, the track would need to be completely dedicated, without direct running on to classical track, and the costs, particularly of approach to city centres, could prove prohibitive. In Germany, it has been suggested that the system might be used to connect airports, thus essentially acting as a substitute for the congested German internal airways; but the problem of access to the centres would be the same as for the air system today. The Japanese have undertaken to construct a completely new maglev line – the Dai Ni Shinkansen, the Number Two Trunk Line – by the year 2000. Conditions are special: traffic along the Tokaido corridor is so dense, with the existing Shinkansen reaching saturation, that it appears profitable to build a new dedicated line.[1]

Trains versus air

To compare these HST variants with air, we need some basic assumptions. Here we assume that for a city centre to city centre journey, a traveller can reach the station in fifteen minutes and can then reach the train in another five minutes; at the other end, fifteen minutes are allowed to reach the destination. For air, we assume a forty-five minute journey to the airport and another sixty minutes check-in and waiting time, plus five minutes exit and another forty-five minute journey at the destination. The total access and waiting time penalty is thus thirty-five minutes by rail and 155 minutes by air. Some may think this biased against air; we would plead that it represents average western European reality, and makes no allowance for air traffic and weather delays.[2]

On this basis, Figure 3 shows that the break-even distance between HSTs and air is 530 kilometres for a 200 kilometres per hour high speed train, 960 kilometres for a 300 kilometres per hour TGV and 2680 kilometres for the 500 kilometres per hour German or Japanese variants of maglev. The significance of these figures can be appreciated by reference to Figure 4, which shows distances along the major north-west European corridor which is now virtually certain to be the route of the first high-speed service. Table 1 sets out some sample results.

It is clear from this that, though HST is a very satisfactory competitor to air for many shorter-distance links between major metropolitan areas – especially within the same country – the adoption of a European scale immediately pushes the advantage to the TGV technology, which greatly opens up the range of journeys within the most densely urbanised corridor. Indeed, most journeys within this corridor become train journeys, with air reduced to a subsidiary role. Since the European network is certain to be a mixed one, with performance and speeds intermediate between HST and TGV, competition with air is likely to be very fierce at the extremities.

That there will be major effects cannot be in doubt. On the Tokaido Shinkansen, actual traffic growth was far in excess of predictions, nearly double by 1975 (350 000 against 200 000) (Kamada 1980, p. 44). The train halved the time, to three hours and ten minutes between Tokyo and Osaka against two hours and thirty-five minutes by plane, of which fifty minutes is in the air (Kamada 1980, p. 43). After the opening of the Shinkansen, Nagoya Airport was reduced from fifth of eighty-eight to nineteenth; passenger volume shrank to one-quarter and took seven years to return to pre-Shinkansen levels (Sanuki 1980, pp. 235–6). The air travel percentage has remained roughly constant since 1969 (Kamada 1980, p. 45).

In France, traffic on the original TGV-SE rose from 12.2 to 19.2 million passengers between 1980 and 1985, higher than foreseen (7 against 5.5 million); between Paris and St Etienne traffic doubled, between Paris–Lyon it increased two and a half times, and between Paris and Le Creusot/Montchanin, where a new TGV station was opened, it rose no less than 7.2 times (Bonnafous 1987, p. 129). The growth between Paris and Lyon came 30 per cent from air, 18 per cent from road, and 49 per cent from induced traffic (Bonnafous 1987, p. 129). Traffic on the French internal airline, Air Inter, between Paris and Lyon fell by nearly half between 1980 and 1985, and the share of total traffic fell from 48 to 17 per cent; it slowed appreciably between Paris and southeast France, noticeably between Paris and Marseilles, but not at all on other routes radiating from Paris (Berlioz & Leboeuf 1986, p. 764; Bonnafous 1987,

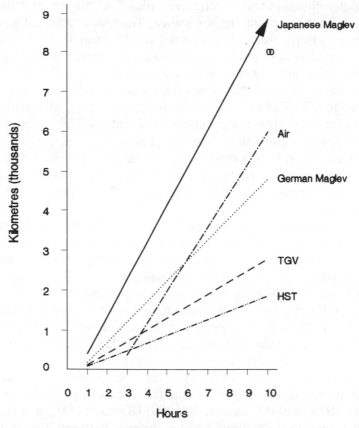

Figure 3 High-speed train versus air.

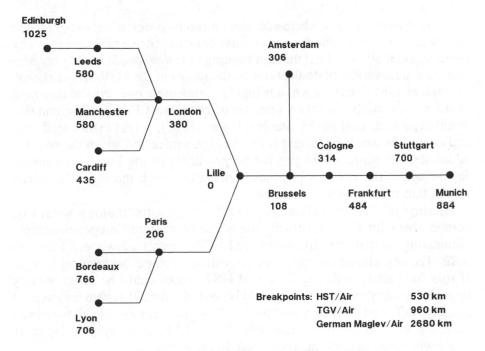

Figure 4 Europe's 'new trunk line'.

Table 1 High speed rail: journeys faster than by air

HST (530 km)	TGV (960 km)	Maglev (2680 km)
Manchester–London	Manchester–Paris	Edinburgh–Madrid
Cardiff–London	[Manchester–Köln]	London–Seville
Leeds–London	Cardiff–Köln	Edinburgh–Warsaw
London–Paris	London–Amsterdam	Lyon–Warsaw
[London–Brussels]	London–Frankfurt	[London–Moscow]
Paris–Köln	Paris–Amsterdam	[Paris–Moscow]
Paris–Frankfurt	Lyon–Brussels	
	[Lyon–Amsterdam]	
	[Lyon–Köln]	

[ ] Journeys marginally over the break-even limit.

p. 130). French investigations show a 45 per cent traffic increase compared with a 'zero-action' situation. The travel times by TGV are about half those of the former service, so that a rough travel-time elasticity of –1.0 can be derived; though these results are not necessarily generalisable (Savelberg & Vogelar 1987, pp. 108–9).

Speed rail as against air thus seems to be the crucial factor in the choice of technologies. Professional railway managers, and some independent researchers, argue strongly for the mixed TGV/HST mode. Though it will be limited to speeds between 200 and 300 kilometres per hour, it can employ sections of existing track where adequate; it can be progressively upgraded to speeds at or near the limit; it requires little or no expensive new access to city centres; and it allows direct through running at lower speeds to give connections to a great variety of destinations, as the model of the TGV-SE has shown. Further, as Table 1 has shown, it is highly competitive over critical distances in the most densely urbanised corridor of north-west Europe. The conventional argument, well put by Stephen Potter (1987), is that extra speed over and above this would be bought at far too high a price and, given the possible additional ridership, would just not be profitable in the European context; Japan, where the corridor population densities reach ten times European levels, thus represents a special case.

Against this is the radical argument. Maglev technology would be competitive with air over virtually the whole of western Europe, effectively eliminating internal air traffic within the EEC except for a few special connections. The key, almost certainly, lies in creating a compatible bivalent system. If this were done, existing TGV and HST tracks could be progressively upgraded to carry maglev, which would become the natural system for the most densely trafficked corridors, feeding – as TGV does now – into conventional services to a variety of destinations. It would be surprising if Japanese engineers were not thinking along these lines.

However, despite the decades of work on high-speed maglev, its operational success is still uncertain. The conclusion in Rhodes and Mulhall's 1981 study – that a complete system still lies in the future, and that a gradual transition via linear motors on conventional high-speed rail is more likely – still seems correct. A Canadian team, who evaluated a number of alternatives – including TRANSRAPID, the Japanese maglev and TGV – for the proposed Los Angeles– Las Vegas high-speed link, concluded that a deployment decision on TGV would be possible in 1987, on TRANSRAPID in 1990 and on the Japanese system only in about 1995, though a higher level of commitment by the Japanese government could advance this to 1992–3 (Boon *et al*. 1987, pp. 239–40). Operational reliability, they stressed, is a major factor in commercial feasibility, and neither maglev system has yet reached commercial prototype stage. While each demonstrates doubts about reliability at present, these could be overcome through established design engineering techniques, but the ultimate reliability remains uncertain (Boon *et al*. 1987, p. 240).

Even if maglev achieves the technical breakthrough that researchers expect, its commercial results will still be in question. Evaluated for TGV Nord, it was cheaper to build per kilometre, but came out more expensive overall because of its inability to use existing tracks. It would achieve Paris–Brussels in one hour and six minutes at 500 kilometres per hour, only a twenty-four minute saving over the TGV. Thus there was no way in which it could generate sufficient additional traffic to substantiate its greater capital cost. Maglev begins to generate such traffic only over 1500 kilometres, when it competes with air, and the risks of large-scale implementation are very great. Thus, Stephen Potter (1987, p. 182) concludes, 'the technology exists, but there is little evidence that there is a real market for it'. As a rule, 'only where market potential is very large is it worthwhile contemplating ground transport systems that require new network infrastructure'; maglev may need passenger flows of the order of 50 million per annum (Potter 1987, p. 188). The general lesson is that 'the existence of a well-developed infrastructure or product support system makes the entry of a rival system based on a different infrastructure difficult or impossible, even though the technology of that rival may be superior to the existing product' (Potter 1987, p. 189).

The resulting logic seems clear. The European railways are right in their present strategy of developing a mixed steel wheel-on-rail system, with a combination of upgraded track for 200 kilometres per hour and new track for 250 to 300 kilometres per hour. But they would also be right to develop a strategy for progressively moving to a maglev system on the new stretches, as and when such a technology were developed on a compatible bivalent basis, and always provided that it proved commercially feasible. The first part of this strategy can and will be implemented during the 1990s. The second stage would logically follow after the year 2000.

The building of the European network

So, of the two areas of the world where HST is especially well-developed, it is western Europe that is making the running on the basis of a mixture of HST and TGV technologies, involving new building and upgrading of the classical railway, all on the basis of steel wheel-on-rail. Down to the present time, all that can be seen is a collection of disparate and unconnected national projects. But soon, as the original railways did 150 years ago, they promise to link rapidly into a European network (Figure 5). In January 1989, the heads of fourteen western European railway systems unveiled a 63 billion pound scheme for a European HST network. To be completed by 2010, it would involve building or modernising 30 000 kilometre plus 10 000 kilometre of link lines in the twelve EEC countries plus Austria and Switzerland, who together form the Community of European Railways (CER). CER estimates that rail travel will increase 400 per cent over the next thirty years, with a particularly big boost after 1992. They think it will be financially viable and should attract private capital as well as national and EEC funds. The total cost would be one per cent of Community countries' GDP or 10 per cent of transport investment over the next ten years (*The Guardian* 25 Jan. 1989).

THE URBAN IMPACTS

We know something of the urban impacts of HST from experience of the existing cases.

On the Tokaido Shinkansen, the number of business trips has increased while their duration has shortened; tourists go further but may spend fewer overnights (Kamada 1980, p. 47). Generally the line has accelerated the growth of the major cities along the line, and speeded up the development

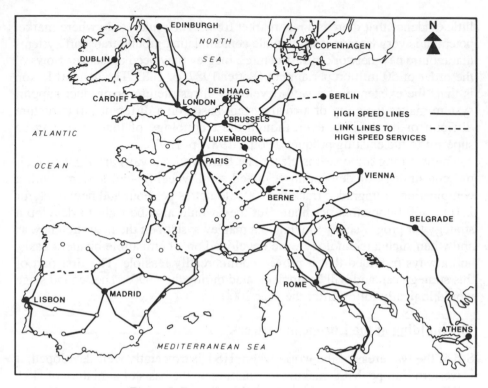

Figure 5 Europe's evolving fast rail network

of a megalopolis. Tokyo and Osaka, especially Tokyo, have generally been strengthened while the position of Nagoya, the main intermediate city, has been weakened (Kamada 1980, p. 48). The Shinkansen has had a major effect on the 'nucleus-controlling' effect of the cities: Nagoya shrank severely, and in certain functions – head office, financial – Osaka–Kobe also lost (Sanuki 1980, p. 236). In commercial and hotel functions, the Shinkansen brought competition between cities, but generally all did better (Sanuki 1980, pp. 238–9).

With the TGV, similarly, the result is that the structural effects have been centred on urban poles and their immediate environs (Bonnafous 1987, p. 129). There is an historic imbalance between the economies of the two regions at the end of the TGV-SE line: Rhone–Alpes has half the population of the Paris region but only one-third of the production, one-fifth of the higher level services, and one twenty-fifth of the headquarters of top companies (Bonnafous 1987, p. 131). Surveys show that high-level services in Rhone–Alpes have benefitted by gaining better access to Paris, while Paris competitors are happy to stay with their own market. Parisians have increased their journeys by 52 per cent to Rhone–Alpes to buy or sell a service, while inhabitants of Rhone–Alpes have increased theirs by 144 per cent (Bonnafous 1987, p. 136). Thus service industries, particularly consultancies, do not need to move to Paris, but can sell their services from Lyon (Bonnafous 1987, pp. 135–6).

However, the effect of a new high-speed link does depend on the way it relates to the economic geography of the region through which it passes. The TGV-SE and TGV-A both follow strong economic axes, as will the TGV-N between Paris, Lille and Brussels; but the proposed TGV-Est would cut transversely across the main economic axis of Lorraine and Alsace, unless an alternative route is developed (Houee 1986, pp. 109–11). Similarly, a new high-speed line with limited stops may completely alter the pattern of regional feeder services, strengthening the points of interchange and weakening others: some places may be bypassed altogether, a particular problem for centres relatively near the capital, such as Amiens, Dijon and Orléans. Within cities, entirely new interchange stations may be developed at locations different from the old, as has already occurred in Lyon and will occur in Lyon and Reims (Houee 1986, pp. 112–16, 123). As the development around the new Part–Dieu station in Lyon so amply shows, the effects on urban structure can be profound. The TGV Paris bypass may be particularly significant in this regard.

Generally, because the commercial advantage of the new trains will lie in competing with air, we should expect that they will strengthen the position of existing top-level centres where the major airports are located. Conversely, as has already occurred in France, the inevitable truncation of express services on the old lines may seriously weaken intermediate centres (Houee 1986, pp. 123–4). On the new trunk line of the European TGV, we should expect to see a reinforcement or enhancement of the positions of London, Paris, Brussels, Köln and Frankfurt and a weakening of intermediate places; the sole exception will be Lille, because of its position as hub of the entire system. Places like Leeds, Manchester, Cardiff, Lyon and Stuttgart may also benefit so long as they are connected into the system, as the French are doing for Lyon.

The moral is that deliberate planning of the network, and its integration into a wider framework of regional developmental planning, can powerfully foster private investment even if it cannot guarantee it. This is the French approach, and it stands in striking contrast to the British government's hands-off policy. This is particularly clear from the French strategy, in which a new TGV bypass line east of Paris will connect key growth nodes in the regional plan, in comparison with the British decision over the high-speed line between the Channel Tunnel and London (Anon. 1989a; 1989b; Journet 1989; Pommelet 1989).

AN ANATOMY OF ELECTRONIC MAIL

Just as there is no single HST technology, so there is no single technology called electronic mail. Rather, there is a family of systems, ranging from telegrams through telex, analog fax, digital fax, interactive videotext and communicating communicators to voice mail (Vervest 1986, pp. 52–4). Many have a surprisingly long history. Fax goes back to 1842, when the Scottish inventor Alexander Bain fashioned an electrically controlled pendulum mechanism, used for synchronising clocks, and developed for the visible transmission of signals over telephone lines. Bain's 'automatic electromechanical recording telegraph' was patented in 1843 (Costigan 1971, p. 2). A commercial system was established in France, connecting Paris with several other cities, in 1865; it lasted about five years. In England in 1850, Frederick Bakewell demonstrated a precursor of the cylinder-and-screw scanning mechanism; Dr Arthur Korn in Germany demonstrated photoelectric scanning in 1902 and established a commercial service in 1907, linking Berlin, London and Paris by 1910 and spanning the Atlantic in 1922 (Costigan 1971, p. 3). A commercial radio facsimile service was introduced in 1926 by RCA for the transmission of news photos; soon, AT&T, RCA and Western Union had established commercial picture services (Costigan 1971, pp. 1, 4–6).

Western Union established an automatic fax telegraph system in the early 1930s and a compact desktop transmitter, the Desk-Fax, in 1948 (Costigan 1971, p. 7). It was very successful and there were nearly 30 000 in use in the United States by 1970 (Costigan 1971, p. 26). In the mid-1960s came fax by phone via a compact desktop transceiver, coupled with an easing of restrictions on the connection of 'foreign' devices; it was still forbidden to connect customer-provided terminals directly to the switched network, but indirect connection via switched couplers became possible (Costigan 1971, pp. 38, 102–3). In the late 1960s came the use of solid state devices and digital transmission (Costigan 1971, pp. 38, 41).

At the start of the 1970s, cheap dial-up machines produced by companies in the United States, Japan and Europe were available in the United Kingdom, but they failed to provide the convenience, speed and flexibility needed to meet the needs of business. The machines were inadequate and customers were disillusioned. The biggest obstacle was cost, since most of the cost of a six-minute transmission was the cost of the call itself; compatibility was also a problem (Barrett & Farbrother 1976, pp. 1–2). The future, a commentary at that time stressed, lay in digital transmission: 'Speeds of a page per half-minute over ordinary telephone lines, at prices that the average facsimile customer can afford, are by no means an exaggerated forecast, nor very remote in terms of time', though standardisation would also be needed (Costigan 1971, p. 257). One report at that time ended prophetically: 'Facsimile is highly developed in Japan because of its ability to transmit documents containing the complex characters used in the Japanese language. So if, or when, the Japanese do market directly in the UK they could have a major impact' (Barrett & Farbrother 1976, p. 14).

The Japanese moved into fax out of necessity: the need to transmit kanji characters (Cawkell 1982, p. 18). They developed new standards for digital machines, which soon became standard, and began to mass-produce very cheap machines (Cawkell 1982, pp. 19–21). By 1981 they were producing 80 per cent of all sub-minute fax machines, with sales of 270 million dollars (Cawkell 1982, p. 21).

There was an open market worldwide. At the start of the 1980s, 24 million pieces of mail were being transmitted every day in the United Kingdom,

150 million in the United States; a very low proportion – 4 per cent in West Germany, the highest – went electronically. Traditional post offices carried the bulk: 74 per cent in the United Kingdom and France, 96 per cent in Germany where private courier services were banned (Connell & Galbraith 1980, pp. 30–1). A survey at this time concluded that because of the rising cost and diminishing quality of conventional first-class mail, there was opportunity for a sizeable volume to be diverted to electronic transmission; there was likely to be a big growth in Group 3 (digital) fax which would take less than a one-minute phone call per page, and in which the cost of machines, then 3000 to 8000 pounds, would drop (Connell & Galbraith 1980, pp. 52, 65, 71–2).

This was one case where the technological and market predictions proved uncannily right – save in one respect.

In the second half of the 1980s, fax enjoyed a boom, with a doubling in the market in Britain between 1985 and 1988, and an estimated 200 000 shipments in 1988, with falling prices, increasing awareness and easy access to an estimated 7.8 million terminals worldwide. The Japanese established a virtual monopoly through the strength of their home market plus economies of scale. The growth was expected to continue through to 1992 (Pyne 1988, pp. 27–8). Nineteen eighty-eight saw a British 'fax explosion', with 180 000 new installations; by the start of 1989, 350 000 fax machines were installed in Great Britain and the number was growing by 60 per cent per annum. Among small British businesses at that date, according to a survey by the Small Business Research Trust, 49 per cent had fax; a further 13.6 per cent said they would be installing it within a year. In the United States, sales were 191 000 and 712 million dollars in 1986, 910 000 and 2.1 billion dollars in 1988 (*The Guardian* 12 Jan. 1989; *The Times* 20 Jan. 1989; *Electronics Times* 16 March 1989).

FAX VERSUS EMAIL

The point that most predictions got wrong was the relative spread of fax and full electronic mail – that is, direct communciation between computers. 'It cannot be long before fax overtakes electronic mail as Britain's favourite piece of communications technology after the telephone – if it has not already done so', wrote one clearly bemused computer journalist at the start of 1989 (*The Guardian* 12 Jan. 1989). As against an estimated 350 000 fax machines, the leading electronic mail system, Telecom Gold, was estimated to have 140 000 users, but not all were regular users. Though there were an estimated 11 million mailboxes worldwide by the end of 1988, as against 7.8 million fax terminals, it is impossible to tell how many are being used regularly, or at all (Pyne 1988, p. 29). Yet fax typically takes a sluggish thirty seconds to transmit an A4 sheet, against five characters a second by telex or thirty to 120 characters a second by email. And, of course, the document is dead when it arrives at the other end: unless it is scanned, it cannot be machine-read and so cannot be further edited or electronically stored.

The commentator asked the obvious question: 'So why is the fax tortoise winning against the telex and electronic hare?' The answer lay in its instant availability. No one knows whether email is there. Email is confidential but this can be true of personal fax. Fax can also send illustrations, though this feature is seldom used (*The Guardian* 12 Jan. 1989).

The same answer came from Michael Cavanagh, president of Cavanagh Associates, a postal and telecommunications consultancy firm in Washington. 'The fax machine seems an anachronism', he said, 'but its simplicity and ease of use are appealing. Fax machines may turn out to be a migration device, helping many people make the transition to a more electronic society' (*Electronics Times* 16 March 1989). Public email continued to be plagued by the problem of compatibility, especially between countries, and also by the need for computer literacy (Pyne 1988, p. 28). A survey found that the most common answer (69 per cent) to the question 'Why do you not use email?' was lack of interconnection (Dean 1987, p. 208). The industry, it has been suggested, is now like the phone services in the United States eighty years ago (Dean 1987, p. 209).

NETWORKING TO THE RESCUE?

The breakthrough in electronic mail thus can only lie in making it as user-friendly as fax; and that must entail complete and easy compatibility. The answer seemed to have arrived by the early 1980s – Open System Intercom-munication (OSI). The basic reference model, establishing an international standard, was followed in 1984 by X.400 Electronic Message Handling, the first complete stack of OSI protocols (Valentine 1987, p. 128).

X.400 has a standard interface to allow incompatible email services to communicate with one another as well as allowing an email user to connect with telex, teletex and fax terminals. On the surface, it seemed the gateway to real electronic mail: a device whereby any terminal could access any other transparently. Coupled with integrated data networks (ISDN), which will replace the present cumbrous interconnections by a single interface, it pro-mised standard interfaces as easy to use as a telephone keypad, plus easy directory and addressing; particularly, it would allow personal computers to communicate over the switched network without the need for special lines (Newman & McFarland 1988, pp. 43–5; Pyne 1988, p. 31). The aim is nothing less than worldwide connectivity for information services (voice, data and image), extending the concept of OSI to multimedia (voice, data and image) communication across international frontiers (Carrelli & Decina 1987, p. 70).

But it has not been that simple: despite great efforts by national telecom-munications undertakings, ISDN is still years away, and there have been many technical problems in implementing the X.400 email software (Pyne 1988, p. 29). As late as 1988, a commentator wrote, 'to date X.400 has encouraged much talk but little action...Among the majority of users...confusion reigns' (Pyne 1988, p. 29). The vendors were waiting for a lead from the carriers, and vice versa (Pyne 1988, p. 30). To succeed, X.400 had to escape from the image of a technology waiting for a problem (Pyne 1988, p. 30). Ironically, the main beneficiary from the new international protocols have been the fax manufacturers.

And this is why, at least for half a decade, electronic communication will take place mainly through a second-best technology.

FAX AND HIGH-QUALITY MAIL

As everyone knows, precisely because fax is such a limited technology, its main impact – apart from the additional traffic which it is undoubtedly generating – is on high-quality commercial mail services (courier services) which transmit mail at the highest possible speed for premium rates. These are operated both by post offices in the form of specialised services like the British Datapost and the United States Overnight Delivery, and by commercial organisations like Federal Express, who built its initial operations almost exclusively within the United States (and from its Memphis hub) and DHL, which has taken the lead in the international market. Figure 6 compares the cost of sending typical paper packages by fax and DHL over certain distances. DHL and its competitors use a broad banding, whereby any package up to five kilograms in weight – corresponding to a document some 1160 pages long, travels at the same fixed tariff for that destination: with fax, where the main element is the phone connection, the rate varies directly with the time of connection and so with the number of pages. To send a document from Britain

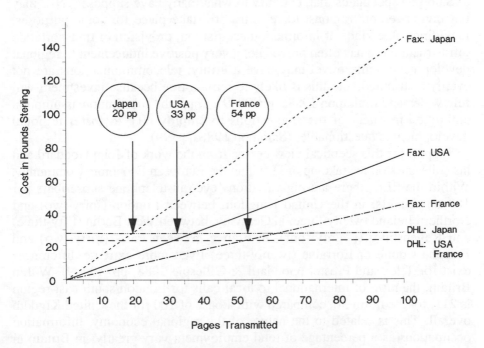

Figure 6 Costs of facsimile versus DHL

to a nearby western European country such as France or West Germany, it becomes more economical to use DHL if the document is fifty-four pages or more. The corresponding length for the United States is thirty-three pages and for Japan only twenty pages. Fax is therefore an extremely economical option for a user wanting to send many relatively short documents, but express mail services are better for the volume user.

THE SPATIAL IMPACT OF EMAIL

Two associated questions arise. First, whether and how far new information technology will substitute for transportation of people and also for high-quality specialised postal services. Secondly, whether in doing so it will benefit some cities and regions, and hurt others.

NIT may have no impact at all on transportation, though this is implausible; it may substitute for it; or it may be complementary to it, as in the use of IT to help the driver (Salomon 1988a, p. 91). The demand for it, like that for transportation, is a derived demand; for the most part, it is not desired for itself but for what it may bring. So market acceptance is associated with the demand for information. The costs are easy to measure, the value to the recipient is far harder. As we have seen, IT currently has some severe limitations: it is sensorily restricted, it is controlled by the sender rather than by the recipient, and it may be indigestible. Teleconferencing and Prestel are examples of technologies that failed to realise market forecasts (Salomon 1988a, pp. 95–6).

Salomon speculates that, contrary to what many have supposed, NIT may not favour remote regions: travel must still take place for some purposes, including some kinds of information acquisition; provision of transportation infrastructure too has often proved not a very positive inducement to regional development; some travel may have a utility; telecommunications are not evenly distributed, and this is likely to remain true because investment will follow demand (Salomon 1988a, pp. 98–9). Thus 'the substitution assumption embodied in many of the suggestions to employ NIT to foster regional development is questionable' (Salomon 1988a, p. 99).

Support for this sceptical view comes from the work of John Goddard and his colleagues on the take-up of IT within the European Economic Community. Within the EEC, there are big variations even in telephone subscribers per 100 inhabitants: in the United Kingdom between London (forty-two) and Northern Ireland twenty-three; in Germany, between West Berlin (fifty-three) and Regensburg (twenty-four); in France between Paris (forty-two) and Franche Comte or Lorraine (twenty-three) Even more extreme differences exist for Telex and Prestel (Goddard & Gillespie 1988, pp. 137–9). Within Britain, the ratio of international to local calls for London/south-east region is 211, for the north 36, compared with a base of 100 for the United Kigdom overall. This is related to the nature of the regional economy. Information occupations as a percentage of total employment vary greatly: in Britain in

1981, from 57.8 per cent in London and 47.3 per cent in the south-east down to 38.8 per cent in the north and 39.4 per cent in Wales. Further, 80 per cent of manufacturing in the north is externally controlled, which helps to explain the low percentage of information occupations in manufacturing and construction, thirty against forty-eight for London (Goddard & Gillespie 1988, pp. 125–7, 139). Even at the consumer level, semi-anecdotal evidence suggests that personal computer ownership in Britain – overall, by far the highest in western Europe – may vary from 35 to 41 per cent in the south-east, down to 7 to 18 per cent in the north, 7 to 9 per cent in Wales and as little as 1 to 7 per cent in Scotland (Batty 1988, p. 162; Steinle 1988, pp. 82–3). In Germany, competence in IT has been found to rise steadily with size of area, being twice as much in larger conurbations as in small, mainly rural and peripheral, communes; equipment is also more widely diffused in the big cities, and familiarity is greater. Thus, despite the potential to develop less favoured regions, the prospects are not good: the larger central areas have the labour, the innovative applications and (because PTTs are market-oriented) the installations (Steinle 1988, pp. 85–6).

These variations are basically a function of the existing information-handling economy, which is highly concentrated in the biggest metropolitan areas and is, if anything, becoming more so. London has 93 per cent of the headquarters of service companies in the United Kingdom, Paris 70 per cent of those in France, Rome 67 per cent of those in Italy, and Frankfurt 53 per cent of those in Germany. Externalisation of internal services, as with computer services for banks, leads to increasing concentration in a few metropolitan centres and just possibly in regional centres like Manchester and Lyon. The EEC has a strong representation in multinational service companies, reflecting a trading and colonial past: thus close on 30 per cent of the 500 largest banks in the world were EEC-based, almost invariably in the leading financial city. And overseas-based companies overwhelmingly base themselves in the core national region. The most innovative small new service firms are also found in core regions and attractive areas (sunbelts) (Howells 1988, pp. 34, 48–50, 68, 83). One recent study concludes that 'the evolution of the service sector over the next ten to fifteen years will militate against the less favoured, peripheral parts of Europe...the major structural, organisational and technological trends in the EC services will have a centralising effect in inter-regional terms, although on a subregional basis there appear to be few constraints on service industry dispersal' (Howells 1988, pp. 96–7).

Related to these huge variations in potential demand, the provision of more advanced IT services may be very uneven, especially at the start. Britain again provides examples. The Packet Switchstream Service for data-handling was originally concentrated on a limited net connecting the largest cities and excluding Newcastle, though it was extended there in 1981. Similarly Prestel was originally available in a limited area though it is now extended to 94 per cent of the country; private VANs are totally concentrated in London and the Home Counties, 125 out of 164 in 1985. The Mercury telephone system, which offers reduced rates to high-volume subscribers, was originally limited to a figure-of-eight and still does not serve much of the country (Goddard & Gillespie 1988, pp. 131–3, 135). Thus, 'what has not been adequately appreciated is that the shift from awareness to adoption of new technology needs a much fuller demonstration of the relevance of the developments to the user's own environment' (Goddard & Gillespie 1988, p. 140).

Within the urban hierarchy, a few key locations are emerging as global sites for data and communication networks. New York, London and Tokyo benefit from being key financial centres, and the hubbing of communication networks has tended to reinforce their position, though companies are becoming more flexible and mobile. The United Kingdom has gained from deregulation and low tariffs, and has 25 per cent of all the network termination points in Europe, 28 per cent in the financial sector, partly reflecting BT's low tariffs which, however, are no longer the cheapest. There is thus an increasing dichotomy between information-rich and information-poor regions (Howells 1988, pp. 150, 153). And, though this conclusion specifically applies to Europe, there can be no doubt that it is generally applicable.

CONCLUSION

In terms of the revised Weberian theory set out at the start of this chapter, the costs of transmitting information – whether in the form of brains attached to bodies, packages of paper or electronic messages – are still high and likely to remain so, despite technological advances. Further, agglomeration economies are undoubtedly even stronger for the information-handling industries than they were for the old goods-handling industries. Because of the subtle relationship between face-to-face exchange and remote exchange, and because the take-up of new technology is so much faster in information-rich regions, a continuous process of synergistic innovation is set up in those regions, resulting in what Myrdal (1957) once called a process of circular and cumulative causation. At most, because of internal cost pressures, there is a process of sub-regional deconcentration of information-handling industries and activities from cores to peripheries of such regions, as evidenced by well-known cases like Reading (England), Stamford (Connecticut) and the Interstate-680 corridor in the San Francisco Bay area. In this process, the peripheral information-poor regions will be left ever farther behind.

NOTES

1 The 590-kilometre corridor along the line has about 34 per cent of the Japanese population and about 60 per cent of the industrial production. The original line had about 3 per cent of national route length but 25 per cent of JNR's traffic volume (Nishida 1980, pp. 11–4).

2 Nearly one in five European flights was delayed for fifteen or more minutes in 1988, as against 15 per cent 1987 and 12.5 per cent 1986, giving a total of 150 000 lost hours,

equivalent to the whole Alitalia or Swissair fleet. Lufthansa alone spent 10 253 hours in stacks at a cost of thirty million pounds. In early 1989, the position had further deteriorated (*Financial Times* 22 Feb. 1989; *The Times* 27 April 1989).

3 A detailed Japanese study gives the breakpoint between the Shinkansen, which has HST speeds, and air at 600 kilometres (Sanuki 1980, p. 240).

4 This of course was deliberately planned as part of a long-term strategy for the revitalisation of the city as capital of a depressed industrial region.

5 Fax includes standard daytime phone rates plus paper charges but not the amortisation of the equipment. DHL assumes a small-volume user; rates for high-volume users (more than four packages per month) would be substantially lower.

PART I

NEW TRANSPORT TECHNOLOGIES AND THEIR SPATIAL IMPACTS

2

FAST RAIL NETWORKS AND SOCIOECONOMIC IMPACTS

John Brotchie

INTRODUCTION

The transition to an information society involves an increasing coordination of communications and transport at regional and global levels, and their closer integration with land use activities. An element of this change is a growing interest in fast intercity rail. The increasing scale of commercial activities, the lowering of national barriers in Europe after 1992, and the high value placed on travel time, are further agents of change in the development of a European fast rail network. This network is planned to extend across the continent and into the United Kingdom via the Channel Tunnel (Chapter 1, Fig. 5; also SNCF 1986). At an estimated cost of 100 billion US dollars, a total of 8000 kilometres of new tracks and 20 000 kilometres of upgraded tracks is planned. The Shinkansen fast rail network in Japan, the first link of which began operation in 1964, also has expansion plans beyond its present network length of 1800 kilometres. Feasibility studies are also being made in the United States, Canada, Australia, South Korea and Taiwan. These developments are occurring in an environment of traffic congestion on roads and in the air, and increasing air pollution with implications for the greenhouse effect and ozone depletion. The new electric fast rail systems, on the other hand, are efficient in the use of land, and much more efficient in energy and emissions than a car or jet plane. There are also increasing opportunities for location of activities along the route, facilitating decentralisation while integrating urban systems and commercial and industrial production.

The new rail networks are based on conventional, electrified, standard gauge, wheel-on-rail systems. The standard gauge facilitates interconnection of national systems as it did for the first generation of railways in the industrial era. Recent electronic advances allow operation under different voltages and frequencies. A feature of these new systems is the carriage of large numbers of passengers – safely, reliably and conveniently – between city centres. A further generation of fast rail systems using magnetic levitation is also under development in Germany and Japan.

INTEGRATION OF TRANSPORT, COMMUNICATION AND LAND USE

These fast rail systems are part of the transition to an information economy, involving the growth of global and regional communication networks, a similar spatial development of transport systems and an extension of organisational structures and markets. This development is also linked with an increasing coordination of service activities at a global and regional level.

An initial aim of fast rail in Japan was to integrate the urban systems that it linked. The Shinkansen had a major impact on these cities (Hirota 1984). Reported growth rates in cities with stations on the Tokaido line increased substantially – from the national average of 1 to 1.6 per cent per annum and to 1.1 per cent per annum for other cities in the corridor. Growth in service industries including food and accommodation was dramatic. At the terminus in Hakata, Hirota reported that the number of hotels increased from twenty with 2060 rooms in 1972 to forty with 5320 rooms in 1974 (in anticipation of service commenced in 1975). At the intermediate city of Okayama, the number of hotel guests increased from 170 000 in 1971 during the period 15 March to 31 May, to 236 000 for the same period in 1972 immediately after introduction of the train. In Mishima City, also on the route but only 110 kilometres from Tokyo, the growth rates in population and number of households, and the annual sales in restaurants almost doubled after the introduction of the rail system and, more significantly, the growth rates in number of enterprises, annual wholesale turnover, and annual retail sales each more than doubled with the introduction of the service.

At an overall economic level, similar impacts were reported. Table 1 compares growth rates for various sectors in Japanese cities over ten-year periods before and after the opening of the Tokaido Shinkansen. Rates for cities with and without Shinkansen stations are shown and indicate a substantial increase in relative growth rates in cities with a Shinkansen station – in each of the sectors – wholesale, retail, industrial production, construction and population. The cities with Shinkansen stations are seen to have had a growth rate significantly less than average in each sector in the decade before the train, and a growth rate substantially higher than average in each sector in the decade after the train began operation. Thus, despite a period of reduced economic growth overall in the second time period, induced growth has been sufficient to substantially reverse the growth rate trends between these two sets of cities in each of the sectors above, and particularly in wholesale, retail and population.

Table 1 Comparison of principal economic growth indices for cities with and without Shinkansen stations, before and after opening of the Tokaido Shinkansen

Item	Annual increase (per cent, ratio)					
	Before Shinkansen			After Shinkansen		
	(A1) Cities with Shinkansen Station	(B1) Cities without Shinkansen Station	(C1) A1/B1	(A2) Cities with Shinkansen Station	(B2) Cities without Shinkansen Station	(C2) A2/B2
Wholesale	12.90	20.80	0.621	11.63	8.70	1.34
Retail	10.10	13.50	0.748	9.96	8.58	1.16
Industrial production	13.70	14.20	0.967	9.48	7.81	1.21
Construction work in area	13.80	14.90	0.926	8.01	6.37	1.26
Population	2.64	3.39	0.777	1.88	1.55	1.22

Notes 1 Growth indices are annual averages over the ten years before and after opening of the Shinkansen.
2 Growth indices after opening of the Shinkansen are consistently smaller than those before opening of the Shinkansen, reflecting stagnant economic conditions.
Source: Hirota 1984.

A further study (Nakamura & Ueda 1989) examined the impacts over the decade 1975–85 of the new lines Joetsu and Tohoku Shinkansen which commenced operation in 1982. Growth rates in population, income and retailing over the period 1981–85 increased in a higher percentage of local regions served by Shinkansen than in regions without Shinkansen. Those regions with both Shinkansen and an expressway showed even stronger growth trends: of regions served by Shinkansen, nineteen of thirty-three (58 per cent) increased in population, compared with sixteen of seventy-one regions (23 per cent) without Shinkansen. In regions served by both Shinkansen and an expressway, seventeen of twenty-seven (65 per cent) increased in population. The Shinkansen carries passengers only. The expressway also facilitates the movement of freight and hence manufacturing industry.

From an examination of employment changes it was found that the number of employees in information-based industries increased significantly in Shinkansen served regions. These industries were classed as information, investigation and advertising services, banking, real estate, R&D, higher education, and political institutes. A characteristic of these industries is their dependence on information and knowledge. Table 2 indicates the higher growth rates in these activities in areas served by Shinkansen and an expressway over those areas with an expressway only.

Table 2 Rate of increase of employees engaged in 'information exchange industries' in regions with population increase in the period 1981–85

	With Shinkansen & expressway (%)	With expressway only (%)
Business services	42	12
Information, investigation & advertising services	125	63
R&D and higher education	27	21
Political institutes	20	11
Other business services	57	28
Real estate agencies	21	3
Total of information exchange industries	22	7

Source: Nakamura & Ueda 1989

For regions with increasing population, those served by Shinkansen had average commercial land price increases of 67 per cent compared with 42 per cent in regions served by an expressway. However, the study also showed that the impacts of Skinkansen differed between the cities it linked, as discussed also by Hall in the previous chapter.

Similar variations in impact are considered (by Hall) between cities in Europe linked by TGV where the impact is more recent and not so well identified. These variations are considered further later.

The major intercity network planned for Europe after 1992 and the lowering of international barriers is apparently beginning to have land use impacts. New developments have occurred around existing TGV stations such as Lyon, while residents in the United Kingdom are reported to be buying homes in Brittany in anticipation of the London–Channel Tunnel–Paris link. The changes in regional development, industry structure and human lifestyle that result, will provide an opportunity for future study and forecasting of impacts of technological change.

A consequence of new technology is the increased opportunities provided for work and leisure, reflected in an increased value placed on travel time. This increased value of time adds to the demand for fast transport and for comfort, convenience and quality of time spent in travel. This time may be used for business or leisure – aided by high quality, on-board communication, providing a further integration of communication, transport and business or leisure activities.

At a freight transport level, an emerging integration of production, distribution, and communication is beginning to facilitate inventory control, just-in-time manufacturing, and production and distribution on demand. Fast rail presently caters primarily for passengers and mail but fast freight is being planned and will reinforce the framework of the regional production system above.

Differential impacts on land use

The discussion above has considered activities stimulated in cities linked by high-speed rail. This activity, however, is noted to vary between cities en route. As indicated in Nakamura and Ueda (1989), impacts can differ among these cities. Growth is generally substantial at line terminals and major nodes. Fast rail, like telecommunications, reinforces the existing major nodes linked. With reduced travel times, the spatial scale of markets increases to the possible disadvantage of smaller centres drawn into those expanded markets. Thus Tokyo and, to a lesser extent Osaka, have generally been strengthened by Shinkansen, while the position of Nagoya, the main intermediate city, has been weakened as far as numbers of head offices and producer services are concerned (Chapter 1; Kamada 1980). Thus, while the average impact is positive and substantial, some cities may lose while others gain. In commercial and hotel functions, however, generally all cities with stations did better than the national average (Chapter 1; Sanuki 1980; Hirota 1984). Similar impacts appear to be resulting from TGV (Bonnafous 1987) where Paris and Lyon have been drawn into each other's market areas. In this case there is some evidence (Chapter 1) that service industries in Lyon are benefitting more than those in Paris from this link. That is, it is more beneficial for the service sector in Lyon to be part of the larger Paris market than for Paris firms to share the smaller Lyon service market. Furthermore, the initial effects may be operational – expanded markets, increased turnovers and mergers between firms. The spatial effects would involve investment and relocation and occur more slowly.

TRANSPORT TECHNOLOGY

This increasing mobility is enabled by a growing network of transport links and modes – road, rail and air. Each mode has a place in the transport market with road dominating for shorter trips, air for longer trips, and fast rail occupying the middle ground (Figures 1–3). The increasing value placed on time is leading to speed increases through technological development in each of these modes. Freeways and tollways are providing faster road travel. Jet airliners are facilitating faster intercontinental and international movement. And fast rail is allowing more rapid intercity travel. Train speed has increased from Shinkansen's cruising speed of 210 kilometres per hour (1964) to TGV-SE at 270 kilometres per hour (1981), TGV-A at 300 kilometres per hour (1989) and TGV-N at 320 to 330 kilometres per hour or more (1993). The Very Fast Train (VFT) (Australia) is planned for 350 kilometres per hour in 1997 (Wild *et al*. 1985; VFT 1988: 1989). Magnetic levitation (maglev) aims at even higher speeds.

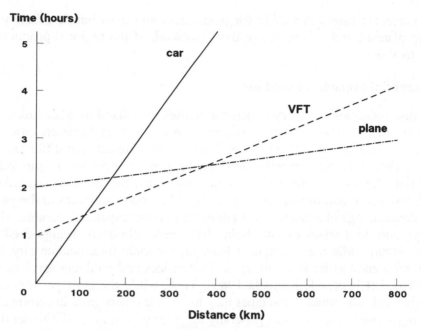

Figure 1 *Travel time versus distance for car, fast rail and plane modes,
indicating competitive range of trip length for each.*

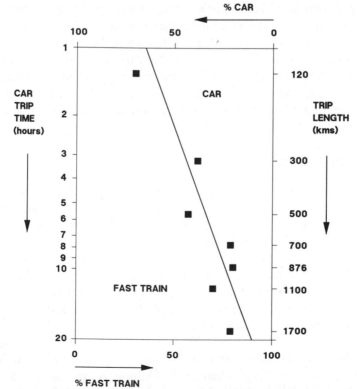

Figure 2 *Relative market shares of car and fast train versus trip length
and travel time by car.*

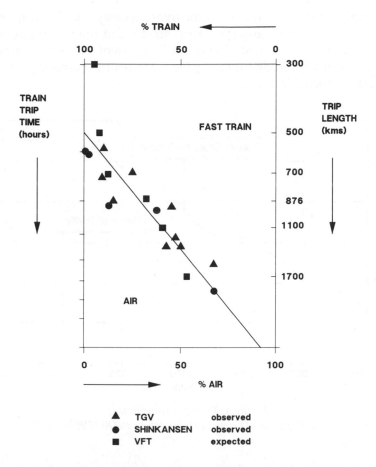

Figure 3 Relative market shares of fast train and air travel versus trip length and travel time by fast train.

The increasing speed of fast rail systems responds to increasing travel distances and the increasing demand for intercity and international travel (e.g. Figure 4) for business and non-business purposes. Viability also increases with these increases in speed and demand (Figure 5).

Environmental impact

An important further impact of the new technologies – both telecommunication and fast electrified rail – is their benign effects on the environment and on the new focii of environmental concern – the greenhouse effect and ozone depletion. Telecommunication produces negligible greenhouse gas emissions and can substitute for some travel under appropriate economic constraints, but it more often has a complementary role. Fast rail is efficient in regard to energy use and greenhouse gas emissions – several times more efficient (JNR 1986) than its principal competitors – the motor car and jet plane. It is also land efficient by a similar factor over freeways, and can relieve the increasing congestion of airports, skies, streets and roads – improving the reliability and safety of intercity travel. It is a system whose time appears to have come. The VFT study for the Sydney–Melbourne corridor gives further insight into expected impacts.

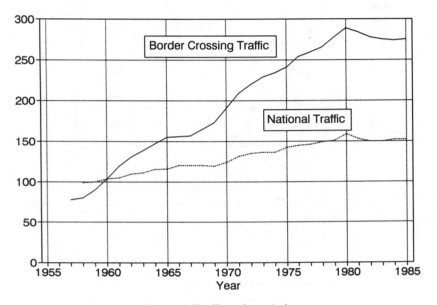

Figure 4 Traffic volume index:
Federal Republic of Germany (Hendricks 1988) (1960 = 100).

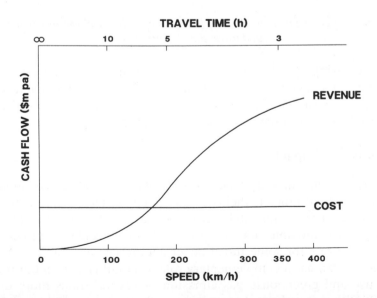

Figure 5 Cost and revenue versus train speed, travel time: Sydney–Melbourne.

VFT-AUSTRALIA

The VFT is a proposed new high-speed rail system to link the city centres of Sydney and Melbourne via Canberra. The system is planned for both passengers and freight. With a cruising speed of 350 kilometres per hour, the VFT could travel non-stop from Sydney to Melbourne in three hours and Sydney to Canberra in one hour. Route length is 876 kilometres. Over forty services per day in each direction are expected, including trains which stop at intermediate stations. Technology will be similar to the French TGV, German ICE, and Japanese Super-Hitari 300, each with speed capabilities in excess of 300 kilometres per hour. The TGV-A and ICE have each exceeded 400 kilometres per hour in test, and the TGV-A has exceeded 500 kilometres per hour in several test runs.

The corridor contains nearly half the population of Australia (about eight million in the corridor in 1995), the majority of its manufacturing and high tech industry, its two largest cities and national capital, financial centres, its snow-fields, much of its energy resources, and many tourist attractions. More than two million visitors entered Australia in 1988, largely through Sydney. The study is now in its feasibility stage, the first part of which was a comprehensive passenger market study (Hensher *et al.* 1989). The study indicated an expected market of over six million one-way Sydney–Melbourne trip equivalents for VFT in 1995. This market would be diverted from air (1.7 million), car (1.5 million), coach (0.7 million) and the rest would be induced (2.5 million). The number of trips per person in the corridor expected on VFT is comparable to the per capita rates for TGV and Shinkansen. The revealed values of travel time are also comparable for each. So are fares per kilometres, and market shares (Figure 3). The Sydney–Melbourne corridor, like the Tokyo–Osaka corridor, accounts for about 50 per cent of national GNP. The estimated cost of the system is 5000 million Australian dollars (1989 dollars).

The market studies have evaluated characteristics of activities and travel behaviour at a regional level. The average adult randomly sampled in the Sydney–Melbourne corridor makes twelve one-way trips (six return trips) each greater than 70 kilometres each year, one-third for business and two-thirds for non-business purposes. The trend is towards more trips of shorter duration. Just over half the trips observed were between the capital cities – Melbourne, Canberra and Sydney. The average intercity trip distance in the corridor varies with mode – air and coach average approximately 700 kilometres and car 240 kilometres. For longer trips, coach has increased its market share, apparently at the expense of car and air. There is also considerable reported latent demand – not satisfied because of the expense of air travel and the slowness of conventional ground modes.

Residents of small cities en route were found to make approximately thirty one-way intercity trips per year of average length 150 kilometres, giving 4500 kilometres of annual intercity travel. Metropolitan residents make fewer but longer trips of average length over 400 kilometres, giving a comparable total distance travelled. Only 18 per cent of trips from smaller cities are for business compared to 37 per cent for metropolitan residents. Fast rail will suit these longer, metropolitan-based trips with their higher business content.

The values of time of intercity travellers are relatively high (compared with that of intra-metropolitan travellers, commuters or shoppers) – at thirty dollars per hour for business and ten to thirteen dollars per hour for non-business. Non-business travel is divided almost evenly into visiting friends and relatives and into recreational travel. As noted earlier, these values of time appear to be increasing over time as income and opportunities for both business and non-business activities increase. Attributes preferred in the survey include the comfort and convenience of fast rail, which is seen to offer quality time during travel – allowing a wider range of on-board activities. Information systems were favoured to assist these activities. The fast rail service was preferred for its direct access to city centres – avoiding the congestion of suburban travel links, and increasing its competitiveness with car and plane. The terminals themselves can be relatively compact, allowing (desired) high quality environments at reasonable cost. Safety, reliability and punctuality of these services are other features preferred by both business and non-business travellers.

Regional development impacts

The system links the central business districts directly with the countryside and almost half the trips expected have one or both ends in a smaller centre. This would allow decentralisation of business and non-business activities, and their development in areas where land is cheaper and where recreational facilities – mountains, rivers, lakes and beaches – are also available. Thus the system could facilitate a broader choice of lifestyles and access to a wider range of housing land. This range would cater both for the first home buyer and for the upper end of the market seeking resort accommodation for lifestyle and investment purposes.

The types of development expected to be induced by fast rail vary along the route but include the following categories:

- commuter cities, largely within an hour's travelling time from a metropolitan city, could provide lower cost land for housing and industry and access to metropolitan support services for business and for residential living;
- commercial developments would be stimulated in some centres by integration of the urban systems in the corridor, and the economies of scale and agglomeration that this provides;
- resort developments could be facilitated by the additional access provided to recreational areas including mountains, ski areas, beaches, oceans and lakes, and allowing integration of recreational, residential and, in some cases, commercial developments. A further potential activity is just-in-time manufacturing industry, including high tech industry, and production and distribution on demand – again providing economies of scale and agglomeration and reducing storage and inventory costs;

- commercial, hotel and parking developments over and around metropolitan terminals, and at larger intermediate stations, are another possibility;
- knowledge-based industries or a multi-function polis – providing a composite of many of the activity types above – would be another potential development.

The system would facilitate the development of tourist facilities along its route. It provides access to metropolitan amenities – almost comparable to that of peripheral suburbs – for each of the centres en route. The VFT would be not so much a separate transport system as an integral component of development in the corridor.

The Shinkansen experience indicates that growth in absolute terms is likely to be greatest around stations at centres close to each metropolitan city, whilst growth rates may be greatest in the smaller centres with stations en route. At a broader level, the system is expected to stimulate development in the south-east of Australia, producing a more balanced development between metropolitan and non-metropolitan regions and between the south-east and north of Australia. The growth rate in the south east is currently just over 1 per cent compared with over 2 per cent in northern Australia and 1.5 per cent for the nation as a whole. VFT has potential extensions to the north (Sydney–Brisbane) and west (Melbourne–Adelaide), linking the major capital cities and the communities between them and possibly creating new communities en route.

Participants

The VFT system is a joint venture of four multinational companies, three based in Australia (BHP, Elders IXL, TNT) and one in Japan (Kumagai Gumi). The system also requires government cooperation for initial access to land along the route and later for its (compulsory if necessary) acquisition, and in defining and oversighting environmental impact processes.

The potential impediments to this development are not so much financial as political and environmental. Opposition comes from conservationists and, to a lesser extent, from some rail unions. Conservationists oppose a planned route through mountain forests and its proximity to national parks. They also focus on train noise. Some rail unions fear the loss of jobs on existing rail systems. Similar opposition has been expressed in Europe, Japan and the United States.

Community benefits

VFT is estimated to provide greater benefits for the community than for the joint venture. Its efficient use of energy and land were noted earlier. It would provide access to cheaper land and lower cost transport. It could arrest the present drift of population, and industry, to the north (Queensland), providing a more balanced regional development. It could also provide a more even development between the capital cities and smaller centres. It would facilitate a more even spread of incoming tourist flights between the already congested Sydney airport and the under-utilised Melbourne airport, reduce congestion, accidents and maintenance costs on interstate highways, and reduce imports of aircraft, trucks and fossil fuels. Like its overseas counterparts, it would be safe and reliable, and reduce transport costs.

Enhanced computer-based tools for planning these systems are being developed. These include land use – transport interaction models, and techniques for optimal location of alignments in three dimensions, for evaluation of financial, socioeconomic and environmental impacts, and for optimising the system as a whole.

Spatial impacts

The spatial impacts of fast rail at the regional or corridor level may be expressed in terms of the two-dimensional space of activity interaction versus activity dispersal, previously introduced (Figure 6; also Wild *et al.* 1985). The triangle ABC represents the limits to this dispersal (BC) and to interaction (AB, AC). A particular land use and travel pattern is represented by a point in this space, e.g. D_1.

The impacts of fast rail at the regional level are:
• to divert some existing travel from other modes representing a reduction in transport costs, time and energy use (but no movement of the point D_1);
• to increase interaction and average trip length in the corridor due to induced intercity travel, particularly to or from minor centres, representing a movement upwards (increased interaction distance, e.g. D_1 to D_2) in the short term;
• to induce decentralisation of some industry and residential development, representing a movement to the right (increased dispersal D_2 to D_3) over a longer period.

Thus, the spatial impact of fast rail in this two-dimensional framework is initially an increase in interactions and in trip lengths in the corridor representing an initial movement upwards in the interaction space, and an increase in dispersal of land use development representing a longer term movement to the right in Figure 6. The increased interactions are accomplished at a net reduction in transport energy use, and the increased dispersal allows a potential further reduction in energy use and greenhouse emissions through telecommunications and some degree of local self-sufficiency.

CONCLUSION

The developed world is entering a further phase of integration of its land use activities, and its communication and distribution systems with the development of fast rail networks. They fill a gap between trunk road systems (freeways and tollways) and faster air transport, catering for intercity (CBD to CBD) travel. They also link the smaller centres in the urban system inducing increased travel and decentralisation of some activities including residential, recreational and associated service industries. They cater for the commuter seeking cheaper land or recreational amenities, those seeking resort amenity and needing less frequent access to urban amenities, and service industries seeking lower cost locations. They also offer the potential for further integration of production, communication and distribution at a regional level as fast rail systems develop for both passengers and freight. This provides opportunities for major changes to land use and living patterns. The extent to which they are realised remains to be seen and studied.

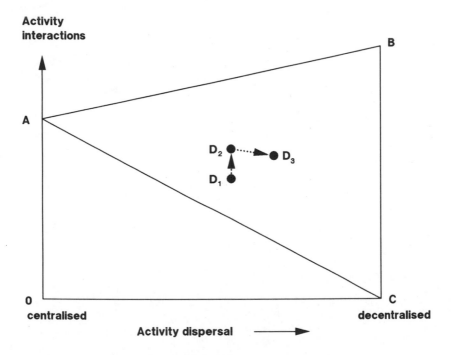

Figure 6 Activity dispersal versus activity interaction, in the fast rail corridor, and the limits to this dispersal and interaction defined by the triangle ABC. The impacts of fast rail are represented by the increased interaction distance (D_1 to D_2) induced in the short term and increased dispersal D_2 to D_3 induced over a longer period.

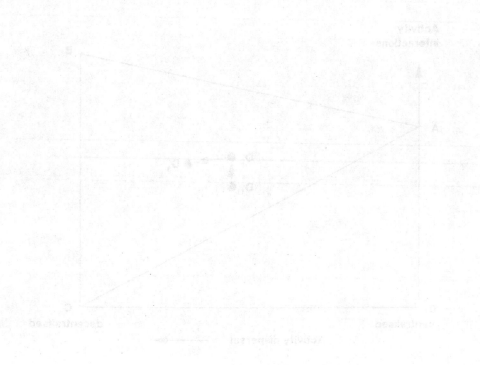

3

THE RAPID TRANSPORTATION SYSTEM AND THE SOCIOECONOMIC RESTRUCTURING OF JAPAN

Kozo Amano, Tsunekazu Toda and Dai Nakagawa

INTRODUCTION

Since early in the twentieth century, Japan has made great strides towards developing a rapid transport system. As a result, it has a high-speed network consisting of the airlines and Shinkansen. However, mainly due to the concentration of urban functions and population in the Tokyo metropolitan area, further transportation problems are being created. Increasing passenger demands are expected to soon exceed network capacities in some parts of the high-speed system. By contrast, there are still some regions to which the high-speed network does not extend. These transportation problems must be considered together with problems of urban concentration.

The technology of maglev and the linear motor is anticipated to be ready soon for implementation. This new high-speed system is expected not only to ease the load on existing systems, but also to play the more important role of alleviating the problems caused by urban concentration.

This chapter outlines the present status of the development of the maglev-linear motor in Japan, and proposes its use in meeting future transport needs. Firstly, a brief history of Japanese rapid transportation is presented. Secondly, a Chuo linear maglev express connecting Tokyo and Osaka is proposed. Thirdly, a quadruplet capitals' project is considered as one of the most effective measures to decentralise capital functions.

A BRIEF HISTORY OF JAPANESE RAPID TRANSPORTATION

The first plan was for a 'bullet train', with a maximum speed of 200 kilometres per hour, between Tokyo and Shimonoseki. The construction of this system started in 1940. However, it stopped in 1943 because of the Second World War, and the plan was abandoned. After the war, 'the business express

Kodama', which connected Tokyo and Osaka in 1958, was the fastest train. Its average speed was eighty-two kilometres per hour and it took six and a half hours to cover the 500 kilometres involved.

In 1957 the Tokaido Shinkansen plan was decided, and opened in 1964 between Tokyo and Osaka. Its maximum speed was 200 kilometres per hour and the trip time was four hours. Currently it takes less than three hours with a maximum speed of 220 kilometres per hour, and the line extends to Fukuoka.

Through the construction of Tohoku and Joetsu Shinkansen, the network now totals 1832 kilometres (Figure 1). Further extensions of the lines to a total of 4950 kilometres are planned. However, almost all plans are suspended for financial reasons.

On the other hand, the airline network is developed among major cities and the increase in passenger numbers is remarkable.

TECHNOLOGICAL DEVELOPMENT OF MAGLEV

The basic research on maglev started at the Railway Technical Research Institute of Japan National Railway (JNR) in 1962, before the operation of the Tokaido Shinkansen, and the first magnetically levitated tram was tested in 1972. Experiments at the Miyazaki Test Center (with a total length of

Figure 1 The Shinkansen network in Japan.

guideway of seven kilometres) commenced in 1977. In 1979, the test vehicle ML500 achieved the world speed record of 517 kilometres per hour at this centre. The next vehicle, MLU001, achieved a manned speed record of 305 kilometres per hour in April 1982, and 400.8 kilometres per hour in December 1987. At present, the MLU002 is under test.

These achievements are at the leading edge of world technology, and show the practical potential of an ultra-high-speed surface transport system. The remaining step before implementation is to run on a test track of more than forty kilometres, which will need to be constructed in advance on the planned route.

This system was developed using superconductors for magnetic levitation by repulsion. Recent advances in higher temperature superconducting materials may be used here when liquid helium gas cooling is superseded. The superconductivity temperature is expected to increase further with future technological developments.

The maglev linear motor system has the following advantages over the present Shinkansen:
- the speed can exceed 500 kilometres per hour as the propulsive force does not depend on friction between rail and wheel;
- as the vehicle is levitated magnetically, less noise and vibration is generated along the line for a given speed;
- the grade may be as high as 10 per cent, which can reduce the length of tunnels, and decrease the total earthworks cost;
- as the vehicle is levitated, the wear on infrastructure is small, saving maintenance costs;
- the linear motor vehicle can make more than two round trips, while the Shinkansen makes only one. This high productivity would reduce the operating costs;
- as the vehicle is levitated without contact with rail and guideway, passengers can have a more comfortable ride.

As mentioned above, the linear motor system has various potential advantages, including reduced construction costs, convenient and comfortable service, lower operation and maintenance costs, and less pollution for residents along the line. Moreover, this system has been developed in parallel with various fields of technology including superconductivity, and an additional impact expected is the induced development of high technology in related fields.

THE CHUO LINEAR EXPRESS AND ITS IMPACTS

The maglev system developed by JNR has already overcome basic technological problems and the remaining work is related to its development for practical use. Therefore, it is expected that a route will be selected for this development as soon as possible. The authors' proposal is to connect Tokyo and Osaka with such a system, along an approximately straight line of about 500 kilometres. One reason is that the passenger demand between Tokyo and Osaka will soon exceed the capacity of the existing Shinkansen and airlines. The other is that this line can play an important part in solving the problems caused by concentration of functions in Tokyo, as later outlined.

The Chuo linear express would connect Tokyo with Kofu, Nagoya and Osaka, and take only twenty minutes between inter-city sectors. This means that the place of Osaka will move to that of Kofu as shown in Figure 2, and Tokyo and Osaka would become one city for all practical purposes.

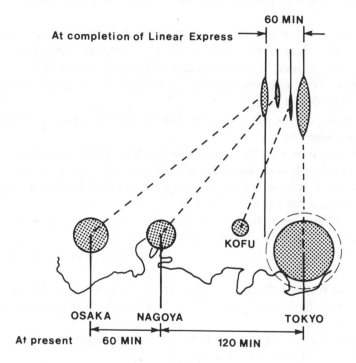

Figure 2 The change of travel time caused by linear express.

QUADRUPLET CAPITALS PROJECT

Decentralisation

The means of decentralisation proposed is the linear motor vehicle. Before introducing this plan, the problems caused by the concentration of urban functions in Tokyo are discussed.

Although wholesale commodity prices are stable, the average land price in Tokyo doubled each year for about three years from 1985. The role of Tokyo as an international financial and information centre has been growing significantly, and the demand for office buildings has come from foreign as well as domestic companies. These phenomena brought a sharp rise in land prices in the limited city centre of Tokyo. The land price in the best part of Marunouchi district reached thirty billion yen per square kilometre, and that of residential areas within a radius of thirty to fifty kilometres increased. As a result, although new buildings will be constructed, adequate infrastructure facilities such as roads, parks and water supply to support those urban activities cannot be expected, and the living environment for citizens will deteriorate. Figure 3 explains the causal relationship generating various problems by the concentration of functions in Tokyo.

In view of these impacts, the scheme proposed for Tokyo is one that aims to restrain further concentration and to decrease the demand on land to match the supply. Moreover, it must be considered not from the narrow perspective of the Tokyo region, but nationwide.

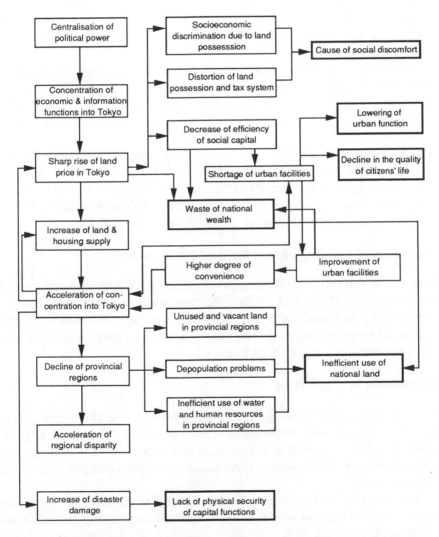

Figure 3 Problems caused by the concentration of functions into Tokyo.

Quadruplet capitals

The proposal for decentralising capital functions follows.

New high-tech cities would be built on vacant lands which are 200 to 300 hectares in area in the suburbs of Kofu, Nagoya and Osaka, and the station for the maglev linear express would be constructed in the centre of each city. These areas are designated as Special Districts, which compose the quadruplet 'Capital Special City' with Tokyo's Kasumigaseki–Marunouchi district (the 'Chiyoda Special District') (Figure 4).

The central government's twelve ministries and eight agencies headed by state ministers, currently concentrated in Tokyo's Kasumigaseki district, should be dispersed across the 500 kilometre region stretching from Tokyo to Osaka. Three or four should be relocated in each of the new districts in Kofu, Nagoya and Osaka. The Kasumigaseki–Marunouchi district which is hundreds of hectares in area will be enlarged to twice or three times the present size at the same time.

As the maximum travel time from Tokyo to Osaka, through Kofu and Nagoya, will be sixty minutes, the requirement of each department or agency to locate at a specific place would weaken, and the most effective alternative can be selected to realise a multi-polar, dispersed pattern of national land development.

Various organisations related to central government, such as the Bank of Japan and public corporations, should relocate following the movement of the relevant supervisory ministry or agency. For example, the Management and Coordination Agency, Cabinet Secretariat, Prime Minister's Official Residence, and Ministry of Justice could be moved to Kofu.

Governmental buildings wired for the high-tech age

Many of the buildings in Kasumigaseki that house government agencies were built in the 1950s and 1960s. The relocation program would provide an opportunity to transfer the agencies from buildings inadequate to house modern data-processing and telecommunications equipment, into smart buildings wired for the high-tech age.

City building in a new field

These governmental buildings would be rebuilt at the three new Special Districts, which would allow for a spacious layout. The most advanced intelligent buildings would be constructed and enough vacant land should be secured. Civil servants working there could move into congenial residential neighbourhoods.

Tokyo businesses would also be encouraged to relocate in these areas, thereby alleviating the city's congestion and improving its residential environment.

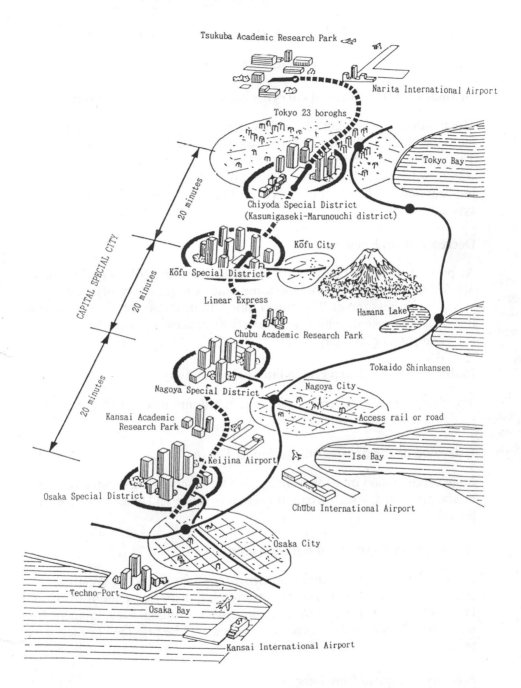

Figure 4 Imaginary plan of special districts in the 'quadruplet capitals project'.

ADVANTAGES OF QUADRUPLET CAPITALS PROJECT

The advantages of this project are summarised as follows.

Dramatic improvement of carrying capacity of the Tokaido line

The number of passengers carried by Tokaido Shinkansen is more than 150 thousand a day and about 270 trains are operated per day in both directions. The system has already reached the limit of its carrying capacity. The best way to solve the sclerosis of the 600 kilometre trunk artery in Japan is the introduction of the most advanced railway technology, the linear motor system.

Decrease of time consumption

At present, it takes three hours to travel between Tokyo and Osaka by Shinkansen 'Hikari'. Almost the same time is required by plane, including access and egress travel. This travel time will be reduced to one hour by the linear motor system, which will save 320 thousand person hours for 160 thousand passengers a day.

Reduction of the sharp rise in land prices in Tokyo

The sharp rise in land prices can be reduced and the basic factors causing land problems in Tokyo can be solved.

Extension of the prosperous period in Tokyo

More concentration into Tokyo along with the deteriorating urban environment can be prevented, which would prevent its decline and extend its prosperous period.

Balanced development of national land

Even if clear decentralisation of urban functions found in West Germany cannot be expected in Japan, the multi-polar, dispersed pattern of national land, proposed in the Fourth Comprehensive National Development Plan, would be realised, and various conditions would be provided in each region to enjoy its economical and cultural properties.

Security of capital functions

Japan is in an earthquake belt and the possibility of a 'Second Kanto Big Earthquake' cannot be denied completely. Although the dispersal of some capital functions from Tokyo might decrease the agglomeration advantages slightly, it can add robustness with a small 'disaster insurance premium.'

Impacts to promote the development of high-technology

The practical use of a maglev linear express would boost technological development in various fields including superconductivity. Visible and invisible benefits can be expected from this system for living and economic conditions in Japan.

Growth of domestic demand

The construction of a linear express would stimulate the construction, steel and cement production industries directly. It would also enlarge domestic demand in other industries indirectly.

Moreover, the completion of the linear express would provide a convenient travel service between Tokyo, Nagoya and Osaka, and accelerate urban and industrial development at various cities along the line, including Hachioji, Kofu, Iida, Nakatsugawa, Suzuka and Nara. Furthermore, if some capital functions are moved into three Special Districts, the construction of infrastructure facilities such as roads, water supply and subways would cause large internal demands, which would relax economic friction with foreign countries.

Therefore, the decentralisation of capital functions is a very effective plan to meet a number of planning objectives.

CONCLUSIONS: WORKING TOWARDS A COMFORTABLE LIVING

The concentration of urban functions into Tokyo has stimulated the Japanese economy in the period of rapid economic growth. However, various environments surrounding Japan were changed dramatically when a foreign trade surplus of 100 billion dollars a year in Japan strained relationships with other countries. One of the main reasons for this problem may be the Japanese attitude to seek efficiency and rationality, neglecting 'humanity.' The concentration of urban functions into Tokyo corresponds to the acceleration of financial problems and tensions in the world.

The world environment requires Japanese society to change from a workers' society to a comfortable and humanistic society. The rigid illusion that 'Tokyo is Japan', neglecting the spirit of the times, should be weakened. The sharp rise of land prices in Tokyo can be interpreted as an alarm bell for this illusion.

Tokyo is a typical city where all urban functions including political power, economy, information and culture are concentrated. Other cities besides Tokyo have various problems because of excessive concentration. If Japan proposes a solution to this problem and executes it by herself, it can become a valuable contribution to human welfare in the world.

4

NEW TRANSPORT SYSTEMS IN EUROPE: A STRATEGIC EXPLORATION

Peter Nijkamp and Adriaan Perrels

INTRODUCTION

In this chapter the claim is made – on the basis of a mainly qualitative socioeconomic and spatial exploration – that a more integrative, advanced and environment-friendly transport system in Europe is needed. It should provide a feasible and promising infrastructure alternative in the light of the great many bottlenecks faced in current transport systems in most European countries at both local/regional and national/international scales. A proposal is made to regard subterranean transport as a realistic option to be investigated more thoroughly.

Europe is in motion, politically, economically and spatially. In the past decade the European transport map has featured a wide variety of problematic developments at both local/regional and national/international scales. Despite the increasing popularity of just-in-time (JIT) systems and related concepts, the actual practice of both commodity and passenger transport is disappointing and often frustrating. Severe traffic congestion phenomena at the urban or metropolitan level (e.g. Athens, Rome, Paris), unacceptable delays in medium and long distance transport during peak hours, unsatisfactory service levels of European railway systems (and public transport in general), unreliable airline connections due to limited airport capacity, and slow technical and institutional renewal of air traffic control in Europe; all these phenomena illustrate the difficult position of the European transport sector. And there is no clear perspective for a drastic improvement of this situation. On the contrary, it is increasingly claimed that a free European market (beyond 1992) and further deregulation of the European transport sector, may lead to unacceptable accessibility conditions in major regions in Europe. Another important complicating factor will be environmental policy. In contrast to the deregulation with respect to the pure transport market phenomena, environmental policy is critically dependent on a great deal of regulation. In particular, technical restrictions are likely to be imposed, e.g. limited emission levels of motor cars or even a prohibition of the use of certain transport modes.

Transport policy makers in most European countries find themselves in exremely complicated situations. A large number of interest groups, ranging from multinational companies to local environmentalists, urges them to take action, however often in quite different directions. On the one hand it has become obvious that the environment poses its limits on the volume, the character and the pace of the extension of the transport infrastructure. On the other hand most companies in (western) Europe are concerned about their competitiveness in a global context due to inadequate infrastructure.

The inadequate infrastructure might hit European business in several ways. The relatively slow development of sophisticated telecommunication infrastructure in Europe may curtail the industries in the possibilities to offer new services. Moreover it may limit the possibilities to speed up international trade in a reliable way. Also, the restricted capacity of inland transport networks may cause higher production cost levels in Europe. However the last item should not be overstated as regards global competitiveness. For instance, Japan also suffers from heavy congestion on inland transport systems, although it should be admitted that Japan invests heavily in (high-speed) railway infrastructure and other rapid mass transit alternatives.

All in all, it is clear that Europe should increase its investments concerning transport and communication infrastructure in order to increase its competitive power. Despite the urgency in some areas, the extra efforts should be allocated with care for both economic and environmental reasons. This raises an extra difficulty, as sufficient care is usually incompatible with swift action. Short-term solutions, as advocated by some – mostly business-oriented – interest groups, will rely heavily on a further massive extension of the European motorway sytem. This option may make some sense for southern and eastern Europe, but for western Europe this option does not seem viable in the long run. Time and again, Say's Law [that each supply (e.g. of infrastructure) generates its own demand] has proven its validity concerning the motorway sytem. Therefore, any extension beyond the level of relieving some unfortunate bottlenecks will only create a next era of congestion on a higher level. Such a scenario will be likely, even if additional measures, such as road pricing, were introduced. Furthermore, it will be detrimental to the spatial organisation of most urban areas as well as to the ecology in western Europe.

Other alternatives in western Europe, such as the extension of public transport infrastructure, both for short and long distances, will necessarily have a long-term character. Although it may be more expensive as regards both the investments and the operational costs, we could receive a better quality of life in a sustainable economy.

As is already briefly indicated above, radical long-term solutions, relying mostly on more or less collective kinds of transport, seem to offer the best prospects. In order to explore more favourable future transport infrastructure options, the Dutch Minister of Transport and Public Works has recently commissioned a study with the explicit aim to investigate new and non-conventional infrastructures which nevertheless should be compatible with the current infrastructure system. In this context, the concept of ITS (integrated transport system), which is based on a high-speed vacuum pipeline system and which existed already in blueprint form on the drawing board, has been further developed and placed in a socioeconomic and spatial context.

The present chapter will report on findings from this exploratory study. First, the essential characteristics of ITS will be described in more detail, then the long-term backgrounds of transport evolution in Europe will be sketched by providing an inventory of structural developments (megatrends), impacts and bottlenecks in the field of spatial development and transport. Finally, we will look at the question of whether – and if so, to what extent – ITS may contribute to a removal of foreseeable bottlenecks in the European transport scene. This chapter will be concluded with some reflective comments.

ITS – A SYSTEM DESCRIPTION

Time and space are important cost factors in all economic activities. Consequently, the design, implementation and maintenance of a fast and reliable transport system is of paramount importance for the competitive situation of our economies. Given the fact that high-speed and reliable infrastructure systems are increasingly facing problems of congestion, environmental externalities and high energy consumption, various attempts have been made to design new infrastructure alternatives. One such option is ITS.

The ITS concept is based on two complementary transport system modules, viz. a high-speed transport (HST) module for fast medium and long distance shuttle transport of both passengers and commodities via an underground vacuum pipeline system, and a collecting and distributing transport (CDT) module for providing a variety of efficient transport connections (mainly based on adapted conventional transport modes) to the terminals of the HST system in major urban agglomerations.

The aim of ITS is to provide a technologically advanced transport system which is nevertheless compatible with the existing transport infrastructure. It serves to increase drastically the capacity of both passenger and commodity transport in Europe, to provide fast and reliable transport at low variable costs, and to reduce environmental stress dramatically due to the underground structure whose construction is based on low-cost tunnelling techniques.

In a final form, ITS is intended to become a European network connecting major economic centres in various countries. Permanent near-vacuum in the underground tunnels allows high-speed trains (in the form of shuttles with a maximum capacity of approximately thirty passengers or ten tonne of freight and a maximum speed of 540 kilometres per hour) to provide reliable and frequent linkages between the HST terminals in major agglomerations in Europe. This new infrastructure system, which is entirely computer-controlled, is suitable for both person and goods transport. It does not suffer from current congestion phenomena (in ground and air transport), environmental externalities (pollution, landscape deterioration) and high energy consumption. The variable costs (per person-kilometre or tonne-kilometre) are extremely low, so that a very high frequency of the service can be offered. The CDT module acts then as a tailor-made complementary system for the local/regional transport of persons and commodities to and from the HST terminals in urban centres.

In general, the design principles of ITS are the following:
- fast, efficient and reliable door-to-door transport of persons and commodities;
- low variable (operating) costs for the HST-part;
- compatibility with existing transport modes;
- minimum surface occupancy (i.e. minimum land use);
- large transport capacity;
- high degree of safety;
- low dependence on fossil fuels;
- low impacts on nature and landscape.

It is clear that all these objectives cannot be fulfilled by a single transport system, so that an integration between existing and new infrastructure has to be striven for. This also explains the subdivision of ITS into an HST and a CDT module. Further details on these modules will be given later.

The HST module

The HST module follows modern advances in the telecommunication, informatics, telematics and new materials technology. Predecessors were the Japanese Shinkansen and the French TGV, whilst at present new developments (e.g. maglev) are underway. All such new infrastructure designs focus attention on advanced, reliable and high-speed transport modes. However, many of these new transport modes overlook social costs emerging from environmental externalities (e.g. noise annoyance, deterioration of landscapes and 'cityscapes') and energy use. ITS is aimed at a drastic reduction in both environmental and energy cost of modern transport by providing for its HST module an underground low-cost tunnelling infrastructure which, through its (almost) vacuum tubes, leads to drastic energy savings, whilst the CDT module ensures an efficient linkage of HST terminals to existing transport infrastructures.

The feeder lines to the HST terminals are tubes in which the shuttles have a modest speed (up to 200 kilometre per hour), whilst the main lines allow a maximum speed up to 540 kilometre per hour. The general features and advantages of the HST module are:
- high average speed (maximum speed 540 kilometre per hour) (compare the speed of TGV-Atlantique of 300 kilometre per hour);
- enormous capacity (e.g. in the Dutch context already sixty-four million person kilometre per hour);

- extremely low energy use (0.025 kilowatt hours per tonne kilometre) (compare the energy use of TGV of 0.52 kilowatt hours per tonne kilometre);
- reliable service due to a computer-controlled system which is independent of weather conditions;
- minimum waiting time and transfer problems;
- high frequency of service and high capacity (up to 1800 shuttles per hour per tube);
- negligible environmental effects;
- negligible surface and landscape destruction;
- high degree of safety;
- considerable time savings at medium and long distances.

The HST system vehicles are cylindric aerodynamic shuttles in which the air pressure is kept atmospheric constant. The low pressure in the (almost) vacuum pipeline system and the related energy efficiency on the one hand, and low maintenance and personnel costs on the other, make this system suitable for an inexpensive extension of its capacity. Shuttles can be fully automated and sent to any desired terminal. For instance, it has been calculated that the shuttle transport of a car including passengers over a distance of approximately 1000 kilometres will not cost more than approximately Dfl. 100, while the travel time is approximately two hours. Similar developments are also taking place in other countries (e.g. the United States; see Davidson 1987).

The CDT module

The CDT module enables the integration between local/urban/regional infrastructure facilities and the HST system. It is made up of a variety of medium-scale, small-scale and tailor-made transport solutions for both passengers and goods, ranging from trains and trucks to small neighbourhood buses and small specialised pick-up vans. This means that an optimal reconciliation with the existing transport infrastructure at the local/urban/regional level has to be found. In any case, it would be necessary to have, whenever possible, a radial penetration into population/industrial centres from the HST terminals by means of efficient, reliable and frequent public transport without drastic changes of road infrastructure at the local/urban/regional scale. The entire system should function as an integrated hierarchical system, in which each sub-system is used for those purposes to which it is best suited. Such a design may produce a very efficient transport system in terms of both natural resources and costs. Thus the CDT module, as part of the ITS system, is complementary to the HST system. It serves various purposes, such as efficient commuting, just-in-time delivery of commodities (mainly in containerised form), recreational trips, and medium and long distance business journeys. The general features and advantages of the CDT module are:

- relatively high speed in urban areas due to efficient organisation;
- transport of both passengers and commodities;
- integration with public transport and private transport;

- short waiting times for transport to HST terminals due to computerised calling systems;
- (if desired) use of private car to HST terminal;
- need for only marginal adjustments in existing infrastructure;
- possibility of door-to-door transport.

Thus, there is a variety of transport modes within the CDT system – private car, taxi, tram, metro, bus, truck, conveyor car, etc.

ITS: a new perspective

ITS has – in comparison to other infrastructure solutions – the following evident advantages:
- relatively low environmental stress;
- relatively low energy use;
- a high degree of safety and reliability;
- low exploitation costs;
- full use of modern technologies (telematics, new materials, etc.);
- high-speed transport;
- high frequency of service;
- door-to-door transport.

The safety issue is of course extremely important in this context, ranging from operational (systemic) and material safety to personal safety. In a way comparable to airline safety measures, systematic procedures have to be developed (in terms of monitoring and checking procedures). Naturally the interior design of the shuttle has to meet the psychological perception of travellers. The economic feasibility is of course of decisive importance. The construction costs of such advanced infrastructure are high, but this is compensated by excessively low variable transport costs. An assessment of the travel time curve of various transport modes is given in Figure 1. It will be clear that both the CDT and the HST systems should maintain a high average velocity compared to the individual competing systems (car and airplane). Otherwise ITS will not develop a sufficiently large market and consequently the unit costs will be too high.

Having described systematically (although briefly) the main features of ITS, we will now describe which developments and bottlenecks in the transport sector may be expected, followed by a treatment of the question whether ITS may provide a proper response to such bottlenecks.

LONG-TERM DEVELOPMENTS IN THE TRANSPORT SECTOR

In the light of the economic restructuring of the European economies, of the changing international trade patterns after 1992 and of the adoption of new telecommunications/informatics technologies, the transport sector will become a decisive determinant for the future developments of Europe. In the context of the present study, we will focus attention successively on emerging megatrends, foreseeable consequences and emerging bottlenecks.

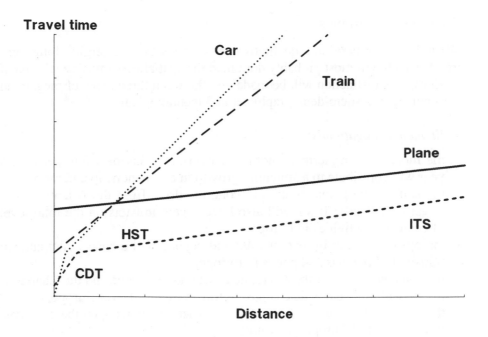

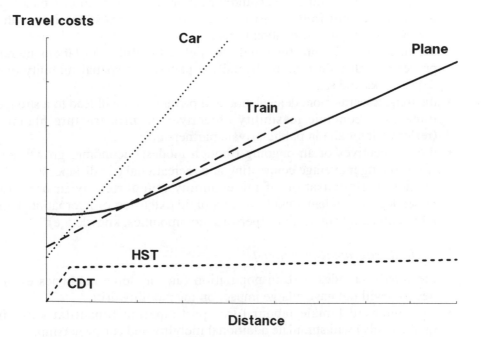

Figure 1 Indicative travel times and costs of various modes.

Emerging megatrends

We will present here, in a qualitative sense, a series of emerging long-term trends which will most probably dominate the spatial-economic development of Europe. A distinction will be made here between three types of megatrend – 1 economic, 2 socio-demographic, and 3 technological.

1 Economic megatrends:

- the moderate long-term economic growth prospects of a few per cent a year will contribute to a structural growth in car ownership and mobility;
- the shift of the global centre of economic drive from the Atlantic Basin toward the Pacific Basin will also have severe impacts on the total level of economic activities in Europe;
- the open market in Europe in 1992 and beyond will increase international transport of persons and goods in Europe;
- the southward shift of the economic heartland of Europe and the Channel;
- tunnel will induce drastic changes in traffic flows all over Europe;
- the rapid shifts in eastern Europe will drastically impact upon the economic development of Europe as a whole;
- the rapid penetration of telecommunication and information technology will create a shift from industrial production to business services with a major emphasis of information transfer;
- the increase in leisure time and the higher flexibility in labour market processes will induce more diversified patterns of spatial mobility over days, weeks and seasons;
- the trend towards more deregulation and privatisation will lead to a stronger impact of economic feasibility objectives in infrastructure planning (reflected inter alia in public-private partnership);
- the perspectives of an ongoing (though modest) economic growth also leads to longer average commuting and recreational trip distances;
- the internationalisation of the economy (supported by information technology and telematics) leads to a rapid extension of international and intercontinental connections (persons, commodities, knowledge).

2 Socio-demographic megatrends:

- the relative modest rise in population (and in some countries even a decline) will not have a large impact on the mobility drift;
- the increased female labour force participation (quantitatively and qualitatively) will stimulate additional mobility and car ownership;
- the demographic aging processes will lead to a society in which a considerable part of the population, having plenty of leisure time and an appreciable purchasing power, will show a highly mobile behaviour, notably by car;
- new lifestyles (two person households, etc.) will lead to a rise in mobility reflected inter alia in multiple holidays a year;

- foreseeable higher education levels will also lead to more international mobility, both for leisure and business;
- the intensification in business relationships will also lead to more international (and intercontinental) traffic movements.

3 Technological megatrends:

- the increasing importance of telematics will drastically increase the number of interpersonal interactions, which for routine matters may be a substitute for physical interactions, but for non-routine activities there will be a need for more face-to-face contacts;
- new technologies (e.g. new materials and super-conductivity) will lead to spectacular changes in conventional transport modes beyond the year 2000;
- there is a tendency toward an increasingly large-scale European infrastructure (the Channel tunnel, the TGV, the Trans-European Motorway, etc.);
- the development of new logistic structures (e.g. JIT, INTIS, Sagitta) leads to an integration of production and distribution of commodities and hence to a dramatic increase in the efficiency of commodity handling;
- new developments in the telecommunication area (e.g. ISDN, IBC) will intensify rapid international contacts and hence increase the efficiency of international commodity transport.

Foreseeable consequences

The foreseeable consequences of these megatrends are manifold and will be listed here in a qualitative sense under three systematic headings – 1 transport, 2 environment, energy and safety, and 3 land use.

1 Transport:

- the mobility drift based on private car use will continue to rise in the foreseeable future;
- the mobility in business transport over long distances will also structurally increase in the medium and long term;
- conventional public transport will face serious difficulties in terms of capacity, service level, reliability and financial results;
- rapid intercity transport is likely to create a relatively favourable position;
- the road, railway and telecommunication infrastructure in and around large agglomerations will be facing serious capacity problems, not only during the peak hours but even during many hours of the day;
- there will be a serious lack of parking space in urban areas;
- the spatial mobility for social, cultural and recreational purposes as a consequence of the increase in leisure time, car ownership and rise in income, will drastically increase;
- there will be an increasing potential for large-scale, rapid and environment-friendly mass transit systems.

2 *Environment, energy and safety:*

- environmental deterioration will increasingly take place as a consequence of transport mobility (air pollution, smog, solid waste, etc.);
- in the long run the increasing use of primary and secondary raw materials in car production will lead to a further exhaustion of scarce natural resources;
- the threats to the environment will induce new vehicle and infrastructure technologies which serve to ensure ecological sustainability;
- the open character of Europe leads to an internationalisation of environmental problems;
- in terms of safety, a relative shift from more frequent small-scale to infrequent but (very) large-scale accidents is likely to take place in the future.

3 *Land use:*

- the conventional infrastructure will increasingly use a considerable part of scarce land in densely populated areas, especially in the case of surface transport;
- a further extension of traditional infrastructure will lead to a large number of intersections through ecologically valuable areas, so that the 'wholeness of a natural system' is affected.

Emerging bottlenecks

Given the aforementioned megatrends and their consequences, a variety of serious threats to the transport sector may be expected:
- a structural threat to environmental quality, as ecological sustainability standards are likely to be violated in the future;
- an increasing congestion in urban agglomerations, especially on ring roads outside the centre;
- a serious lack of parking space in urban areas, with many negative consequences for the quality of life and safety;
- limited possibilities for expansion of conventional infrastructures in densely populated areas;
- lack of capacity and of service levels of conventional public transport;
- unsatisfactory maintenance and management of existing infrastructure;
- increasing serious congestion in air traffic, so that, especially during the peak hours, time schedules become entirely unreliable.

The general conclusion from the previous qualitative observations is that a structural incompatibility of long-term transport developments with socio-economic environmental and safety conditions is likely to emerge. In the light of these observations two questions have to be raised:
- Do we have a sufficient spectrum of policy options for coping with these bottlenecks?
- Does ITS provide a satisfactory potential for coping with these problems?

These questions will be dealt with in the next section.

POLICY OPTIONS AND THE POTENTIAL OF ITS

In view of the bottleneck phenomena in European transport developments, various policy initiatives and bottlenecks can be imagined, ranging from incremental to integral changes. However, piecemeal and incremental policy actions are likely to be unsuccessful, as they do not account for the drastic restructuring processes of most European countries. A passive transport and infrastructure policy neglects too much the far-reaching importance of geographical accessibility for all regions and nations of western Europe, and hence transport and infrastructure planning cannot afford to be trend following; it should be more active and steering.

Indeed, since the last years of the past decade, ambitious transport plans are proliferating across Europe. In particular, railway technology is receiving a lot of attention. Many railway companies include high-speed lines in their future plans. However, it remains to be seen to what extent the plans will actually materialise. To date, France is far in the lead with one line in operation (Paris–Lyon ±400 kilometres) and a next line to be opened in 1990 (Paris–Bordeaux ±550 kilometres). The Federal Republic of Germany has several high-speed 'stretches' (the longest is Hannover–Wurzburg ±300 kilometres) on which high-speed trains will be operated from 1989. Italy has reached about the same stage as Germany as regards the line Roma–Milano. These three countries intend to expand their high-speed railway networks. Fast trains with somewhat lower speeds (±200 kilometres per hour) are operated in the United Kingdom and the USSR. Other high-speed projects are reported in Sweden, Austria, Spain and Switzerland.

It is very striking that all these plans have an outright national character. The only international project is the extension of the French system to Brussels, Amsterdam and Cologne. Further development of border crossing connections is required to generate more benefits from these high-speed systems. Even if these interconnections are realised, various impediments remain due to the different technologies applied. Obviously the lack of international thinking in the beginning of the various projects has transformed itself in a structural shortcoming of the upgrading of the European (rail) infrastructure.

It would also be desirable to design and implement more environment- and energy-friendly transport modes, as ecologically sustainable economic development objectives are of paramount importance for an appropriate long-term balanced evolution of our economies. Technology policy and transport policy are of crucial importance here.

As an intermediate step 'polluter pays' principles and road pricing policies may be meaningful (and in the future probably electronic road pricing) to reduce emissions by cars and to induce selective car use, but such policy actions do not aim to achieve an integral and dramatic improvement of environmental quality.

Clearly, in the area of physical planning, alternative complementary measures can be foreseen, such as compact city planning and reurbanisation (although the traffic consequences of such options are not by definition favourable), combined transport mode planning (e.g. rail/road, road/air, water/rail), enhancement of the service level of public transport (including before and after transport), etc.

To overcome the urgent problems and to alleviate the pressure in general, national and regional authorities could resort to intermediate measures. What will be effective will depend largely on regional or local circumstances. Two kinds of measures are worth mentioning as they already receive some attention in several European countries. In the first place, tele-communication could be promoted as a substitute for transport, e.g. teleconferencing and telework. In some areas or countries this option will offer very limited possibilities due to general capacity problems in the telecommunication network. Second, the organisation of work times and opening times of shops and services may be rescheduled in a more flexible way. That means a larger range of choice of opening and closing times together with an overall increase of production time. Due to increasing capital intensity in various industries, this option has already gained some popularity among entrepreneurs. The difficulties, not only in the company organisation but also at the micro and macro level in the society in general, should not be underestimated. However, limited rescheduling, both in terms of diurnal patterns and the number of sectors involved, should be feasible in the short run.

All such policy directions are meaningful, but it is still questionable whether such initiatives will ensure the aforementioned compatibility requirement between high-speed and reliable transport on the one hand and environmental, safety and socioeconomic conditions on the other hand.

In this context, it is meaningful to reconsider the potential role of ITS. A variety of bottlenecks has been listed, viz. unacceptable environmental impacts, congestion, lack of parking space, lack of space for expansion of infrastructure, inadequate conventional public transport, lack of maintenance/management of existing infrastructure, and congestion in air traffic.

ITS may provide a new potential for both offering a high quality service and removing these bottlenecks. Referring to economic theory, the system design strives for a maximum utilisation of the efficiency envelope. In terms of quality, ITS has the following favourable characteristics:

- it is not competitive with, but complementary to, existing transport modes;
- it offers high-speed transport at low costs, high reliability and high safety (the HST module);
- it uses a variety of existing transport modes (including public transport) to ensure efficient before and after transport (the CDT module);
- it exploits the potential offered by modern informatics and telematics, and may act as an incubator for even more advanced technologies;
- it meets very strict environmental standards (in terms of noise annoyance, pollution and landscape deterioration) at excessively low energy costs;
- it ensures a just-in-time and door-to-door delivery of commodities at extremely low variable costs; and

- it provides an infrastructure that is appropriate for an open Common Market in which internationalisation of transport of persons and goods is an important feature.

Of course, it should be mentioned that ITS is not a panacea for all transport problems. Moreover, in all sections of the transport industry, the problems mentioned have certainly been noticed. Several initiatives are underway to produce solutions largely based on existing systems, for instance the automatically guided electric car. However, ITS is an important alternative which offers a huge potential in combination with the (adjusted) existing infrastructure. From a technical point of view, it is able to remove the major congestion problems in densely populated areas and in air traffic, while preserving the quality of landscape and the environment.

To acquire more insight into the potential of ITS, a social cost–benefit assessment will be carried out. This assessment study is quite a challenge as it endeavours to compare several future transport systems in terms of market share opportunities. The future transport systems to be considered are ITS, high-speed trains such as TGV and ICE, magnetic levitation vehicles such as TRANSRAPID and automatically guided electric cars. Apart from these four rather advanced alternatives, upgraded versions of conventional transport modes such as inland shipping are included.

CONCLUSION

In the light of the great many foreseeable structural changes in the western economies, notably the changes in distributional patterns of persons and commodities, the need to reflect on new forms of infrastructure which meet the demands of the twenty-first century is evident. Such new forms have to be designed, based on a multiplicity of objectives: speed, safety, convenience, flexibility, low energy use, low environmental impact, low land use claims and economic efficiency. Only a system which provides a surplus value on top of the existing infrastructure may be regarded as a plausible option for the future: synergy is a sine qua non.

The conclusion from the previous section that ITS may provide such a meaningful option needs to be demonstrated by means of a further feasibility analysis, e.g. on the basis of an experimental pilot study for a concrete sector (e.g. Amsterdam–Brussels or Rotterdam–Ruhr area). The socioeconomic and geographical spinoffs could then be studied in more detail. In all cases, compatibility with existing transport modes offering tailor-made solutions – in the form of CDT modules – for the terminals of ITS systems has to be given due attention. In this sense, ITS may really become an integrated European transport system at both local/regional and national/international levels.

PART II

NEW INFORMATION AND COMMUNICATION TECHNOLOGIES AND THEIR SPATIAL IMPACTS

5

NEW TELECOMMUNICATIONS NETWORKS AND THE SPATIAL CHARACTERISTICS OF MARKETS

William Melody

INTRODUCTION

The convergence of rapidly improving computer and telecommunications technology is having a profound impact upon economic and social institutions. The growing significance of electronic information and communication networks has highlighted the overwhelming importance of information and communication, aspects of life that generally are taken for granted in economic analysis. The characteristics of information gathering, storage, processing and dissemination fundamentally affect the nature of markets and the structure of industry, as well as the competitiveness of firms and the prosperity of regions. They affect the internal structure of organisations and the information environment through which consumer behaviour is formed.

When information and communication networks undergo major change, traditional explanations of economic and social phenomena are rendered obsolete. The new information and communication systems are often more complex than the old. Ironically, in an age where information and communication systems are more sophisticated and comprehensive than ever before, the planning horizons for decision makers of all kinds are continuously being reduced because of a growing inability to forecast even short-term future developments. Seldom in our history has a subject attracted such attention, yet yielded so little critical insight into its long-term implications.

The fundamental reason that changes now taking place in the information and communication sector are so pervasive is that they affect the characteristics of essential information and communication networks. But most theories attempting to explain the characteristics of the primary institutions in society, such as economic markets or political democracy, assume a stable state of perfect information and communication. This may be tolerable under relatively stable institutional conditions. It is not acceptable when the underlying information and communication structures are undergoing significant change.

Major technological advances in telecommunications have pushed back the extensive geographical limit of markets in an increasing number of industries from local and national to global dimensions. Major technological advances in microelectronics and the computer industry have pushed back the intensive limit of information markets by reducing the cost of generating more and more kinds of data. What are the implications of markets without geographical limits, and an enormous expansion of information? The conventional economic theory of markets would suggest that more information and better (and cheaper) communication can only improve the functional efficiency of markets. It must lead to expanded competition and an increased role for the market in allocating resources in society. More considered analysis, and the experience of the last decade raises questions about this oversimplified analysis. In particular, it raises the possibility that improved information and communication networks may be fundamentally altering the structure of markets so that, at least in many instances, they function less efficiently and play a less significant role in allocating resources. This chapter investigates some of the implications.

INFORMATION, COMMUNICATION AND INSTITUTIONS

The definition and structure of all institutions are significantly influenced by the state of information. Institutions are created from the development of a desire to share information, thereby cultivating patterns of interaction, that is, communication or information exchange. Institutions become structured in particular ways to achieve desired internal and external information flows. The institutional structure changes when, for whatever reason, the communication processes and information change. Institutions die when the incentive or the ability to maintain the information flows and communication links ceases. Institutions can be described according to their informational characteristics, and one way to study institutional change is to focus directly on an institution's changing information and communication structure.

Equally significant for economic analysis is the fact that institutions also generate information for the external environment that is employed by other institutions and individuals for decision making. For any particular institutional structure in society, there will be an associated information structure that will influence how that society functions. Some institutional structures will provide conditions for incentives conducive to the creation and diffusion of more information than others. The structure and quality of information is likely to change as a result of changes in institutional structure. If institutional change is desired, it may be necessary to change the information structure as a prerequisite to, or as an essential aspect of effective institutional change.

The importance of information flows and communication patterns to the establishment and maintenance of particular institutions has been well understood by economic policy makers since earliest times. Trade routes and communication links were deliberately designed to maintain centres of power and to overcome international comparative disadvantages. Britain still benefits substantially from its historically established communication links with its former colonies, long after the empire's formal demise. Universal telephone service was adopted as a policy objective in many countries to encourage economic and social interaction within the country. The European Economic Community is attempting to foster a new European identity by promoting increased communication and information exchange as a basis for stimulating increased trade among its member countries and completing the single European market in 1992. Those factors that influence information and communication structures are central to the study of all institutions, and sometimes are controlling with respect to economic institutions.

Essentially the information and communication sector of the economy consists of microelectronics; computer hardware, software and services; telecommunications equipment and services; the mass media and a plethora of new database and information services; as well as the more traditional forms of information and communication such as print and postal service. Stimulated by rapid and continuing technological change, this sector has experienced a high rate of economic growth in recent years. Moreover, the direct economic effects are compounded by the fact that major parts of this sector provide important infrastructure services or enabling functions that affect the operation and efficiency of almost all other industries, as well as government agencies and most other institutions.

Many analysts believe that information gathering, processing, storage and transmission over efficient telecommunication networks will provide the foundation upon which technologically advanced nations will close the twentieth century as so-called 'information economies', or 'information societies', i.e. societies that have become dependent upon complex electronic information and communication networks and which allocate a major portion of their resources to information and communication activities.

The expansion of the information and communication sector serves to integrate domestic economies more easily into the international economy by means of efficient international information and communication networks. As international economic integration expands, the impact of domestic public policies in all nations is reduced. Control over the domestic economy by national governments is weakened.

These developments are forcing national governments to recognise the need for a full range of international trade policies addressed not only to direct trade in information and communication equipment and services, but also to the implications of worldwide information and communication networks for other industries.

Growth opportunities are opening in a wide variety of information and communication service markets, trading in both public and private information. Although these markets are adding value to information, they are very imperfect markets. They raise important policy issues relating to government regulation of monopoly power in national and international markets, and government policy with respect to access by the public to traditional types of public information. Determination of the appropriate limits to place on the commoditisation of information must be a subject of in-depth research, public debate and the fashioning of informed public policy.

THE POWER OF THE INFORMATION ASSUMPTIONS

Major issues of debate in economic analysis and in public policy development hinge crucially on tacit assumptions about the characteristics of information and its efficient and effective communication. This is perhaps most clearly evident in the assumptions of economic theory with reference to the characteristics of markets.

The general definition of a market is the provision of exchange opportunities between buyers and sellers. Without exchanges, or transactions, there is no market. The rate of exchange is the market price, which is determined by the conditions of supply and demand. Certain aspects of the market can be examined as an abstract exercise in logic by assuming that the only matter of significance is a single exchange price at a moment in time. But this grossly oversimplified analysis leaves out a lot. It focuses on a few surface character- istics of markets and a method of calculation, ignoring the institutional foundation of the market and many important structural aspects of markets, all of which are essential to preparing the ground for the ultimate market exchanges.

An exchange can only take place if there is a commodity, or service, to be traded. Trade requires ownership, i.e. enforceable property rights in the commodity being traded. The specific characteristics of property rights in tradeable commodities have varied significantly over the last several centuries and do so today among different countries, and even among localities within countries. The notion of property rights embodies a large collection of specific rights that define the terms and conditions for the use and exchange of property. It is a dynamic concept subject to ongoing change, as current debates in many countries relating to changes in patent and copyright laws demonstrate. The vast majority of goods and services that are exchanged do not carry with them total freedom for the owner of the property to do with it whatever he/she pleases. Zoning regulations, product safety standards, and cultural norms illustrate some of the constraints on the terms and conditions of trade.

The historic debate in economics between the relative merits of the market versus central planning as the best mechanism for allocating resources most efficiently in society hinges crucially upon the role attributed to information and communication. Hayek's (1945) seminal article (see also, Arrow 1974; Koopmans 1957), *The Use of Knowledge in Society*, presented the case for the superiority of the market as cogently as any when he stated:

The various ways in which the knowledge on which people base their plans is communicated to them is the crucial problem for any theory explaining the economic process. And the problem of what is the best way of utilising knowledge initially dispersed among all the people is at least one of the main problems of economic policy – or of designing an efficient economic system.

The system that is most efficient, argued Hayek, depends mainly on the question – 'under which of them we can expect that fuller use will be made of the existing knowledge?'.

The knowledge that is needed is the overwhelmingly massive amount of detailed unorganised information with respect to the particular circumstances of individual buyers and sellers. Such information cannot hope to be captured in time, if at all, to facilitate coordinated central planning. The beauty of the price system is that it is a mechanism for capturing and communicating all this detailed unorganised information that reflects the myriad of individual buyer and seller, day-to-day decisions under continuously changing circumstances. Economists cannot disregard the 'unavoidable imperfection of man's knowledge and the consequent need for a process by which knowledge is constantly communicated and acquired', argued Hayek. 'To assume all the knowledge to be given to a single mind in the same manner in which we assume it to be given to us as the explaining economists is to assume the problem away and to disregard everything that is important and significant in the real world.'

Most neoclassical economists marvelled at the triumph of the market, but they have not followed up Hayek's early analysis. Having accepted the apparent fact of real world information deficiencies to reject the central planning option as unacceptably imperfect because of its untenable assumption with respect to information and communication, neoclassical economics has neglected to take up the challenge of examining information deficiencies in real market systems, preferring instead to maintain the idealistic perfect information assumption of theory. This, of course, begs the real issue that Hayek raised. To date, there has been no serious testing of Hayek's information hypothesis, although the work of Machlup (1980–84) and others can be seen as offering potentially relevant insights on this issue.

Hayek assumed perfect knowledge on the part of individual buyers and sellers with respect to their own individual alternatives, preferences, circumstances and ability to maximise their own best interests. He relaxed the perfect knowledge assumption only with respect to the knowledge that individual buyers and sellers would have about the behaviour of all other buyers and sellers, or about the complex set of market interrelations in the economy. But he also assumed that individual supply and demand would be unaffected by developments about which the individual sellers and buyers had no information. Thus, he assumed that individual demand was independently determined, and not influenced by the demand of others or any other external events. It was exogenous to the analysis.

The problem Hayek addressed then was how to use this known 'perfect information' that individuals had about their own circumstances most efficiently to allocate resources in the economy. But the advantage Hayek claims for the market only applies to a condition of perfectly competitive markets. When markets are imperfect, individuals do not have sufficient information to know what will best serve their own interests. On this point, K.E. Boulding (1960, p. 6) has observed:

> It is one thing to look at a price tag and to know that any amount can be bought or sold at this price. It is quite another thing to discover a demand function, which is a set of *possible* prices and *possible* quantities, only one of which is given in present experience. Thus making what seems like a simple extension of the model from perfect markets to imperfect markets actually involves us in an information problem of first magnitude.

Moreover, even if the prices in imperfect markets did capture the perfect knowledge by individual buyers and sellers with respect to their individual circumstances, those market prices would not bring about an efficient allocation of resources. Under monopoly conditions, for example, this information would simply result in a monopoly price. In imperfect markets, a requirement for an optimal allocation of resources would be that prices *not* be set on the basis of this limited set of perfect knowledge by individual buyers and sellers.

Hayek's assumption about independent atomistic decision making based on individual preferences made in a vacuum, and uninfluenced by other individuals, institutions and developments in the economy, is necessary to keep his market alternative from being defeated by the same information complexity problem that he attributes to central planning. In addition, Hayek's analysis does not address the issue of coordinating non-price information, a common function for social institutions; nor does it entertain the possibility that in some circumstances collective decisions may yield better results for all individuals than the sum of individual decisions. Moreover, since information does not conform to the classical properties of privately supplied commodities, it is likely to be underproduced relative to what would be obtained if it were a perfect private good. Further, many types of information take on the characteristics of public goods.

Hayek clearly has not demonstrated the superiority of the market as the most efficient system for allocating resources. He has drawn attention to one aspect of the problem that has highlighted an advantage of coordination of certain types of information through market prices. But his real contribution has been to focus debate on this longstanding economic controversy on the role and characteristics of information in the institutional structure, a crucial aspect of the issue that far too often is neglected. It is disappointing that the debate on this important information issue has not been sharpened significantly since Hayek's article. An efficient allocation of resources in society will require an institutional structure that contains elements of both planning and markets. It is important that the structure be designed to reflect the comparative advantage of each in the areas to which they are applied. On the basis of the present state of knowledge, economists can offer few guidelines on this fundamental policy issue because of their inadequate knowledge of the real conditions of information and communication.

More recently, O.E. Williamson (1985) has used an updated version of the Hayek analysis to argue the opposite case. He has used the concept of 'transaction costs' to recognise that in imperfect markets involving complex technologies – almost all directly associated with the new information and communication technologies – the costs of negotiation may become significant. According to Williamson, transaction costs are driven up by bounded rationality, opportunism and asset specificity, i.e. inadequate information, a failure of communication and a high degree of uncertainty. Because market transactions are too complex and costly, it is more efficient to integrate vertically and horizontally, thereby avoiding the market and the necessity for settling on a price. By avoiding the market, large conglomerate corporations will be in a better position to plan and to supply their products more efficiently. Apparently large-scale planning is now seen as superior to the market in coordinating at least some types of economic activity. Williamson does not attempt any empirical tests of his theory; nor does he discuss the relative merits of public versus private planning. His case also rests on untested assumptions about the information and communication characteristics of the market transaction in a technologically advanced economy.

By parallel analysis to that above, it could be shown how other fundamental concepts underlying market theory are dependent upon implicit assumptions about the state of information and communication processes. Consumer preference is governed by the state of information (or misinformation) and the extent to which it has been communicated throughout the consumer community. The limits of scale and scope economies are explained as the point at which increasing administration and management costs, i.e. information processing and communication costs, force total unit costs to rise with larger scales of production. Indeed it would appear that the new information and communication technologies are extending the limits of economies of scale and scope for transnational companies in many industries.

THE EXTENSION OF MARKET BOUNDARIES: THEORY AND PRACTICE

According to conventional market theory, an expansion of available information, together with enhanced and improved telecommunications, should permit more efficient decision making and the extension of markets across geographical and industry boundaries. It should increase competition. It should allow resources to be allocated more rapidly and efficiently. The conditions of real markets should approximate more closely the assumptions of theory, where markets are frictionless and operate under conditions of perfect information. Indeed much of the literature on the information economy considers these developments to provide unmitigated benefits to society.

But closer examination indicates that the benefits of these technologies are not likely to be distributed uniformly across markets, that certain segments of society will be made poorer both in absolute as well as relative terms, and that the structure of markets in many industries will be made less competitive.

These new technologies permit many markets to be extended to the international and global level. But it is the largest national and transnational corporations and government agencies that have the greatest need for, and the ability to take full advantage of these new opportunities. For them the geographic boundaries of markets are extended globally, and their ability to administer and control global markets efficiently from a central point is enhanced. These changes have been a significant factor in stimulating the wave of mergers and takeovers involving giant transnational companies in recent years. The diseconomies of size and scope provided by the increasing administrative costs and reduced effectiveness of information processing and communication in very large organisations can be reduced substantially by the application of information and communication technologies.

6

TELECOMMUNICATIONS: ABOLISHING SPACE AND REINFORCING DISTANCE?

Ian Miles

INTRODUCTION

This chapter is concerned with New Telematics Services (NTS).[1] These services enable new spatial distributions of activities, and are among the innovations that are heralded as bringing about dramatic changes in the locational features of industrial societies as they enter the 'information age'. This chapter argues that the potentials of NTS are shaped, and in many respects limited, by social and organisational factors.

NTS combine the information-manipulation and information-transmission powers of new Information Technology (IT). They are computer-mediated services (to date mainly using text or graphics to convey information, although voice mail may be regarded as an NTS, and video services are also anticipated). Furthermore, they deliver information through a telecommunications system. And the services are typically interactive. Traditional broadcast and recorded media involve the 'passive' delivery of information, where the user does not play a role in shaping the output provided by the NTS, at best selecting among available material at the point of delivery (although this information may subsequently be manipulated by means of the user's own skills and/or equipment). Interactivity is one of the key features of new IT, and NTS are frequently highly interactive: even if drawn from a database, the package of information delivered is responsive to inputs from the user (and the database is usually updated on a frequent basis). When NTS involve new communication services, rather than providing access to stored information provided by the service providers themselves, the interactivity is between users as well as between users and the system.

New IT, 'the convergence of computers and communications', enables data to be handled in NTS in such a way that they are readily processed by a variety of (micro)electronic systems. Information can be transmitted through or stored in a wide variety of media, and manipulated via computer processes to form databases, 'hypertexts', and other types of information product.

NTS are among the 'value added network (or data) services' (VANS, VADS) identified, with variations of detail, in national telecommunications regulations.[2] NTS can be classified both in terms of specific services (such as electronic mail) and broad service systems (such as videotex, which offers email along with other facilities). Considering the first dimension, three main groups are readily distinguishable (see PA Computers and Telecommunications 1986; Thomas & Miles 1988; 1989).

- *Information services*, such as accessing databases. Until recently, such on-line services were the main form of electronic publishing and NTS. Interactive on-line database services only distribute information in response to a user request – as distinct from such new services as, for example, broadcast teletext, where the user simply selects among material that is being transmitted continually. NTS also differ from information delivery via storage media such as CD-ROM, which uses optical discs (rather than telecommunications facilities) to deliver databases.
- *Communication services*, such as messaging of various kinds. Users can communicate with each other via electronic mail, bulletin boards, computer-conferences and analogous services. These contrast with conventional mail or voice telephony which have traditionally involved, respectively, non-electronic recording/display of text and graphics, and real-time audio connections, with the data not being encoded in a form suitable for manipulation by computer systems.
- *Transactional services*, such as electronic data interchange, or ordering and paying for deliveries on-line. These contrast with conventional modes of invoicing or direct payment involving mail or physical presence, and the exchange of money or cheques.

This approach classifies NTS by function. Further subdivisions can be made, of course – for instance, between long-term, archival information and that which is updated from minute to minute; between real-time communication and stored messages; between transaction services devoted to purchasing goods, booking tickets or transferring funds; between bulletin boards, computer-conferences, and 'conventional' email; etc. However, this classification provides a useful starting point. Some common problems apply to all types of NTS, if they are to take root and become widely used; and each type of NTS has its own problems to overcome. A number of major problems are set out below; we shall elaborate on aspects of this in due course.
Problems common across NTS:
- slow development of standards, proliferation of proprietary and specialised standards;
- poorly designed terminal equipment (e.g. low portability);
- problems of privacy and data protection.

Information services:
- equipment problems: reading material on-screen is difficult, printers are low-quality;
- unclear tariffs, and complex tariff structures over services with multiple means of access;
- legal problems: lack of clarity concerning copyright, libel, sub judice and other features of electronic publishing.

Communication services:
- need to establish new communication norms (sometimes called 'netiquette' to deal with characteristics of powerful but limited media – to deal with junk mail, inappropriate behaviour, etc.;
- problems associated with lack of traditional means of personal contact (e.g. handshake, voice and body language, ability to display graphics, etc.);
- doubts about professionalism of material used in electronic media.

Transactional services:
Due to their involving financial operations, these services raise particular issues as to:
- operational security;
- authentication of instructions and verification of identity;
- liability for loss due to fraud, failure or error;
- irrevocability and finality versus countermand or reversal of instruction;
- priority of claims in cases of insolvency, etc.;
- burden of proof in disputed cases.

NTS contribute substantially to many of the changes in organisation and production processes which are associated with the use of IT and the changed roles for information-processing which it facilitates. Commonly cited among these changes are: increased flexibility in corporate operations, with closer matching of supply and demand; globalisation of production; the development of networks of firms, with new user-supplier linkages and new opportunities for small and large firms alike. All of these examples are liable to require contribution from NTS, allowing inter-organisational communications, rapid processing of strategic information from a diversity of sources, and the externalisation of key producer services. A failure to exploit NTS is not the whole story, but it is likely to be part of the explanation for the slower realisation of the capabilities of IT than pundits had foreseen. Likewise, the use of NTS by the population at large is often portrayed as a defining feature of information society, one which permits new employment opportunities and new ways of life to emerge.

This paper sets out to discuss some of the key obstacles facing both suppliers and would-be users of NTS, to discuss responses to these obstacles, and, in particular, to consider how these factors are influencing the use of NTS and the spatial implications of this pattern of use. Two caveats are necessary. First, our focus will be on NTS traded between companies – many of the points made here apply equally to the use of new information systems within organisations, but there may be specificities to intra-organisational telematics activities which we have not identified. Second, spatial issues have not been at the core of our empirical research, so the conclusions we reach on these topics may be less than ideally systematic.

UNFULFILLED FORECASTS AND UNDERDEVELOPED DATA

Let us consider an example of how NTS forecasts have met the challenge of market trends. In August 1979, *The Economist's* briefing on new business communications media presented Mackintosh forecasts – persuasive trend graphs and text. These predicted that by the late 1980s the use of communicating word processors (electronic mail and teletex systems) would have overhauled facsimile transmission (fax). Email would be well into the phase of explosive growth, while in the United States fax would have passed its peak and be declining.

These forecasts imply a model in which demand for rapid communication is growing, with a substitution process between media in which the more advanced technological solutions substitute for less advanced systems. Thus email, which harnesses the power of new IT to provide cheap and accurate transmission of text, with facilities to store-and-forward, send multiple copies to mailing lists, etc., was seen as the superior solution. It uses the text (and, in advanced systems, the image) processing capabilities of (micro)computers to transmit and manipulate characters (especially ASCII characters, where common standards exist) and other data.

Fax, in contrast, scans and breaks down the letters and illustrations on a page, into a stream of signals that represents the page as a large grid and simply indicates the presence or absence of markings at particular locations on the grid. It is a long-established technology (first developed in the 1840s: an international fax message was sent in 1901); while being rendered cheaper and more sophisticated by the incorporation of microelectronics, it is slower and more costly than email.[3] Email can be based on existing personal computers (PCs) (though a modem attachment, or link to a Local Area Network (LAN), will be typically required); fax requires its own apparatus.

It seems clear which technology is superior – at least until future generation (Group 4) fax allows mixing of ASCII text and visual images. But the 1980s – especially the last few years – have seen the triumph of fax. In the United States, public email systems have been losing money. (Federal Express has dropped its Zapmail service, and the Postal Service sold its email system.) Fax sales practically quadrupled over the 1986–88 period; fax equipment is now commonplace, being sold alongside PCs and telephones in electronics stores. In the United Kingdom, the largest public email system, Telecom Gold, has shown healthy growth – 138 000 mailboxes in late 1988, overhauling the 95 460 terminals attached to the public videotex service, Prestel (launched with a headstart at the beginning of the decade – and with much fanfare – we return to this later). But Gold has been eclipsed by the suddenly booming market for fax equipment: over 200 000 terminals were sold in 1988 alone.[4]

The technical virtues of email have been eclipsed, it seems, by organisational issues. First, other than intra-firm email systems (many of which have been successful) there is the requirement to register with an email service. In most countries, fax machines are used much like regular telephones, with no additional registration. There are time and money costs of registration (and there is the choice of which email system to join), though there are some advantages – email registration means that the service providers store messages in users' postboxes, so there is no need for a telephone line to be devoted to electronic messaging, unlike most current fax systems. But there are also interconnection problems between different email services, while any fax machine can be reached by simply dialling the phone number. Achieving access to users of other email services can be a tortuous task. Additionally, it is necessary to know their postbox numbers: there is still no overall directory, and for some services there is no public directory at all.

The relatively slow take-off of email also reflects the need for individual and organisational change in behaviour. Consider the steps typical users will need to check their post (admittedly some current commercial offerings make these steps much easier): start the communications software running on the PC (this may well mean exiting any other program one is running); log in to the email service, giving ID and password (often unmemorable, error-prone and cumbersome); inspect one's mailbox; either display contents on the screen or print them out for perusal; decide whether or not to reply immediately; log off; exit the communications program. Several of these steps are fiddly and interfere with other activities. Users rapidly grow discouraged when the upshot of their efforts is a message that they have no new messages. Email services begin to be underused by those who have mailboxes: a vicious circle develops, with messages lying unread, and even the keener users getting deterred. Equally problematic is electronic junk mail: while many stories are probably apocryphal, most users will have had experiences of other users getting carried away with the ease of circulating redundant material.

Fax is, equally, only rendered functional by the existence of a community of fax users. But it is easier to locate and send a message to a fax number, and there is no need to check to see if the message has been inspected by at least someone in the recipient organisation. Using fax is much more like using a telephone than is the use of email; it requires few skills (even ability to operate a keyboard is unnecessary, since handwritten documents can be mailed). It has achieved the critical mass to be a standard office requirement, while email remains by and large restricted to specialised communities of users. The take-off of fax reflects various factors, not least of which is the cheapening of fax equipment by Japanese producers.

In the email-versus-fax case, we have access to forecasts and data covering the same period. Many forecasts currently being bandied about deal with the future: thus validating them against statistics is a task to return to after the passage of time. But, more generally, assessment of the scale and diffusion of NTS activity is difficult. Adequate statistics (for example, on market size and share, customer base and profitability) are largely missing, while there is plenty of hyperbole (usually praising one NTS, one network, or one type of technical solution over all others). Statisticians and users are uncertain as to needs for accurate reporting on NTS as well as other new IT-related activities (cf Miles *et al*. 1989), and these activities are poorly captured in the reporting procedures required for many traditional media and telecommunications services. The absence of data and proliferation of hype is also in the interests of many NTS suppliers, who are reluctant to reveal that their services are yielding little revenue, or have captured only a small market share.

Despite the data problems, there seems to be a reasonable degree of consensus on four features of NTS development:

1 Sizeable NTS markets have been established in several countries – though at lower levels and rates of growth than forecast. Thus, the sample of UK firms recorded in *Business Monitor SDQ 9*, for example, as supplying VANS notched up billings of over fourteen million pounds in 1986; consultancy forecasts for 1990 put the UK VANS market in the several hundred million pounds by 1990. Some trade sources estimate that on-line database services alone were already taking over 200 million pounds in 1986, and would be over one billion pounds by 1990 – while the US market was already at this size by the mid-80s. Eight hundred and sixteen VANS services were registered with Oftel in mid-1986; as we have seen, British Telecom's (BT) Prestel and Telecom Gold services both now have around 100 000 users; around 1000 UK companies (and 5000 in the United States) regularly use Electronic Data Interchange (Coathup 1988); etc.

2 Much NTS activity is concentrated in the areas of transactional services and transaction-related information and communication services: e.g. financial information services, telestockbroking, travel booking services, etc. Markets have also been established for scientific and technical services of various sorts (e.g. information for lawyers).

3 Most of this activity involves professional and business-to-business services rather than services to final consumers. Furthermore, business NTS use tends to be concentrated among larger firms and a number of leading sectors. In some of the latter (e.g. the automobile and travel industries), large firms have often been able to draw their customers and/or suppliers into use of transactional NTS. While this trend is expected to grow to include more sectors and a wider range of information, there are problems in some sectors associated with the development of competing systems among different firms.

4 The French experience with Minitel/Teletel demonstrates that consumer markets can be established by appropriate 'pump-priming' interventions. There is less consensus, however, over (a) how far such pump-priming is required to stimulate mass markets, and whether they can develop more or less rapidly as a result of market mechanisms; (b) whether intervention will be undertaken by public agencies or the private sector on a sufficient scale in other countries; (c) whether this take-off will be sustained in the

longer-term; and (d) how far the sorts of consumer NTS demonstrated by Minitel are broadly socially acceptable in many countries.

IMMATURE TECHNOLOGIES?

The take-off of a product towards its full market potential frequently involves a shift in the pattern of activity (Abernathy & Utterback 1978). In earlier phases of development, emphasis is stronger on product innovation. Suppliers compete to produce designs that will establish themselves firmly in the marketplace. Technical inputs from users, and information on their needs play important roles here in shaping still-fluid designs. Later, however, emphasis shifts to process innovation. Competition centres on price (and on minor modifications within the standard design), with one design or design class now dominant. Teece (1987) refers to these as 'preparadigmatic' and 'paradigmatic' stages in the product cycle. Typically successful products either embody design developments that reduce the need for new user skills, or prove themselves so useful that skills are willingly established around a design paradigm.

Most NTS appear to be still in the 'preparadigmatic' stage, with limited take-off, and considerable uncertainty about what the features of the mature products are likely to be – about which new modes of service delivery will succeed in establishing themselves in specific applications. There has been a proliferation of procedures to use, say, different on-line databases or email facilities. (This resembles computer applications software, where every word processing package has its own idiosyncrasies – although spreadsheets do tend to share many common features.) NTS suppliers face choices over whether to abide by de facto emerging standards (with the advantage of less new learning required for users) or to pioneer new (perhaps more powerful or application-specific) approaches. No dominant paradigm has yet emerged for most classes of NTS: hence there is uncertainty for users and suppliers alike. One of the factors limiting the spatial impacts of NTS is this uncertainty: potential users are deterred, potential applications are underdeveloped, and the scope for organisational change is thus restricted.

The mixed fortunes of videotex form an informative case. Videotex systems derive from an attempt to establish a dominant paradigm for the delivery of NTS of all types (for mass markets). The original design of videotex, undertaken in the 1970s by engineers in what is now BT, was informed by views of what features an NTS would need to be able to win mass use. Home computers were unfamiliar: NTS were seen as combining two familiar domestic technologies, television and the telephone. It was believed necessary to develop modes of presentation which would be attractive for non-professional use. Videotex thus presents information a 'page' at a time, with relatively large letters which can easily be read on a TV screen, simple but potentially colourful and interesting graphics and layout possibilities, and a system of menus enabling use of a simple keypad to route one the desired 'pages'.

Prestel, the BT videotex service, was marketed initially as a TV-based system. At first consumers would have to buy a new TV to use Prestel (the TV manufacturers hoped to revive flagging markets), and they would typically have needed new telephone sockets to be fitted in their homes. The early keypads were unsuitable for user input of more than a few symbols at a time, such as would be needed for messaging. Gateways to the computers of service suppliers were not initially available, which meant that real-time teleshopping – difficult enough with the keypads – was effectively ruled out. The menu structure of the service was also cumbersome, becoming increasingly irritating as one gained experience of the system, as one found it necessary to go through the same sequence repeatedly, and as the potential for mistakes was high. The information provided was of very uneven quality – content quality had been neglected in the enthusiasm to get a technically advanced system running (one might work through a chain of menus, only to find a final screen admitting the required data was not yet on tap). The pricing structure also confused potential users, while the information was often remarkably similar in appearance (and, in the cases of news-type services, content) to the information services becoming available at the same time on broadcast teletext.

Prestel did not appeal to the mass public, which has little enthusiasm for accessing databases. Forecasts of millions of residential users made in the late 1970s proved over-optimistic by two orders of magnitude.

In France, in contrast, the PTT's distribution of terminals has led to mass public use of Minitel (notably for messaging purposes). The decision to distribute terminals was of course important here, but so too were design features. Minitel users were provided with a standard simple computer-type terminal-cum-VDU; they were motivated to gain experience by the strategy of putting the telephone directory on-line. Minitel allowed for search by keyword rather than by progression through menus (introduced to Prestel in 1987). Messaging proved to be a major consumer application of Minitel – this was not originally foreseen by the suppliers, but it was designed in as a facility after it emerged as important in pilot studies. Gateways were provided to service operatives from the outset, allowing for teleshopping and related applications.

Another contrast with Prestel is BT's own Telecom Gold. BT had made several attempts to design a sophisticated email service, but design problems, heavy investment costs and (post-Prestel) uncertainty about demand, led to Gold being an 'off-the-shelf' package, licensed from the American company Dialcom. It could be hosted on relatively inexpensive minicomputers and expanded in modular fashion as demand increased. It could transfer data on the X.25 packet switched networks, which were becoming standard for both national and international data traffic and which facilitated the implementation of gateway services. Its 1982 launch was aimed at business users (Dialcom had a reasonably large corporate user base); and market research suggested that most of the initial traffic would be intra-organisational, so inter-computer data transfer could be minimised. Blocks of mailbox numbers on a single computer were allocated to a user company to distribute; the pricing structure set a standard corporate rental charge (irrespective of the number of mailboxes allocated), with other charges reflecting actual use and file storage. This increased the attractiveness of the system to potential subscribers, by increasing the (apparent) number of users.

Design flexibility is important in a preparadigmatic phase of a new product; in the NTS case, investment committed to specific architectures, from which migration may be necessary, is thereby minimised, as seems to have been the case with Gold. Advanced technology is not a sufficient basis for success in the NTS field: a design paradigm is more often created through experiment and interaction with users, than it is born fully-fledged in the designer's inspiration. For example, Prestel was launched without adequate field trials and pilot studies to test its suitability for a mass market.

Its design, however, proved suitable for some applications – especially once relatively cheap videotex terminals for business use became available. Videotex has established an important role in the UK travel industry, where staff are able to access information on flight availability or insurance rates, and to book seats or order components. Here, and in some other sectors such as insurance and the motor trade, time-urgent information is at a premium and much time was being wasted on telephone calls – and Prestel is now faced with commercial competition from private videotex services, of whom perhaps as many as 1000 are operating. (Thus the number of videotex terminals in use in the United Kingdom well exceeds Prestel subscriptions.)

Prestel has moved toward a niche market approach, searching for 'trigger services' which would motivate substantial use of videotex within limited markets, and hopefully eventually encourage these users to turn to other NTS offered via Prestel, as the telephone directory was seen to have done for Minitel. The product needs to be well-tailored to suit niches; thus BT Travel Services and BT Insurance Services have bought in people with substantial experience of the relevant sectors. Symbiotic relationships may develop between NTS suppliers and users. (With a sophisticated understanding of the market, suppliers may be able to sell their products on the basis of quality as much as, or more than, price.) Examples of such successful niche services can be found in many areas, including legal services, market analysis for advertisers and financial information/dealing services. The sector in question must have many specialised features, making it difficult for firms supplying a wide range of NTS to tailor these to fit the area (even so, there are signs that larger firms are buying up some niche NTS).

NTS have had to learn the importance of market research, pilot studies and trials as ways of assessing user requirements. Equally important is maintaining close contact with the user community – for instance, trade associations, which give access to a wider spread of opinion than just the vanguard users, and which can help develop industry-wide strategic thinking and forward standardisation activity. The situation varies according to whether the NTS application is specific to a relatively small market or is one that is relevant across a great many industries – or, indeed, to a mass public. Niche markets offer the scope for NTS suppliers to closely relate to user communities. Such user contacts may be slow in developing, in part, perhaps, because it is difficult to stop them benefiting present and future competitors. Thus several business users have used their experience on Prestel – as suppliers of services to third parties, or as closed user groups for intra-corporate communication – to evaluate videotex and prototype their own systems. These users are now among leading private videotex services in the United Kingdom, operating outside the Prestel framework through the telephone network or through one or more of the competing data networks.

This section has raised a number of key points for understanding the slow realisation of NTS potentials. Its central theme is the lack of generally accepted paradigms for NTS in many important application areas. This design uncertainty is fuelled from several sources: competition among suppliers; continuing progress in the power of the heartland technologies, making mini-revolutions in performance both real and anticipated; and failure to adequately understand user requirements and develop appropriate facilities. Associated with these problems are uncertainty over standards and systems, and problems with developing combinations of skills and organisational features which can effectively use the technological potential. Let us consider these factors.

USER UNCERTAINTIES

Among the largest source of bafflement to users are standards and tariffs. Competition in the NTS field is often a very imperfect phenomenon. Ironically, information flows in the field are very imperfect. It is difficult for users to get a comparative assessment of the virtues and limitations of alternative NTS suppliers – for instance, there has been a proliferation of on-line databases in a number of areas. This has meant that some NTS have survived despite being, for instance, relatively costly and/or clumsy to use, or offering poorer quality information (unhelpful abstracts, less frequent updates).

Additionally, as suggested above in discussing user-supplier relationships, suppliers face problems in capturing returns on their investments. To the general features of network technologies are added the difficulties that conventional methods of intellectual property protection such as patenting and copyright are only partially applicable to NTS. Meanwhile, service concepts are often rapidly emulated and aggressively challenged: new entrants can appear in many NTS markets from areas not previously seen as competing with existing service providers – e.g. banks, building societies, insurance companies, major retailers and other organisations are realigning and competing in newly-opened financial services markets. Controversy is still raging about how far copyright and other modes of protection can be applied to software, and NTS are likely to go through analogous battles. (This looked like happening within the United Kingdom videotex community in 1987, when BT threatened to pursue its patent rights on a particular feature of the videotex format – a threat which receded as mysteriously as it had arisen.)

Given the problems of using the formal means of protecting intellectual property, suppliers often seek to gain an edge in the market by means of 'lock-in'. This is rendered more possible than it might otherwise be by the time and money costs users face in experimenting with NTS. Provision of training sessions and other means of ensuring familiarisation with one set of services – while providing no information on others – is one method of achieving lock-in.

Users may be tied more 'physically' to particular terminals or to specific sets of standards. In the United Kingdom, 'standards wars' have been prominent especially in transactional services linking manufacturers to dealers and to component suppliers, or distributors to retailers. An example is the automobile trade, where manufacturers run videotex systems, enabling dealers to locate cars (at manufacturing plants or other dealers nearby) meeting customer requirements. Links have also been added between manufacturers and their component suppliers, with orders being placed and invoices sent using electronic data interchange (EDI). Manufacturers' growing 'just in time' concern leads them to demand that suppliers use EDI. Suppliers who traded with several manufacturers found that they had to subscribe to several incompatible services. Despite the existence of an active trade association being urged by its members to simplify matters, it proved difficult for the motor trade to move towards fully standardised protocols: gateways between services have been conceded by some, but not all, suppliers. Despite years of discussion about standards, one supplier (of metal pressings) was reported in early 1989 as having 'three terminals in his office...His internal computer systems have to be slightly different to cope with the dialects on each service [Ford, Austin Rover and IBM]. He would like gateways between the services, and more standardisation...' (Sarson 1989). Discrepancies between British and international standards add to the problems.

NTS suppliers often attempt to have their ways of doing things accepted as a de facto standard: but they may find themselves instead locked into standards incompatible with the way everyone else is working. Unless there are strong forces working for the diffusion of the NTS, such uncertainties about standards can delay uptake; and conflicting standards can restrict the inter-operability and utility of NTS. In the EDI field, attention is now being paid to 'equivalence of meaning' across systems, so that messages can be automatically translated from one standard to another.

Suppliers may attempt to lock-in users in early stages of NTS development; but as users gain experience of the technology and see opportunities for using and linking a variety of services, pressure for standardisation should grow. 'Physical' modes of lock-in, such as special terminals or incompatible communications protocols should then be less important.

In addition to standards, tariffs are a regular source of confusion amongst users and would-be users. Users, wanting control over their costs, will typically want simple tariffs and 'one-stop billing'. Complaints are legion about inscrutable tariffs, especially for international data traffic (where telecommunications operators are coming under increasing pressure from transnational regulators such as the EC); but even database directories contain many confusing accounts of charging systems. The complexity is fuelled by the burgeoning of methods of accessing NTS – multifunctional terminals and rapid changes in the number of different speeds and network routes whereby a given service can be accessed. Service providers have often accordingly sought to make separate charges for distinct component elements of the NTS, such as connect time, time of day, data transmission speed, number of data packets sent and/or received, number of references 'hit', number of references printed out, etc.

The resulting complexity makes it hard to assess individual services or to compare different services. Big users, or those organised in powerful trade associations, may pressure suppliers to offer simplified or reduced tariffs. For instance, trade association pressure has meant that the network costs of travel and insurance services in the United Kingdom are frequently borne by the tour operators and insurance firms rather than by the independent travel and insurance agencies.

Reinforcing, and in some cases underlying, these problems of standards and tariffs – and thus the uneven diffusion of NTS – are four further complexities of the NTS decision environment:

* NTS compete with traditional ways of accessing and using information;
* NTS compete with other NTS and IT-based modes of accessing and using information;
* NTS decisions are taken in the midst of many other IT decisions, and in a context of continuing uncertainty;
* NTS can be delivered over competing telecommunications networks.

As service innovations, NTS often compete with other modes of service delivery;[5] with established information services and products (e.g. libraries, books), communication services (e.g. conventional mail, telephony), and transactional services (e.g. shopping) – and with other IT-based modes of delivery. These include, for instance:

* fax versus email;
* optical discs as means of delivering database information (challenging on-line services, and complementing them in the case of some databases);
* teletext as a way of broadcast delivery of news (challenging the similar-looking videotex services);
* cellular telephones as means of accomplishing messaging (challenging text-based systems).

The development of NTS is affected by complementary and competing services delivered by the same means (telecommunications networks, PCs, etc.) and via other routes (broadcasting, optical discs, conventional telephones, etc.).

Meanwhile, traditional modes of delivery may themselves be reshaped by the application of IT (e.g. library automation, advanced rapid delivery systems). It is often far from clear what the virtues and costs of different modes of using NTS are in practice.

Even where NTS use is already widespread, decisions about its use can overlap uncomfortably with other IT-related decisions. The UK travel agency sector features near-universal use of videotex to obtain flight availability information and to book tickets from tour operators. There is now a clear move toward integrating front-office videotex access and back-office PC-based administration and word processing (their separation leads to wasted effort in re-entering data). But this entangles choices about NTS access equipment with overall IT strategy, which may be realistic, but which is liable to make decision making slower and more complex. For sectors where there has been less of an impetus toward NTS, the introduction of equipment and software may well be delayed by the priority given to other uses of existing or proposed IT systems.

An additional complication is that a given NTS can, in principle, be accessed through various channels. A growing variety of telecommunications networks exists, including, in several advanced industrial countries, private networks (both Local Area Networks and Wide Area Networks), managed data network services, the public telephone network, and other facilities (such as cable TV networks, data broadcast, etc.).

Consider UK travel agents again. *Travel Data* (May 1988) lists almost sixty videotex services for them: apart from direct dial through the public telephone network, services are available on two private networks (Istel and Fastrak) as well as from BT's (the travel services division, which allows access to Prestel). Few are available across the whole range of options; some are only on one private network service. Outside the travel sector, too, some NTS may be exclusively available on a private network system. Others are offered on several networks: one can access many of the best-known data-bases, for example, through the public telephone network, through one of a number of specialised computer networks, etc. Each network has its own particular advantages and disadvantages, has its own access conditions and imposes its own set of charges – making the process of choosing a mode of delivery more complex and complicated. It is usually possible in principle to communicate across networks; in practice, incompatible standards, restrictions on access, and other organisational factors often cause difficulties.

Many NTS suppliers are attempting to simplify matters for users, often by 'bundling' different services on a common 'host system'[6] – reducing the need to log in to and acquire familiarity with the peculiarities of numerous services. A supplier's competitiveness is enhanced by bundling together complementary services into a package which others find it hard to emulate.

In the on-line database industry hosts such as Dialog, Pergamon (Orbit) Infoline, Datastar, and ESA-IRS, seek to provide databases from various sources and covering numerous fields, and to make use easier by instituting common search languages. More sophisticated methods of bundling further reduce users' need to know about the contents and relative prices of different databases – 'Easylink', for instance, features an interface which questions the user about the sort of information required, determines the appropriate databases, and conducts the search at a standard charge rate.

Email suppliers also bundle services – for example, by providing 'gateways' between the computers hosting their email software and the hosts of other services, and also by adding services other than email to their own computers. Thus, for instance, Microlink in the United Kingdom offers a variety of information, transactional and communications services charged at standard rates (a mixture of basic subscription, file storage and access time), and provides gateways to external services which levy their own charges in addition, such as fax, telex, and databases such as Newsbytes. (Microlink has run on BT's Gold service, but in 1989 shifted to Istel on the grounds that this permitted it to interconnect with more services, including international email, than BT allows it to.)

Network providers, such as BT itself, also bundle services; BT bundles NTS offered via videotex and ASCII display formats. Such integration is perhaps more a move towards a Total Service Package than bundling. VANS providers, such as Istel and Fastrak, who offer managed data network services, strive to run a mixture of their own services and other NTS. These suppliers emphasise the value of network management as an important asset in running NTS. Reliability and continuity of operation are vital ingredients of most NTS, especially transactional services. (Custom may be lost, money may be lost due to failure to respond to market prices, etc.) Security is a concern of users, who do not want 'hackers' or frauds using their systems.

Bundling simplifies matters for users, but may support lock-in and raise entry barriers for potential competitors. Teece (1987) has outlined how complementary assets are important determinants of successful innovation – or rather, of who is able to succeed in commercialising innovations. We have already discussed one set of complementary assets for NTS suppliers in niche markets: familiarity with a specialised sector, having the skills to package information tailored to it, having established links with the actors in this sector, and having access to data that can readily be put on-line. 'Insider' knowledge of markets, and the information/media skills germane to a particular class of content may also be bought in. The ownership of a telecommunications network, with its body of subscribers, is a major complementary asset for NTS supply on a wider scale.

The high costs of establishing networks, together with the economies of scale associated with them, may dispose new entrants to piggyback on existing ones. Some new entrants, however, may derive from the marketing of existing intra-corporate networks as telecommunications services. Geographically dispersed firms may have established their own networks as well as a competence in NTS: Istel is an example, where the dispersion of the Austin Rover group led to an elaborate network structure being set up; and where the need for user-friendly videotex services for a variety of actors in the motor trade provided experience in NTS. Likewise, large firms may be able to find new uses for already existing IT resources and thus overcome barriers to entry into NTS. In the mid-1980s one of the smaller banks (the Bank of Scotland) attempted to extend its customer base, without having to invest in an extensive branch network, via 'telebanking'; but once the larger financial organisations secure a footing here, as they now are attempting in various ways (sometimes using telephones instead of microcomputers or videotex terminals), this goal is less likely to be feasible for other small banks.

This section has outlined a range of factors that make the use of NTS a complex matter, one which typically requires user investments of time and money in acquiring appropriate skills. While a number of developments have been noted which promise to reduce these problems, the continuing pace of IT innovation, and the development of entry barriers in NTS, may well mean that they will continue to inhibit the uptake of NTS and the reorganisation of activities to use their potentials. Let us now consider a related issue of skills which lies at the core of many of these problems.

CONVERGENT TECHNOLOGY AND DIVERGENT SKILLS?

NTS are prime examples of computer-communications convergence. But convergence at a technical level often means collision at organisational levels.

Briefly, different cultures and skill bases are associated with computer and communications firms and professions. Bringing these together in workable combinations – into a new skills complex – proves a daunting challenge. But this is not all. Since the products involved are generally information services or involve a high presentational component, suppliers also require skills in selecting, presenting and packaging information to render it useful for the intended market. Thus, skills in 'media' and/or in understanding the require-ments and information contents of specialised user sectors are additional parts of the skills complex.

Forming the appropriate combination of skills is one of the major challenges facing NTS suppliers. A lack of appropriate skills is liable to mean that NTS fail to meet user requirements in one way or another, however good their technical quality. Individuals with the ability to cross these skill boundaries are at a premium – and are relatively rare, since training and educational bodies have yet to recognise the problem.

Managing to combine successfully the groups of skills is proving difficult for many large organisations. Their personnel and other senior managers tend to approach problems from the perspective of one or other of the 'three cultures'. But large firms are relatively better placed than others when it comes to recruiting the new skills or to buying in consultancy services. They may acquire smaller firms with relevant skills or enter into joint ventures with them, as well as adopting conventional recruitment and 'headhunting' methods; BT uses a combination of the two. Telecommunications network providers, in particular, will already have some access to at least computing and communications skills. The uncertainty in the area has led to a cautious attitude from big firms, who presumably reckon that they will be able to buy out any small actors who are able to establish healthy markets.

Another widely-encountered problem involves both skills and organisational practices: the use of NTS and information products does not always fit easily into organisations' existing budget headings. The technical accountancy literature is beginning to note a general problem of organisational adaptation to new IT-based operations, one encountered intensely when justifying investment in information services. Industrial interviews yield accounts of investments only achieved by subterfuge or by overruling accountants; the need for such steps points to requirements for financial skills of various kinds among NTS suppliers and users. Many suppliers also argue that they face 'ideological' problems in convincing potential customers that they should pay for information which they believe should be available more cheaply on other, more familiar, media or which are 'value-added' repackaging of official statistics or public domain material.

Organisational change will place demands on management. Clear lines of responsibility for the introduction and management of new services are required; for larger firms, at least, this will often mean appointing overall IT managers at board level. Of the sample of larger IT users in the United Kingdom featured in the 1987/88 Price Waterhouse *Information Technology Review* (1988), those we would expect to be leading in NTS use, have as yet allocated no responsibility for NTS facilities like email or use of VANS. Less than 30 per cent have overall IT managers to whom DP managers report. However, there is a trend toward more coherent IT strategy, as indicated in a drop from over 30 per cent (1981) to under 20 per cent (1986) of IT/DP managers not reporting to anyone at board level (40 per cent of these managers forecast that by 1991 they would be reporting to the CEO).

RIGHT SOLUTIONS, WRONG PROBLEMS?

The potential of NTS is only slowly being realised, in large part because of social and organisational problems. Partly because of these problems, there is considerable room for mismatching of what NTS can currently provide, what they are marketed as delivering, and what users actually expect and require. Many of the forecasts of substantial change in the spatial distribution of activities, for example, are based on the assumption that NTS can substitute perfectly for traditional means of communication – including telephony and face-to-face contact. But this is far from always the case. It is sometimes said, for instance, that a major use of email is for individuals to establish mutually convenient times when they can talk on the telephone! Even systems as technically complex and costly as video-conferencing seem to lack important features of conventional meetings: it is not that there is no scope for substitution, but the scope is more limited than the engineers expected. Thus it is not simply that potential users fail to recognise the value of suppliers' offerings: quite often NTS designs are (still) inadequate for the intended users' needs.

An example from consumer telematics is teleshopping. This is an engineer's dream, which would free up valuable retail property. To date, videotex has been the main medium used in teleshopping systems in the United Kingdom. (The Keyline system about to be launched – with plans to distribute 500 000 free terminals in the first year of operation – uses a simpler, text-only interface.) But various limitations have become clear with videotex teleshopping systems.

Hardware barriers:
- a limited amount of text fits onto a conventional screen;
- eyestrain may be associated with reading it, especially when a poor TV or home computer is used;
- the screen and keyboard are often not very portable (not very comfortable on one's lap, let alone in the bath!).

Software/information barriers:
- interfaces are not generally particularly user-friendly, and unless one is already using telematics services are liable to be time-consuming to master;
- methods of 'finding one's way around' the goods and services on offer are typically cumbersome: the menu systems used on most videotex services make it difficult to scan items and use the material in a highly interactive way;
- graphic quality is inferior to a printed catalogue or to video/TV-type presentation, and is no basis for inspecting goods.

Social and system barriers:
- limited diffusion of appropriate hardware and software, limited experience of telematics;
- choice may be narrowed as only a few (generally large) retailers have a presence on the system;
- delivery schedules pose a problem: unless delivery times are efficiently negotiated, or storage systems introduced, consumers have to wait around for goods.

Initial enthusiasm has often quickly waned as users have found that as soon as more than a few items are on offer, they have to wade through a series of menus in order to reach their final destination – if they ever get there. Product information is inferior to that yielded by physical presence in a shop. And, of course, delivery remains a problem. (Recent service developments have attempted to offer consumer choice over which of a number of time ranges delivery is required in, and the ability to replicate or modify a personalised shopping list, but to date in the United Kingdom the right formula remains elusive.)

The most successful teleshopping experiments, aimed at housebound and disabled people, have been organised as much as social services as commercial activities. They have demonstrated the value of teleshopping to sectors of the population for whom shopping is an almost unalleviated burden. Their success has been linked to subsidisation of services and terminals for a clear target population, with close involvement of retailers and equipment suppliers.

While some retailers are seeking the successful teleshopping formula, much of the industry argues that although the affluent and busy people whose disposable income could provide a profitable basis for commercial teleshopping are most motivated to relieve themselves of routine, low-value shopping, they enjoy shopping for high-value items. Physically visiting shops provides social rewards that are absent from teleshopping. Still, the high diffusion of videotex in France has made it possible for teleshopping to make a mark on mail order (over 1 per cent of the turnover of La Redoute, the largest French mail order company) and the 'Caditel' system has shown that there is scope for teleshopping for everyday groceries.

Whether or not current teleshopping efforts succeed, then, the scope for teleshopping would seem to be enhanced by developments in consumer IT (Miles 1988), leading to:

* increased consumer familiarity with IT systems of all kinds (keyboards, 'mice', speech synthesis, telematics services, electronic funds transfer, etc.);
* increased IT power located within the home (and car), with corresponding scope for linking consumer devices to external systems in effective ways;
* increased manufacturer willingness to invest in new consumer ITs, cheapening their price and improving their quality, and increased awareness on the part of software writers and service suppliers of the requirements for useful services and interfaces.

The following suggests how these developments might be used to overcome the barriers to teleshopping that were identified earlier.

Overcoming hardware barriers:
* limited text on screen, eyestrain problems: better screens (high resolution, flat screens);
* lack of portability of screen and keyboard: smaller systems, mobile communications, multiple phone sockets/data networks in homes.

Overcoming software/information barriers:
* non-user-friendly interfaces: improved interfaces using, for example, 'mice', trackerballs, remote controllers;
* cumbersome menu systems: simulated shopping environments, personalised 'shopping lists', natural language systems;
* inferior graphic quality: photovideotex, video quality images delivered via various media – cable TV, ISDN telephony, 'downloaded' catalogues broadcast on TV and stored on videorecorders, interactive compact disc, satellite broadcasts, etc.

Overcoming social and system barriers:
* limited diffusion of hardware, software and telematics: development of a wide range of consumer information technologies (home informatics);

- limited choice of services: expanded range of services as critical mass of users established and as more retailers use computerised stockholding, ordering and transactional systems, electronic funds transfer, etc.;
- problems with delivery schedules: social innovations, facilitated as economies of scale in delivery possible – flexible delivery times and schedules, neighborhood deposit centres (e.g. post offices), and household deposit centres (refrigerated post boxes, new types of doors?).

As for the problem of low-quality images and unlifelike interactivity associated with teleshopping – and certain other NTS – two paths of technological development may be particularly important.

First, broadband communications supplied by cable TV systems or telecommunications companies would allow for transfer of the volumes of data required for interactive video (and allow for the use of sophisticated software) so that teleshopping could simulate physical shopping. Broadband is planned for households in the 1990s in several countries: in the United Kingdom the prospects remain uncertain, though improvements in telephone networks (ISDN – the Integrated Services Digital Network) are, at least, on the cards.

Second, optical data storage systems are likely to diffuse to households as manufacturers like Philips and Sony extend the compact disc into a medium for video and computer data of all kinds. Just as department stores and mail order firms publish catalogues of consumer durables, so retailers could move to CD publishing of catalogues – the consumer's system would interrogate the CD for basic product details and video images (with software perhaps emulating a stroll through the shelves and arcades) and then use conventional phone systems to ascertain product availability, current costs, and delivery arrangements. This is particularly appropriate to shopping for consumer durables, but is quite conceivable for more frequent shopping arrangements, provided the CDs can be frequently updated as product ranges change.[7]

Teleshopping may be a special case of NTS; the social rewards of shopping may be very different from those of formal work settings which other NTS challenge. Nevertheless, there may be parallels in terms of social dimensions of communications, as is suggested by the video-conferencing case. At least with current technology, NTS seem inadequate for the intense and nuanced interchange of information that characterises many face-to-face encounters. This suggests that they may have less impact on non-routine, knowledge-intensive interactions, and – if they do have a spatial impact – this will mainly be for more routine interactions.

Furthermore, this consumer NTS case suggests that organisational change may be more of a longer-term problem than technical change per se. Telematics networks need to be complemented by physical networks – and by new social and organisational habits and practices, which can often be a long time forming.

CONCLUSIONS

NTS may be slow to take off, but it can be forecast that they will play an increasingly important role for many firms. This forecast derives from the view that market, technological and strategic considerations are involving closer (and more flexible) integration of components of production, distribution, exchange and administrative processes. This involves communication between organisations as well as within them. Suppliers and users of NTS will confront the challenge of integrating their internal communications and information systems with external networks and services. Often, they will need to adopt new forms of organisation, and establish new skills complexes, in order to gain competitive advantage from the new opportunities.

Some commentators argue that NTS use should be rapidly extended from its rather narrow business-oriented base into mass markets. The normative argument for this tends to dwell on equity of access to information resources, and the consequences that follow for social power and choice. A more economistic argument views contemporary change in terms of a new 'regime of accumulation'/'technoeconomic paradigm'/'sociotechnical system'. This requires the establishment of new ways of life and new patterns of demand, making use of new technological opportunities alongside their use in formal production processes. The mass-market supply and use of interactive services would provide the population with an extended skill base (in telecommunications, software, information management, graphical design, etc.) from which further advances could be made. The development of such a scenario currently seems highly contingent upon interventions by the state, or by concerted groups of large business actors – the patterns of demand development and the social needs serviced could be very different in distinct cases.

Further factors are likely to facilitate the growth of NTS: the first is the process of liberalisation of telecommunications regimes. Associated with this, the internationalisation of service markets is already well underway, given the international scope of many of the firms best placed to offer certain elements of NTS packages (notably the provision and management of value-added networks); it will be spurred on by the efforts of the EC telecommunications directorate to facilitate the creation of one element of the 'single European market'. (This leads to some fears that the liberalisation and modernisation of telecommunications might pave the way for the domination of NTS markets by foreign suppliers – a 'spatial impact' we are not considering here, but that is worth further study.[8])

Another factor leading to the emergence of more NTS, and the further honing of NTS against evolving market requirements, is the 'spinning-off' of NTS from in-house corporate services. Firms with a heavy investment in telematics may wish to externalise NTS as well as networks. Those whose internal networks are not on a large enough scale for use as general carriers may wish to export their internal NTS through gateways to other networks. This may lead to greater private sector interest in the development of (more or less) universal, high quality public networks; or in the expansion of, and collaboration among, private networks that might carry NTS. Regulatory issues may be raised with the proliferation of such networks, especially concerning their interconnectivity.

This study has identified some of the factors currently leading to a very limited realisation of the promise of NTS. They involve a mixture of technological, economic, organisational – and, perhaps above all, strategic and policy – issues. These issues should not be interpreted simply as slowing or speeding the 'spatial impacts' of NTS. They help to shape these 'impacts', which are by no means logical consequences of autonomous technological change. While some technical constraints may be important (it is very costly to install broadband systems at present, for instance), we would argue that attention to the social shaping processes is now crucial – both to account for patterns of development and to influence them.

NOTES

1　This paper was prepared while the author was funded under the Economic and Social Research Council's Programme on Information and Communication Technologies (PICT). I would like to thank the PICT and my colleagues in the Programme and in SPRU for material and intellectual support. This paper draws heavily upon earlier studies carried out with Graham Thomas, initially supported by the Leverhulme Trust, to whom I am also indebted.

2　However, not all VANS are necessarily NTS: for instance, we would exclude services that offer prerecorded messages or 'chatline' several-way conversations for our scope.

3　The pace of innovation is such that practically every technical statement made in this discussion of fax and email could be qualified. New devices and services are being developed to overcome the limitations mentioned, but since most of these innovations are recent and only diffused to a limited extent, so the discussion should be accurate as an account of circumstances currently prevalent.

4　British Facsimile Industry Consultative Committee figures.

5　See Gershuny and Miles (1983) on changing modes of service delivery as a major dimension of socioeconomic evolution.

6　A host is roughly equivalent to a publisher, offering on-line information services that may be produced by quite distinct 'authors', so that users need not make contact with each service through an independent route.

7　Keyline proposes a more immediately accessible model (though one that is less interactive) in which night-time TV broadcast catalogues are stored on videorecorders.

8　Parallel research at SPRU by Jagger and Mansell is addressing this issue.

GLOSSARY

BT—British Telecom; EC—European Community; EDI—Electronic Data Interchange; IT—Information Technology; LAN—Local Area Network; NTS—New Telematics Services; PC—Personal Computer; VADS—Value Added and Data Services; VANS—Value Added Network Services.

7

TELEMATIC UNDERPINNINGS OF THE INFORMATION ECONOMY

Peter Newton

INTRODUCTION

Eras which represent a transition from one major bundle of technologies to another or one dominant economic system to another present peculiar problems for foresighting – rooted as occupants of such periods are in the familiarity of the past, the immediacy of what constitutes the present and the uncertainty of the future. Under such circumstances it is often instructive to read accounts of earlier periods of technological transition. One such account is Oxford economist H. de Beltgens Gibbins's (1901) review of the Industrial Revolution and its progress through the nineteenth century. At the outset of his treatise he entreats those who search for '…the great and sudden industrial changes of (their) time' to consider that many of the causes had been operating for some time 'beneath the surface'. In other words, look for the historical antecedents for the current 'revolutionary' conditions; much is evolutionary. And what of the nature of changes wrought by 'a revolution in manufactures'? Gibbins's (1901, p. 3) description: 'It was a revolution which has completely changed the face of modern Europe and of the New World, for it introduced a new race of men – the men who work with machinery instead of with their hands, who cluster together in cities instead of spreading over the land in villages and hamlets; the men who trade with those of other nations as readily as with those of their own town'.

Ninety years on, society is experiencing another set of revolutionary technological changes – changes which are extending the powers of the mind rather than muscle (Stonier 1983); change which is knowledge-based rather than energy-based; change which has the potential for countering the central-ising tendencies characteristic of the Industrial Revolution, but whose disper-sive capabilities are yet to be fully explored (Kellerman 1984). The labelling of our current era 'post-industrial' (after Bell 1973), sits uncomfortably for some (e.g. Cohen & Zysman 1987) who argue that contemporary standards of living depend upon the competitiveness of the manufacturing base of the economy. Returning once more to Gibbins (1901, p. 10) and his nineteenth century perspective, we find: 'It [agriculture] is the industry upon which ultimately all others must rest, for it is the industry which of all others deals most directly with Nature, and which can subsist alone without external aid...The manufacturing industry, though necessary to the well-being of a nation, may yet exist for ages in a very rudimentary form before the wants it fulfills are deeply felt...But in the present age we are inclined to under-rate the importance of agriculture and the necessity of supporting it in a flourishing condition'.

Substitute manufacturing for agriculture and we find much the same flavour in the industrial restructuring debate of the 1970s and early 1980s; that is, a belief that there was a limit to the contribution of services to national economic growth – that manufacture of goods must be made more efficient and productive. The period of high economic growth characteristic of advanced societies in the quarter century following the second world war, however, has been identified as a period which fostered the growth of what have come to be termed high technologies; which include computers, software, micro-electronics and telecommunications (although many of their origins can be traced back to the nineteenth century (see Beniger 1986)). These new technologies, as well as contributing individually to enhancing efficiency within the longer established sectors of industry (primary, secondary, tertiary), have become integrated into a generic technology, termed, alternatively, information technology or telematics – denoting a bundle of technologies associated with the economic arrangements by which information is collected, stored, processed and distributed.

THE INFORMATION ECONOMY

There is now little debate concerning the existence of the information (or quaternary) sector in national economies, although the size and importance of that sector will vary between countries according to their level of development (Mandeville 1987a). This sector has continued to exhibit growth over a long period, as information has increasingly formed an important part of the economy – but most notably since the 1940s (Beniger 1986, p. 24). Pioneering research by Machlup (1962) and Porat (1977) in the United States has been replicated in other countries (Hepworth 1988; Lamberton 1988) in respect of measurement of the size of the information sector. For example, in Australia, the size of the labour force involved in what could be classed as information-related activity is now in excess of 40 per cent; and the primary information sector's[1] contribution to gross domestic product is 36 per cent (Lamberton 1987; 1988). Both represent the continuation of a trend extending back at least several decades.

The information sector has emerged primarily in response to the increasing complexity of the economic system (Robinson 1986; Engelbrecht 1986;

Karunaratne 1986) and the increasing demands this places on information handling – given that each economic transaction is necessarily associated with a flow of information. Again, an historical perspective is informative. As that flow of economic transactions intensified and extended beyond local economies to national economies and ultimately to a world economic system, it precipitated what Beniger (1986) has termed a crisis of control which demanded new means of communication. The communications infrastructure we have today is a cumulation of networks developed over many decades designed to direct and mediate, in the most efficient possible manner, the flow of information, people and goods between areas and sectors of the economy. For a time, particular 'communications' networks dominated the transshipment of people, goods and ideas (viz. canals, railways, automobile, air), and engendered major changes in patterns of living and working in the process. This chapter seeks to explore the manner in which the new bundle of telematic networks and services (some of which will come into play in the 1990s), that some writers have termed a new long wave of 'informatisation' (Kogane 1988), likely to impact on spatial patterns and processes.

THE ROLE OF TIME AND PLACE IN THE INFORMATION ECONOMY

The geography of the information economy

At present, a range of national and state industry and settlement policies are being advanced which have information- and knowledge-intensive industry and telecommunications infrastructure as their centrepiece (e.g. Victoria's high technology precinct policy (see Edgington 1989); and the joint initiative by the Australian and Japanese governments in respect of a multi-function polis – MFP). Laudable as such 'market leading' initiatives might be in their desire to stimulate development in a number of areas hitherto underdeveloped, they run the risk of foundering in the absence of fundamental market analysis. Urban policy makers and technologists both tend to share a common trait of believing they have more control over the environment than they actually have. Indeed, it was in the context of the MFP that Langdale (1988a, p. 12) concluded, '...we know very little about the role of telecommunications in the contemporary information economy; consequently, forecasting the future is likely to be a very risky business. Our ignorance about the contemporary information economy is likely to be a problem which will bedevil planners in a wide variety of areas'.

Measurement

The information economy is traditionally comprised of firms involved with information products or information services. Such firms may be classed as primary if they generate a final, marketable product. The taxonomy of the primary information sector (PRIS) employed in the present study is a composite derived from insights and classifications documented in Machlup

(1962), Porat (1977), Hepworth (1988) and Drennan (1989), but constrained to follow as close as possible to the OECD (1981a) scheme. OECD (1981a, p. 24) segments the PRIS in the following manner:

1 Knowledge and information production industries which '...create new knowledge and information or package existing information into a form appropriate to a particular recipient'. A wide spectrum of activity is included, ranging from basic through applied research to consultancy activity. For the most part the activity is not routine and is undertaken in response to some need, internal or external to the organisation, either technology push or demand pull in nature. Examples of information production industries include: real estate and property consultants, consulting services to business, management, engineering, etc., legal services, accounting, health services, market researchers and so on.

2 Information distribution and communication industries which '...are primarily concerned with conveying information from the initiator to the recipient'. The education and communication industries convey knowledge and information that currently exists. Both industry groups include elements of information production (e.g. university research activities), but the primary activity is considered to be distributive.

3 Information processing industries which '...are primarily concerned with receiving and responding to information inputs. The response may be to decide, to administer, or to perform some manipulative operation on the information inputs'. Typical of this class are brokerage industries, advertising and marketing, insurance and finance, and the primary governmental information and regulatory services.

4 Information infrastructure industries which manufacture, wholesale, install, operate and repair the machinery and technology used to support the other categories of information sector industries (that is, industries associated with telecommunications, office equipment and a range of telematic products, including computers).

Data

In studies undertaken to date, such as that by Porat (1977) and Drennan (1989), recourse is made to data on industries arranged according to the Standard Industrial Classification (SIC) system. The major problem inherent in relying exclusively on such an approach is that the SIC system currently available in Australia (i.e. ASIC) is dated, designed for an industrial structure circa 1970s, and if applied in the present study would not identify the newly emerging information technology-oriented industries. The Yellow Pages Directory emerged as the preferred data source for identification of all primary information sector industries with the exception of knowledge-based industry (the source of data on the latter class of establishments was CSIRO's Directory of Scientific and Technical Research Centres). The 2700 separate business descriptors employed by Yellow Pages to characterise its 156 000 establishments within the Melbourne region were assigned a five-digit code to designate their alignment with a particular category of information- and communication-intensive industry (ICII). Individual establishments with common ICII codes were aggregated by postcode area, facilitating production of maps depicting the spatial configuration of Melbourne's information economy.[2]

Spatial patterns

In an earlier study (Newton & O'Connor 1987) of the location of high technology industry in Australia, a pattern of suburban and central city selectivity was identified that appeared to be strengthening a distribution of well-off and less-well-off areas within the city. It was a pattern indicating that location of high technology industry was clearly reinforcing historically established trends. The present analyses move beyond what was essentially a small, albeit important, segment of the national economy (high technology industry) to the broad group of primary information industries within the Melbourne metropolitan area as they existed early in 1989. Figures 1 to 4 represent, respectively, the distribution of industries associated with knowledge and information production, information distribution and communication, information processing and information infrastructure. The lowest category in each map depicts those areas which have a below average representation of that specific class of industry, the middle category up to one standard deviation above average and the top category over one standard deviation above average. Metropolitan Melbourne also extends well beyond the borders depicted in these maps, but concentrations of information-intensive industry in the outer suburbs remain at the lowest levels. The patterns clearly mirror the social geography of the city and present yet another, and hitherto unidentified, dimension of inequality within our major cities which continue to bedevil state planning authorities and their policies designed to engineer change.

Time and the information economy

The spatial differentiation inherent in the information economy underlines the significance of connectivity – the need for and ability of business of different types (both within the information sector and outside of it) to exchange information as well as goods and services over space. In pre-industrial times where most markets were localised, information exchange was typically undertaken face-to-face: same time/same place. With the movement toward highly differentiated industrial economies which span major cities, continents and indeed the globe, communications technologies have continued to be sought which would come as close as possible to producing a real time information system: facilitating a same time/different place type of connectivity. Indeed, over the past century, new technologies have been developed to facilitate real time communication – initially with telephony (voice), then telework (incorporating, in addition to voice, the ability to transfer two principal 'currencies' of the business economy – data and text) and lastly telepresence (incorporating image). Technology provides, at any point in time, the limits on, as well as the opportunities for the form of telecommunication capable of being undertaken.

These limits are well illustrated in Table 1. Directing attention in the first instance to the column that relates to transmission speeds of 1200 Kbps – a rate characteristic of much information transfer in the late 1960s and early 1970s – it is evident that for many different types of 'document' or 'message' transfer, the time required for transmission and its monopoly of the communication channel (and setting aside the question of cost) exceeded that considered appropriate for efficient practice. At such speeds, rather than utilise voice mail, it would be more efficient to leave a message with a secretary or

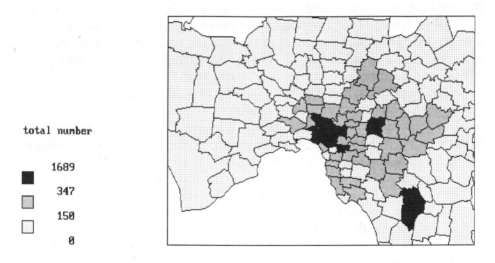

total number

■ 1689

▦ 347

□ 150

□ 0

Figure 1 Melbourne: Knowledge and information production industries, 1989.

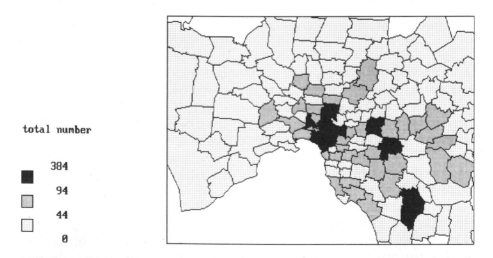

total number

■ 384

▦ 94

□ 44

□ 0

Figure 2 Melbourne: Information distribution and communication industries, 1989.

receptionist; catalogues would be more effectively posted out than committed to electronic data interchange (EDI); image refresh times for videophones, videoconferencing and PC screens were not conducive for interactive applications; and for transfer of large files, courier services would prove speedier than the public switched telephone network (PSTN) or dedicated data lines. As one progresses to higher transmission rates, however, telematic applications become increasingly suited for real time use. Indeed, we are still on the threshold of a move to high-speed services. As recently as 1988, 97 per cent of data services in Australia operated at speeds of 9.6 Kbps or less (SNP 1988). While ISDN (Integrated Subscriber Digital Network) now provides for 64 Kbps transmission over ordinary telephone wire, 2 Mbps effectively represents the limit for copper wire – and optical fibre is only beginning to

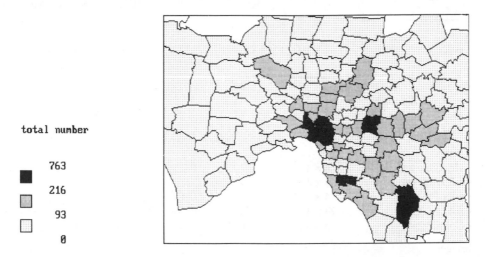

total number

763
216
93
0

Figure 3 Melbourne: Information processing industries, 1989.

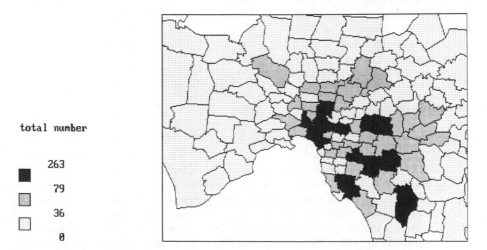

total number

263
79
36
0

Figure 4 Melbourne: Information infrastructure industries, 1989.

penetrate sectors within our cities (trunk routes between major cities now possess fibre optic capability). Clearly it is likely to be well into the 1990s before broadband ISDN and fast packet switching provide for an extensive network at speeds of 20 Mbps and above.

Table 1 Transmission times for telematic applications on networks of different speeds

Transmission content/ message type	Typical number of bits	Approximate transmission time (s,m,h,d,w)				
		@ 1.2 Kbps	9.6 Kpbs	64 Kbps	2 Mbps	20 Mbps
Voice						
• voice mail	2×10^6	28 m	4 m	31 s	1 s	0.1 s
Transaction						
• airline reservation	2×10^2	0.2 s				
• EFT/ATM transfer	5×10^2	0.4 s				
• EDI invoice/order	1×10^4	8 s	1 s	0.2 s		
• EDI catalog	24×10^6	6 h	42 m	6 s	0.2 s	
Text						
• videotex screen	8×10^3	7 s	0.8 s	0.1 s		
• telex/telegram	4×10^2	0.3 s				
• email/memo	4×10^3	3 s	0.4 s			
• A4 fax (G3)	24×10^4	3 m	0.4 s			
• Colour fax	5×10^6	1 h	9 m	1 m	3 s	0.3 s
Image						
• PC screen – LR	26×10^4	4 m	27 s	4 s	0.1 s	
• remote sensed image	34×10^6	8 h	1 h	9 m	17 s	1.7 s
• colour TV frame	1×10^6	14 m	2 m	16 s	0.5 s	
• colour HDTV frame	4×10^6	56 m	7 m	1 m	2 s	0.2 s
• videophone frame – LR	41×10^4	6 m	42 s	6 s	0.2 s	
• videoconference frame	15×10^5	21 m	3 m	23 s	0.8 s	
• video mail	41×10^4	6 m	42 s	6 s	0.2 s	
File transfer						
• 5.25" floppy disk	36×10^4	5 m	38 s	6 s	0.2 s	
• 3.5" floppy disk	14×10^5	19 m	2 m	22 s	0.7 s	
• mag tape 1600 bpi	32×10^7	3 d	9 h	1 h	3 m	16 s
• CD-ROM, 5.25"	44×10^8	42 d	5 d	19 h	37 m	4 m
• 12" WORM	24×10^9	33 w	29 d	4 d	3 h	20 m

Note: Table refers to transmission times only for 'standard' document; times for logging in, establishing electronic 'handshakes' are not included. Examples of standard documents include: 30 s voice message, 10 word telex, half A4 page memo, low resolution PC (320 x 200 pixels), remotely sensed image (1024 x 1024 pixels by 32 bits depth), low resolution videophone frame (176 x 144 pixels x 16 bits/pixel).

Timing

It takes time for any innovation to penetrate the marketplace. Even successful products such as TV, the VCR, and microwave ovens have taken decades to diffuse through a mass market. The history of the facsimile machine clearly illustrates this concept and the range of factors that operate to dictate the 'ripeness' of a market. Considered by many as a product of the 1980s, the concept of facsimile was actually patented in Britain in 1843 and employed for much of the next century as a message sending medium to supplement the telegraph service, principally in the dispatch of weather maps (Costigan 1971). For the thirty years following the time when the first Desk-Fax was launched (1948, in the United States), most fax transmission was within large fax networks (discussed later in greater detail). The massive uptake of facsimile from the late 1970s (see Figure 5) has been due to the following mix of factors:

- prior to 1976 when CCITT began to introduce standards for Group 1 and 2 fax, the various makes of fax units were mostly incompatible with each other;
- group 3 fax provided for higher transmission speeds, lower prices (one quarter that of early 1970s) and more programmable features than earlier models; and CCITT initiated an additional set of standards in 1980 for G3 to enhance connectivity within the PSTN (Voros 1989);
- persistence of Japanese electronics and communications companies in their development of fax technology because of the ease with which it facilitated transmission of Kangi symbols (Roberts & Morrison 1989).

Fax, like other telematic products before it, such as the telephone, the xerox machine and the computer, has now become what Voros (1989) terms a self-generating technology: '...the more it penetrates the market, the more useful it becomes'. But it did not happen overnight. In a similar manner to the time required for telematic services to diffuse through the market, there is likewise a temporal and spatial lag in the installation of new terrestrial telecommunication networks. Introduction of Integrated Services Digital Networks (ISDN) is a good example. Lazak (1987) comments from a German perspective that as ISDN is now available, advanced users of network systems are trying to install it as soon as possible, yet it is estimated that it will take from thirty to forty years to switch over from old to new networks throughout the entire country. The spatial implications for the transition period are a 'landscape of ISDN islands, both nationally and internationally'. At the international level, Lazak (1987, p. 229) envisages advanced networks with access and distribution nodes, termed teleports, providing user access to the most advanced communication systems worldwide irrespective of the status of networks throughout particular countries. At national levels, Zamanillo (1985) describes what is typical of phased introduction of ISDN over the PSTN: trunks first, then exchanges, then subscriber lines – initially in areas considered most likely to exhibit high levels of demand. The recent moves by major international corporations to establish their own private global communications networks is another example of early entry into a new system by particular categories of industry (see *We're Sharp*, July 1989, for details of initiatives by Sharp; see *Financial Review* 26 June 1989, for General Electric Co. plans).

TELECOMMUNICATIONS INFRASTRUCTURE OF THE INFORMATION ECONOMY

Set in historical perspective, the past twenty years have seen the most revolutionary developments to date in both hardwire (terrestrial) and softwire (satellite, microwave) telecommunications infrastructures, providing increased capacity for the growing array of network and telematic services which they

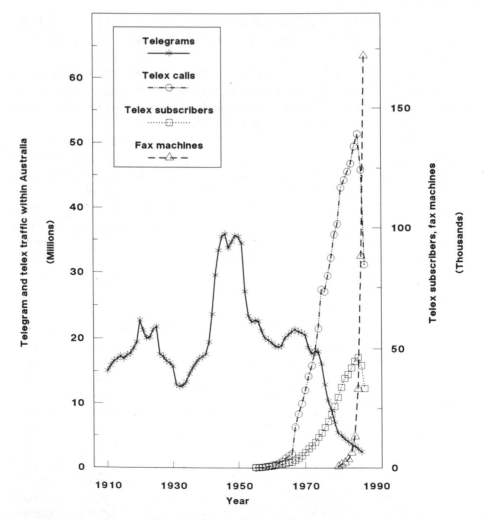

Figure 5 Text services within Australia.

host and which are discussed in some detail in the following section. It is a period in which global communication has boomed (see Figure 6), underpinned by factors such as the following:

- growth in transmission capacity of cables (e.g. the COMPAC cable which commenced operation in 1963 linking Australia to Europe via North America with sixty circuits; its 1984 replacement, ANZCAN, employed 1380 circuits. The SEACOM cable, with its ninety-six circuits, providing links between Australia and Europe via South-East Asia commenced operation in 1967 and in 1986 was replaced by the AIS cable with 1380 circuits. Tasman 1 cable provided links with New Zealand in 1976, while in the same year APNG cable linked Australia with Papua-New Guinea);

- introduction of increasingly powerful communication satellites (Australia was linked to Intelsat 2 in 1968 and thereafter at regular intervals to Intelsat 3, 4, 4A, 5, 5A and 6, whose capacities have increased from under 500 circuits to over 30 000);

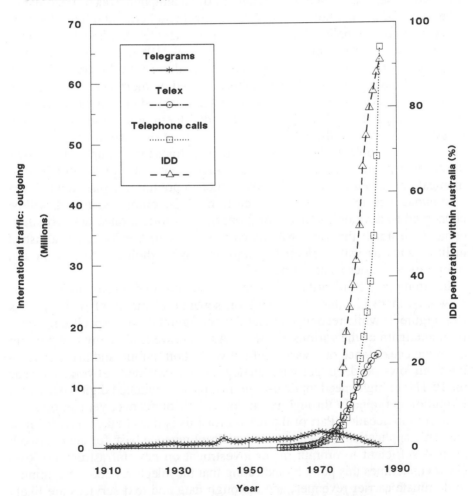

Figure 6 International telecommunications traffic outgoing from Australia.

- growth in telematic services in countries with which Australia interacts and provision of linkages which increase connectivity; for example, in 1959 Australia had telex links to 27 countries, over 100 by 1968 and over 200 in 1975. While local telex traffic in Australia has now begun to decline (see Figure 5), international telex traffic is merely plateauing, reflecting slower take-up of facsimile in other countries compared to Australia;
- provision of services which automate telecommunication connectivity between countries; for example, international direct dial (IDD) was introduced in Australia in 1976 providing links to thirteen other countries. Two years later, IDD services had been established between Australia and seventy countries; by 1988, over 90 per cent of telephone subscribers in Australia had IDD connectivity (see Figure 6).

One hundred years earlier, residents of Western Australia were celebrating their telegraphic link to the east coast via Adelaide. Transmission speeds were forty words per minute and the throughput of telegraphers was of the order of seventy messages per hour. Such technological and human bottlenecks were exacerbated by the political organisation of post and telegraph services – then a state rather than federal responsibility. Moyal (1984, p. 50) vividly describes the activity in the telegraph offices at the South Australia/Western Australia border in 1877: '...telegraphists, seated on their respective sides of the operating table, took down the morse signals tapped out from their capitals – in differing telegraph alphabets – decoded them and passed the written message through "hand-holes" in the head high partition to their appropriate number'. No problem with the measurement of transborder information flows during that period. Indeed, we appear to have entered a phase in telecommunications development in the 1990s where a premium is placed on secure communications by major corporate customers. Governments, in turn, will be concerned to develop methods for monitoring information flows (volumes, content) in much the same way as currently occurs for longer established utilities such as water, electricity and gas. Why should information and information utilities be any different?

In attempting to identify trends in the evolution of telecommunications networks, there is value in focusing on separate elements of such systems (see Figure 7) while recognising that the configuration of a specific network is an amalgum of the various elements. As such, we find at any one point in time, the coexistence of a variety of networks both public and private, ranging from low-speed, copper wire, analog, circuit switched networks (such as the PSTN) to high-speed, optical-fibre, fast packet switched digital networks. Evolution is typically through technological obsolescence, yet can often be measured in decades. Part of the reason for this is that it takes time for new telematic applications to generate a significant revenue base for their network hosts – sufficient to prompt major investment on new infrastructure. Ross (1982) underlines this point by indicating that the telephony service continues to dominate carrier revenues, and although data and text services are likely to grow relatively faster through the 1990s, they will still represent a small share of total revenue (see Figure 8). According to Ross, the future for broadband high-speed services is uncertain and, up to the 1990s, revenues from such services remained small in relative terms. The rate at which they are likely to grow in the 1990s and beyond is open to dispute, but the introduction and integration of the full range of telematic services listed in Table 1, into the economy, will depend on investment in high-speed digital networks.

Transmission media

Competition between hardwire and softwire networks has been underway for over a quarter of a century and over this time capacities of each network have increased substantially. The present copper wire media, which provides the most extensive telecommunication network, is limited to a bandwidth of

- **Transmission Media**
  terrestrial: copper wire ⟶ coaxial cable ⟶ optical fibre
  satellite: growth in circuits from ‹ 500 to › 30 000

- **Transmission Speed**
  low speed (300 bps) ⟶ high speed (155 Mbps +)

- **Transmission Signal**
  analog ⟶ digital

- **Switching System**
  circuit switching ⟶ packet switching ⟶ fast packet switching

- **Level of automation in telephone exchanges**
  manual ⟶ computerised

Figure 7 Trends in the evolution of telecommunications networks.

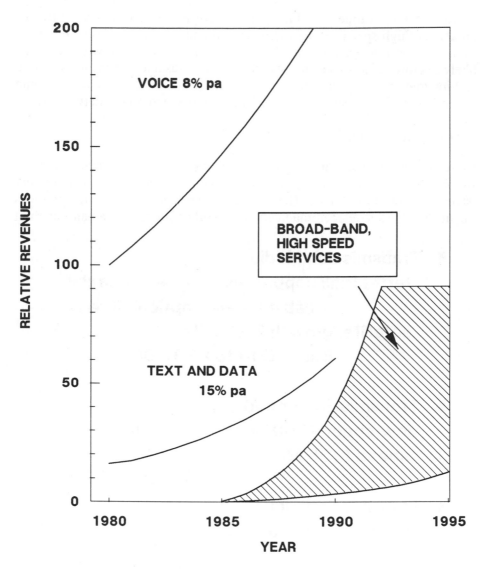

Figure 8 Telecommunications revenue trends (source: Ross 1982).

approximately 4 kHz, which is satisfactory for voice, but severely limits the ability to transport digital services. For data rates above 1.5 Mbps, it is preferable that other transmission media be considered. For provision of new networks to more remote areas, microwave radio has provided a viable alternative to copper cable. For example, mining, railway and pipeline companies have been among the pioneers in creating private microwave networks to link their geographically dispersed locations. Digital microwave systems have also been employed in an attempt to meet the need of voice, data and image transmission, but performance levels have been disappointing (Jacobs 1986): there is a sensitivity to atmospheric conditions (e.g. rain), electromagnetic interference (common in large metropolitan areas), and lack of security. Coaxial cable, the dominant medium in long distance telephony (as well as TV in many countries) has larger bandwidth, lower crosstalk, and better immunity to electromagnetic interference than twisted copper pairs (Burmeister 1985).

Satellite communication opened up another avenue of competition in transmission, particularly in the transmission of data and video. Satellites have proven to be cost-effective over long distance, low volume routes, and are particularly useful to regions or countries which lack a well-developed telecommunications infrastructure; and provide a network for point-to-multipoint applications such as television (Langdale 1988b). Satellite transmission has been found to be less satisfactory than surface lines for interactive communication because of the requirement to send information 35 000 kilometres up into space and return. This introduces an undesirable delay in interactive transactions between distant sites. However, it is well suited to the transmission of large quantities of information in one direction at a time. Organisations such as large retail chains, that have many dispersed locations and must transmit large batches of data between these locations and a central site can use satellite transmission effectively, although developments in fast packet switching (see later) may alter the situation again.

A new era of competition between transmission media has emerged with fibre-optic cable, whose addition to the telecommunications infrastructure has been in response to increased telephone traffic (see Figures 6 and 9) and emerging demands for a full-scale data service and video transmission system. The advantages of fibre optics have been identified by several writers, and include: wide bandwidth which provides for large capacity transmission (multiplexed); reduction in duct congestion (due to small size); reduction in load on buildings (due to different volume of copper versus fibre optics required); lack of appreciable crosstalk; immunity to interference; and lower life-cycle maintenance costs. Studies which have attempted to evaluate the relative costs of competing media point to the likelihood of fibre-optic systems becoming increasingly competitive (see Ross 1982).

Transmission signal

Much of the current terrestrial communications infrastructure was installed to support voice communication employing analog signalling (i.e. conversion of sound waves to electrical current for transmission then reconversion at receiving end). Use of the analog PSTN for digital data transmission has been in operation since the 1960s via the application of modems. The move towards a fully digital network began in a number of countries with the introduction in the late 1970s and early 1980s of digital data networks, providing dedicated (fixed) point-to-point and multipoint data services. The dedicated networks arose in response to the fact that the switched circuits simply could not accommodate the high data transmission rates required by most users. The principal advantages of digital over analog transmission includes significantly higher transmission speeds (affecting the relative performance of a wide range of telematic services – see Table 1), lower error rates and ability to mix information of multiple types (data, voice, image, text) on the same circuit. It is a significant factor in the development of integrated telematic products. The introduction of ISDN (Integrated Subscriber Digital Network) in Australia in 1989 represents the first stage in the development of a fully digital public switched network with global connectivity at a total aggregate channel capacity of 144 Kbps (2 x 64 + 16). Yet even at the time of its introduction there were claims that it will be overtaken by broadband ISDN offering interface rates at 600 Mbps or higher.

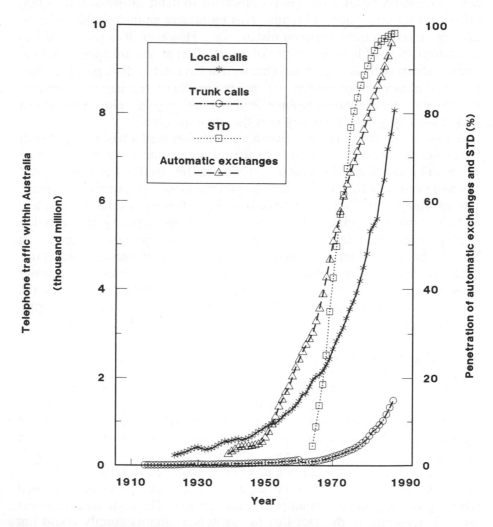

Figure 9 Growth of telephone traffic within Australia.

Switching system

Currently there are two basic switching types – circuit and packet switching. Before the mid-1960s the only switching technology available was analog circuit switching used in the public voice network. Data, therefore, were initially switched through the PSTN. With circuit switching, once a link is established between origin and destination it remains completely dedicated for the duration of the communication. The principal disadvantages associated with this mode of switching relate to the time required to set up the circuit (Clare 1984), speed selection limitations, and the unavailability of the line for other communications (Zorkoczy 1984). Consequently, circuit switching is rarely used for data networking.

Packet switching is relatively newer, first proposed in the United States in 1964 and now used worldwide. It employs computers to control data flow and does not require a dedicated physical path between origin and destination. Data files or messages to be transmitted are split into packets which are transmitted on an appropriate route (or routes) determined by network software. Major advantages of packet switching include minimising circuit and node congestion, optimising utilisation of available bandwidth of the transmission channel (Zorkoczy 1984) and error checking. Accompanying such benefits, however, was the disadvantage of delay in the packet store-and-forward process, making the technology unsuitable for voice and other non-data signals (Bender 1987). By the late 1970s it had become apparent that neither packet nor circuit switching systems as they stood could satisfy the diverse demands of data, text and video with their very different transmission speed requirements (Gerla 1985). On the supply side, the availability of low cost transmission capability offered by optical-fibre systems also stimulated thinking about new network switching structures (Bender 1987).

A solution to the problem was found by operating the switches at extremely high speeds so that real time delays are dramatically decreased (see Table 1). The fast packet switching technology now available (Kirton *et al.* 1988) enables integrated voice, text, data and video information to be transmitted at very high speeds (at least 155 Mbps) linking LANs with metropolitan area networks (MANs) to provide national as well as international services. It has also been agreed that broadband ISDN will be based on fast packet switching and that the standard line rate will be 155 Mbps (Park 1989).

THE SHIFT FROM CENTRALISED TO IN-HOUSE TO MOBILE TELEMATIC SERVICES

There is a certain fuzziness in the literature concerning the nexus between telecommunications and patterns of spatial development. Take Kellerman's (1984, p. 242) conclusion to his paper on telecommunications and the geography of metropolitan areas: 'Telecommunications is thus perceived as a powerful communications device that may assist people, industry, business and society to achieve goals that are determined, in principle, independently of communications. It is, therefore, suggested that telecommunications may lead to more than one geographical pattern'. Clearly so. Given the time required to install new network services – such as the new digital network ISDN discussed above – lags, of themselves, will translate as spatial opportunities for some areas but not others. Furthermore, the increasing array of telematic products and services, some of which are listed in Table 1, have entered the market at different times, at different levels of sophistication and at different rates within particular sectors of industry. Most, if not all, tend to follow a general trend however: initial introduction as a centralised service, progressing subsequently to in-house adoption and finally to a mobile telematic service (see Figure 10), usually following some major technological development, a decline in cost, appearance of complementary products,

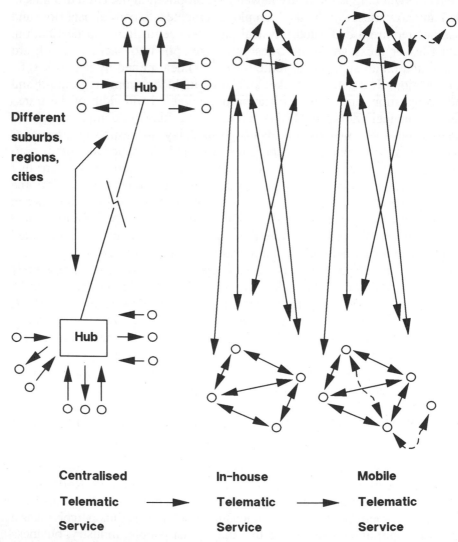

| Centralised Telematic Service | ⟶ | In-house Telematic Service | ⟶ | Mobile Telematic Service |

Figure 10 Trend in diffusion of telematic services.

integration with another telematic product or introduction of standards that facilitate connectivity of systems which open up the market (viz. example of CCITT standards for Fax, introduction of MS.DOS for PCs, uniform standards for compact disks – see Schnaars 1989, p. 179). In-house (or more specifically within-establishment) introduction as a stand-alone telematic product, tends to progress further over time to a desktop device, servicing the needs of an individual worker; a principal factor behind statistics which reveal decline in number of workers per establishment, but increase in floorspace per worker. A further phase of product development is the personal transportable telematic service. The settlement implications of the trend from centralised to in-house to in-home to personal mobile telematic services is a freeing of individuals and organisations from a need to locate in close physical proximity to hub providers of telematic services, allowing other factors to come into play in the locational decision. Some examples will illustrate this trend.

Voice

The 'plain old telephone system' (POTS) has been in existence since 1879 in Australia and over the century which followed, constituted the principal vehicle for delivery of new telematic services: transmitting text, data and image as well as voice – albeit at low speed. The telephone has achieved 'in-house' (office, home) penetration to a higher degree than any other information technology product, with the possible exception of television. Rate of penetration was relatively slow, however, prior to the second world war (Figure 11); in contrast to that of public telephones (in a sense a centralised service) which were close to their maximum penetration by the late 1950s. Proliferation of party lines in the decade following the war became the means by which the pressure of public demand could be accommodated against a background of shortage of urban infrastructure in general and communications infrastructure in particular.

The history of mobile voice telecommunication in Australia extends back to 1950 with the introduction of the mobile radio telephone (Moyal 1984): a private, dedicated, single-user radio dispatch system used most commonly for public safety applications such as police, fire, ambulance and so forth; for the most part relatively centralised services, oriented to a small number of hubs within a metropolitan area. Cellular mobile telephones, introduced during the 1980s, represent an extension of the PSTN, increasing connectivity of voice systems, facilitating calls from mobile units (typically automobiles) to fixed locations, from fixed sites to mobile units and from one mobile unit to another. The commercial introduction of cordless telephones in 1991 (in Australia) at one-tenth the price of cellular mobile units (approximately $350) will increase the market for mobile voice communication despite the fact that it will only facilitate out-going calls made within a 50 to 100 metre radius of a 'telepoint'. Some measure of connectivity is planned with the integration of the pocket pager with the cordless telephone (CT2). A little discussed impact of CT2 on urban form will be the manner in which accommodation for parking is resolved at telepoint locations.

The consistent trend of all telematic services, and none more so than voice services, is towards increased connectivity between subscribers. The progressive automation of telephone exchanges put an end to silence and isolation at night (particularly in the country areas) and provided twenty-four-hour communication for social and business purposes. Increase in telephone traffic paralleled this trend in automation (Figure 9) in the same manner that penetration of subscriber trunk dialling (STD) stimulated growth in long-distance communication. Telephone answering machines, voice mail, paging systems and mobile telephones further promote connectivity over both space and time.

Growth in 008 services, which permit long-distance telephone calls at local rates and commonly on a twenty-four-hour basis, have the potential for

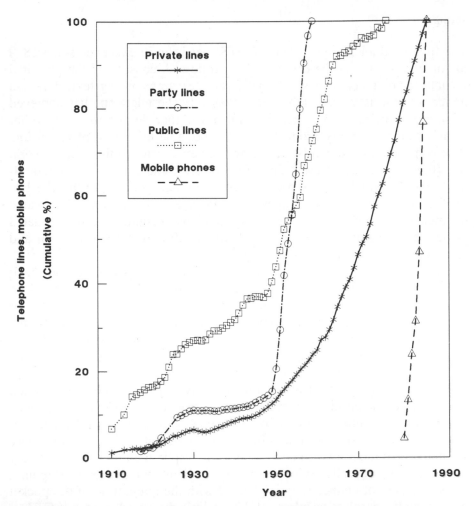

Figure 11 Trends in telephony services in the State of Victoria, Australia.

extending the market catchment for a particular private or public sector enterprise to national boundaries and beyond. The industry and settlement implications are difficult to anticipate. In theory, 008 services provide for location of business establishments in either urban or non-urban realms. In practice, they appear to be centralising in the most populous city (Sydney) in the most populous State, New South Wales (see Table 2). Four sectors of industry dominate the demand for 008 services: wholesale and retail trade, representing almost half of all subscribers; manufacturing industry; recreation, personal and other services; and the finance, property and business sector (see Table 3).

Table 2 Distribution of 008 subscribers by State, 1989

State	Share of business establishments (%)	Share of 008 subscribers (%)
NSW (including ACT)	35.5	43.1
Victoria	25.8	26.2
Queensland	18.2	15.3
Western Australia	8.8	7.1
South Australia (+ NT)	8.9	6.2
Tasmania	2.8	2.1
Total	100.0	100.0

Source: 008 – Telecom Australia, 1989.
Business establishments – IRIS Database, Australian Bureau of Statistics, 1989.

Table 3 Demand for 008 telephone service by industry sector: Victoria, 1989

Industry sector	008 subscribers (% of total)	Business establishments (% of total)
Agriculture, forestry & fishing	0.5	0.6
Mining	0.1	0.3
Manufacturing	16.5	8.4
Utilities	0.0	0.2
Construction	3.0	13.5
Wholesale & retail trade	49.1	33.5
Communication & transport	0.7	5.1
Finance, property & business services	12.9	15.9
Community services	2.9	12.2
Recreation, personal & other services	14.3	10.0
Public administration & defence	0.0	0.3
Total	100.0	100.0

Source: Telecom Australia, 1989.

Transactions

Economic transactions are closely associated with information flows. During the 1980s, telematic products such as videotex and electronic document interchange (EDI) have been introduced in a number of countries with varying degrees of success. Videotex facilitates a range of electronic transactions in-house via computer, and was launched in Australia in 1985 under the trade name Viatel. The market performance of Viatel in respect of subscribers and service providers is outlined below (source: Telecom Annual Reports).

Year	No. of subscribers	No. of Viatel service providers
1985	4500	112
1986	6000	250
1987	28000	300
1988	30000	200

Offering services such as shopping and banking (access to which is also available, respectively via teletext and voice mail), it was expected to serve a mass market and act as a major soft infrastructure for the information economy. Instead, it has touched only a small segment. Several reasons for this are advanced by Schnaars (1989) who suggests that videotext provides few, if any, services that people consider essential, that there is a preference still for examining merchandise before purchase, and for dealing face-to-face. Furthermore, browsing databases have not yet captured the imagination as a free-time passive activity, and costs of equipment and subscription do not yet pass price/performance thresholds. The extent to which heavily subsidised services (as with Minitel in France) and niche videotex services (as with Elderlink in Australia – a rural service) can generate higher penetration rates is worth monitoring.

Electronic document interchange (EDI), in contrast to videotex, is entirely business-oriented and is concerned with the exchange of standard format business documents between computers. It aims at improving communication between companies by replacing the traditional process of printing a business form from a computer, putting it in the post and re-keying the information into a computer at the receiving end. Along with other telematic products, such as electronic mail, it has the potential for reduction in paper messaging within the office environment, as well as a reduction in the volumes of mail to be transported via couriers or government postal services. In the 1970s, a number of individual organisations or trading partners whose business generated high volumes of paperwork had begun to experiment with paperless trading through the exchange of magnetic tapes. This was subject to very specific one-to-one arrangements and was quickly overtaken by the concept of data exchange via the telecommunications network. The next step, point-to-multipoint connections, brought a number of significant problems relating to standards for the interchange of information. As with facsimile, a key to the widespread development and optimal utilisation of EDI services is adoption of international standards (for both communication protocols and document structure), and moves towards such a standard are occurring with the United Nations and International Standards Organisation (ISO) initiative called EDIFACT (Electronic Data Interchange for Administration, Commerce and Transport).

The sectors of industry most interested in EDI include manufacturing, where EDI is central to just-in-time techniques (i.e. manufacturing products, specifically as ordered, for delivery on a particular date, eliminating stock-piling; the automobile industry in Australia has been a leader in this area (see Plunkett 1989)). Just-in-time is also becoming increasingly important in retail trade, where shops are attempting to order on the basis of sales figures to prevent accumulation of unpopular goods (K-Mart is one Australian retail chain using EDI). Transport and distribution sectors are interested from the point of view of cargo tracking, and transmission of documents to enable shipment of goods to clients with minimum delay.

As with any new technology, there are many factors which can slow penetration into the market place. At present a number of large Australian companies are trialling EDI to assess benefits against the initial set up costs. Issues of security, error checking, confidentiality and legal status of EDI transactions are also under examination (Draper 1988). And a recent study (Takac & Zinn 1988) raised the matter of cooperation between Australian companies as central to EDI's success, clearly, connectivity is required at an industry-wide level: '…its [EDI's] biggest savings will come only when and if the maximum number of companies – which will often be in competition – are connected through the same or compatible networks'.

Text

Transmission of text represented the earliest application of a telematic service with the introduction of the electric telegraph over 150 years ago in the United States. The railway and the telegraph developed as complementary technologies and, in Australia at least, shared much of the same infrastructure (viz. telegraph lines followed the rail routes and telegraph stations could frequently be found at railway stations). Both technologies were fixed route and formed backbones of linear, centralised settlement systems. As a telecommunications technology for text, the telegraph was dominant in Australia until the 1970s, when telex began to exert its influence (see Figure 5). The boost to telegram traffic evident during the war years was related to Australia's emergence as the communications hub of the South Pacific following the fall of Singapore and the significant increase in telecommunications infrastructure installed during that period (Moyal 1984).

The advantage that telex held over the telegraph was its ability to transmit point-to-point messages with no need for intermediaries or surface delivery. Text messaging had moved in-house. With the conversion to fully automatic telex switching in 1966 (Moyal 1984), traffic boomed. As we shall see with other networks, a combination of connectivity and automation (ease of use) is a powerful formula for penetration of telematic services into the market. Cost is also a factor: telex was cheaper than a trunk telephone call. Telex would dominate until the facsimile developed to a point where its cost/performance capabilities clearly outshone those of its competitors. The facsimile machine is not, however, a recent entry to telematic services.

Facsimile emerged as a service for business communication where delays of a day or more were prohibitive (e.g. in transmission of news pictures, weather maps, in commercial transactions between head office and branches and so on) and where complex information unsuited to telex or teletype needed to be exchanged (graphs, symbols, plans, etc.). The absence of standards for facsimile manufacture and transmission until the mid-1970s promoted the development of several large fax networks in the United States wherein certain standards were adopted – connectivity outside such networks being poor. By the early 1970s there were at least six such networks operating throughout the United States, ranging in size from about thirty stations to over 1000 (Costigan 1971). Operators of such fax networks leased blocks of telephone lines between cities, and as the cost of transmitting copy over a given distance was determined by volume of use, the centres were able to transmit material from city to city cheaper than could a business operating its own system at lower volume. (Similar fax networks are likely to emerge in the 1990s with the introduction of colour capability.)

With the appearance of the G3 fax in the late 1970s, advances in technology had made facsimile equipment easier to use (e.g. programmability, unattended transmission), more attractive to the office environment (small, odourless and relatively quiet), cheaper, and faster in transmission. CCITT standards provided for wide connectivity. The 1980s growth in fax usage and in-house penetration within organisations is a reflection of these sets of factors. G4 fax, now available to organisations on 64 Kbps digital networks (G3 operates over the analog PSTN), provides for transmission times of less than three seconds per page, and potential for significant savings for high-volume fax users whose network is national or global. According to Voros (1989), several companies in the United States are establishing a backbone network of G4 machines on their private digital networks with the more numerous G3 faxes feeding into their local G4 'gateway' for fast-forwarding across the digital network, with retransmission to G3 destinations. A throwback to a centralised network? In concept, yes. It represents a necessary, albeit temporary, accommodation for the current period of analog-to-digital transition, but all transactions remain electronic.

Prospects for increased penetration of fax machines into the home are certainly closer than they were in the late 1930s, at a time when several newspapers in the United States were issuing fax editions and forecasts were for fax recorders to become as commonplace in the home as radios (Costigan 1971). Commercial TV ended any prospect for such a service – and today, via teletext, provides a still limited but interactive and entirely electronic version of public text transmission (videotex offers a wider range of services).

Householders in Australia who wish to use fax can now do so via Australia Post's Faxpost service, introduced in 1989 on a network of 720 sites nation-wide (hosted on Olivetti M280 PCs), providing either a two-hour or next-day service. Mirrored on the business fax network of the 1960s and 1970s it offers a service during a transition phase while fax moves in-home and in-car (interfaced with cellular telephones). Again, it will take time, further reductions in cost in absolute terms and relative to other text delivery services (e.g. ordinary mail) and an ability to meet a need in the market, at present somewhat obscure.

Are there any spatial implications of this trend for telematic applications to translate, over time, from a centralised service to an in-house service? Moss (1988) proposes that telecommunications is creating a new urban hierarchy which reflects the variable concentrations of information-intensive industries nationally and internationally. Using penetration of facsimile machines as a measure of telecommunication-intensive firms, Moss identifies several cities (San Francisco, Washington DC, Atlanta, Boston and Pittsburgh) with signifi-cantly higher concentrations of facsimile machines than would be suggested by their population size, joining other centres such as New York, Chicago and Los Angeles which rank highly on both criteria. Are there cities in Australia which also dominate as centres of information exchange? Yes, but they do not disturb the existing urban hierarchy (see Table 4) in the manner documented by Moss for the United States. There is, however, a clear division between the five largest cities where telematic services (as measured by fax) are concen-trating at levels appreciably higher than city size alone would suggest.

Video and image

Of all the telematic products discussed in this paper, perhaps none more than those which incorporate the transmission of image have attracted the label of failed innovation or unwanted benefit. Here we include interactive TV, the picture telephone and videoconferencing. Schnaars (1989) is particularly damning of these services: interactive TV failed because consumers preferred passive rather than active entertainment; the videophone, introduced in the United States in 1964, attracted few customers, largely due to cost. For video-conferencing, a product which evolved from the videophone, lack of market penetration is seen as reflecting a need for 'high touch' (see Naisbitt 1982) and trust (Meier 1985) in business operations – a sustaining of established, even embedded, face-to-face practices. Schnaars's (1989) dictum: 'Personal interactions will never be replaced by technological innovation for anything more than mundane repetitive transactions.'

Strong words indeed. Are there any real prospects for videoconferencing in the future? While the major suppliers of videoconferencing in various countries (such as Telecom in Australia, NEC in Japan, Bell in the United States (see Douglas 1989) and British Telecom (see Tyler 1988) have their own well-established 'centralised' networks linking selected offices in major

Table 4 Penetration of facsimile by urban centre, 1989

Urban centre	Population	Per cent of national population	Fax machines (% of total)
Sydney	2 989 000	18.7	24.5
Melbourne	2 645 000	16.5	21.7
Brisbane	1 037 000	6.5	10.1
Adelaide	917 000	5.7	6.5
Perth	895 000	5.6	8.4
Newcastle	255 000	1.6	1.5
Canberra	248 000	1.6	1.3
Wollongong	206 000	1.3	0.5
Gold Coast	163 000	1.0	1.5
Central Coast (NSW)	162 000	1.0	0.6
Hobart	127 000	0.8	1.1
Geelong	125 000	0.8	0.6
Townsville–Thuringowa	96 000	0.6	1.4
Darwin	72 000	0.5	1.6
Toowoomba	71 000	0.4	0.7
Launceston	66 000	0.4	0.8
Ballarat	63 000	0.4	0.5
Cairns	54 000	0.3	1.4
Rockhampton	54 000	0.3	1.5
Bendigo	53 000	0.3	0.6
Australia	16 018 000		

Note: Data on fax machines derived from 25 per cent sample of National Facsimile Directory 1988/89, Telecom Australia; population data from Australian Bureau of Statistics, 1986 Census.

cities – a service used in-house by employees and available for commercial hire by outside organisations – sales of the systems have been slow and amount to but a handfull in Australia. Stimulus for change can be classed as either demand side or supply side. On the supply side, the following changes will affect price/performance relationships:
- the penetration of integrated services digital networks (ISDN, and later broadband ISDN) will provide international digital connectivity (given that videoconferencing encompasses voice, text and image sub-systems); commercial introduction of ISDN will be underway in several countries by 1990;
- CCITT is also to have developed standards for videoconferencing in the 64 Kbps to 2 Mbps range by 1990 (Douglas 1989);
- algorithms have been developed to place entire coded functions (the compression of full motion colour images to 64 Kbps from raw transmission speeds of 90 Mbps) on chips for use in PCs (Nelson 1988), enabling desk-to-desk videoconferencing at costs as low as $30 000 (Tyler 1988) compared to half a million dollars in the earlier days of videoconferencing (Douglas 1989);

- fast packet switching, when established in the 1990s, will enable video-conferencing on a switched rather than the now common dedicated network – enhancing connectivity.

On the demand side, the trade-off for travel inherent in arguments for videoconferencing appears not to be gathering momentum if business travel statistics are any guide. Principal demand at present appears to be associated with major corporations with offices in more than one country. Savings of travel time and expense appear to be of the order of twice the cost of installation and operation for these organisations.

Greater demand is likely to be experienced in the 1990s for high-speed digital networks that can provide the connectivity for a range of computer-based graphics applications which include the following:
- land information systems – textual and graphic registers of property data capable of being interrogated on-line by a range of clients, including government departments, solicitors, and real estate agents;
- remote sensing systems – used in real time monitoring activities such as weather forecasting, defence, and environmental analysis;
- geographic information systems, which integrate property data with remotely sensed data and socioeconomic data for a wide variety of strategic planning and marketing applications;
- CAD/CAM, which includes a wide spectrum of design professions, ranging from textiles and fashion, through architecture to mechanical engineering.

At present, interchange of large textual files or graphics files within and between these systems is typically undertaken by transferring data to disk or tape and via courier or post to its destination. The emerging data networks operating at speeds above 2 Mbps (see Table 1) will provide for efficient electronic exchange of textual and graphic files on high-speed public switched networks (Newton *et al.* 1990). Current efforts of many organisations are being directed towards development of comprehensive fully integrated collections of textual and graphic information for use across a wide spectrum of applications: 'With some minor exceptions, the main effort at present is to organise, collect, evaluate, clean and structure data drawn from existing databases. Once the data collection phase has been completed, and maintenance procedures in place, the use of these data sets is expected to grow exponentially over the medium term' (Zwart 1989).

The movement towards high-definition television (HDTV), whose introduction is expected towards the end of the 1990s, represents potential for replacement of up to 600 million sets (Grewlich 1989). Unlike many new telematic products, we are dealing here almost entirely with a substitution issue, but one still dominated by fundamental marketing factors of price and performance. From a performance perspective HDTV will represent a quadrupling of pixels (from 180 000 to 700 000), providing a picture quality characteristic of 35 mm cinematic films, together with compact disk quality sound. The question which cannot be answered at present is whether households will consider the quality increment worth the price tag. Several other significant issues also await resolution, among the most significant being the absence of a global standard. At present there are two competing standards – one centred on Japan (and the United States), the other on Europe. Given the size of the potential market for what is now an ubiquitous service, the political economy behind moves toward a universal standard are complex. Yet HDTV offers a unique opportunity to establish a worldwide standard for television – something which currently does not exist, but is basic to any prospect of global telepresence and the 'supranational exchange of programs' (Grewlich 1989). Competing interests are also evident as to what will constitute the delivery medium for HDTV: cable (coaxial, fibre) or satellite. In the Australian context, this means competition between Telecom, who see HDTV as a vehicle for delivering fibre to the home (although the cost of laser detectors will need to fall before such a scheme is economic) and the nation's domestic satellite company, AUSSAT, a relative newcomer to the telecommunications industry in Australia (1985 was the year in which AUSSAT's first satellite was launched).

Computers, file transfers and data networks

Transmission of computerised information over the PSTN in the early 1960s represented the start of computer networking. Modems were employed to convert the digital computer data to analog form suitable for transmission along telephone wires. Large private and public organisations developed their own computer networks (e.g. CSIRONET) to link scattered branches or departments with the 'centre's' mainframe computers. Such centralised systems reached their zenith, in Australia at least, in 1971 with the introduction by the Postmaster-General's Department of its Common User Data Network (CUDN), designed to service the computing needs of the Federal bureaucracy. Its brief history is documented by Moyal (1984): established in all mainland capitals by October 1975, before a customer base had been successfully recruited, it was scrapped in 1980. Like all centralised computer systems of the time, it proved unresponsive to the needs of a majority of its users and tended to lack the flexibility to accommodate new computer technologies, most notably the personal computer. The decade of the 1980s saw marked advances in the PC: memory, operating systems, capacity of CPU, speed, graphics, programming languages (see Newton *et al.* (1988) for a more detailed description). This period has seen widespread in-house penetration of PCs within organisations – almost exclusively as stand-alone devices and frequently in the face of opposition by 'gatekeepers' in the EDP sections of organisations.

Advances in development of high-speed digital networks (discussed in the preceding section) now provide the basis for integration – not necessarily centralisation – of PCs, workstations and mainframes without the delays characteristic of interactive use during earlier periods. Local area network (LAN) and wide area network (WAN) interconnection[3] via optical-fibre digital networks employing fast packet switching will provide for interchange of information (voice, text, data, image) between different LANs at their own internal speeds, which can be of the order of 10 Mbps and above. (In the short-term future, however, such networks are likely to be embraced only by a relatively small percentage of organisations.) Networking solutions are available for either a centralised or distributed database structure for organisations (see Newton & Cavill 1989). To implement a centralised structure, however, might well be attaching new technology to an organisational structure which some writers (e.g. Sweeney 1982) see as inefficient, from an information processing perspective (in its inability to respond to change or produce further technical progress). Close interlinking and integration – that is, networking – among smaller productive units is seen as an emerging trend for organisations in the information economy. For a number of computing, organisational and management reasons, distributed processing and data management has become all but *de rigueur* with large central processes with multi-terminal access all but assigned to antiquity. The introduction of WAN technologies could, however, see a reversal or a slowing down of this trend, as networked topology will become largely irrelevant (Zwart & Newton 1990): 'Speeds and network capacities will be such that whether a terminal is connected to a local or distant host will make little difference. Other factors, such as the availability of trained staff, system security, data management, and quality control are generally easier to solve in non-distributed environments'. Broadband telecommunication networks, whether public or private, will give managers much greater flexibility in how their information systems are organised and managed.

CONCLUSION

The information economy has been evolving and growing for over a century. From the historical perspective adopted in this chapter, it is clear that it takes time, often decades, for new technologies, related to telecommunications networks and telematic products and services alike, to penetrate the market and for substitutions to take place. Significant discontinuities or 'break points' can be identified and the explanations sought. In this chapter, principal attention has been given to an exploration of the technological underpinnings of the information and communications sector of the economy, although it is clear from the examples discussed, that a mix of factors is at work in dictating when, where and at what rate a new product or service will penetrate the market. The mid-1960s in particular appear to have been a significant period in the take-off and usage of new telecommunications networks and services – a reflection in part of the growing nexus between computers and communications developments in network speed, digitalisation, connectivity, automation, standards, cost and performance, provided a further stimulus to network growth and usage.

The telecommunication network of the future – the broadband digital optical fibre network – has proven itself in limited trials. Its widespread implementation, however, will await a growth in demand for broadband services, in particular video-graphics, interactive file transfer, EDI catalogues, and a range of integrated (voice/data/text image) telematic products. Penetration will be well advanced by the end of this century, but a complete transition to a fully digital network has been estimated to take twenty years and more for technologically advanced societies. In the meantime, there will be variations between areas in the type and performance of their telecommunications infrastructure, variations which will translate as barriers to development for some localities with superceded networks, and opportunities for others with access to the latest equipment. The improved levels of performance demonstrable for telematic products hosted on the high-speed digital networks will appeal, in the first instance, to leading edge users (which typically include the major private and public sector organisations) who generally face needs that will become common within the marketplace, but do so earlier than most users (von Hippel 1986). According to Roberts and Morrison (1989), the ability of leading edge users to set the pace of development is jointly predicated upon 'the demonstration effect that they have and on the economic imperative of other companies having to follow them to survive'.

In attempting to assess the spatial implications of technological change in telecommunications, an examination of the utilisation of telematic products and services by industry (and households) reveals a general trend: initial introduction as a centralised service, progressing subsequently to within-establishment adoption and ultimately in-home or personal-mobile use. The settlement implications of this trend is in the freeing of individuals and organisations from a need to locate in close physical proximity to hub providers of telematic services, allowing other factors to come into play in the locational decision. Likewise with developments in the telecommunications network. With high-speed digital networks, organisations will be in a position to decide for themselves whether to instigate centralised or decentralised information systems independently of any networking restraints. High-speed broadband networks can provide the connectivity between regional/branch offices and a centralised database with the desired throughput instantaneously. It can also provide connectivity between distributed (dispersed) offices and their information systems at required performance levels. Information-intensive industry does, however, appear to be favouring certain locations for their operations – whether viewed at inter-metropolitan or intra-metropolitan scale. Such patterns of concentration are likely to become increasingly familiar features of the information economy in the future.

NOTES

1 The primary information sector (PRIS) comprises industries which participate directly in the marketplace for information goods and services. Secondary information sector (SIS) activities could be classed as 'in-house' or 'hidden', comprising intermediate inputs which are used within each sector of industry, but are not marketed; for example, accounting activity undertaken within an organisation whose principal economic activity is steel making. SIS activities represent a measure of what Rubin (1988) terms a 'bureaucratisation of the production process'; activities which many organisations are now 'contracting out', thereby bolstering the PRIS.

2 These analyses form part of a larger study being undertaken jointly by CSIRO and Telecom Research Laboratories to develop GIS and market forecasting tools applicable to telecommunications networks and services. The author gratefully acknowledges the contribution of several colleagues in this project: Marina Cavill, Simon Greener, Jill Connor and John Crawford.

3 A wide area network (WAN) is a computer-based network which allows communication over distance, as opposed to local area networks (LANs – and PABXs) which are typically restricted to individual buildings or a geographically close group of buildings, such as a campus. Fibre-optic LANs are a basic infrastructure of 'intelligent' buildings.

8

POSITIONING AND PARTNERSHIP: CORPORATE ALLIANCES IN TELECOMMUNICATIONS

Philip Cooke and Peter Wells

INTRODUCTION

The most striking feature of contemporary Information Technology industry dynamics is technological convergence between the two key fields of communications and computing (C&C). Because the traditions of the two industries are so different in the European and US contexts, yet firms in both economies have increasingly to compete with the more integrated Japanese corporations, strategic alliance formation is to be expected.

This process is further encouraged by three phenomena. Firstly, the tendency – well-established in the United States and the United Kingdom – for state regulatory regimes to be relaxed or at least very substantially changed, has introduced competition in the hitherto protected environment of state-run telecommunications services (the PTTs) and equipment supply.

Secondly, the European Open Market of 1992 is further forcing former 'national champions' to collaborate in cross-national alliances for position in a vastly increased market threatened by large Japanese and US corporate competitors. The GEC-Siemens purchase of Plessey is precisely the kind of response to be expected in this context, running ahead as it does of the hitherto national UK alliance between GEC and Plessey in telecommunications (to form GPT, the UK market leader in 1988). Other such UK alliances have included Plessey-Racal to form Orbitel, the new digital-cellular mobile telephone equipment supplier. In computing, ICL-Fujitsu, DEC-Fiat (Camau) and Logica-General Systems (Italy) are illustrative of the increasingly inter-national scope of alliance-formation, in some cases also taking the form of equity joint ventures. On the European front, alliances such as those between AT&T, Philips and Italtel, AT&T and Istel, CGE and ITT, and NEC and Telefonica (Spain) further signify the scale and dynamics of these emergent forms of corporate collaboration.

Thirdly, major users of these technologies are increasingly globalised, and are therefore seeking global telecommunications integration. There is a premium placed on the attainment of 'seamless' network interfacing, especially on very high volume optical digital communications networks, with demand fuelled by international finance and multinational companies of many types. The attempt by Cable and Wireless (C and W) to develop a Global Digital Highway can be understood in this context. Through a series of strategic alliances with PTTs and private telecommunications firms, C and W has sought to introduce 'one-stop shopping' for firms with global telecommunications requirements, and has linked together the world's major financial centres.

THE FORCES BEHIND CONVERGENCE

The reasons for the evident convergence at an inter-corporate level between C&C companies are extremely complex. Moreover, as Morgan & Mansell (in press) have shown, companies themselves are by no means agreed about the degree or even desirability of technological convergence between the two technologies, although, on the face of it, they all agree about the need for rapprochement between activities, not least because of market demand. The latter is something of a new phenomenon for firms in both sectors. In the past, PTTs provided services and the customer was constrained to operate in a 'take-it-or-leave-it' environment. The power of PTTs limited the scope and enterprise of telecommunications equipment suppliers to producing the limited range of products demanded by the PTTs. In computers, a comparable situation prevailed. The major players (IBM, ICL, etc.) produced mainframes and controlled the supply of technology. The aim was to achieve an installed base in user organisations and anticipate renewed orders for the latest equipment as and when budgets allowed. The deregulation of PTTs and the arrival of distributed computing, office workstations, and the companies capable of competing by supplying non- hierarchical systems (notably DEC, Prime and Unisys) changed all that, and placed considerable competitive pressure on, for example, IBM.

Competition has produced new challenges and opportunities but also new problems for both industries. These problems overlap in some areas as the technologies have begun to move closer together. Problem and opportunity areas can be conceived as falling into three main categories, each of which has a particular relevance, for the moment, to the technical envelope surrounding the core technologies of the equipment providers in the two industries. The categories concern standards, services and software.

Technical standards

When the computing world was dominated by the hierarchical systems supplied by the large mainframe suppliers, basically all other computer companies either ensured their products were IBM-compatible or if not they faced the danger, when insisting on their own proprietory system standard and protocols, that their customers might ultimately move to their larger, more innovative competitor. The experience of ICL in Britain is testimony to the difficulty of competing with IBM on its own ground. However, once DEC came along with a different basic concept of computer systems – one that was both compatible with but also, because of its flexibility, capable of competing with the hierarchical, installed base systems of the large mainframe producer – they were in a stronger position to impose their own software standards upon customers. As a result IBM, though still the most powerful single computer firm, has felt it necessary to join the movement towards the inter-operability of different firms' products.

Interfacing problems arise because computer systems are increasingly being linked in networks. Over the years users had built up many disparate 'islands' of computing embodying the products of many different firms. DEC, for example, began by producing midi- and mini-computers that could be used at departmental level in an organisation that would typically have an IBM installed base. In time the midis and minis gave sufficient networked power and flexibility to leave corporate organisers wondering why they needed a mainframe installed base at all. Now microcomputers and workstations are challenging minicomputers (Kehoe 1989a), hence the competition from distributed networks for traditional mainframe computer systems and their producers. Hence also a market niche for network management firms who manufacture the multiplexers and modems to transmit data from telephone lines. So to try to maintain market share, all producers now need to form alliances or at least formal agreements with their competitors to ensure interfacing.

In computer-based telecommunications, standards are required in four main areas: computer-computer communications both within a firm's product range (i.e. proprietory systems architectures) and between different firms' products (i.e. open systems interconnection); computer-software communications, notably in terms of operating software; computer-operator communications where the ways in which information is presented and manipulated are crucial; and computer-network communications. Coherent standards are best developed in the first area, computer-computer communications, where open systems interconnection (OSI) is adhered to by all manufacturers and standards setting bodies. Even IBM, which attempted to remain outside OSI and force the world to accept its operating architecture as standard, has adopted OSI rules on interconnectivity.

The second main area, that of computer-software program communications, shows the greatest conflict over standardisation. The core of the debate concerns operating systems, the software computers need to operate their internal workings and, more importantly, the interaction with software application programs. For largely historical reasons there is only one standard operating system, UNIX, developed by AT&T and licensed by them to other firms. Many firms have, however, created their own versions of UNIX, for example IBM (Xenix) and DEC (Ultrix). AT&T recently tried to monopolise the development of the next generation of UNIX in partnership with Sun Microsystems. IBM, DEC, Hewlett-Packard and other major computer firms reacted by creating the Open Software Foundation, dedicated to the development of a rival standard UNIX. Meanwhile, AT&T established UNIX International, a consortium of fifty members, behind its version. Thus the computing-telecommunications world has been split into two sides in a 'standards war'. At a broader level, another standards body, X-Open (which includes most major firms except IBM) may be able to provide common ground between UNIX International and the Open Software Foundation (Kehoe 1989b).

For telecommunications companies the question of standards is equally, if not more important, since increasingly it is they who are responsible for installing the interfacing systems by means of which computers speak to each other. It is no coincidence therefore that it was AT&T that originated the UNIX standard. Thus, telecommunications companies have similar reasons to form partnerships in standards agreements for the same reasons as computer companies do – the ability to maximise communicability between information bases. Moreover, this requirement is matched by that involving the industry's own form of distributed network, through the development of private automatic branch exchanges (PABXs), local area and wide area networks, not to mention virtual private networks such as those installed by General Motors, Ford Motor Co., Westinghouse and GEC. Such systems clearly need to be capable of interfacing with competitor systems of communication. And to the extent that developing telecommunications systems actually embody computer technologies to undertake message-switching, the element of convergence between the system protocols applying to the hardware of both industries becomes transparent.

However, questions of standards are of importance to telecommunications companies in a wholly different area. There are numerous global and continental standards within which telecommunications services must operate, ranging from GATT, ITU, CCITT, CEPT and so on at a world scale to agreements on Common Area Interface and GSM digital cellular telephone standards for mobile telephone services. Though influenced by corporate opinion, to the extent that it is believed in the industry that 'standards are determined by whoever shouts loudest', these are increasingly the responsibility of supra-national regulatory agencies. Cellular telephone, for example, has reached its second phase of development (CT2) which will be on the market in the first half of 1990. UK companies are developing alliances with other countries' producers (e.g. Orbitel with Matra in France and Ericsson in Sweden) to seek ensurance that the CT2 standard to which they adhere will be adopted as the European standard. Through this and the GSM ground-base infrastructure system, a European cellular network is in the process of being constructed in standards discussions with seventeen European PTTs. If this standard is not adopted it is clearly a setback for those partners who have moved together down that particular road. Currently digital cellular standards are incompatible within Europe as well as being totally so between Europe, with its 900 megahertz waveband, and the United States on 800 megahertz. Hence, the future is uncertain and for some time to come it is likely that the advantages of CT2 – a personal telephone number with total telephone user mobility – will be limited by the difficulty attending the development of standards, making local, national and international interfacing difficult on occasions, if not impossible where communication across different systems is concerned.

Moreover, the state is active in promoting universal standards and inter-corporate alliances, in collaborative pre-competitive research at both national and European community level in such programs as ALVEY, ESPRIT and RACE (Arnold & Guy 1986). Research and Development in Advanced Communications Technologies for Europe (RACE) sees tele-communications as the central growth focus for electronics in Europe, and as the essential basis for European competitiveness in all industries and services. Specifically it is concentrating on the development of integrated broadband (i.e. digital, high volume) communications infrastructure. Despite this pan-Europeanism, however, distinctive national characteristics remain evident in the nature and organisation of telecommunications services (Morgan & Webber 1986).

Services

As the relative costs of hardware decline in relation to those of software in the total cost incurred for system installation, there are three tendencies in the organisation of system provision. First, companies capable of supplying customised software applications to meet the variety of market demands are growing in both output and employment terms. Second, there is an emergent process of vertical integration on the part of hardware companies to acquire or otherwise form alliances with leading software houses. Often such relation-ships, even where they involve acquisition, leave the acquired company as a relatively autonomous business unit. Examples of such a relationship include AT&T and Istel, Microsoft and IBM, Olivetti and EDS, Plessey and Hoskyns. Microsoft remains independently quoted on the New York Stock Exchange while Hoskyns has recently distanced itself from its acquirer Plessey's opposition to the GEC-Siemens bid. These are indications of the importance such agreements or acquisitions have for the parent companies. Thirdly, there has been an accelerating restructuring of the software industry itself. While the top firms in the United Kingdom have regularly grown over 20 per cent per annum over the last few years, the world market has been growing at 30 to 40 per cent per annum. There were too many firms of insufficient size to compete on the world market, and this resulted in a surge in mergers and takeover (up 80 per cent by value to 530 million pounds in the first six months of 1988) and increasing internationalisation (1985 exports were 7 per cent of total sales, by 1988 this had reach 19.7 per cent). The mergers of System

Designers and Scicon, and Sema Group and CAP, and the purchase of Data Architects by Logica are examples of this restructuring. As a result, the industry has become bifurcated into a few major firms, and a larger number of small specialist firms.

The new services which are already or will shortly become available are extremely wide in range and difficult to classify (Mansell 1988). For simplicity they can be divided into three: value-added network services (VANS or TNS), logistics systems and support systems.

Value-added network services

The emergence of area networks, either local (LANs) or wide (WANS) through private automatic branch exchanges (PABXs) has enabled developments such as the 'electronic office' based on cells of linked workstations, financial trading systems, teletext, electronic mail and many kinds of specialist data and information network systems to be accessed within and between offices, within and between corporations on a local to a global scale. Moreover, most of the PTTs in the OECD countries are in the process of, or have already established, public data networks to enable more widespread access to value-added services, a market capable of yielding significantly enhanced profit margins. These profit margins are, in general, sufficiently high for companies that have hitherto been solely equipment suppliers to be developing strategies that will position them in the VANS market. Plessey's purchase of the Hoskyns software house is an example of this, and they are on record as seeing a major part of their future corporate expansion (the GEC-Siemens deal notwithstanding) being in the network services market. In the past this ambition had been thwarted by Plessey's dependence upon British Telecom as a customer of Plessey's equipment, and the difficulty of becoming a competitor to its customer. Now, however, liberalisation has made that less of a problem, especially as BT itself now sources switching equipment from non-UK suppliers such as Ericsson and Northern Telecom.

A comparable example is DEC which is principally a supplier of distributed network computing equipment. Within the software industry, though, DEC is increasingly seen as a systems house. Whereas previously systems engineering used to be subcontracted to third parties when DEC systems were being installed to user-specific requirements, now this work is increasingly being performed in-house, thus competing with independent software and systems engineering houses. In West Germany, DEC already functions as a systems house rather than primarily as a hardware manufacturer. Thus, VANS is a significant growth area, one in which telecommunications and computer companies clearly have shared as well as competitive interests. Until now, the interfacing of technologies and the sale of specialist electronic services have been the province of smaller, freestanding software and systems engineering houses. But such is the growing scale of the market, that vertical integration must be a strong influence on the likely structure of the VANS industry in the foreseeable future.

Logistics systems

Many of the new C&C systems and services now available have the potential to 'collapse space and time'. This means simply that information can be made instantly available so that the movement of material can be speeded up because it is better, more efficiently coordinated. However, the demands made of IT equipment and services are that much greater in consequence, and the flexibility required by customers, each with their own specific requirements for service customisation, demands the highest quality systems engineering. Thus, far these logistics problems and their solution have been primarily the field of operations of the specialised systems and software houses such as Logica, SEMA-CAP (now Sema Group), CAP-Gemini, EDS (Electronic Data Systems), SD-Scicon and Software Sciences. As Table 1 shows, these are dynamic, output and employment growth companies. While it is difficult in the UK context to be precise about employment growth in the industry because the SIC does not distinguish software and systems engineering from computer maintenance, it is clear from Table 2 that the category 'computer services' has been outperforming other IT sectors in recent years.

All software and systems houses are, to a greater or lesser extent, involved in designing logistics systems. Examples include expert systems such as those designed by Logica which aid product formulation by interfacing an intelligent knowledge-based system with a computerised sensor-system to ensure correct chemical mixes in, for example, the vinyl coatings industry.

Alternatively expert systems are required in the materials handling industry, and transport, health and water industries where packet-switched data communications facilities enable local and remote terminals of various kinds to communicate with centralised computer facilities.

Precise timing, often down to microseconds, is required within industrial plants operating flexible manufacturing systems, linking computer-aided design and manufacturing facilities. Moreover, as more firms operate just-in-time delivery systems, so the requirement for precise external logistics becomes essential. The Philips corporation has recently estimated that with advanced logistics systems it will be able to reduce the average delivery time of its products from factory to retail outlet within Europe (intra- and extra-EEC) from thirty to fifteen days, thereby doubling its capital turnover time. As a consequence, distribution depots in many countries are being rationalised and an increasing proportion of their materials handling will be undertaken from a few central depots. However, external logistics also involves the integration of long-distance transportation, legal services and insurance services as well as customs and excise clearance (Janssen & Machielse 1987; Janssen & Van Hoogstraten 1989). Integrating these is now feasible with distributed telecommunications and computer technologies, and the expert systems engineering available from the specialist software houses. In this way, corporations such as Philips will be better positioned to compete with the already integrated Japanese 'trading companies' such as Mitsubishi, Matsushita and so on.

Table 1 Illustrative growth rates for SD-Scicon, Logica and CAP

		SD-Scicon	Logica	CAP
Turnover (£m)	1983	102	–	–
	1984	150	50	26
	1985	210	62	36
	1986	235	87	50
	1987	252	110	78
	1988	–	132	113
Staff	1983	3 300		900
	1984	4 600	1 563	1 006
	1985	4 700	1 843	1 200
	1986	4 800	2 348	1 400
	1987	4 700	2 682	2 000
	1988	–	3 256	2 900

Source: Company reports.

Table 2 Employment change in selected IT industries 1981–1984

		1981	1984	Change	%
3301	Electrical control systems	26 746	34 418	7 672	29
3302	Electronic data processing equipment	56 799	71 225	14 426	25
3444	Components: electronic equipment	29 735	29 290	–445	–2
3453	Active components & sub-assemblies	75 654	64 712	–10 942	–14
8394	Computer services	54 772	78 699	23 927	44

Source: Department of Employment (NOMIS)

Support systems

One of the key requirements of companies involved in providing and using
C&C services is improved internal operation and management, particularly
in relation to customer services. Thus, there is growing demand for software
systems that can deal with billing, the logging of calls, routing of calls and
efficiency of switching. These questions of internal data processing require
integrated database systems which can manage data processing automatically
in respect of front- and back-office linkage, customer management, accounting and resource management. Moreover, where confidentiality is at a
premium, rapid supply of information on changes to authorisation codes is
essential. Software which enables monitoring of performance, route-tracking
and problem identification is in growing demand. Call accounting, traffic
measurement, call handling, data retrieval, file transfer and directory updating

are other areas for which software engineering is supplying necessary systems support.

The key question surrounding systems support, most of which is now customised, is whether it should remain so, and hence remain a lucrative business for specialist software houses, or whether standardised packages should be developed to meet these growing requirements. At present there are serious technical problems in standardising currently customised services because of the lack of appropriate CASE tools (techniques for automatic generation of core elements of complex software packages) (Cane 1989; Manchester 1989). Moreover, were standardisation (or semi-standardisation) to be the route chosen, there are the questions of standards and transportability to be faced, let alone the prospect that vertically integrating equipment suppliers could take a share of the market either alone, or through their alliances with standardised package producers. At present the question does not seriously arise but it is a concern faced by the system integrating software engineering companies.

Taken in the round therefore, the convergence of telecommunications and computer industries has produced technological and service network dynamism. Much of the practical convergence has been managed by independent software and systems engineering houses. These are amongst the fastest growing employers of highly qualified intellectual labour. European countries have some edge over US and certainly Japanese competitors in the field. Yet UK firms face considerable uncertainty over the future configuration of the market. In particular there is inadequate overview information of the likely needs and strategies of users and suppliers of IT equipment, and as a consequence uncertainty as to the developmental directions to be pursued. Some of these uncertainties are discussed in the following section.

Software

It is clear that software and systems engineering companies are playing a crucial role in the convergence of telecommunications and computing, but in the process they face a number of uncertainties. They are primarily bespoke firms tailoring products to detailed customer needs. It is likely that their special, independent skills will remain in short supply, not least because of the developments in Open Systems Architecture which will keep demand for network interfacing high. However, it is also clear that the larger equipment suppliers are eyeing the lucrative market – worth seven billion dollars in the United Kingdom alone in 1989 (*Computer Weekly* December 1988) – for software and services supply, and have been acquiring or forming alliances with these dynamic business units.

One key question, as yet unresolved, refers back to the core technology around which much of this convergence, or supposed convergence, is focusing. This core is switching technology. With the arrival of digital switching such as GPT's System X or Siemens' EWS-D, the possibility has been raised that computers could actually take over from switches as conventionally understood.

Switching has been the central product of the large-scale public telecommunications equipment providers. The argument that computers could replace
them is based on the trend to distributed networks in telecommunications and
computers. The key to this is the growth of VANS. Whatever happens, existing switches have to be upgraded to enable the full range of these services
to be supplied. The question is whether a digital switching system such as
System X can accommodate these. In Britain, the Plessey and GPT view is
that it can. It simply requires new software to be written, making the new
services available to all served by the switch. Another British producer, STC
(excluded by BT from final involvement in System X) believes the future
lies with programmable digital multiplexers (PDMXs) which distribute the
software out into the distributed network. A system of this design has recently
been produced by STC for BT in the form of the Flexible Access System
(FAS). If STC are right this means a decline in the relative importance of
switches as carriers of software and a probable growth in the market for less
centralised forms of software production and services. But if computers take
over the 'intelligence' from switches it may make software companies even
more vulnerable to acquisition since the activities are logically more closely
tied than is the case with telecommunications companies (see Morgan *et al.*
1989). However, if software firms do become tied to particular hardware
firms they will lose their independent status which users value because it is
a guarantee of unbiased advice.

Confronted with these and other uncertainties, software companies appear
to have particular problems in knowing which route to take regarding
standards, CASE tools, the particular question of UNIX, likely developments
in logistics systems, and, further into the future, developments in artificial
intelligence and, particularly, intelligent knowledge–based systems.

There are questions regarding the preferability of developing and staying
with niche markets, depending upon the continuing growth in demand for
customisation and specialising in certain functional areas. Alternatively, it may
be that growth and continued relative independence can be better assured by
seeking to develop more standardised or part-standardised solutions to software problems. This is seen as necessary in the industry anyway, though the
technology to do this, CASE tools, is as yet scarcely available. Finally, there
is the issue of what kind of alliances to get involved in. Can they continue to
play off telecommunications against computer firms, or do they make a guess
that multiplexers are the future and develop systems in that rather than the
more traditional switching software that they have been used to? The route
followed in Europe (outside the United Kingdom) has been to become
partners of the large management consultancies. This may prove an optimal
solution in the UK case also (Moulaert *et al.* in press).

In spatial terms, it is clear that the transformation of software away from its
craft/cottage industry status towards a more mature, customer- and product-
orientated industry dominated by a few large firms has significant spatial
implications. In particular, the growth and decentralisation of employment

away from central London is an emerging feature, powered as it is by both cost-push (central London locations are highly expensive) and demand-pull. The feature of the industry is that staff must spend a great deal of time at customer premises, and this is helping to create a more decentralised spatial structure.

On the face of it, the C&C industry faces a contradictory developmental dynamic between centralisation and decentralisation. Software and systems engineering houses are centrally involved in the integrative core activities of the convergent technologies, yet the equipment companies are far from agreed that convergence will actually reach into that core. As a consequence there is a great deal of uncertainty surrounding future development trajectories, an uncertainty of which the players themselves are only too aware.

CONCLUSIONS

It is clear that the C&C industry is in a particularly dynamic developmental phase. There are perhaps three salient features to be observed. First, it is noteworthy that the deregulation of communication services and the challenge to hierarchical computing have forced the large corporate equipment providers in C&C to change corporate strategies significantly. Competition has replaced complacency as a dominating factor in their shared outlook.

Second, and as a consequence of the competitive challenge, firms in all sectors of C&C have become far more market-facing and customer-conscious. The threat of Japanese invasion of domestic European markets led European firms first into US arms and more recently into each others to build Fortress Europe. Whether or not these alliance strategies will succeed in this objective remains to be seen.

The third feature of contemporary C&C in the face of European integration is that, as well as forming partnership with complementary hardware producers, C&C firms perceive safety in the healthy profit margins hitherto enjoyed by the systems integrators who exclusively met customer need (Teece 1986). Hence, there is widespread interest and intent by C&C companies to take over this lucrative business previously dominated by the software and systems engineering companies. The latter, faced with uncertainty caused by techno-logical convergence combined with a bifurcating C&C technological paradigm (hierarchies versus distributed systems), are in something of a fix. Do they allow themselves to be acquired, compromising their functional independence, or do they form alliances (such as CAP and SEMA) to preserve functional integrity while losing company identity? In the new world of global and con-tinental markets, corporate alliances of one sort or another seem unavoidable if firms are to gain or maintain significant market position.

ACKNOWLEDGMENTS

This research is funded by ESRC. We are grateful to our collaborators, Patrice Grevet, Kevin Morgan, Frank Moulaert and Olivier Weinstein for their assistance. The usual disclaimer applies.

9

URBAN INFORMATION NETWORKS: THE EVOLUTION AND PLANNING OF COMPUTER-COMMUNICATIONS INFRASTRUCTURE

Michael Batty

INTRODUCTION: THE NETWORK PARADIGM

The rapid and fundamental change which marks the information revolution through which contemporary urban society is passing can be approached from several different theoretical perspectives. One which seems increasingly appropriate yet continues to resist extensive research is the idea that cities are complex forms of interlocking networks through which information and people continually flow in pursuit of their daily activities. Moreover, urban change can be conceived in terms of changing networks based on the provision of new links, the renewal and abandonment of old, and the substitution of physical flows based on energy for those of information. Indeed the current notion that urban change is often abrupt and discontinuous is given further credence by the network paradigm. As Andersson and Batten (1987) say: '...urban transition may in fact be triggered simply by the addition of one small but important link in the network. Furthermore, slight differences in the pattern of network development may result in large differences in the final commodity production capacity'.

Yet, despite the promise of this paradigm, there are considerable difficulties in its use as a framework for explaining and understanding the information city. Although network infrastructures involved in moving people and goods are easy enough to identify, the emergence of multifarious information networks poses problems of detection, observation and measurement which increasingly makes them 'invisible' to sustained research. The development of information networks involves complex substitutions between flows of information and energy, new opportunities for reorganising work and leisure, as well as the realisation of new types of communication. There are new forms of supernet or 'internet' emerging, as networks are linked in diverse ways and as complex patterns of access develop, enabling various groups to be 'locked in' or 'locked out' of the means to secure valuable data and information.

Notwithstanding these difficulties, the network paradigm is so suggestive that there is already considerable work in its use to explain new spatial patterns. The ideas of 'wired cities' (Martin 1978; Dutton *et al.* 1986), of new forms of interaction based on telecommunications (Kobayashi 1986), of new production methods linking consumers to producers, demand to the supply of information (Tsuchiya 1988), and of the competitive advantage associated with information technology (IT) (Bar & Borrus 1989) are all being pursued in terms of networks. In this chapter, we will concentrate on particular forms of information network, specifically those which are based on the synthesis of computers and telecommunications, and we will begin our analysis by discussing the various components which make up such networks. Our emphasis will in fact be mainly from the perspective of network infrastructure rather than network services, although we will attempt to provide a balanced characterisation.

We will then develop three examples of rather different network structures based first on real, fairly smoothly but nevertheless rapidly evolving infrastructures in research environments which exist across the full hierarchy of spatial scales from local to global, second on a highly integrated plan for a 'network society' serving many sectors, in the city-state of Singapore, and finally, on a speculative proposal for a network city at Kawasaki, an inner suburb of Tokyo. These examples will enable us to demonstrate several themes which are important in the development of networks. First we will explore the development of special-purpose networks for single sectors or agencies in contrast to more coordinated proposals for city-wide information networks. Second, the extent to which plans for networking are realistic or speculative will be illustrated, and third, the way these new forms of network based largely around computers are impacting on traditional network services and infrastructures based on telecommunications, will be presented.

In the rest of this chapter, the networks which will be described are those which involve the use of computers and, as such, exclude traditional forms of single purpose telecommunications such as telex and telephone. These networks involve communications between user-to-computer, or computer-to-computer, or user-to-user via computer(s). The networks in question have the possibility of being multipurpose and, as such, usually exclude those based on dedicated circuits such as those in traditional telephone systems (Kahn 1987). These have only emerged in the last decade and their development is in its infancy. Accordingly, before we present our examples, we will describe the components of such networks, emphasising their multifarious functions, sketching their technological development, and introducing some terminology.

COMPONENTS OF COMPUTER-COMMUNICATIONS NETWORKS

Before the convergence of computers and communications, which began some two decades ago, the traditional technology of telephony was based on single-purpose dedicated lines of communication. The technology involved switching circuits to provide a single line between origin and destination and thus the technology was self-limiting in its potential to handle more than one link to or from any user at any one time. Computers, on the other hand, have since their inception dealt with more than one user at a time. Initially this was in the form of time-sharing, but more recently this has been through networking. The technology developed to handle the interaction of many users with many computers on a network departs radically from the single dedicated link, and as such rests on the notion of many links existing at one time in the form of the messages broken down into bits or packets and switched in such a way to enable virtual single-user dedication. This packet switching versus circuit switching constitutes the major difference between computer communications and traditional telecommunications.

Without developments in wiring technology, the difference between these two technologies would be largely academic. Traditional telecommunications infrastructure is based on the twisted-pair (of wires), whereas the newer and much bigger capacity wires are based on coaxial cable as used in cable television or on optical fibres. Most computer networks are based on a combination of these wiring types, but there are still rapid technological developments in all these mediums (Roberts 1988). So far, the anticipated convergence between voice and data has not occurred in practice, although the development of infrastructure such as the integrated services digital network (ISDN) is bringing the older telephone and the newer computer technologies together. In fact, developments in networks other than those based on computers have been much slower. Cable television networks have proved to be something of a 'white elephant' so far, in that the sorts of interaction and use originally envisaged have not been borne out (Laudon 1987). The same is true of the development of networked services in the home based on interactive services such as videotex. The only new service which has taken off dramatically is facsimile transmission, which was not anticipated. The present view is that although many of the new telecommunications services are technologically possible, they are not economically feasible, thus preventing their widespread application so far.

Computer-communications networks are designed for four main services. The most basic of these is electronic mail (email) which depends on such networks enabling total connectivity. The use of such networks for file transfer is also an important service as is their use in accessing large databases. The most selective use is in remote log-in to computers attached to the network which clearly depends on the speed and capacities of the network to enable interactive use. The extent to which this is possible depends on distance between computers or between user and computer; the further away the transmission, the more difficult it is to engage in interactive computing. These types of network assume the connection of any user to any other or to any computer, as well as the connection between any pair of computers attached to the network. This is quite different from traditional telecommunications which are designed to only enable user-to-user communication although, with the provision of network services over leased telephone lines, this distinction is breaking down.

The hierarchy of computer-communications networks spans the global to the local. At each level of the hierarchy there is a basic network, often referred to as the 'backbone'. This may be based on a mesh of connections but often it is, as the term suggests, a kind of electronic super-highway which enables networks at the next level of hierarchy down to be interconnected. For example, in the United States, major national networks such as ARPANET and the newer NSFNET are based on meshes of links in contrast to BITNET which is mainly for mail and file transfer, and whose topology is based on a tree-like structure (Jennings *et al.* 1986). In the United Kingdom, the national network linking universities and research institutions together, called JANET (Joint Academic NETwork), is also based on a simple mesh-like form. There are an increasing number of such national networks in developed countries and worldwide networks are beginning to emerge which involve connecting different nets together using gateways to effect the appropriate linkage. Constellations of these networks are referred to as internets, based initially on the development of ARPANET which is still the most developed of such networks in the United States. For example, it is now possible for an authorised user to communicate across several networks, assuming an appropriate charging policy. Communications through ARPANET, NSFNET, CSNET (a network in the United States for computer scientists), UUCP (a network for UNIX users), and across the European research backbone net, called EARN, are possible through a hierarchy of gateways which are continuing to evolve.

At the more local level, of the campus for example, networks which have evolved around different computers usually within buildings or building complexes are called local area networks or LANs. These are linked to campus backbone networks which in turn enable access to higher level wide area networks (WANs) and in turn, to national and worldwide networks. The topology of the LAN is important. Originally, users were linked to host computers in the form of a star network but as more and more computers have become accessible to a single user, these stars have been replaced by token rings or by line networks known as 'buses' whose most common form is the ethernet. Various types of rings and ethernets can be arranged as meshes, but what is emerging is a stricter hierarchy of networks, linked together by gateways which enable appropriate translation of electronic languages and special filters to constrain transmission.

A strict hierarchy is required because, as the network in question covers larger and larger areas, the rates of transmission fall accordingly. At the building complex or LAN level, rings and ethernets are high-performance nets operating at speeds of at least 1 Megabit per second (Mps), while at the campus backbone level, the network usually operates at kilostream (Kilobits per second – Kps) rather than megastream. Rings and ethernets, although originally developed by IBM and Xerox respectively, are non-proprietary forms of networks but, at the local level, there are many nets associated with specific hardware which have to be linked into some wide area form. For example, Mackintosh machines are linked by Appletalk, DEC VAXs by DECnet, IBM PCs by Fidonet and so on. To link these networks, special link nodes called bridges are required to filter out and translate data which are to be communicated to computers and networks based on different proprietary systems. There is a complete arsenal of communications linkers such as repeaters, multiplexers and other types of switch enabling transmission, and the possibilities for transmitting greater and greater data volumes is increasing almost daily.

Apart from capacity of transmission, which relates to the physical limits on bandwidth and the constraints on speed already mentioned, the other major constraint on communications between computer and computer or users and computers, relates to the languages used. For example, at the University of Michigan in 1985, there were 101 different types of computer produced by different manufacturers, all linked to the network (Marks 1988). To enable communication between the various proprietary operating systems, it has long been accepted that there should be gradual migration towards some internationally agreed standards based on what is called the open systems interconnection (OSI). To facilitate this transition, the various languages or 'protocols' used for transmission are arranged through a series of layers, seven in all, various standards being applied to each layer. Network protocols are converging towards these standards but only slowly. This means that it is often necessary to write different software for the appropriate translations, this inevitably being a limiting factor on the ability to communicate between different computers.

Email tends to be the easiest of services to support, but in any data transmission this is limited by the smallest capacity of any network in the hierarchy of communication. This means that it is virtually impossible at the present to provide any remote interaction with respect to data which involve high resolution graphics and although this may be serious with respect to scientific computing, it is probably an even greater constraint on more public systems which rely on the communication of data in pictorial form. For example, although state-of-the-art LANs can handle graphics processing at speeds which are appropriate to a scientific user, such computing over long distances, which might be necessary if users require supercomputers or national information services, cannot be supported remotely. At the level of access to databases and other forms of information system, the present technology is still highly constraining although the prospects here are good. For example, Negroponte who directs the MIT Media Laboratory, has said that present technology can deliver up to half a gigabyte of data per second to the home using fibre optics and it is only a matter of time before the economics will come out right (quoted in Brand (1987)).

There are of course many other types of global and national information network, but these are mainly internalised to various companies, particularly computer firms. For example, the Digital Equipment Corporation (DEC) supports a network called Easynet for their internal operations, while IBM have several in-house networks such as VNET (Quarterman & Hoskins 1986). The Xerox Corporation who developed the ethernet have their own internet (XIN), while there is a variety of networks for production purposes in the newspaper and related media industries (Hepworth 1987a). At present, because our knowledge of networks is so rudimentary and what knowledge we have is internalised to particular developments, it is extremely difficult to do more than describe what exists and then speculate on how these developments may impact on urban structure and form. With respect to what we know about such impacts, it would appear at present that considerable restructuring of existing development is taking place, in that the new media are being rapidly introduced into existing structures. We do not have a clear view about how spatial form is responding to such impacts because the possible repercussions are so indirect and diverse that we are only likely to get at these by engaging in some in-depth study. Most observations we have are based on macroscopic changes whose precise causes are difficult to isolate. Our picture of urban information networks which we have built up so far, is largely in terms of physical infrastructure. We have ignored the market and pricing implications of such media; these are likely to be as constraining as the physical limits we have already defined. In the three examples we will now describe, we will attempt to examine both infrastructure and services, but this is very much a beginning and in some senses raises more problems than it resolves.

REALISTIC NETWORKING: RESEARCH NETWORKS BASED ON AN EXPLICIT SPATIAL HIERARCHY OF COMMUNICATION

What is manifestly clear in the study of computer-communications networks is that a high degree of central coordination and planning is required to enable sub-networks to communicate with one another and to enable a common infrastructure to develop. We will begin our discussion with a couple of examples of LANs linked into a campus backbone which in turn provides gateways to the rest of the hierarchy. The University of Michigan has been involved in networking its computers for nearly twenty years and indeed was a pioneer of its own WAN, Merit, before the US national networks were established in the 1970s and 1980s. Michigan is a large campus university with some 35 000 students, and the campus-wide network which has developed rapidly during the last fifteen years now enables access to over fifty different host computers from some 6000 ports. In fact, there are many sub-networks connected to the campus backbone, in particular linking some very computer-intensive rings and ethernets such as an Apollo ring of 400 workstations, several Appletalk nets, various DECnets, SUN NFS and Hewlett-Packards. There are in fact two backbone networks on the main campus, namely a coaxial cable for computer communications and an optical fibre for the university's own telephone system (see Figure 1).

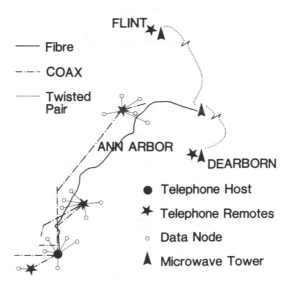

Figure 1 The campus backbones in the University of Michigan (after Marks 1988).

Extremely ambitious plans to serve up to 30 000 workstations on campus are being implemented with the basic systems already installed. Administrative and library computing is also integrated with academic computing in that they share the same infrastructure (Marks 1988).

The Michigan example stands at one extreme of the spectrum with respect to wide area networking. It also illustrates the various pitfalls associated with the provision of a common infrastructure taking voice and data communications, as well as problems of security when common infrastructures are used for diverse applications. An example at the other extreme is St Andrews in Scotland, a university a tenth the size of Michigan (see Figure 2). This university is at present implementing a very clear policy of networking based on the local hierarchy of building complexes and application areas defined by the research and teaching functions of the university. An optical-fibre backbone links some twenty 'computer villages' based on various forms of ring and ethernet LANs. The backbone is connected by an X.25 line to a Telepac switch which provides the gateway to the outside world in the form of access to JANET, while there are also some direct X.25 lines from the various villages to the outside world.

As in many academic computing environments, the infrastructure which is evolving is becoming more strictly ordered in that various specialist processing is being associated with different levels in the hierarchy. Campus networks are more and more based on workstations served by different

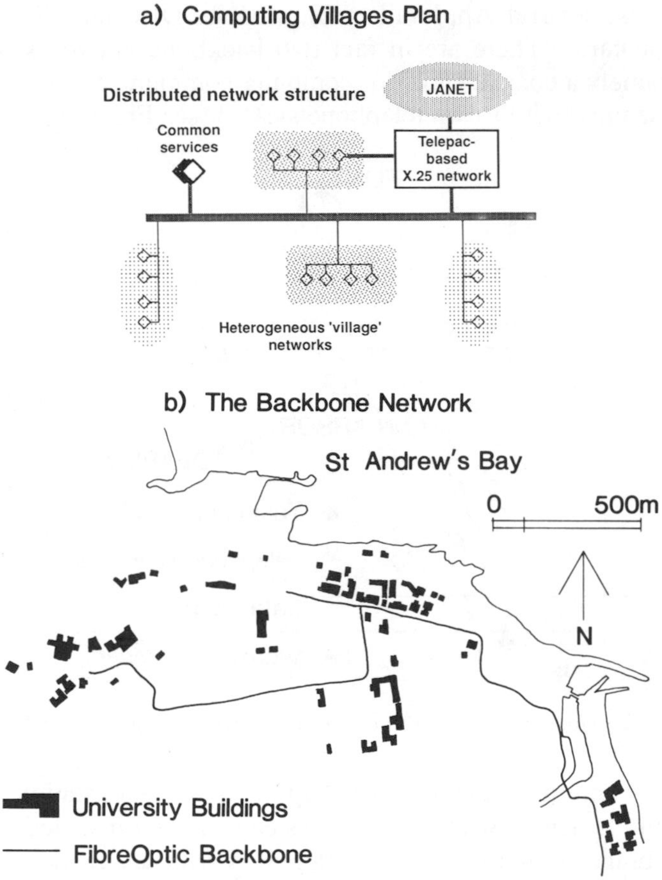

a) Computing Villages Plan

Distributed network structure

JANET

Common
services

Telepac-
based
X.25 network

Heterogeneous 'village'
networks

b) The Backbone Network

St Andrew's Bay

0   500m

N

■■■ University Buildings

——— FibreOptic Backbone

Figure 2 Computing villages and the campus backbone in the University of St Andrews.

devices on the network, while large mainframes are being centralised to deal
with computationally-intensive and data-extensive computing. In the extreme
case, this involves users interacting with large remote supercomputers
dedicated for very specialist applications at national centres. This is the
pattern that is emerging in the United States, United Kingdom and Germany
and, one suspects, elsewhere as well.

Most higher education and research institutions are beginning to evolve
network infrastructures which embody elements of those depicted in Figures
1 and 2. There may be important differences due to resources available and
different management structures, but the notion of networking is becoming
central to the way universities and like institutions are beginning to deliver
resources. The same is certainly true of other services provided by government, such as health, other forms of education and training, welfare services
and emergency services which require real time control. In the next section,
we will examine the implications of such networking for comprehensive
service delivery in the city-state of Singapore, but for the moment we will

continue to concentrate on academic and research services for which an explicit spatial hierarchy has evolved.

JANET, which provides the national infrastructure for networking between universities and research centres in the United Kingdom, was originally established in the early 1980s in response to the need for specialist shared services as well as the need for more rapid communication between communities of researchers. It is significant that in the United Kingdom there is only one such network which is managed and funded centrally, in comparison to the United States where several national networks have evolved simultaneously and are now linked as internets. The present configuration of JANET is illustrated in Figure 3. The network is a backbone mesh net based on six nodes, two of which are national research laboratories, the others universities. The backbone and its links to the rest of the academic sector are based on kilostream lines leased from British Telecom. At present these lines are being upgraded, some to megastream in JANET Mark II, and there are proposals for Super JANET which will take this upgrading much further as well as combining with other public and private agencies anxious to participate in the research activity made possible by this network.

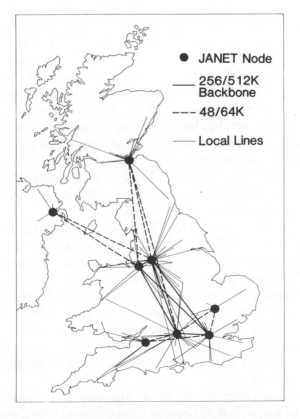

Figure 3 The Joint Academic NETwork (JANET) for the United Kingdom.

The pattern in Figure 3 is illuminating in that it provides a picture of access which is based both on the location of universities, which follow the general distribution of the population, and on the particular demands which reflect the eminence and specialisms of the universities and research laboratories concerned. In this sense, it is quite clear that the national network mirrors trends in other patterns of information technology which reveal the dominance of southern England. This largely reflects the evolution of a network designed to serve the present pattern of demand which in turn reinforces existing inequalities between information-rich and information-poor regions. In the United States, the same is true of the evolution of national networks, although these are more geared to the pattern of computer science and military defence research than in the United Kingdom. The basic network is ARPANET which was started in 1969 by the Defense Advanced Research Projects Agency (DARPA), part of the Department of Defense (Rheingold 1985). The original network has now been split into military (MILNET) and non-military (ARPANET itself) sub-nets which comprise the original Internet. Other networks of note which evolved through the 1970s and 1980s are CSNET (Computer Science NETwork), BITNET (Because It's Time NETwork – the base network for academic email), MFENET (Magnetic Fusion Energy NETwork), and the more recent NSFNET (National Science Foundation NETwork) which is primarily designed to provide access for researchers to the six recently designated national supercomputer centres as well as acting as a major facility between many of the other research-related national networks.

BITNET and NSFNET are shown in Figure 4. ARPANET and those other than the NSF backbone run at kilostream speeds, ARPANET itself at 56 Kps, BITNET at the much lower speed of 9.6 Kps (Jennings *et al.* 1986). The NSF backbone, however, has been designed to run at megastream (1.5 Mps) and rapid upgrades to the speeds and capacities of all these networks are planned. There are two sub-nets which were developed as part of BITNET, namely NETNORTH, which links BITNET to Canadian institutions, and EARN (European Academic Research Network), thus enabling BITNET to extend to Europe and the rest of North America.

National networks such as JANET connect to BITNET through various gateways and, in turn, BITNET connects to other networks in the same way. Gateways certainly exist between all national academic networks which have so far been developed, and even into various private networks, particularly into computer companies. But a clear picture of what linkages there are and what types of traffic use these nets does not exist. This obviously makes the demand for more descriptive research very urgent, for it is quite possible that links are being forged which are generating the sorts of discontinuities in spatial development alluded to by Andersson and Batten (1987) with little prospect of our knowing.

The networks we have looked at in this section are those which enable communities of researchers to develop what Webber (1964), over a quarter of a century ago, called the 'non-place urban realm'. These types of networks

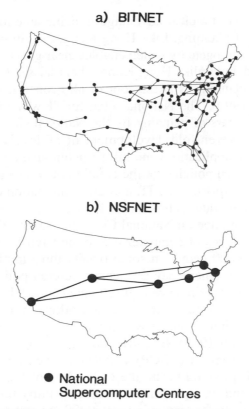

Figure 4 BITNET (Because It's Time NETwork) and NSFNET (National Science Foundation NETwork) in the United States (after Jennings et al. 1986).

are of global significance in their potential to rearrange individuals and groups in research and academia, and in this sense only give the most partial picture of spatial impact. Nevertheless, these networks do provide one glimpse of the sorts of complexity which must be occurring in a variety of other sectors as well. Although we have emphasised physical infrastructure rather than associated services provided, this represents a convenient starting point in assessing what are clearly complex patterns of spatial impact. In contrast, these networks might have been studied without any real attention to their physical structure, although as a distinct spatial hierarchy is necessary for their operation, any discussion should involve some reference to their physical form. In our next example, we will move to the other extreme and examine a plan for a network city in which the physical structures remain implicit.

ALMOST REALISTIC NETWORKS: THE HARD WIRING OF SINGAPORE

The only country in the world (as yet) to have a National Plan for Information Technology is the small island city-state of Singapore. Singapore has a population of some 2.6 million and is a completely developed, compact area of some 620 square kilometers. The size of the country as well as its excellent economic record give it a clear advantage in being able to articulate highly centralised forms of planning. Like Hong Kong, the city-state has a degree of uniformity and homogeneity which enables clear goals to be set and plans to be implemented; but unlike Hong Kong where laissez faire dominates the economy, central planning is at the root of all economic policy making in Singapore (Batty 1990). The National Plan for IT was announced in 1986 after five or more years of planning by the National Computer Board. The plan is based on a seven-fold development of IT involving proposals for industry, manpower, applications and infrastructure in the context of organisational and educational policies for the creation of an IT culture, the support of creativity and enterprise using IT, and the coordination of IT strategies in both the public and private sectors (NCB 1987).

In 1980, the Committee on National Computerisation (CNC) was formed to examine the problems of computer use in the Civil Service. The Service employed some 70 000 people in some twenty-three ministries which deal with everything from emergency services to foreign policy and trade. The Civil Service then had a single centralised data centre which provided computer services, and the need to scrutinise its workings was clearly motivated by the huge applications backlog which was growing ever longer year by year (Ko Kheng Hwa 1988). In 1981, the CNC proposed a Civil Service Computerisation Program (CSCP) which has been and continues to be implemented. This program meant the disbanding of the traditional central computer service and its replacement with some thirty installations serving some ten ministries, so far employing some 400 computer professionals and technicians, and involving the development of around ninety applications packages. The ultimate intention of the CSCP is to develop 200 or so applications and to develop computer use in all the ministries comprising the Service.

The development of this widespread computerisation of the government has been aided by several strategies. First, the plan does not involve using much standard software. It was recognised early on that the sorts of application required had not generated standard software marketed on a worldwide basis, and therefore the Service had to develop its own. Second, the object of the plan was complete computerisation and the real bottlenecks to this were not technological but in terms of specialist manpower. The development of an IT culture in the Service would help to smooth the implementation of policies and bring enormous benefits. In fact, by 1988 the program had already established that 'benefits' exceeded 'costs' by over 100 per cent and this had been achieved against a background of a 6 per cent loss of staff. In 1980, there were only 800 IT professionals and technicians in Singapore and it was recognised that any computerisation effort would clearly fail unless this pool of talent were to be increased dramatically. Part of the plan was therefore based on the provision of training programs and incentives to increase this number of professionals, which now stands at around 8000 (Batty 1989). Networking is clearly central to this plan for computerisation in that the thirty installations are based on some seventy mainframes and minis which can be accessed from over 3000 workstations or dumb terminals. Yet the provision of the networking infrastructure is regarded as being of secondary importance to the development of relevant application packages, the provision of skilled manpower, and the development of an IT ethos.

The development of the CSCP program in 1981 was the first task of the newly created National Computer Board (NCB), the Board being set up '...to drive Singapore into the information age' (Ko Kheng Hwa 1988). The success of the CSCP so far is thus clearly dependent upon the whole range of operations which the Board has responsibility for and, in this way, manpower planning in the IT sector as well as the provision of common and specialist infrastructure can be easily coordinated with policies that depend on this provision. So far the computerisation of the Civil Service has cost over $US20 million in terms of capital equipment, and IT-related activities are now costing in the order of $US35 million per year. A variety of networks is being developed such as CSNET (Civil Service NETwork), NALINET (NAtional LIbrary NETwork), MEDINET (the MEDical Information NETwork), ECOMNET (Economic COmmission Monitoring NETwork), as well as many real time controls systems for emergency services, housing management and welfare (Kuo 1987).

Other projects which depend on the existence of a large pool of IT professionals as well as applications software, involve the attempt to computerise the import–export trade in the country through the development of a computerised information system called TRADENET, and the development of a public information system at the domestic level called TELEVIEW which has similarities to the MINITEL system in France. TRADENET will provide massive automation of Singapore's basic function as an entrepot for the Asia–Pacific region. The value of Singapore's trade is three times its GNP in value and estimates of the cost of the paperwork involved in import–export transactions are put at about 7 per cent of this value. The system will be based on electronically communicating and processing inward declarations and manifests, and on access to databases giving pertinent economic information, all set against the background of a network linking relevant public agencies to each other and to the private sector. The TRADENET system will save the island $US50 million each year, this being perhaps the clearest example of the effects of total computerisation on the economy.

Since the early 1980s, Singapore has begun to develop massive network infrastructure based on a variety of communications media. Fibre-optic submarine cables linking the ASEAN countries in the region have been installed, while the provision of a '...backbone infrastructure based on ISDN' (NCB 1987) is undergoing field trials. This will be based on the 8000 kilometers of optical fibre which was installed to link all telephone exchanges in 1986. A dedicated high-speed (64 Kps) digital network as the basis for leased lines is to be developed, while there is a variety of broadcast media being installed based on satellite earth stations. A rich set of services will be available in the near future, ranging from travel information to the real time control of public and private services as diverse as hospital care and economic forecasting.

These developments in Singapore largely depend on the production and implementation of a highly coordinated and integrated plan not only for infrastructure but also for manpower and applications software. It is difficult to see how such a plan could be realised without very strong central control, for the economics of the venture are highly dependent on the provision of common infrastructure and software, on centralised purchasing strategies and on the lead given by the public sector. Nevertheless, there is little controversy over the National IT Plan for the implementation of IT is regarded as essential as the country begins to diversify its economy away from the manufacturing branch plant economy which dominated its first two decades of economic success. The precise form of network infrastructure would appear to be largely independent of the plan in spatial terms at least, but there still remain some crucial issues relating to how networks are linked to one another at the local as well as at higher levels.

SPECULATIVE NETWORKS: JAPAN IN GENERAL, KAWASAKI IN PARTICULAR

So far we have presented examples of highly explicit physical networks crossing a range of scales but based on rather specific sectors of the space economy, as well as implicit networks at the metropolitan scale but covering a wide spectrum of sectors and services. These differences are not simply a matter of presentation. Networks which link local to global are much more important to articulate in physical terms than networks which cover entire urban areas where the emphasis is on coordinating services and providing access to various forms of data and information, as in Singapore. The last types of network we will deal with here represent much more speculative forms of planning. These are often never intended to be implemented in their proposed form. They are introduced purely to focus ideas on what might be possible as well as to compete with other agencies and areas also bidding for the same resources. The examples we will present are taken from Japan and we will concentrate on the widely publicised plans for Kawasaki which is promoting itself as the prototypical advanced information city (Batty 1987).

Over the last decade, Japan has pursued the development of information technology with a single-mindedness and zeal which cannot be surpassed by any other nation state. This is manifest at all levels in the belief that information technology will enable economic and social solutions to many of the deep-seated paradoxes and dilemmas facing the modern Japan. This extends quite visibly to urban development and planning. As Newstead (1989) says: 'There is an almost obsessive attachment to the concept of information cities which feature in the national plans of central government agencies and the strategic plans of municipalities'. The first evidence of this interest goes back to the development of the new town of Tsukuba as a 'science city'. In the late

1950s, there was mounting concern about the development of Greater Tokyo and, as a result of planning to reduce urban congestion, two birds were killed with one stone, so to speak, when Tsukuba was designated as both a new town and a high-tech city in 1962.

For a variety of reasons, mainly relating to the difficulty of countering the dramatic centralisation of Japan about its two metropolises Osaka and Tokyo, Tsukuba has never been considered a successful venture (Tatsuno 1986). Nevertheless, high-tech fever still ran high in the late 1970s, and the Ministry of International Trade and Industry (MITI) decided to designate various regions as 'technopolises', which by 1985 had reached sixteen. These regions were beneficiaries of a variety of special grants and subsidies designed to generate high-tech development (Tatsuno 1986). Hard on the heels of the technopolis concept came a variety of initiatives in which the Ministries of Posts and Telecommunications (MPT), and of Construction, began to compete with MITI. First, in 1983 there came MPT's 'Teletopia' concept which has so far led to 128 zones in urban areas being designated for high-technology networking infrastructures. Then MITI introduced its 'new media community' project in which fifty-five cities were identified to receive various benefits associated with computers and communications (Miyakawa 1985). In 1986, MITI extended this initiative into their 'Advanced Information Metropolis' project, increasing the areal extent of the benefits available. Most recently, beginning in 1987, the Ministry of Construction has begun its 'intelligent cities' project, of which thirty-six have been selected so far.

Apart from the '...overwhelming conviction that IT promises solutions...' (Newstead 1989), the competition between central government ministries is enormous and is only matched by the intense rivalry between the candidate cities themselves. The result is that most urban areas in Japan have been selected for one or more of these initiatives, and this is further complicated by the difficulties of identifying the impacts of these projects. The hard wiring of Japanese cities is made even more complex still by the existence of several local projects promoted by the various municipalities themselves which often have a higher profile than those of central government. The example of Kawasaki is one of the most well-known in that its current land use development plan is now entirely based on IT, the plan having been selected through international competition (Droege 1988). Kawasaki is an inner industrial suburb of Tokyo with a population of about 1.2 million, bounded by the port of Yokohama on the south. For over twenty years, the area has been plagued by the closure of heavy industries which were at the basis of Japan's earlier industrial miracle, and the major policy response by the city government has been to diversify the local economy through introducing and encouraging high-tech industries and services, a policy which has already met with some success. The city government now sees the explicit development of an 'information city' combining the advantages of computers and communications as the logical next step in the further diversification and strengthening of the local economy.

The plan is to develop eighteen 'intelligent plazas' which will be based on both new and existing focii in the city. These plazas will be constellations of 'smart' or 'intelligent' buildings, all intensively wired with LANs along the lines of other building complexes in Tokyo, such as the Ark Hills project (Sakamoto 1988) and Mitsubishi Industries' Marunouchi Intelligent City (Nobuyuki 1986). These plazas will form the beads in a chain running along the spine of the city which will be linked together by a high-performance optical-fibre cable some thirty kilometers in length. This network is shown diagrammatically in Figure 5. The plazas will provide gateways to this network, which in turn will be connected to the cross-Japan cable running from Tokyo to Osaka, known locally as the 'bullet train or Shinkansen of telecommunications' (Tatsuno 1986).

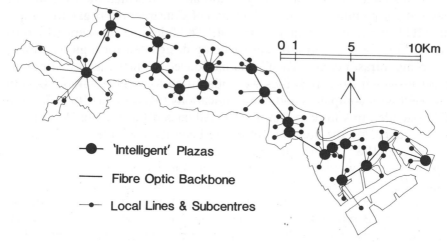

Figure 5 The optical-fibre backbone linking the intelligent plazas in Kawasaki.

Kawasaki's plazas and their link network will lie along the route which already contains over 100 high-tech industries. These have been grouped into four broad land use zones. On the western edge, newer technologies involving microprocessor applications have been developed and these are to be rationalised and further encouraged in the designation of this area as a 'techno-venture park'. Adjacent to this zone is the centre of the older industrial technologies which will be established as a 'techno-community', thus enabling regeneration through access to new information services. The existing commercial heart of Kawasaki is to be called 'Technopia' and here, sandwiched between the port on the east and the 'techno-community' on the west, will emerge the many business and financial services as well as local government and municipality functions so essential to the success of this high-tech world. Lastly, the port itself, called inevitably 'techno-port', will be renewed through the development of robot technologies for the physical movement of goods as well as the development of information services similar to Singapore's TRADENET.

The eighteen plazas are planned to represent the focii of these four broad zones and will enable users from industry, business and the community at large to access a range of public and private information services through the gateways established in each of these centres. These services will be available either on a value added basis or will be provided free if they involve government functions based on public information or social–community services. Users will be able to rent nodes or computer ports in these centres thus enabling interaction within Kawasaki or more likely with the outside world of Greater Tokyo in particular, the rest of Japan and the international community in general. Each plaza will be modelled on the idea of a neighbourhood office which will contain an intensive array of information technology. The idea of these offices is to persuade many of the workers who travel daily to other parts of Tokyo to work nearer home in these complexes which will be provided with all the services these workers require. The plan is for each office to accommodate up to 1000 workers, and to provide some 200 fax machines, and medium-speech data circuits on an ISDN network distinct from the fibre-optical backbone network although gatewayed to it. There would also be 200 data-only dedicated channels to the various information services available from outside the city, while there will be fifty picture phone systems and ten wideband channels for video-conferencing and like media.

Each optical fibre pair in the cable will be able to support ten or more such offices requiring the transmission of at least one gigabit of information each second. But of more interest in this proposal in the cost-benefit analysis Kawasaki municipality has attempted, which shows that simply on the basis of reducing travel costs alone, the proposal would be viable, costing no more than $US2000 per worker (Newstead 1989). There does not, however, seem to be any clear design for the detailed implementation of the system, although the city government has allocated about $US200 million for the provision of the basic infrastructure (Batty 1987). Apparently the broadband fibre-optic cable is being laid along routes already available for new and existing utilities provided by the city. What is somewhat unclear, however, is the way this initiative will link to others which are already ongoing in Kawasaki. For example, the city is the recipient of at least five central government initiatives in high tech, namely those associated with MITI's advanced information cities project and MPT's teletopia project. These involve the existing central area of downtown Kawasaki. The Ministry of Construction's intelligent cities project is also being implemented in three locations in Kawasaki. Adding even more complexity, Tatsuno (1986) noted that the fibre-optic cable project for the whole of Japan was first tested in Kawasaki with the development of a 15 kilometer cable laid in the city in 1983, and this would appear to be suspiciously like the present proposal for such a backbone network. One of the difficulties of evaluating the feasibility of the Kawasaki project is the fact that the project is so speculative with respect to the various information services to be provided. Doubtless the provision of such infrastructure will make Kawasaki more and more attractive for the location of leading edge industries as well as services to support these new developments. A snowball effect is anticipated, but only if the attraction of Kawasaki in these terms were much greater than other municipalities in Tokyo and the rest of Japan. This is doubtful. Although such proposals may be necessary in competing with other similarly placed local governments, the Singapore case shows that at this level it is probably not the network which is important but the availability of special services which in turn require new databases and software not readily available. In other words, the development of the sorts of high tech envisaged in Kawasaki depend on applications packages being available, on how this network relates to others in Kawasaki itself, the rest of Tokyo and Japan and the rest of the world, and how workers and other potential users are to be attracted away from their present pursuits to partake of the high-tech paradise being provided by the city.

CONCLUSIONS: THE USEFULNESS OF THE NETWORK PARADIGM

Notwithstanding the powerful imagery evoked by the network paradigm, its use in understanding the spatial impacts must be qualified. Of our three examples here, the first which was based on a clear and explicit spatial hierarchy, and which has evolved the most 'naturally', provides a useful picture of network development which is helped by concentrating on the development of physical network structures. We did not emphasise the development of services associated with these research networks for several reasons, the most obvious being that much of the development of IT itself has been based around these networks. For example, the development of network topologies and protocols has been partly the prerogative of the very universities and research institutions who have been developing and using such networks, while the provision of other services has been largely geared to research communities whose demands on computing and networking are somewhat open ended. In fact, it is worth emphasising the point that alongside the development of these academic networks, there have been major developments of software and applications which involve a very wide community of computer scientists, programmers and scholars. The fact that we are able to separate out the physical structure of these networks is partly due to the fact that they depend on this massive backcloth of applications and services which has paralleled network development.

The second example of Singapore shifts the focus entirely away from the physical form of the network to the services and manpower required to make the application of IT feasible in terms of relevant application areas. Quite clearly some of the major constraints on the introduction of IT to the public in general, particularly in information services such as cable television, concern the provision of services which are relevant and easy to use. Such services also need to be priced in such a way that their demand is assured. Singapore has broached these issues directly, and notwithstanding the fact that the scale and density of the city make the development of the actual physical form of the network infrastructure of lesser importance, the need to develop the whole range of functions associated with the use of computers and communications is clearly a vital factor in the development of any plans for integrated urban information networks.

Our last example of the proposed hard wiring of Kawasaki is plagued with uncertainties. Although the plan for the information city has been clearly articulated in network terms, the almost complete dearth in the proposals, of plans for information structures and services which parallel the infrastructure, means that the plan remains a speculative venture until such services are specified. There is always the possibility that the city is actively concerned with developing such services, and that it is simply difficulties in communication, the Japanese penchant to cartoon their media, and our simple ignorance of what is happening which makes the Kawasaki example so obscure. Nevertheless, as in the example of Singapore, the development of 'information services' paralleling 'information infrastructures' would appear to be a prerequisite to the successful implementation of this advanced information city concept.

The other issue which we have not been able to resolve here involves the extent to which information networks are able to interlink in terms of common infrastructure and services. It is easy to see how networks might develop for a single sector across a wide hierarchy of spatial scales and, although more complex, it is a comparatively straightforward task to see how government might develop infrastructures and applications which serve the community at large. But we have found it extremely difficult to develop any real understanding of the extent to which diverse public and private agencies might share the same infrastructure and services, and the extent to which this is already happening through both ad hoc and formal connections between like and unlike networks. There is an urgent need to begin work on unravelling the vast complexity of the modern city in network terms. What is also required is a way of classifying different types of urban networks, not just in terms of their physical form which is straightforward, but with respect to common applications areas, and their scope in serving the multifarious needs of diverse urban populations. If we can conclude anything, it is that the development of a better understanding of the effect of new technology on cities must be based on painstaking empirical work and must abandon the almost idealistic characterisation of IT which still conditions much of our research.

10

NON-UNIVERSAL SERVICE?
POLITICAL ECONOMY AND
COMMUNICATIONS GEOGRAPHY

Andrew Gillespie and Kevin Robins

INTRODUCTION

In an earlier paper (Gillespie & Robins 1989), we endeavoured to challenge the prevailing view of communications innovations as space-transcending and, therefore, necessarily decentralising in their geographical manifestations. Starting from the political economic perspective of Harold Innis (1950; 1951), we attempted to confront the 'spatial bias' of the new communications technologies. Innis argued that the bias of these technologies would tend to facilitate the binding of centres and peripheries together, and would in consequence facilitate the centralisation of power and control over space rather than the converse. For Innis, communications technologies were at the heart of the 'problem of empire', the articulation of relations and patterns of domination across, and through, spatial arenas. His important realisation was that these relations and patterns, and the spatial inequalities which they engender, are not contingent, but rather constitutive, aspects of communications technologies (Hepworth & Robins 1988).

This chapter is concerned with the changes currently taking place in communications networks and in the new services which they support. Advanced networks are of considerable importance because of their much enhanced significance for processes of urban and regional development in the so-called 'information economy' (see, for example, Goddard & Gillespie 1986; Hepworth 1986; Gillespie & Hepworth 1988; Gillespie & Williams 1988). In particular, we are concerned with the geography of these networks, and especially with the availability of services in different locations. In the contemporary environment, the geography of advanced network provision is becoming an increasingly central issue as we see a complex amalgam of technological, economic and regulatory changes bringing pressure to bear on long-standing assumptions of geographical universality in network and service provision.

It is upon these pressures that we focus. Our approach is one of political economy, and starts from the premise that communications networks are integral to particular social formations and, as such, are shaped by their prevailing power structures and social relations. In developing an understanding of the geography of advanced networks, we need to begin with a consideration of the forces that are shaping the development of these networks, including changes to the regulatory structures within which they are embedded. We need to ask who is designing the new networks, on whose behest, and in whose interests.

THE CHALLENGE TO UNIVERSAL SERVICE

According to Marshall McLuhan (1964, p. xiii), the new media of communication 'in effect abolish space and time alike...electric technology is instant and omnipresent and creates multiple centres-without-margins'. Wilson Dizard (1982) extends this argument into the post-industrial future, suggesting that a 'global knowledge grid' will be created, resulting in the unimpeded free flow of information, and underpinned by 'a universal electronic information network, capable of reaching everyone everywhere'.

But will the global grids in fact facilitate the 'unimpeded free flow of information'? Will they really be 'universal'? And if they are indeed capable of 'reaching everyone everywhere', will there be restrictions or constraints on this capability, on who is reached and for what purposes? It is our contention that there are grounds for questioning the assumptions of universal, unimpeded access to the global knowledge grid. The development of electronic communications networks, in so-called 'deregulated' environments at least, suggests very clearly how and why these assumptions of universal access are being undermined.

The concept of universal service has traditionally been an implicit, if usually unspecified, cornerstone of telecommunications policy in most western countries. As Garnham's (1989) comprehensive review for the OECD makes clear, the 'universal' of universal service is usually taken to mean access to the telephone network both in terms of geographical location and price and level of service. The first of these elements, universal geographical availability, has been intimately associated with the development of nation states as political and economic realms with distinct territorial configurations, and with communications infrastructures functioning as potent forces of national integration. The second element concerns non-discriminatory access to these services, and has been associated with a politico-philosophical conception of access to 'public service' telecommunications as a basic right of all citizens.

Both of these aspects of universal service are now under threat from a complex interplay of technological, economic and regulatory changes. The advent of digital communications technologies, in conjunction with the widespread computerisation of larger firms and institutions, has made possible a proliferation of new specialist data networks and value-added services. These serve to 'naturally' segment the customer base, most obviously into those that require only 'basic' service (i.e. voice telephony) and those that require, in addition, access to the new 'advanced' digital services. Further, the requirement of a number of the new services for end-to-end digital connection has necessitated the development of digital overlay networks to overcome the constraints of analogue technologies, particularly in the local loops, such that we now need to talk not of 'the network' but in terms of a range of technologies which constitute separate networks.

If new technologies are making possible the segmentation of the telecom-munications market, the strategies of the service suppliers are making such possibilities a reality. In line with the marketing strategies of other commercial enterprises in the current period, telecommunications companies are actively responding to (or is it creating?) segmented markets, in which customers are increasingly differentiated according to the nature of their demand and in which service supply becomes increasingly demand-led. In political environ-ments in which belief in the notion of a healthy public sphere of communica-tion is subject to denigration, and in which public service principles are seen as something to be exorcised, regulatory adjustments are facilitating the creation of increasingly fragmented network and service structures. As Geoff Mulgan (1989, 9. 226) asserts,

> In the UK and US in particular networks are evolving into a complex patchwork of private networks, LANS, overlays, microwave towers and satellite transponders, cable television nets and so on. Each special purpose network can be built in response to demonstrable demand.

But what exactly is the nature of the 'demonstrable demand' to which the telecommunications companies are increasingly responsive? Here the evidence seems clear. In essence, it is the demand of large corporate users for their own private networks that constitutes the driving force behind the strategies of the telecommunications companies, at least in the more competitive and market-driven environments of the United States and Britain, upon which we shall be concentrating. In these environments, a major shift has taken place from the supply-led concept of universal service provision, to a demand-led concept of differentiated services targeted at key customers in high-growth, high value-added markets (Gillespie & Williams 1988). The nature of this shift can be seen in the very different conceptions of the integrated services digital network(s) (ISDN) in 'traditional' as opposed to deregulated markets.

In traditional or supply-led environments, the development of ISDN 'can be seen as responsive, first of all, to the needs of major telecommunications equipment companies to create and exploit new markets' (Schiller 1985, p. 106). This understanding of the forces shaping the development of ISDN in monopoly environments is shared by Eli Noam (1986, pp. 21–2). What he terms 'hegemonial ISDN',

...combines the institutional self-interest of the PTT with the economic interests of its affiliated 'postal-industrial complex', in particular of traditional equipment manufacturers whose domestic demand is plateauing while their international competitiveness is slipping...But these conditions may not prevail in the long-run; like a Greek tragedy, the unified system of hegemonial ISDN will unravel, because it reflects the needs of a bygone era.

In the non-monopolistic environments which Noam favours, ISDN is seen much more as a telecommunications companies response to a competitive threat, not only from rival telecommunications companies but, crucially, from the possibility of large users 'bypassing' the telecommunications companies networks altogether and creating truly private networks. As J.E. Olson (1988, p.378), Chairman of AT&T until March 1988, put it:

> We, the providers, must accommodate the demands of our customers, or they will meet their own needs. And they can. They have the same access as ourselves to information technologies. They can build their own networks and in the process bypass the PTOs or even bypass entire nations. Our customers have very real options, options which put a premium on us to have the flexibility to change and to deliver what they want.

The bypass threat, and the competitive response of the telecommunications companies to the threat, is heavily concentrated on the large corporate customers who dominate the revenue base of the advanced service vendors. In the case of AT&T, for example, 90 per cent of its business toll revenue is generated by a mere 12 per cent of its business customers, with 300 corporations responsible for 25 per cent of AT&T's total business revenue (Morgan & Pitt 1989).

As a result, in the United States the implementation of ISDN has proceeded as a series of customised, tailored solutions for individual corporate and institutional customers, termed 'ISDN trials' or 'ISDN roll-outs' by the Regional Bell Operating Companies (RBOCs) (Dordick & Kyrish 1989). AT&T meanwhile are actively promoting a customer-designated integrated service (marketed as Tariff 12), by which they combine or 'bundle' different services and types of equipment according to customer requirements, with the whole package sold at steeply discounted rates: 'this new departure is AT&T's response to the changing requirements of corporate America's most sophisticated users' (Morgan & Pitt 1989, p. 26).

There can then be little doubt as to whose interests are being directly served and represented in the development of advanced digital networks in the United States. If in much of Europe the hegemonial ISDN model continues to serve primarily the interests of the PTT monopoly provider and, in Noam's (1986) acerbic words, its surrounding 'postal-industrial complex', in the market-driven telecommunications environment of the United States the balance appears to have shifted decisively in favour of a relatively small group of users. In this context it needs to be stressed that the notion of a 'user' has changed dramatically in function and significance. As Darmaros (1989, p. 10) persuasively argues,

> Users are aggressively demanding their own role in shaping the various ISDN islands and are moving from being ISDN customers, to ISDN designers...This type

of approach effectively passes the ISDN development initiative from carriers to users, especially big ones. *It may lead to ISDNs that are largely based on private rather than public network facilities. In other words, ISDN may become predominantly a private network facility* (emphasis added).

For our present purpose, this is the essential message to emerge from the above brief review. In market-driven environments, the challenge to 'universal service', in the senses defined earlier, would appear to lie in the move away from the provision of a public infrastructure, to which all users have access on broadly similar terms, towards networks which in their essential features are private, regardless of how they are provided and who they are provided by.

Thus at one extreme, the telecommunications companies facilities can and are being bypassed completely. Although there is much controversy over the real as opposed to the potential extent of bypass (see Mansell 1986), recent industry figures, cited in Darmaros (1989), suggest a rapid growth in private networks: seventeen billion dollars were spent on private networks in the United States in 1987, more than the total investments of all the RBOCs on infrastructure.

At another level, the universality of service provision is being directly challenged by the marketing strategies of the telecommunications companies in their response to the potential bypass threat. The proliferation of 'customer-specified' networks bears testament to these strategies, revealed most starkly in the offering of virtual private network (VPN) services, which are sophisticated digital networks, fully tailored to individual user needs, but owned, managed and upgraded by the carriers. According to Morgan and Pitt (1989, p. 34), VPN services 'are a vital weapon for the RBOCs in their battle against the private networks'.

Advanced networks and the services based upon them can then increasingly be regarded as private and proprietary, emphasising the inappropriateness of the 'public highways for the information age' analogy which is frequently used in discussing the significance of digital networks (Bar 1987; Gillespie & Hepworth 1988; Gillespie & Williams 1988). The effective privatisation of advanced communications networks in liberalised environments raises a number of distributional questions, not least for the viability of a public sphere of communication. In economic development terms, the concentration of network access in corporate hands has important competitive implications for small and medium-sized enterprises (see Gillespie and Williams (1989) for a preliminary discussion), and also for the geography of network access. It is to a consideration of this geography that we now turn.

THE GEOGRAPHY OF MARKET-DRIVEN SERVICES

The extent to which the development of new telecommunications services will be differentiated by the geography of the markets being served is a matter of some considerable complexity, as is evidenced by the history of the spread of telecommunications services in competitive environments. Part of this complexity is related to the instability of such environments. Although Brock (1980) suggests that competition in early telephone and telegraph systems fostered rapid price falls and rapid diffusion of service, periods of competition tended to be short and followed by longer periods of monopoly, stabilisation and higher prices.

Generalisation is rendered more problematic by the differing geographical characteristics of services targeted at different types of market. It should not be forgotten that a number of service innovations have been designed to meet predominantly localised markets, with the telephone itself being a good example: 'the original value of a telephone was to call the other side of a town or city rather than another region or country' (Mulgan 1989, p. 229). In contrast, other services, starting with telegraphy, have been designed from their onset to meet primarily long-distance communication requirements. Clearly the geography of these networks, reflecting the geography of the markets they are serving, will be entirely different even if both are market-driven.

The example of telegraphy provides an interesting historical parallel with the types of specialist business or institutionally-oriented services with which we are here concerned. Certainly the early competitive period in the development of telegraphy in the United States, between Morse's first cabled message in 1844 and the consolidation of Western Union's monopoly in 1866, saw a very rapid rate of diffusion and the establishment of a continent-spanning network. Yet the availability of telegraphy services was highly skewed in favour of big cities. As Richard DuBoff (1983, p. 269) has described,

> Larger cities, and the businesses attracted to them for their superior access to market information and their auxiliary services, were precisely the ones the telegraph first linked together (New York, Philadelphia, Boston, Washington, New Orleans, St. Louis). Relative ease of access to the telegraph thus became a matter of 'queuing'. Availability was limited by geographic and institutional factors, combined with technical considerations of maximum wire capacity. In concrete terms, telegraph users in smaller towns often found that the lines were tied up by heavy volumes of messages traveling between and within major cities.

Nor should it be supposed that these networks were necessarily publicly accessible. By the mid-1880s, Western Union's leased-lines business had become so profitable that the company seriously considered ceasing to convey public messages in favour of concentrating entirely on the provision of private networks. In many ways, then, the prime beneficiaries of telegraphy were the nineteenth century forerunners of the multi-locational companies and institutions that dominate the development of today's digital networks. The geographies which the telegraphy networks delineated were those of the commercial empire builders of the day. In the remainder of this section we examine the extent to which the development of contemporary advanced networks, in the market-driven environments of the United States and Britain reflect (and by implication serve to perpetuate) the interests of the corporate-metropolitan control centres.

This is certainly the interpretation put on the geography of advanced networks in the United States by Mitchell Moss. He asserts that the opening up of the telecommunications industry to market forces 'is leading to the creation of a new telecommunications infrastructure designed to serve the information-intensive activities of large metropolitan regions' (Moss 1988, p. 162). The long distance fibre-optic systems 'are designed to serve heavy traffic and thus must reach the largest metropolitan regions that are the information hubs of modern society' (Moss 1986, p. 2), while major investments are taking place in high-capacity digital networks within the metropolitan centres.

Thus, more than one-third of all the Bell System's optic fibre has been installed in New York Telephone's service area (Moss 1986), while the key commercial asset of the most extensive teleport in the United States, Teleport Communication, now 95 per cent owned by Merrill Lynch, is its Manhattan optic-fibre network. These competing concentrations of infrastructural investment are responding of course to demand from some of the largest and most sophisticated telecommunications users in the world and they have made New York the 'bypass capital' of the United States (Morgan & Pitt 1989). More generally, of the fifty-five teleports in the United States which are operational, most are located in the metropolitan business centres in the eastern half of the continent (Hanneman 1987).

In Britain, the liberalisation of telecommunications has been of more recent origin, but already a similar basis to the geography of network and service provision to that which has emerged in the United States can be discerned. The terms of British Telecom's licence impose conditions on the licensee for the 'universal provision of telecommunications services' and for the 'provision of telecommunications services in rural areas', but British Telecom have made it clear that they do not plan to extend these conditions to new services, which will be market-driven (Garnham 1989). Following the trials of their pilot ISDN offering, integrated digital access, based on four System X local exchanges (two in London and one each in Birmingham and Manchester), for example, BT are planning to introduce the service not on a universal basis but only where there is sufficient demand for it.

The service offerings of Mercury Communications, the competitor carrier to BT which began operating in 1984, are, as would be expected, driven more overtly by demand, though it should be noted that there are some important conditions in Mercury's licence which require it to 'provide near national coverage within five years'. Considerable pressure was placed upon Mercury during the negotiation of the licence to accept the national coverage provision and, as a result, the geographical location of the required network nodes are specified in the licence. Already, the originally planned 'figure of eight' fibre-optic network linking London, Bristol, Birmingham, Manchester and Leeds has been extended geographically. A microwave extension up the east coast has been opened, providing service to Newcastle and Scotland, as have spur networks to the south coast of England and to South Wales (Figure 1).

The geography of the availability of Mercury's services remains far from universal, however. Large parts of the country are excluded from Mercury's

Figure 1 Mercury Communications: United Kingdom Trunk Network, 1988

existing or planned network, while the availability of service is further restricted to an area within a maximum twenty-five mile radius of a transmitter or distribution node. In practice the radius is often much less than this, for line-of-sight access via a microwave link is required in order to be able to receive direct Mercury service. In Newcastle-upon-Tyne, for example, a number of Mercury's potential customers, such as Procter & Gamble and the Northern Rock Building Society, are not yet able to receive Mercury service more than a year after the Newcastle network node opened for business. Mercury are addressing the local access problem in certain key metropolitan locations with city centre cabling schemes, providing direct optic-fibre access into the trunk digital network. Beyond the West End and City of London, where several hundred kilometres of fibre have been laid in recent years, seven local cabling schemes are in progress: in Bristol, Manchester, Birmingham, Heathrow, Reading, Leeds and Edinburgh (Whitehorn 1989). As in the United States, therefore, investment in the most advanced communications networks is heavily concentrated in the metropolitan centres of the 'information economy'.

Even for those smaller cities and towns that are passed by Mercury's trunk network, the economics of demand-driven service provision severely limit the extent to which the business communities in these locations can benefit from Mercury's service offerings and their competitive prices. Even the creation of a new node on the existing trunk network requires an investment of about five million pounds, and Mercury is only prepared to consider an investment of this order if there is firm interest from potential customers with a combined telecommunications expenditure in excess of 300 000 pounds. Nor can this be achieved by aggregating the demand of a large number of small businesses; Mercury will not provide less than a two megabit link (equivalent to thirty exchange lines) to a single customer location (Economic & Transport Planning Group 1989). Access to Britain's only competitor network to BT is, then, restricted both geographically and by size of firm. The market to which they are responding is predominantly comprised of large corporations operating in metropolitan locations.

The final example of the geographical implications of introducing more immediate market pressures into the provision of advanced telecommunications networks is provided by the scenario work undertaken by the PA Consulting Group for the Department of Trade and Industry (DTI) as part of the latter's review of prospective developments in the electronic communications infrastructure of Britain (PA Consulting Group, 1988; see also DTI Communications Steering Group 1988). The likely development of broadband networks and services under three contrasting scenarios were explored, these being:

- a *Lightly Regulated Competition (LRC)* scenario, in which the current policy regime is assumed to continue, with the prime role of government being the oversight of fair competition, only intervening in market operations to restrict any unfair use of market power by dominant players;
- a *Laissez-Faire* scenario, encompassing very rapid deregulation without controls on the dominant players. The most important single relaxation, in terms of the future development of broadband communications, would be to allow BT and Mercury to carry entertainment television as well as telecommunications services over a single local network;
- a *National Grid* scenario, in which the government is more specifically interventionist than in the recent past, with the aim of ensuring the creation

of an integrated national broadband network within a timescale which market forces alone might not bring about.

Under the LRC scenario, PA believes that the installation of local broadband networks between now and 2010 would be limited because of the nature of oligopolistic competition in reducing the economic viability of major infra-structural investments with their long pay-back periods. Broadband commun-ications under this scenario are thus likely to be limited to 'fibre islands' in the major urban business centres, with interconnection between these local-ised broadband networks enabling some new broadband services in certain sectors such as financial services (PA Consulting Group 1988, pp. 30–2).

Under the Laissez-Faire scenario, PA predicts that the prospects for the development of local broadband networks would be improved because of the possibilities for BT and Mercury (and indeed other carriers) to provide broad-cast entertainment services on their networks. Nevertheless, PA anticipate that there would be significant regional and local differences in the provision of broadband networks and services (PA Consulting Group 1988, pp.32–3).

Finally, under the National Grid scenario, PA estimates that by 2010 the majority of Britain could be connected to the national integrated broadband network – perhaps 75 to 85 per cent of homes and 90 to 98 per cent of business users (PA Consulting Group 1988, p. 35). In considering the regional development impacts of the three different scenarios, PA made assumptions concerning the varying geographical availability of broadband services (PA Consulting Group 1988, p. 97):

> Under the National Grid scenario...it was assumed that all commercial users in all regions would have access to the new technologies. Under the other two scenarios, however, coverage would include all of London, East Anglia and the South East but only large corporate users and users in the major conurbations in the rest of the UK...We calculated that 42.4% of firms in the 'rest of the UK' would not be covered under these two [i.e. LRC and Laissez-Faire] scenarios.

The future scenario work undertaken by the PA Group points then in the same direction as the existing evidence from both the United States and Britain. This is that in market-driven supply regimes, the availability of advanced services will be markedly geographically differentiated. Only the largest corporate users will be able to escape the uneven geography of telecommunications provision, either through building, where permitted, their own private networks, or by having sufficient market power to make the services they require available via customised overlay networks.

CONCLUSIONS

We would contend that there are important urban and regional development implications associated with the emerging uneven geography of advanced communications networks in market-driven environments (Goddard & Gillespie 1986; Gillespie & Hepworth 1988). This is not to suggest that the problems of declining or peripheral regions are likely to be solved by their connection to the new digital networks. Indeed, as Melody (1987, p. 4) persuasively argues, the new digital highways may provide external interests with competitive advantage over local and regional interests, providing 'an efficient system for sucking out the economic benefits and opportunities that otherwise would be generated in the region'.

We would nevertheless suggest the 'external interests' of which Melody writes, in the guise of the multi-locational corporations, will anyway be able to exploit the new technologies, and their own scale-derived power in telecommunications markets, to develop 'private' networks (whether real or virtual) which meet their requirements. We would further contend that the fragmented, private access, non-universal services that are developing in liberalised environments are precisely those that best serve the competitive interests of the major, frequently transnational, corporate players. As Dan Schiller (1985, p. 106) suggests, with respect to the development of international ISDN networks:

> At every level...from initial planning and technical design to actual implementation, ISDN incarnates only the private interests of the transnational corporations that will engineer, supply, install and make use of the emerging global grid.

Our conclusion would be that, from a regional development perspective, there is a very strong case for ensuring that an unfettered market-driven route to service development is not allowed to prevail, particularly so in the highly imperfect and concentrated markets which are evident in the telecommunications sphere. From this perspective, telecommunications networks are more likely to function in the interests of peripheries and the less-favoured regions if their development is integrated rather than fragmented; if they are publicly accessible rather than private; and if they adhere to universal service principles rather than to the narrowly-framed demand-driven principles currently in vogue in the United States and the United Kingdom.

Clearly this stance need not, nor indeed should it, imply a return to the old cosy ways of complacent and unresponsive monopoly service providers – though as an aside we should point out that, as the French experience with Minitel has demonstrated, monopoly provision and public service principles are in no way inimical to radical service innovation. Indeed, as the PA Consulting Group (1988, p. 19) conclude in their review of recent developments in telecommunications services:

> The most successful and well-known developments (INS, BIGFON and Minitel) have been achieved within climates of significant pressure and investment from central planning authorities with the financial and regulatory authority to steer developments down a preferred path of both technology and market development.

Rather than getting side-tracked into the well-worn discussion over the respective merits of monopoly versus competitive supply, however, we wish to conclude with a plea for the re-regulation of telecommunications markets, whether monopolistic or competitive, in order to ensure that advanced networks and services become available outside favoured core regions. The introduction of competition into existing stable supply environments can in itself act as a stimulus for making explicit such goals. As Nicholas Garnham (1989, p. 127) points out, 'in the UK it is only with liberalisation that the provision of universal service has been made both an explicit aim of government regulatory policy in the Telecommunications Act, and a specific obligation laid upon BT and Mercury in their licenses'. As he goes on to suggest (1989, p. 133), the goal of universal geographical access can be specified and defined within a process of re-regulation. Thus,

> ...an operator could be required to make available given standards of connection for a specified range of services in different regions and different-sized population centres within a specified time-period. The extent to which certain regions were being prioritised, and the cost/benefits of such prioritisation, could then be made transparent. Failure to meet targets could then, in a regulated commercial system, be subject to penalties and in a public system would be more open to political accountability.

We would go even further and envisage a re-regulation process which attempted to discriminate positively in favour of service provision in disadvantaged or peripheral regions, rather than in merely attempting to ensure that they were not further disadvantaged by telecommunications development plans. Certainly we must concur with Ron Abler (1987a, p. 125), who has recently argued:

> Despite de-regulation...the fact remains that regulation exerts more control over what services are available to what classes of customers at what places and at what costs – that is, over the basic geography of telecommunications services – than any other single variable. It seems to me to follow from that fact that a geography of regulation and de-regulation must be one of the first priorities in advancing the geography of telecommunications...

11

THE MUNICIPAL INFORMATION ECONOMY

Mark Hepworth

INTRODUCTION

The last decade has witnessed rapid technological change in the local authority sector of the UK economy. Council investments in information technology (IT) are expected to climb beyond one billion pounds by 1993, in England and Wales alone.[1] Given that local authorities are under severe financial stress, it is reasonable to conclude that IT innovations are crucial to their survival. More accurately, the growth of these capital investments points to the enormous strategic value of information to local government.

This chapter briefly examines the nature and significance of local authority involvement in the UK information economy. It begins by highlighting the 'Cinderella' status of local authorities in the Government's influential Information Technology Advisory Panel (ITAP 1983) report. The growth of the municipal information economy is then related to the Conservative program of local government reform. In the remainder of the chapter, recent trends in local authority IT innovations and information services are examined and then discussed.

THE 'MISSING LINK'

To plagiarise George Stigler (1961), local authorities appear to 'occupy a slum dwelling' in the UK information economy. This contrasts with the central role that the Government sees itself playing in the 'Fifth Information and Communication Kondratieff' (Freeman 1987). For example, according to the Cabinet Office's Information Technology Advisory Panel (ITAP 1983, pp. 7–8) report:

> Government has four major roles that affect the tradeable information sector. It sets the legal and regulatory framework for information services, it is the largest

processor of information in the country and, as a major supplier, it also influences the market for new services; it can act as the national focus for new developments or policy issues; and it can provide financial support.

What is conspicuously missing from the ITAP report is due appreciation of the considerable role that local authorities play in the information economy. Local government is, for example, one of the biggest sectoral markets for IT, with a diffusion rate which exceeds that of most other industries (Grimshaw & Haddad 1988). Further, after the Government and the media, it is probably the biggest provider of information services to business and households – the vast bulk of which are, significantly, provided as 'public goods'.

The results of survey research also reveal significant growth in local authority expenditures on advertising to attract mobile inward investment (Hepworth *et al.* 1989). Quite apart from its potential effects on the locational dynamics of the information economy (and the advertising industry), this growth is indicative of the degree to which local authorities are increasingly absorbing the risks of economic development in Britain. A more accurate interpretation of this feature of 'urban entrepreneurialism' (Harvey 1989) is that, with the Government's preference for monetarism (over Keynesianism), the burden of risk has shifted from 'Whitehall' to the 'Town Hall' (i.e. from the national to the local public sector). Therefore, local government's omission from the ITAP report is surprising.

The realities, of course, are that risk absorption in the information economy does call for local authority involvement. Of particular significance is local government's central role in infrastructure provision – not telecommunications (by dint of the existing regulatory framework), but property and land redevelopment, and human capital. Where would the information economy develop, if not on the newly-emerging office, media and high technology parks, which local councils are busily planning out? And, can the information economy do without local roads, sewers and other basic infrastructure?[2]

Focussing on local authorities, therefore, provides a significant, disaggregated view of recent developments in the information economy. In my view, it provides the most useful starting point for looking at the impacts of IT on urban and regional development.

TWO 'REVOLUTIONS' CONVERGE

The 'information revolution' in Britain's town halls has coincided with – and, indeed, been fuelled by – the last decade of radical local government reform. In essence, the so called 'Thatcher revolution' has cast local authorities in the role of 'quasi firms', whose survival depends on mobilising information resources to achieve higher levels of competitiveness, efficiency and flexibility. What local authorities now confront is privatisation in its many different guises (Pirie 1988).

Central to these Conservative reforms is the political economy of information adumbrated in public choice theory (PCT). Closely associated with the American scholars, Buchanan, Tullock and Mitchell,[3] PCT has found greatest expression in the various primers on institutional design that emanate from the Government's main think-tanks – viz. the Institute for Economic Affairs (IEA) and the Adam Smith Institute. Some idea of the political flavour of PCT – and its ideological appeal to Conservatives – can be gleaned from the titles of IEA pamphlets, such as *Welfare Without the State* and *Transport Without Politics*. As McAuslan (1988, p. 683) remarks:

> It (PCT) has grown, perhaps descended would be a better word, from description to prescription; from a method of analysis of government and politics, to a justification for present government and politics, or more accurately anti-government and politics. In short it has become an ideology.

The 'control-theoretic' role of information in PCT is best illustrated by its application to local goverment. The Community Charge (or poll tax), for example, has the effect of substituting the information-transmission role of the 'ballot box' for the 'price mechanism', in revealing public choices for local authority services.[4] Similarly, the basic intent of compulsory competitive tendering (CCT) legislation is to force local authority bureaucrats to reveal more information about service-delivery conditions (including costs and trade union practices), under the threat of open competition from private firms.[5] And, in its watchdog role, the Audit Commission's value-for-money (VFM) principles of financial evaluation have the basic effect of transforming authorities into federations of (mutually competitive) cost centres: with inform-ation acting both as a unit of account and a unit of exchange (see Stoker 1988, pp. 173–244).

The operation of these information principles, of course, has created strong pressures for IT innovation in local authorities. In essence, they have dramatic-ally raised the transaction costs of public services provision, and thereby the information requirements of local councils throughout the United Kingdom. A major result has been to open-up the local authority sector as a burgeoning market for IT products and services.

TRENDS IN INFORMATION SERVICES

This section briefly summarises the results of a nationwide survey of UK local authorities, entitled *Information Technology, Information Services and Local Economic Development* (Hepworth *et al.* 1989). Given the wide scope of our original investigations, only part of the survey findings, on information services, is presented below.

Business information services

Local authorities are a major source of producer services used by the private sector. These council services are now a vital component of local economic development strategies (Sellgren 1987), and, as information subsidies, their general effect is to reduce the transaction costs of user firms.[6] As such, their rationale is to enhance the competitive advantage of local economies in the current period of growing territorial competition for new investment and jobs (Harvey 1989).

Local authorities, of course, offer a wide array of information services – producer services as public goods – to private firms through face-to-face contacts (e.g. economic development units), documentation and telephony. These media are now increasingly complemented by IT-based information services, which make councils important new entrants to the so called network marketplace (Dordick *et al.* 1981). Some examples of these IT innovations taken from the survey returns, are listed below with local authority users named in brackets.

- marketing databases, or local trade and product directories (e.g. Cleveland, Avon, Preston);
- computerised registers of local sites and premises for industrial and commercial development (e.g. Hampshire, Hamilton, Tonbridge, Malling);
- databases on local labour market, including skills and training requirements (e.g. Mansfield, Tameside);
- databases on financial assistance schemes for businesses (e.g. Grampian Region, South Lakeland);
- computerised listings of planning applications and permissions (e.g. Sheffield, Northumberland);
- viewdata networks advertising council services (e.g. Coventry, Basildon, Richmond-upon-Thames);
- scientific and technical databases on patents, copyright, etc. (e.g. Halifax, Renfrew);
- databases on local housing market (e.g. Hertsmere);
- EEC business collaboration network (e.g. Tendring);
- social and demographic databases (e.g. Birmingham).

Local authorities also provide a large volume of 'raw' data to private information vendors at a nominal price (e.g. electoral registers). These 'quasi-market' transactions, of course, form a small but vital link in the value-added chain by which information is converted into a market commodity. However, local authorities are proposing to capture more of this value-added by entering the information business directly (Figure 1). The broader implications of this recent development are discussed below.

Consumer information services

Local authorities have also increased their budgetary expenditures on consumer information services. Part of these public information activities are directed towards promoting the private consumer services sector of the local economy – shops, restaurants, hotels, and tourism more generally. Some examples of IT applications in this area include the Glasgow On-Line Scheme, the Sheffield Tourist Information Network, and viewdata networks linking up local libraries and public places in Milton Keynes, Brent, Gateshead and Richmond-upon-Thames. The general effect of these information services,

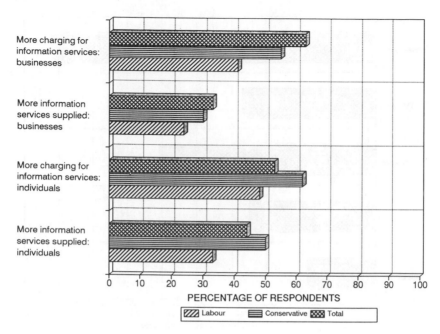

Figure 1 The 'pay-per revolution' in UK local government (source: Hepworth et al. (1989)).

in this case, is to reduce the consumption-related transaction costs of local businesses.[7] Their rationale is to promote local economic development through the consumer services sector, which absorbs a growing share of employment in all parts of the United Kingdom.

Consumer information provided to resident users of local authority public services is another major area of expenditure growth. In essence, advertising and marketing council services have been fuelled by the Government's legislative reforms, that promulgate both 'entrepreneurialism' and 'consumerism' amongst local authorities and their customers (Hambleton 1988). Nearly 70 per cent of survey respondents (authorities) claimed to be providing significantly more information services than five years ago, in order to stimulate 'market' demand.

Civic and local newspapers are still the dominant media of information services provision, together with the local library (Figure 2). However, in attempting to 'get closer' to their markets, some authorities are increasingly looking to new cable networks and viewdata innovations, as complementary media. Coventry and Bracknell, for example, provide consumer information services using weekly cable programs. And, Strathclyde's viewdata network offers information on welfare benefits, leisure and recreation, adult education, grants, funding and training, and labour and housing market opportunities. A further example is Enfield's so-called one-stop information shops, which provide a single IT-access point to all (computerised) information pertaining to the council's services.

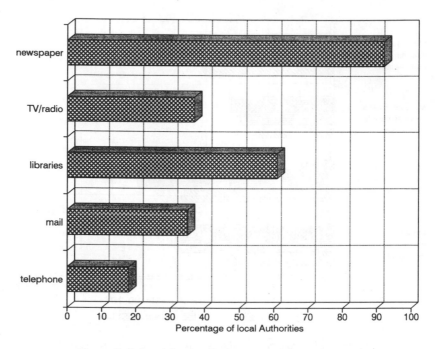

*Figure 2 Advertising media for promoting service usage
(source: Hepworth et al. (1989)).*

The spectre of 'smart card' technologies for consumer transactions is also evident in the local authority sector – for example, the Wakefield 'Passport' and the Thamesdown 'Gold Card'. As in the private sector, these IT-based transactional innovations provide superior consumer information, as a basis for 'fine-tuning' marketing and (services) production strategies. Their potential for real-time marginal cost pricing of services is equally (if not more) significant, given that one traditional welfare economic argument for collective consumption – and the need for state intervention – has been the technical impossibility of obtaining information on individual preferences for public goods.[8]

In sum, UK local authorities are expanding their provision of information services to both firms and consumers, with IT innovations being increasingly used to deliver these services. These recent trends in the municipal information economy have the dual rationale of promoting local economic development and maintaining (or 'legitimating') the role of local government as multiple providers of public services. As suggested below, however, financial pressures to 'make a business of information' may act to undermine these basic objectives of local authority information policies.

DISCUSSION

The survey findings revealed that local authorities in the United Kingdom are considering the possibility of making a business of information (Figure 1).

According to Mosco (1988, p. 5):

> New technology makes it possible to measure and monitor more and more of our communication and information activities. Business and Government see this as a major instrument to increase profit and control. The result is a pay per society.

It should, however, be noted that existing legislation prohibits UK local authorities from entering the information business, on a significant scale. Information charges are set centrally and nominal. Further, opinion is divided on these business prospects, with Conservative councils being relatively more in favour of privatising information services. The pay-per revolution does, nevertheless, create a policy dilemma, with respect to both business and consumer information services.

Charging firms for information services, of course, would generate new sources of business revenue for local authorities. This would partly compensate for the effects of the Local Government (Reform) Act, by which 'Whitehall' has appropriated powers over local business taxation. However, by introducing a local information tax for firms, authorities would effectively be negating the information subsidies which play an important role in their economic development strategies. The increasing centrality of transaction costs in spatial agglomeration suggests that these types of information taxes could seriously undermine the competitive advantage of local economies (Scott 1986; Storper & Christopherson 1987).

Charging for consumer information services produces another dilemma. Its general effect would be to undermine the traditional redistributive function of council information services. That is to say, poorer sections of the local community may be denied access to basic public services, due to their 'inability to pay' for ancillary information. In this respect, it should be noted that the Government is now considering the possibility of 'privatising' library services, through competitive tendering and the imposition of direct user charges (see Figure 2).[9]

This possible outcome of the so-called pay-per revolution, of course, makes nonsense of the Government's view that IT should assist in creating more efficient and equitable markets for public services. Consider, for example, the following argumentation of public choice theory (Lepage 1978, pp. 210–1):

> All that theories of imperfect exchange do is to remind us that information is, in our world, a costly resource. They show us that market imperfections, which serve as a pretext for the expansion of government, are a consequence not of capitalism as such (the fact that there are income disparities) but of the cost of information. The higher this cost is – relative to other economic costs – the more imperfect exchange will be, the more 'unjust' markets will remain, and the more justified liberals will feel the corrective intervention of the state to be. But lower information costs make exchange less imperfect and state intervention less justified. As long as capitalism goes on lowering relative information costs, the more assured we can be that freedom of exchange will lead to more and more perfect real democracy.

Clearly, while IT may reduce the transaction costs of consuming council services (e.g. viewdata terminals in libraries, or cable programming), this does not guarantee 'more and more perfect real democracy' – as public choice theorists would insist. If information is charged for, the general effect would be to make the 'freedom to choose' – i.e. political choices – dependent on each individual's ability to pay. The pay-per revolution', therefore, might be the panacea to Britain's economic problems (as the ITAP report argues), however, it might very well undermine local government, as democratic political institutions (Starr 1987) (see Friedman quotation[4]).

CONCLUSION

In most UK towns and cities, the information economy does not centre on on-line industries, international head offices, high tech industry – or, on teleports, intelligent buildings and 'silicon' factory estates. Rather, it pivots around public sector institutions, created during the post-war golden years of Keynesianism and the Welfare State. Local authorities, as such, are probably the dominant sector of the information economy in most areas of the United Kingdom. For this reason, they merit considerable analytical attention, if our basic objective is to develop an understanding of the geography of the information economy and its social ramifications.

NOTES

1 *Estimates from Local Government in Britain* An ICL Report on the impact of information technology, London : Paragon Communications/KL (UK).

2 For my views on 'transportation and the information economy', see Hepworth (1989).

3 See, for example, Buchanan (1962), Tullock (1976) and Mitchell (1988).

4 For a critique of PCT on this point, see Arrow (1979). Note, for its political and social implications, the following statement by Milton and Rose Friedman (1980, p. 8):
    The price system is the mechanism that performs this task (efficient resource allocation) without central direction, without requiring people to speak to one another or to like one another.

5 For an exemplary application of information economics to contracting out in the public sector, see Laffont (1987).

6 Oliver Williamson has published several books on transaction cost economics. I have cited one of his seminal works (Williamson 1975) in the references.

7 For formal economic analysis, see Klein and Leffler (1981).

8 Using IT to solve this technical aspect of the information problem does not, of course, necessarily mean that public goods will be transferred to the market.

9 *Financing our Public Library Service: Four Subjects for Debate* (A Consultative Paper), Parliamentary 'Green Paper' Cm 324, HMSO, London, 1988.

Part III

New Technology-based Settlement Systems

12

THE INFORMATION CITY IN THE
GLOBAL ECONOMY

Mitchell Moss

INTRODUCTION

One of the paradoxes of contemporary society is that the abundance of advanced telecommunications services, such as cellular telephony, electronic funds transfer, and computer-based communications, has not reduced the attractiveness of large cities as places to transfer, process and exchange information. Indeed, cities such as New York, London, Tokyo and Los Angeles have flourished as centres for international finance and advanced business services at the same time that new technologies designed to facilitate communication without face-to-face contact have proliferated. How can we explain the growth of telecommunications technologies designed to overcome traditional barriers to communication with the emergence of major cities as hubs for communication – both electronic and face-to-face? In order to fully understand the relationship between information technology and urban development, we need to go beyond the current areas of research on issues such as the location of office activities, the internationalisation of business services, employment and labour force skills, and regional development policy – and look more closely at the way in which changes in the function of cities are reflected in the development of different patterns of physical development and transportation and communications infrastructure (see, for example, Gillespie & Hepworth 1986; Goddard & Pye 1977; Gottmann 1983; Hepworth 1987b).

This chapter consists of three sections: a review of the way in which technological changes influence the physical pattern of urban development; a discussion of how information moves within and among cities, with a specific emphasis on the location of such activities in the New York City central business district; and a discussion of the new telecommunications and transportation infrastructure in large metropolitan areas.

TELECOMMUNICATIONS, OFFICES AND PHYSICAL DEVELOPMENT

Each era gives rise to a type of physical structure which symbolises the principal function of the city. As Cowen (1961, p. 25) observes, 'the main symbols of the city, for several hundred years prior to the mid-eighteenth century, were the castle, the cathedral, the palace, and the market place'. With the rise of industrialisation, the factory became the dominant urban symbol, and with it came the 'factory towns' dominated by steel mills, textile plants and the employer-owned housing built for industrial workers. The growth of business services at the start of the twentieth century was the impetus for the skyscraper, which Gottmann (1966) has called 'an expression of a social and intellectual revolution characteristic of our era...the first skyscraper in Chicago and some of the early ones in New York were built by insurance companies – that is, by companies whose business is entirely bureaucratic. Their work is all on paper and in transactions'.

The office building – initially designed to accommodate everyone from the executive to the clerical worker – has been reshaped and reconfigured with the advent of computers and advanced telecommunications. The clerical worker is now equipped with a computer workstation linked by telephone lines that allows the worker to access more information and thus perform more tasks than could be done with a typewriter or adding machine. In 1987, 'there were thirty million computer work stations [in the United States], a number that is expected to double by 1995 so that nine of ten white collar workers will be so equipped' (Parker *et al.* 1989, p. 41). Computer terminals and related equipment impose new demands for space and supporting infrastructure, and, with the reduction in cost and size of information systems, there has been a proliferation of printers, fax machines, and related equipment. As Dowall and Salkin (1986) note, 'new technologies beget new machines which must be housed'. The office, rather than diminishing in importance, has become even more important as the hub for the flow of information – by electronic means, on paper, and in-person. As a study by the US Congress Office of Technology Assessment (1985, p. 7) states:

> The office plays the same role for an organisation that the brain plays in a living organism. It receives information flowing in from all parts of the organisation (or organism) and from the external environment, processes that information and sends back responses, instructions, and commands through an extended nervous system – established channels of communication.

Traditional categories of front-office and back-office are no longer appropriate for classifying the activities that occur in the office environment. Automation may not have improved worker productivity, but it has altered the structure and scope of office functions. Computer-based activities are no longer confined to routine activities – such as check processing and claims settlements – but have been expanded to encompass a vast array of functions including customer service, retail shopping and equipment repair. The General Electric Company, for example, uses an 800-phone system to respond to inquiries about appliances and to provide on-line telephone assistance, prior to assigning personnel to repair equipment.

The growth of computer-based office functions has created a demand for a new generation of buildings designed for computer operations and telecommunications-based activities. Huge floor areas with large weight loads are needed to accommodate computers, raised floors and ceilings are required for electrical and communications cables, and increased energy capacity is required for operating and cooling office equipment. Just as mass assembly manufacturing led to the decline of the old industrial loft building and to the construction of single-storey, horizontal factories, so has modern office technology led to the need for new office buildings capable of meeting modern technological and spatial conditions.

Duffy and Henney (1989, p. 33) have identified the key challenges that information technology present for urban planners, developers and architects: 'The more information is handled, stored and retrieved electronically the more vital it is that buildings have the capacity to accommodate information technology (IT). Buildings have become, in a sense, an extension of the computer'. While several studies (e.g. Daniels 1985; Thrift *et al.* 1987) have analysed how telecommunications has affected the movement of office activities out of the central city to the suburbs, it is also important to recognise how information technology and the high value placed on face-to-face communication has changed the physical pattern of urban development.

In New York City, the preference for newer and larger office buildings – that provide prestige as well as a modern information infrastructure – has fostered a vacancy rate in downtown Manhattan that is almost 40 per cent higher for older buildings than for new office buildings. The migration of the Manhattan financial district from the narrow caverns of Wall Street north to the World Financial Center on the Hudson, and to large parcels on Water Street next to the East River, reflects the demand for mega-structures that can be built on landfill rather than on the narrow urban street-grid of the early twentieth century. The stock market is no longer defined by a place – such as Wall Street – but is what Duffy calls 'an aggregate of activities' located in trading rooms linked to each other and to stock exchanges.

Similarly in London, the financial district – once defined by proximity to the Bank of England – has been extended to encompass new sites on the Docklands and over railroad land that can meet the spatial and technological requirements of the financial services industry.

Instead of 'location', investment banks and securities companies want buildings with large clear floors for trading, high floor-to-ceiling heights to accommodate a raised floor, and high-performance mechanical, electrical and telecommunications services. The ability of buildings to meet these requirements now rivals location as the most important factor. Only the Lloyd's Triangle and to a lesser extent the Baltic Exchange provide a precise physical location for their markets. The new, more fluid locational rules for banks are clearly shown by the rapid take-up of space in Broadgate, which is partly in Hackney; in London Bridge City, which is in Southwark; and in Salomon Brothers' move to Victoria (Duffy & Henney 1989, p. 19). As technology has accelerated, the movement of electronic information in, out, and through the office building, the value placed on face-to-face interaction and the specialised information conveyed through personal interaction have also intensified. While routine office functions that do not involve face-to-face transactions have been dispersed to suburban settings in the United States, advanced business services dependent on immediate access to specialised expertise have concentrated in selected central cities. As Richard Meier (1961, p. 64) wrote more than a quarter of a century ago, 'the need for face-to-face contact offers perhaps the best explanation for the strong attraction retained by the urban centre'. Moreover, the deregulation of financial markets has led to the emergence of new, complex financial instruments that require direct and reliable contact to produce and explain these new financial instruments. Although the buyers of the new financial services can be located anywhere on the globe, the sellers – the information producers – are concentrated in a few major financial centres.

As Thomas Allen (1979, p. 42), in a study of engineers and organisations, has pointed out, 'human beings are the most effective carriers of information... and the best way to transfer information between organisations or social systems is to physically transfer a human carrier'.

Thrift's (1987, p. 208) analysis of international financial centres highlighted 'three interrelated reasons the organisations of commercial capital tend to group together in these centres...to be near clients...to be in close proximity to relevant markets...to tap into information on markets and the operations of banking and industrial corporations and the state rapidly and efficiently'.

The principal function of major world cities today is to provide access to information users and providers engaged in the provision of advanced business services. As a result, technology-intensive office buildings are being built in high-cost urban centres – albeit in new locations – and advanced business services are continuing to concentrate near each other. In New York City, the movement of corporate headquarters to locations in Connecticut, New Jersey, Westchester County and other parts of the country has not stopped the migration into New York City from other nations and other parts of the United States, of law firms, advertising agencies and financial service firms that require access to the high value and specialised information-based activities situated in Manhattan.

Furthermore, Gordon Clark (in press) argues that the popularity of mergers and leveraged buy-outs has reinforced the hegemony of financial capitals where productive corporate assets can be converted into financial assets. The decision to move the headquarters of RJR Nabisco from Atlanta to New York City is based on the need to be in an 'arbitrage centre' rather than in a traditional production centre. 'In essence, the logic of centralised control and decentralised production (so fundamental to textbook treatments of the geography of corporate management) has been taken-over: centralised control in other centers is now necessary for the efficient conversion of assets and decentralised production networks are assets to be sold rather than managed.'

The high value that advanced business service firms place on proximity to clients and to each other is shown in Figures 1 to 5, which illustrate the clustering that occurs with regard to the location of foreign banks, advertising agencies and law firms in Manhattan. Law firms, which were initially situated near corporate headquarters or the downtown courts, are located near each other and their major clients in mid-town. Advertising agencies maintain their traditional concentration on Manhattan's east side, and foreign banks are located in distinct nodes based on nation of origin.

THE MOVEMENT OF INFORMATION BETWEEN CITIES

If information is the key product of cities, how does this information get transported from one place to another and how does information flow affect the relationships between cities? Clearly, individuals remain the principal means for transporting information – whether in the office, from seller to buyer, or from city to city. In addition, a plethora of telecommunications systems supplements the human being and provides virtually instantaneously, flows of information designed to enhance office productivity. Timeliness is crucial; the US Office of Technology Assessment (1985, p. 307) observes: 'Information is ephemeral. It must be available when and where it is needed; too late, it may be useless'.

Measuring the movement of information thus must take into account the flow of people and the flow of information. Government agencies and transportation researchers have developed an elaborate set of measures for

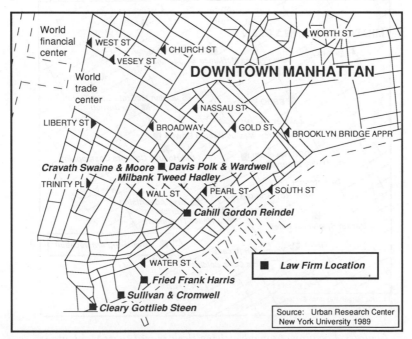

Figure 1 Location of top twenty law firms in downtown Manhattan.

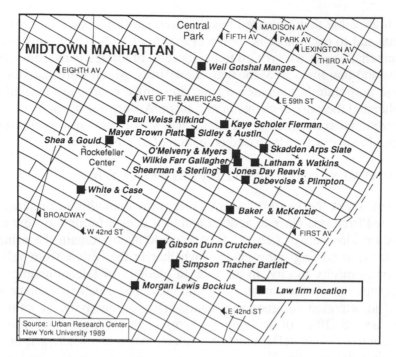

Figure 2 Location of top twenty law firms in mid-town Manhattan.

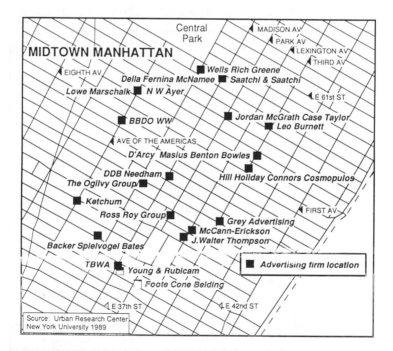

Figure 3 Location of top advertising firms in mid-town Manhattan.

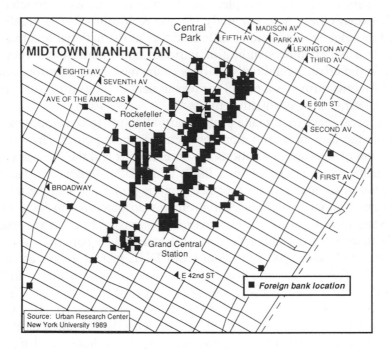

Figure 4 Location of foreign banks in mid-town Manhattan

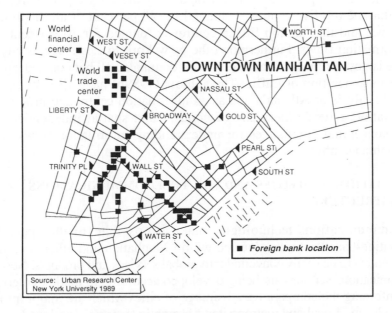

Figure 5 Location of foreign banks in downtown Manhattan.

the movement of cargo and people, but virtually no data exist on telephone traffic between cities. A recent study (Staple & Mullins 1989) highlighted the need for telecommunication traffic statistics at the national level in order to provide a better understanding of national and international economic activity. At the urban level, Pred's analysis of the movement of information in colonial America provides a model for researchers of inter-urban information activity patterns in the twentieth century.

Urban researchers have made preliminary attempts to develop new ways to measure the flow of information between and among cities. However, the deregulation of telecommunications in some nations and the privatisation of telecommunications in other nations, limits our capacity to develop systematic measures of voice and data traffic since there is no longer a single telecommunications provider and competition creates an incentive to keep market data private. New measures of information systems and traffic are essential if we are to improve our understanding of urban activity patterns.

One study (Moss 1988) used data from DHL private overseas mail to examine the flow of information between Tokyo and US cities and also identified the largest origination points for DHL private mail, revealing that London, New York and Tokyo were the leading sources of DHL overseas mail. A recent study by Wheeler and Mitchelson (1989a) relies on the data drawn from Federal Express Corporation's overnight letters and packages sent to analyse the flow of information among forty-eight metropolitan areas in the United States.

Wheeler and Mitchelson's analysis of Federal Express data found that New York generated 14 per cent of all traffic among the forty-eight metropolitan areas, that the top five centres accounted for 40 per cent of all the information flows, and that the top fifteen centres accounted for 70 per cent of all the information flows. Furthermore, the New York to Los Angeles city-pair was the largest traffic route, and New York dominated all but one metropolitan area in its generation of traffic. The authors (1989b) have also conducted a detailed analysis of Atlanta's role as an information centre and propose that 'information genesis, hierarchy of control, and spatial independence are useful conceptual alternatives for understanding information flows among metropolitan centres'.

INFORMATION ACTIVITIES AND THE TELECOMMUNICATIONS INFRASTRUCTURE

Telecommunications technologies make it possible for the specialised information-based activities located within Manhattan and other central city office centres to be easily converted into global services and products. New telecommunications services are being developed according to market criteria and are reinforcing the comparative advantage of cities which are major information producers. Local and metropolitan fibre-optic systems – designed to serve major business centres – are being developed by the regional telephone companies and new competitors in the United States. Firms situated in the major business districts will have the benefit of competition in selecting fibre-optic local carriers, while in rural areas copper cable is unlikely to be replaced by fibre optics. A study by the US Department of Commerce, National Telecommunications and Information Administration (1988, p. 261) noted that, 'since the high-capacity feature of optical fibre offers little advantage where traffic and future growth are low and the remote sites are dispersed, some companies (e.g. Pacific Bell) have chosen not to abandon their substantial capital investment in copper-based systems'.

There is also a fundamental question about the future architecture of telecommunications networks in which Peter Huber, author of *The Geodesic Network: 1987 Report on Competition in the Telephone Industry*, argues that reduction in switching costs will lead to a decentralised network, while others (e.g. Flamm 1989, p. 61) believe that 'transmission costs have dropped much faster than switching costs and, with the advent of fibre optics, have continued to do so'.

The development of local fibre systems that bypass public networks and link large users to national and international telecommunications networks, demonstrates the way in which large metropolitan areas – with multiple fibre systems – become more attractive to communications-intensive industries. In the United States, local bypass is 'a $400 million business growing at 22 per cent a year. Twelve cities from New York to Orlando and Chicago to Boston are wired with 774 miles of fibre and another three cities and 215 miles are planned' (Siler 1989). New firms have been created, such as Teleport Communications and Metropolitan Fiber, and hence provide large firms located in major downtown areas with low-cost access to long-distance networks. This pattern of competition in telecommunications resembles the initial railroad era when 'the competitive points, enjoying lower rates than rural towns on a single line, absorb[ed] all the growth of a region' (Weber 1969, p. 199).

CONCLUSION

This paper has sought to identify the way in which information-based activities are influencing the physical pattern of development in cities, the movement of information between cities, and the development of telecommunications systems in metropolitan regions. The evidence presented here suggests that there is a synergistic effect in which the rise of advanced business services generates a demand for technologically-sophisticated buildings and a high value on those urban settings in which face-to-face transactions can occur. In addition, the deregulation of telecommunications has reinforced the comparative advantage that large information hubs have in gaining access to the latest and lowest-cost telecommunications services. Further research on the relationship of information flows to cities is essential to understand how urban centres can form economic development policies that build on information-based industries.

13

NEW TECHNOLOGY AND THE GEOGRAPHY OF THE UK INFORMATION ECONOMY

John Goddard

INTRODUCTION

This chapter outlines some of the preliminary findings from a major program of research on the implications of the spread of information and communication technologies for the development of cities and regions within the United Kingdom. The research is a contribution to the Program on Information and Communication Technologies (PICT), sponsored by the UK Economic and Social Research Council. PICT can trace its origins to a growing concern amongst UK policy makers about the role of information activities in economic development. Prior to the establishment of the program, major decisions were having to be made in a wide range of information policy arenas, in the absence of well-grounded research, on the implications for economic and social development of various regulatory regimes. Examples included policy towards international trade in services which are currently under discussion in the GATT round, on regulation of telecommunications being considered in the upcoming review of the telecommunications duopoly in the United Kingdom, and on the regulation of information-intensive industries like the media, proposed in the Broadcasting Bill now before Parliament.

One of the reasons for this knowledge gap was that, in the past, policy makers had placed most emphasis on the 'T' of 'IT' and neglected the role of information generation, capture and transmission or communication in economic growth and change more generally. This neglect was surprising given that the demand for IT derives from a growing demand for information.

There are, however, exceptions to such generalisations about the orientation of public policy debate. One of these is closely associated with the name of Charles Read. Through the Cabinet Office's Information Technology Advisory Panel (ITAP) he played an important role in producing the report *Making a Business of Information* in which many of the intersecting information policy domains and their links with the spread of new information technologies are discussed (ITAP 1983). Amongst other things, that report called for more research on the implications of the use of the advanced information and communications technologies and systems for individuals, for organisations and for economic and social change. This challenge has been taken up by the ESRC through the PICT program.

Unfortunately, there was not a corresponding response from the policy making system; indeed ITAP was wound up soon after its report was published. The regulation of the information sector has remained with a number of separate public and private bodies such as trade associations, OFTEL, IBA and separate divisions of DTI. The public interest questions raised by the interconnections between different policy arenas has no forum within which it can be debated.

A similar overemphasis on technology and neglect of information is apparent at the sub-national scale, particularly in relation to urban and regional development, where a great deal of attention has been paid to the location of information technology production (e.g. Hall & Breheny 1987). The success of high technology corridors like the M4, fortuitously underpinned by state support for research laboratories and defence spending, has led development agencies to seek to create the conditions for high technology production in lagging regions and ailing cities – for example, through the promotion of science parks and, in other countries if not the United Kingdom, the science park's big brother, the technopolis. Current debates on local economic development do consider the greater flexibility that new technology is bringing to the organisation of production in different regions, and the possibility of creating industrial districts based on a new division of labour between small firms (e.g. Scott & Storper 1988). However, attention has tended to focus on the workplace and not on the new flexible geography of multi-site organisations made possible by telematics.

An information economy perspective would suggest that this emphasis fails to come to grips with one of the key dynamics in contemporary economic restructuring. It is as if the fundamental economic development issue in the nineteenth century related to the ability to build steam engines and not to the spread of steam power into a wide range of products and processes and the changes in the systems for organising production that the rapid improvements in communication made possible.

Partly because of a lack of previous research on the information economy, many policy decisions are still being made with little understanding of their spatial implications. For example, few agencies promoting local or regional economic development are aware of, let alone engaged in national debates on the regulation of telecommunications and broadcasting. Cable franchises are being established, but the first time many local policy makers begin to appreciate the possible implications is when the franchise holder requests planning permissions.

National policy debates are often equally blind to spatial issues. OFTEL's formal interest is confined to telephones in rural areas; and although the Broadcasting Bill supports the regional dimension of Channel Three, the connections between broadcasting and regional development received little discussion of substance in the preceding White Paper. And yet the spread of ICT in conjunction with the 'informatisation' of the economy carries with it implications for the location of activities and the development of cities and regions as profound as the spread of railways, roads, electric power, the telephone and newspapers, in relation to the development of the industrial economy.

The essence of the information economy from the geographical perspective can be captured in four interrelated propositions.

The first proposition is that although it has always been an important factor, information is coming to occupy centre stage as the key strategic resource on which the effective delivery of goods and services in all sectors of the world economy is dependent. Far from a transformation from an industrial to a post-industrial economy in which the emphasis is placed on a shift from manufacturing to services, an information economy perspective would suggest that manufacturing and service activities are becoming equally dependent on effective information management. The city is – and always has been – the focus for information processing and exchange functions; as information becomes more important in both production and distribution, so the pivotal role of certain cities is reinforced.

The second proposition is that this economic transformation is being underpinned by a technical transformation in the way in which information can be processed and distributed. The key technical development is the convergence of the information processing capacity of computers (essentially a within the workplace technology) with digital telecommunications (essentially a technology linking workplaces). The resultant technology of telematics is emerging as a key spatial component in the technical infrastructure of the information economy. Because of their historic role, major cities are becoming the nodes or switching centres of this network-based economy.

The third proposition is that the widespread use of information and communications technologies is facilitating the growth of the so-called 'tradeable information sector' in the economy. This transformation embraces traditional information activities like the media and new activities like on-line information services. Moreover, many information activities previously undertaken within firms can now be purchased from external sources at lower cost in the 'information market place' – the growth of the advanced producer service sector can, in part, be accounted for by the externalisation of information functions from manufacturing and other firms. While the use of integrated computers and telecommunications technolgy (ICT) permits an increasing volume of inter-organisation transactions, interpersonal contact is still sufficiently important, particularly in relation to the development of new services and relationships, for the role of cities to be further enhanced.

The final proposition is that the growing informatisation of the economy is making possible the global integration of national and regional economies. As the arena within which this highly competitive process of structural change is worked out widens, so the pattern of winners and losers amongst cities and regions is likely to become more sharply differentiated. Far from eliminating differences between places, the use of information and communications technology can permit the exploitation of differences between areas, for example in terms of local labour market conditions, the nature of cultural facilities and of institutional structures. It is therefore very important to see contemporary changes in a longer-term historical perspective and in the context of the specificities of particular national space economies. Even in the information economy, geography matters!

This last point can be illustrated by the following brief historical and geographical account of the UK urban system from an information economy perspective (Goddard 1989). The account highlights the interconnection between the way the economy has been organised and regulated and the ability to move information over space. It also seeks to make clear that the way communications technologies have been used has been shaped by a wide range of influences prevailing in different periods. The technologies for information communication have therefore created possibilities but not determined the trajectory of development.

Within Britain, the key issue relates to the dominance of London over the rest of the urban system. During the middle years of the nineteenth century, cities such as Newcastle, Birmingham, Manchester, Sheffield and Liverpool emerged to challenge briefly the hegemony of London. They became not only centres of production but foci for information-based activities like finance, legal services, education and the media. Many leading British banks had their origins outside London. Universities were endowed by provincial industrialists to support local research and training needs.

The period from 1890 to 1914, however, saw London reassert its dominance (Robson 1986). London financial institutions were able to find a ready market for the profits of northern industry in the expanding empire. In this process London drew provincial institutions into the city; there was a spate of mergers between banks leading to the emergence of the big five by 1918. The roots of the future decline of provincial cities can thus be traced back to the particular form of British financial capital with its preference for portfolio investment overseas. A further key factor facilitating this centralisation was the emergence of the national railway system which made possible the easy transfer of information in the form of people and the mail: this system radiated from London.

The inter-war period saw further centralisation, this time in the form of the control of industrial companies. The financial crisis of the depression led to a major restructuring of such companies to eliminate excess capacity. National companies like ICI emerged to replace regionally-organised companies, the majority with corporate headquarters in London and production spread around a number of cities. A key feature of the period was the widespread introduction of the telephone into larger companies. This communications innovation, like the railways earlier, assisted the interregional separation of production and administration, a division which had previously only taken place on an interregional basis to the advantage of provincial cities.

Developments in another important part of the information economy, the mass media, further accentuated these tendencies. The establishment of the BBC as a national broadcasting organisation eventually led to the emphasis on national news and views. By 1939 the number of provincial daily newspapers had fallen to thirty, half of which were controlled from London (Robson 1986).

The post-1945 period not only witnessed the continuation of these tendencies towards administrative centralisation, but also saw the emergence for the first time of a strong process of production decentralisation and a resultant net decline in the overall economic base of London and all other major cities. This new process strengthened after the mid-1960s with the spatial scale widening to embrace first the peripheral regions of Britain and then the developing world. In this period of relatively stable products and production technologies, the main emphasis was on the search for economies of scale in manufacturing through the use of capital and space-intensive assembly-line methods using low-cost and less skilled labour than was available in the cities. The consequence of this shift was a widespread de-industrialisation of British cities.

In contrast to manufacturing, very few economies of scale were being reaped in the information or control sector of the economy. While computers were being introduced to assist information processing within office functions, there were few technical innovations in the ability to communicate information between sites – the telephone remained the dominant technology and it merely diffused more widely through the economic system. Because growth in productivity in information activities was so low, the increasing scale of organisation necessitated the employment of more and more coordination staff. And because of the limitations in the essentially paper- and personal-based intra-organisational communications systems, hierarchical structures were required to connect production and distribution sites via intermediate levels to higher decision-making centres; in this process, provincial cities became relays in the intra-organisational information system, housing regional or divisional office functions. It was thus possible to point to the isomorphism between the corporate hierarchy and the urban hierarchy at the national and international scales (Goddard 1978).

Such developments need to be seen in the light of fundamental changes in the regulation of the British economy that emerged in the post-war period, particularly the growing role for the local and national state. Increased state ownership of enterprises in many sectors resulted in a centralisation of headquarters control in London. With the increasing indirect role of the state through public purchasing, through support for research and development, and through grants and loans, private sector companies found it increasingly desirable to transfer their headquarters to London which was the focus for state regulatory activities. The growth of collective wage bargaining through national sector-based unions was a further centralising influence. In the sphere of personal services, local government and health services grew in provincial cities, often administering centrally-determined policies. The hierarchical ordering of national space around provincial cities as administrative centres for the public sphere thus paralleled developments in the private sector.

It is now widely recognised that this mode of industrial organisation and regulation of production and consumption, loosely referred to as 'Fordism', collapsed in the mid-1970s with profound implications for the development of cities in Britain and elsewhere. One way of conceptualising what happened is to view it as a 'crisis of control' in which the scale and rigidities of many organisations had inter alia outgrown the capacity to handle the large volumes of information necessary to maintain effective control (Roobeek 1987). In manufacturing, for example, major problems of structural overcapacity appeared in many sectors with excessive inventories produced by rigid production technologies (the so-called 'hard' automation). Contrary to the needs of the market, these technologies allowed little flexibility in production volumes. Economies of scale needed to be accompanied by economies of scope, but this required new production technology, new forms of organisation and new labour processes. Similarly, the national and international dispersal of production inevitably meant more 'travelling' capital and less contact with the market. Rigid bureaucratic corporate structures were not well placed to respond to the requirements of rapid market change.

Events over the past ten years may be interpreted in terms of a struggle to reassert control through more flexible forms of organisation. ICT has been central to this struggle. As a result of the use of ICT, many of the old hierarchical structures of organisations and the related distribution of functions and management of territory have been subject to challenge. These changes have been intimately related to significant shifts in political and institutional structures, shifts which have given greater emphasis to flexible patterns of employment and a revised role for the state as regulator of the markets rather than the provider of services, including telecommunications and broadcasting. These changes have had profound implications for the management of territory and the urban hierarchy.

I will now introduce some of the research findings which map out some of these contemporary changes in more detail. The research has involved investigations into the geography of three components of the UK information economy (Figure 1). First, the adoption of telematics in organisations in the public and private sector, and in manufacturing and service industries, and the linking of this adoption to the geographical division of task between workplaces within and between organisations, and the territories over which they operate. Second, the study of the spatial development of the UK telecommunications system, focusing on BT itself as a complex organisation with its own interregional relations. And third, a geographical analysis of the development of a tradeable information sector par excellence, the audio-visual production sector. These investigations have involved in-depth studies of individual organisations, survey research, analysis of secondary data and

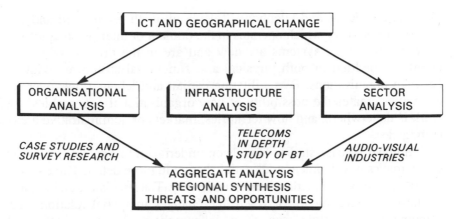

Figure 1 Approaches to analysis of the geography of the information economy.

conceptual work on the relationship between ICT and geographical change. Finally, by synthesising findings geographically, the research has sought to highlight the threats and opportunities for area development in the information economy in a peripheral region like the north-east of England in order to point to the possibilities and limitations for pro-activity on the part of development agencies.

TELEMATICS

The idea of a computer network as a spatial system has been used as a central concept in much of the analysis (Hepworth 1987a) (Figure 2). Figure 2 is an highly simplified map of an intra- and inter-organisational network connecting different workplaces. While the network might make use of the public switched telephone system, it is important to stress the fundamental difference

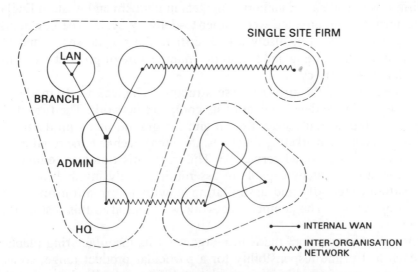

Figure 2 A hypothetical 'networked' organisation.

between telematics and telephony. Telephony is an established and widely diffused technology which operates in the domain of inter-personal communications. Telematic systems are new and are in the process of becoming deeply embedded in both physical and functional structures within and between organisations. By facilitating capital and labour flows over space, telematics creates the possibility of new organisational geographies – what work is done where, and how territories, markets or administrative areas are managed.

A number of case studies have been undertaken to explore the trajectory of telematics development and spatial change in more detail. Three examples can be used to illustrate the changes underway. The first is for an organisation in the manufacturing sector where the changes in spatial relationships are principally intra-national, the second is from the public service sector where the changes are essentially local, and the third from the private service sector where the changes are global.

The first example is a Doncaster-based manufacturer of doors, windows and related components for the building industry, which has used a computer network to assist its adjustment to the changing geography of its markets (Figure 3). In its early development, the firm concentrated on being the least-cost producer in locally defined markets, chiefly for local authority housing. Subsequent expansion involved duplication of production across the whole product range in different areas. The use of ICT at this stage of the firm's development was restricted to finance and cost control functions. The network was therefore used to reinforce a strategic objective of being least-cost producer.

Over a period of three years from 1979, the company's locally differentiated markets collapsed; the firm was left with an organisation suited to securing its growth in market conditions that no longer prevailed. The orientation of the firm was towards local authority markets in northern and western England and to manufacture on a ten-week order-to-delivery cycle. The new market conditions manifested themselves in a shift to the private sector and DIY markets in south-east England and to the manufacture of product on a three-day order-to-delivery cycle.

The response of the firm to these structural changes in its market are interwoven with the development of its computer network. The firm had to bring about the spatial reorganisation and integration of its production, as well as its sales and marketing functions, in order to achieve the requirements of a three-day order-to-delivery cycle. This reorganisation was centred on a new information strategy capable of assembling, analysing and integrating information externally and assimilating it with information on its own internal operations. The computer network was central to this restructuring of the firm.

In terms of production, the firm reorganised its manufacturing plants so that each had prime responsibility for a particular product range, so as to achieve economies of scale in production. Product specialisation rather than

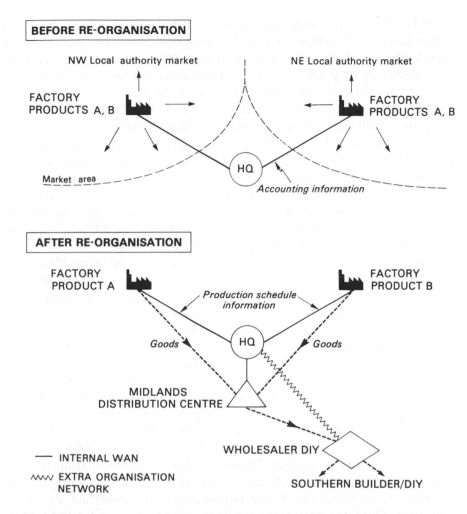

Figure 3 Networked-based reorganisation of a manufacturing firm.

diversification at the individual plant level has now become the norm. Each branch plant despatches output to central warehouses which are responsible for deliveries to the market. The sales function was also centralised and its geographical focus reorientated towards the market in south-east England.

The integration of these spatially fragmented functions of manufacturing, distribution and sales is now managed through the computer network. New relationships have been established whereby the activities of the company are determined by the actual uptake of product in the market. The company has also sought to align its sales activities with several of the large merchant chains through the development of inter-corporate networking. In so doing, it has attempted to use its computer network to exert greater influence on the market and to secure for itself the distribution of product into new geographically defined markets.

Finally, the spatial restructuring of the company has occurred within its existing locations. Through the use of information flows over the computer network, the firm has managed to assert its territorial claims to markets in the south-east of England without new investment in this high-cost area. In short, the development of computer networking has allowed the spatial reorganisation of the company and ensured the integration of different functions, as well as facilitating its entry into new markets.

The second example is a county library service in north-east England (Figure 4). The council has introduced a network-based circulation and control system into its multi-site library service to integrate the details of stock holding against issues, receipts, reservations, overdues, catalogue searches, and the production of statistical information (for example, the recovery rate of overdue books and the success rate for different kinds of reservation, not only for each library, but for the service as a whole).

These systems had been manually-based, contained within each library and committed significant labour resources to back-office activities. A network solution to circulation control has allowed the library service to remain geo-graphically dispersed yet to be integrated around an 'information axis'. This development in the circulation control system is facilitating change in a number of ways. First, it is enabling local book stocks to be tailored to local customer requirements, allowing spatial differentiation rather than duplica-tion in the book stock. Considerable differences in consumer preferences occur in different locations, and information flows are permitting these to be both formally identified and subsequently better matched to local book stocks. As a result, the number of duplicate books has been reduced and the savings made are being spent on extending the range of books available. Second, issue analysis permits 'product range' experimentation through mixing normally separately classified books, thereby increasing overall consumption. In effect the system is facilitating an intensified use of the book stock. Third, the technology is also permitting more rapid and reliable book circulation from within existing stock, further reducing the number of

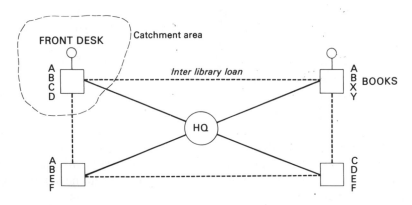

Figure 4 Network structure for a county library service.

duplicate copies of a book and thereby releasing funds to widen the overall stock. Fourth, the total collection is made available via the computer network to all users regardless of the location. The stock can then be conceptualised as 'virtual', permitting access regardless of the physical locations of the books and of the uses. Fifth, the emerging 'new library service' is being further enhanced by the release of staff from the back-office into the front-office, where broader advisory and information functions are central. In short, the adoption of a network solution to the delivery of library services has permitted new spatial structures to evolve which are increasingly sensitive to the differentiated needs of local communities yet do not deny the user the advantages of a large integrated collection because of their location.

The third example is based in the City of London. The company started life as a specialist publisher of financial magazines. Information was gathered through personal contacts and paper records and edited in the City. Magazines were printed in the United Kingdom and sold principally to City institutions. After 'Black Monday' the company's sales plummeted. However, it was able to refinance itself to provide electronic database services (Figure 5). The core data are provided by the annual electoral registers which are collected from all local authorities in Britain. The registers are key-punched in India and the data shipped to a computer bureau in one of the desert states of the United States. The files are then accessed from London by a satellite link. Information is therefore gathered in different localities within Britain, a major labour input is provided in another continent and a major capital item in the production process, in the form of the mainframe computer, is located in a third continent.

To the basic data of around twenty-five million records is added further information from localities in the United Kingdom, such as house prices, and from a range of institutions located in London – for example, share holdings and probate information from Somerset House. Access to the data is often gained through the personal contacts created through City networks. Information on individual consumer behaviour and lifestyles obtained from regular market research surveys are is added to the database.

The company's clients are national and international businesses seeking to identify and size market segments for different goods and services, often

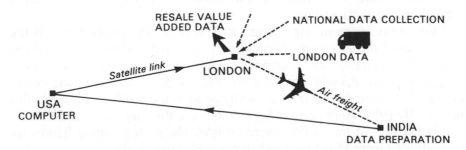

Figure 5 Network structure for an information services business.

for direct marketing purposes. Geography has little meaning for this type of target marketing. In marketing terms there may be more communality between, for example, Jesmond in Newcastle and Camden Town in London than between Jesmond and Wallsend or Camden and Hackney. There may also be greater affinities between Camden Town and the seventh arrondissement in Paris, and in pursuit of such opportunities, the company is now actively exploring database construction in several European countries by establishing subsidiary operations.

From these examples it is clear that telematics can be used as a major weapon in supporting organisational and geographical change and in deriving competitive advantage. It has been closely involved in a new relationship between information flows and physical flows – 'wires' and 'wheels' are obviously related technologies. However, in other organisations, networks have been 'ring-fenced' in accounting and financial control activities and have so far not been used as a basis for reconceptualising the organisation and its relation to the outside world. In order to assess the extent and significance of telematics penetration and use, 25 per cent of the organisations headquartered in four BT districts – the City of London, East Anglia, Manchester and north-east England – representing areas in the core, industrial heartland and periphery of the UK economy, have been surveyed. Six hundred organisations or 40 per cent of the total approached responded. The survey has been used to identify the trajectory of telematics development since 1983 and, when linked to other data on the companies, to explore the association between network use and economic performance in different regions.

The survey revealed an accelerating rate of network adoption, especially after 1985 (Table 1). In 1989, 40 per cent of all organisations were networked, half of whom had installed the network after 1985. It also revealed increasing numbers of users of the network as telematics penetrated deeper into organisations; thus in 1989, 24 per cent of organisations had over 100 users, compared with only 5 per cent in 1982; functions like purchasing, production, marketing and distribution are increasingly using telematics. A higher proportion of these users are also on-line, which is a further indication of integration into organisational processes. Indeed, in 1982 over 50 per cent of networked organisations had no on-line transactions compared with only 8 per cent in 1989. Now nearly one-third of organisations have 100 per cent of their network transactions on-line.

While there were no significant differences (between areas) in the proportions of the surveyed organisations possessing a network, the contrast in network penetration within organisations between, for example, the north-east and the City of London is stark. In 1982, 18 per cent of organisations in the City had more than 100 users, while none in the north-east reached this number. By 1989, 40 per cent of organisations in the City had over 100 users and 41 per cent of transactions were on-line. The corresponding figures for the north-east were 15 per cent and 16 per cent respectively.

Table 1 Computer networks and United Kingdom Organisations

Users of computer networks within organisations

	% of organisations with <10 users		% of organisations with >100 users	
	United Kingdom	City of London	United Kingdom	City of London
1982	69.4	59.2	5.9	11.2
1985	50.0	46.4	11.6	17.9
1989	23.6	15.4	28.1	40.3

Volume of on-line transactions

	% of organisations with <25% of transactions on-line	% of organisations with all transactions on-line
1982	68.9	13.1
1985	42.6	17.8
1989	15.6	28.3

Source: CURDS Computer Networks Organisations Survey, 1989

By comparing firms who have adopted networking with those that have not and linking this to data on employment, turnover and profitability growth, it is possible to examine the association between the presence of telematics and organisational performance (Table 2). The contrasts are significant – for example, a 20 per cent difference in average employment growth and an 11 per cent difference in profitability growth between networked and non-networked firms. While these differences were apparent in all regions, they are most pronounced in the north-east followed by the City of London. In the case of the north-east, this would suggest the use of telematics to compensate for problems of peripherality, whilst in the City of London telematics would appear to be an essential component in product innovation in the highly turbulent financial services market.

Not surprisingly the survey revealed that the size of organisation was a major factor accounting for the adoption or non-adoption of telematics (although this does not fully explain the differences between organisations and regions). In general it is the largest companies that have adopted telematics, chiefly for intra-corporate transactions. Another survey, of 2000 workplaces – the Workplace Industrial Relations Survey (WIRS) – undertaken by the Department of Employment in 1984, revealed that at that time only 5 per cent of single-site establishments in Britain had a network link compared

Table 2 Computer networks and company performance 1985–87

	North-east	North-west	East Anglia	City
Average employment change (%)				
Networked	36.3	19.5	15.4	23.7
Non-networked	9.1	0.1	4.6	-4.6
Average growth in turnover (%)				
Networked	73.5	42.9	48.9	104.4
Non-networked	27.6	18.9	25.6	3.8
Average growth in profitability (%)				
Networked	17.5	4.1	9.1	11.9
Non-networked	0.7	0.6	1.4	-3.4

Source: CURDS Computer Networks Organisations Survey, 1989

with an average for all establishments of 26 per cent (W.W. Daniels 1987) (Table 3). The highest incidence of links to other organisations recorded in WIRS was fourteen per cent in the case of large head offices of multi-site organisations. In comparison, 39 per cent of large administrative or back offices had a network link internal to the organisation. Given the concentration of head offices in London, it is not surprising to find in the WIRS survey that London is the hub of computer networking in the United Kingdom, with 30 per cent of firms there having a network link compared to 20 per cent in the northern region.

Table 3 Organisational structure and computer networking
by type of establishment (% with networks)

	Manufacturing	Services
Single site	4.3	5.9
Head office	15.9	37.8
Administration office	65.7	37.1
Other*	29.5	28.6

* e.g. shop, office, factory
Source: WIRS, 1984

These figures suggest that the United Kingdom has a long way to progress towards a 'networked economy' in which transactions between firms, particularly between large firms and small firms and between small firms themselves, are mediated by electronic means. Far from facilitating a new division of labour between firms as a basis for economic development within the peripheral regions, the analysis of WIRS suggests that telematics are being used to reinforce a long-established interregional and intra-corporate division between relatively low-level production tasks in the north and control tasks in the south. Whilst an increasing division of functions between small firms is emerging, especially in the south where there is a stronger entrepreneurial tradition, the overall low incidence of networking in single-site firms suggests that this division is underpinned by traditional means of communications not telematics.

Some confirmation of these suggestions can be found by relating technical change in WIRS manufacturing establishments to the skills profile of their workforce and the characteristics of the local labour market. Such an analysis reveals that local labour markets in the peripheral regions which have a poorly qualified population, are characterised by large factories employing relatively unskilled workers. Advanced technical change in production is not common but computer linkage to other parts of the organisation is. In stark contrast, rapidly growing labour markets in the outer south-east and East Anglia are characterised by small establishments with a high skill intensity, high rates of advanced technical change but a low incidence of computer networking.

Further support for this suggestion comes from a recent survey of the use of telecommunications infrastructures by a matched sample of manufacturing establishments in the north-east, the north-west, the west Midlands and the south-east regions, undertaken for the Department of Trade and Industry by Diamond and Spence (1989). This revealed that expenditure on transport and communication as a percentage of total operating costs is highest in the south-east followed by the north-east (7.5 per cent and 7.1 per cent respectively). Breaking these figures down revealed significantly higher absolute expenditures on all forms of information transaction (business cars, air and passenger costs, and telecommunications) in the south-east. These figures are indicative of a much more transaction-intensive economy in the south-east region.

The growth of the information economy and interregional differences in its scale are clearly reflected in the aggregate distribution of occupations whose primary function involves the processing and exchange of information (Porat 1977) (Table 4). Applying a classification scheme developed by OECD to occupational data from the Labour Force Survey, suggests that in 1984 47 per cent of the total employment in Britain was in information occupations. This compares with 40 per cent in 1975.

In the south in 1984, this figure rises to 53 per cent whilst in the peripheral regions it is only 42 per cent. Through the teeth of the 1979-83 recession, the south gained 800 000 information jobs while other regions recorded net losses as traditional industries shed both production and information labour. Part of the explanation for these figures is the south's large share of employment in

**Table 4 The distribution of information labour 1975–1984
(information workers as a percentage of employment by region)**

	1975	1979	1984
South South-east, south-west, East Anglia	43.1	44.2	52.4
Heartland West Midlands, east Midlands, Yorkshire and Humberside, North-east	41.8	43.9	44.9
Periphery North, Scotland, Wales, Northern Ireland	34.4	38.1	41.6
United Kingdom	40.1	42.6	47.1

Source: Labour Force Surveys

what OECD calls the 'primary information sector' information-based services and IT production – in which information occupations accounted for 78 per cent of employment in 1984. Nevertheless, over one-third of all employment in non-information goods and services sectors can also be classified as informational. The important point here is that while information activities are concentrating and growing rapidly in the south, they are significant everywhere in the UK economy.

Details on the expansion of information occupations beyond 1984 are not available. However, analysis of the growth of employment in the information-intensive financial and business services sector reveals that London has gained 273 000 jobs in this industry since 1983, a 41 per cent increase in six years. The sector now accounts for one-quarter of London's jobs. While financial and business services have grown outside London, the position of the capital is still dominant with many of the provincial centres increasing their share of this sector at the expense of smaller centres within each region. Growth rates have also been higher in office centres in the south-east outside London, reflecting the relocation of information-intensive back-office functions. According to surveyors Jones Lang Wooton, few relocations have been beyond the south-east – of the 115 moves recorded by the company between 1979 and 1986, 78 per cent were confined to the south-east. Analyses of the trade-off for individual organisations considering relocation between rent and salary savings, and the additional communication costs arising from a non-London location, suggests that the communications damage can outweigh the other savings for moves beyond the Midlands (Goddard & Pye 1977). The exception is provided by telematics-based activities like BT's London directory enquiry service, parts of which have been successfully located to the north-east.

To summarise these findings, it is clear that there is a very uneven geography of information capital and information labour within the British economy. The supply and demand for information services is growing most rapidly in London and the south-east. Elsewhere it is concentrated in major provincial office centres. Nevertheless, it is clear that important opportunities exist for enterprises throughout the northern regions, and not just in the major centres, to use telematics to gain competitive advantage and restructure their activities. Public services within the region can also become more efficient through the use of telematics. The information economy is therefore not just a phenomena of London and the south-east.

Telecommunications infrastructure

What does this very uneven demand for telematic services, the most profitable, most rapidly growing and most competitive segment of the telecommunications market, mean for the development of the telecommunications infrastructure within the United Kingdom (Goddard & Gillespie 1986)? This question has been addressed through an in-depth study of the evolution of BT from a public sector monopoly provider to a telecommunications business. In this study we have focussed on the changing centre-periphery or field-function relationships within the company. The study has been set in the context of the evolving regulatory environment, including early attempts by development agencies in the north to promote telecommunications as part of the necessary, if not sufficient, conditions for regional economic development. There are some extremely complex issues here which cannot be treated fully in the space available, so what follows is an over-simplification and in the process some important points may be glossed over.

BT is charged with providing plain old telephony (POTS) throughout the United Kingdom on a uniform basis. It is evolving from a supply-led and territorial-based public service organisation towards a market-driven business seeking to address competition in various market segments. In relation to voice services, this competitive environment nationally can be conceptualised in terms of a number of layers – POTS, cellular services (mobile telephony), telepoint and the personal communication network (PCN) (Figure 6). Competition is structured horizontally in each layer by the presence of two or more providers and vertically by customer pressures – for example, telepoint users of the public switched telephone network. Further competition in the local loop may come from cable operators. However, this so-called 'national model' only applies in London, the majority of the south-east and major provincial centres. Only in London are all services universally available. As one moves North availability of service within each region decreases as does the extent of competition within and between layers (Figure 7). There are

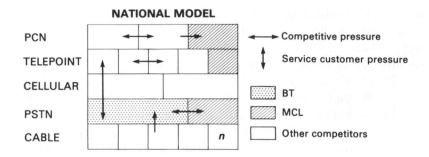

Figure 6 National model for telecommunications regulation.

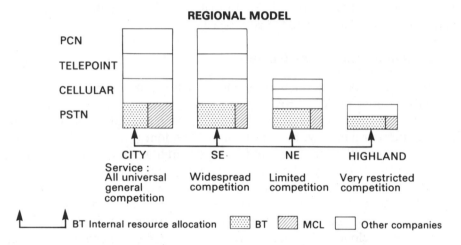

Figure 7 Regional model for actual telecommunications regulation.

also intra-regional differences between city centres and the surrounding areas where important parts of the UK manufacturing industry is located but where competition is limited. Similar and more stark contrasts could be drawn for telematic services.

The national competitive model assumes that the principal regulatory forces are the vertical and lateral competitive pressures mediated where appropriate by OFTEL. In addition there are pressures from industry lobbies like the Telecommunication Managers Association (TMA) representing the largest users generally based in London and the south-east. User pressures in the regions are, however, weaker – for example, in the whole north-east district there are only ninety business users with more than twenty BT lines out of a total of 100 000 customers.

Residential telephony is therefore the primary market. In Scotland, the Telecommunications Advisory Committee established by OFTEL is, by their own admission, not well known 'with many customers unaware of its functions'. Agencies like the Scottish Development Agency have been largely passive on telecommunications issues compared with road, rail and air transport.

As the omnipresent public service supplier, BT faces considerable tensions between its territorial inheritance and responsibility and the needs to respond to market opportunities and competitive pressures in its most rapidly growing market segments and geographical areas. A major part of its initial restructuring towards a more market-orientated philosophy was to break the power of the regional divisions through a policy of districtisation and functional division. This strategy had some unexpected consequences, partly because of the different labour market situations the company was facing in different parts of the country. The research suggests that the north-east district, which was experiencing only a small increase in demand, was able to retain many of its staff and, in comparison with the labour turnover faced in the south-east, was able to press ahead rapidly with network modernisation. In London, however, the break-up of the old London Telecommunication Region into a number of districts, coupled with staff losses and escalating demand, created severe problems for the strategic planning of the network.

These shortcomings have now been addressed and resources are being switched to where the growth in demand and competitive pressures are greatest. In the periphery, advanced services are being provided only where demand is justified; in smaller centres where there are too few users to bundle together to justify the supply of a facility like Kilostream, the service is not being provided. Nevertheless, in areas like the Highlands where BT faces no real competitive pressures, it is acting as a public service agent in concert with the Highlands and Islands Development Board in providing advanced facilities in key locations ahead of obvious demand.

This brief discussion should serve to illustrate that regulation must be seen in the context of the uneven pattern of demand and the important role that telecommunications can play in regional economic development. The present pattern of competition is extremely complex within and between regions. In southern areas, competition may bring benefits; in others, monopoly provision may be necessary to meet the desired economic development objectives. Nevertheless, it should be clear that national regulation of telecommunications in effect means regulation for London and the south-east; the costs and benefits arising in the rest of the United Kingdom is largely incidental and unplanned. The similarity with current inflationary pressures in the UK economy, which have been driven by house price rises in the south-east and leading to high interest rates which severely affect investment in northern manufacturing, cannot have escaped attention.

Broadcasting

This review of the geography of the information economy in Britain concludes with a brief reference to the audiovisual industries. What follows is a simple description of the regional structure of the industry and some of the factors shaping its spatial development. It highlights a possible widespread ignorance or perhaps lack of interest in the regions in a part of the information economy which has been dominated by London opinion, taste and fashion.

The industry centres on the traditional broadcasting companies but includes feature films, production distribution and exhibition, independent television production, the corporate video business, computer graphics, interactive video and post-production facilities. It is an important sector of the British economy and is playing an increasing role in regional development in terms of direct employment and as a provider of specialist services to other sectors. Less directly, as part of the cultural industries, the audiovisual sector is contributing to changing the image, identity and morale of older industrial regions. This sector is also strategically placed in relation to the convergent markets and technologies of broadcasting and telecommunications.

Most data sources indicate the absolute dominance of London as the centre of activity in the sector. The BBC has been hierarchically ordered and vertically integrated with headquarters in London and national production centres in Birmingham, Bristol and Manchester, centres in Scotland, Wales and Northern Ireland, and seven regional production sites. However, over 70 per cent of employment is in London and over 70 per cent of network programming is produced there. The Corporation is now entering a period of cost cutting through contracting out various functions, freezing recruitment in selected areas and moving staff away from the high-cost south-east, partially merging BBC north-east and BBC north-west with a combined headquarters in Manchester. This will eradicate a layer of middle management, and result in fewer regional opt-out programs shown in fewer but larger combined regions.

ITV is organised as a regional/federal group of companies divided into three sets. The five major companies, based in London, Manchester, Birmingham and Leeds, dominate production for the network with 35 per cent of program output compared with 12 per cent for the ten regional companies. The majors account for 60 per cent of net advertising revenues and 50 per cent of employment. Extensive reorganisation is in train involving externalisation of functions, the institution of new working practices and a program of corporate diversification. This process is increasing demand for audiovisual services in a limited number of cities.

Channel Four was founded in 1982 as a publishing house making no programs for itself but rather commissioning programs from the ITV companies and independent producers. Its establishment has encouraged the development of a growing sector of independent production companies, associated service facilities and a freelance labour market. The 1987 quota for independent production for the BBC and ITV with a target of 25 per cent independent production by 1992 has further boosted the sector. However, two-thirds of independent production is based in London and the south-east. The pattern which is emerging in the independent sector is one of a few large companies, which are awarded the lion's share of commissions and a fringe of small companies producing a few programs a year.

Cable and direct broadcasting by satellite represents an alternative means of distributing television programs. Prospects for broadband cable television in Britain are perhaps better now than at any time in the past, particularly within the higher density and concentrated industrial cities. The saturation of the US market combined with the removal of barriers to US investment in UK cable, and the possibility of combining telecommunications and television, has created the possibility of rapid expansion. Cable provides an obvious system for distributing satellite programs. Competition for cable franchises in northern industrial cities has been strong and promises to strengthen the audiovisual sector outside of London.

These various components of the audiovisual sector, together with corporate video and film production distribution and exhibition, comprise a highly integrated sector of the information economy at global, national and local scales. Technological and regulatory change are breaking down the old vertically integrated and hierarchically structured organisations and increasing the degree of interdependence between firms. But, as with telecommunications, the local interrelatedness is not always recognised in national regulatory policy. However, the significance of the audiovisual sector at the local scale is increasingly being recognised in a range of urban and regional initiatives. The sector in Tyneside is an example. At a conservative estimate, it has a total turnover of 80 to 100 million pounds and a direct and indirect employment of between 1500 and 2000 jobs. In addition to Tyne Tees Television and the BBC, there are fifty independent production companies and corporate video producers. Comment Cablevision, a joint venture with US West, has established its headquarters in Tyneside. There is a range of studio and training facilities and a network of economic and particularly social linkages, the latter reflected in the formation of a Northern Media Forum. The presence of such a range of activities has initiated a search for a local economic development strategy to promote the growth of the sector in Tyneside. Schemes under discussion or in progress include bidding for the headquarters of Channel Five, publishing a guide to audiovisual production for potential purchasers of services, establishing a film office to promote the area for film production and a Northern Film Investment Fund as an offshoot of British Screen, which is promoted by the Department of Trade and Industry. Other developments include the promotion of an international film festival, local programming on the cable network, the provision of training facilities and the establishment of a media centre in the Urban Development Corporation's 'flagship' Quayside project.

However, the scope for local action may be limited given that many major public and private decisions affecting the area will be made outside. Tyne Tees Television may lose the Channel Three franchise which may go to a non-local company; this may subsequently be acquired by a European media business. BBC TV has already downgraded the functions of its Newcastle studios as part of its cost-cutting exercise, and Comment Cable may move its headquarters to Manchester if it wins that franchise. Local independent companies may also be acquired by London organisations.

CONCLUSION

A number of conclusions emerge from the analysis that has been presented. First, far from eliminating the importance of geography, the so-called 'space-transcending' ICTs, when taken together with other factors, are supporting a more uneven pattern of regional development within the United Kingdom. Information occupations and industries have grown dramatically in London and the south-east in the past ten years, reflecting the capital's international as well as national role. This growth has been underpinned by the rapid diffusion of computer networks; these networks are hubbed on London, serving to reinforce its dominant position in the national and international urban system.

Second, there is only limited evidence so far of ICTs contributing to more flexible ways of organising the production of goods and the delivery of services in the way that could benefit smaller enterprises and indigenous development in declining regions. Computer networks are still used primarily for intra-organisational transactions and as a means of reasserting control over organisational processes; very few small firms are networked. However, there are examples of organisations which are using ICTs to create competitive advantage, reconfigure their corporate geography and change the way in which they manage territory. Clearly ICTs have the potential for radically changing the face of Britain rather than simply reinforcing the old order.

Third, the intersection between sectoral and geographical considerations in relation to the development of the UK information economy is poorly articulated in the regulation of information industries or in public policy more generally. At the national level, the implications of the privatisation of BT in relation to its capacity to respond to the changing geography of demand, and the fact that it is a complex territorially structured organisation not a 'black-box', have yet to be fully assimilated. Similarly, whilst the role of broadcasting in regional development is acknowledged, the mechanisms are only dimly perceived by policy makers. At the national and local level, there is little evidence of, but an urgent need for, coherent planning for the information economy which integrates training, infrastructure provision, technology demand, simulation measures, etc., not only as a means of achieving more balanced regional development but in order to ensure that the United Kingdom reaps the benefits of becoming a network-based economy.

Finally, the spread of telematics and the associated emergence of more geographically flexible and market-responsive organisations raises important questions concerning methods of regulating the economy in a way which balances public and private interest. The old hierarchical order of national, regional and local governance and of sectoral and regional policy, has been irrevocably challenged. There are dangers of global integration proceeding hand in hand with regional and local disintegration, of islands of economic growth in the networked economy and economic decline of the network. These dangers may now need to be countered by a new era of re-regulation.

This will require new skills in public administration and the drawing together of knowledge from a variety of sources. Better information flows between central and local government, between different departments of state, and between the public and private sectors, often in a European context, will be increasingly necessary if even sharper regional disparities in the information economy are to be considered. Regional policies for the information economy will certainly be different from those for the industrial economy or the enterprise economy.

ACKNOWLEDGMENTS

The paper is based on research undertaken in the Centre for Urban and Regional Development Studies at the University of Newcastle-upon-Tyne as part of the ESRC PICT Program. The contributions of Andrew Gillespie, Mark Hepworth, Kevin Robins, John Taylor and Howard Williams, together with James Cornford, Ken Ducatel, Irene Hardill, Steve Johnson and Pooran Wynarczyk are gratefully acknowledged. Any errors of fact or interpretation are of course the author's.

14

TECHNOLOGY, INTERNATIONALISATION OF SERVICES AND METROPOLITAN AREAS

Peter Daniels

INTRODUCTION

During the last decade, the service sector has undergone substantial restructuring. This has generated a fundamental re-evaluation of its contribution to the development of metropolitan economies and the international urban system. Service industries have become a catalyst for change rather than simply a parasite. Basic services that make a direct contribution to income and job generation are the key players; the producer services whose output is used in the production of a final good or service (purchased by business and industry) (Greenfield 1966; Marshall *et al*. 1988). The development trajectories of these services and, in particular, the choices which they make about where to locate their establishments is vital to the economic welfare of metropolitan areas. Producer services have expanded most rapidly in large, diversified metropolitan areas where manufacturing industry comprises a diminishing share of all employment (Noyelle & Stanback 1984; Beyers 1989). Such cities are interwoven with other major metropolitan areas at national and international level, by a web of excellent communications (air, road and telecommunications).

The highly selective locations decision making by producer services is significant for metropolitan economies for a number of reasons. Firstly, it creates significant demand for supporting infrastructure such as office floor space, telecommunications services, international air services, and facilities for private and public transport. Secondly, it has a significant impact on the structure of labour demand, notably a requirement for white collar, highly educated/skilled/professional/specialised labour as well as less skilled support staff (often part-time, female) (see, for example, Christopherson 1989). Thirdly, it creates a need for other specialised services. This is part of a more general multiplier effect on retail services, housing and entertainment.

There is evidence that certain metropolitan areas, such as Vancouver, are already devising economic policy initiatives to maintain and, preferably, to enhance the contribution of the service sector. Others, observing what has already happened in other cities, are anxious to move out of economic crisis by simulating the service sector rather than 'traditional' revitalisation of the manufacturing base (Daniels 1989). UNCTAD (1989) has highlighted the national strategic role of services but there is no reason why the case should not apply equally to metropolitan areas. Infrastructural services, particularly communications technology is one of the key strategic factors identified. It is important for the efficient function of service industries, for metropolitan economic development and for the international competitiveness of firms.

This chapter begins with an overview of some of the processes responsible for the internationalisation of services. This is followed by some comments on the relationship between technology and services. An exploration of the link between internationalisation and technology and its significance for metropolitan development comprises a concluding section. It is suggested that although technology, especially information technology, is responsible for discriminating between the actual and potential contribution of services to metropolitan development, there are so many other factors at work that the contribution of technology should not be overstated.

INTERNATIONALISATION OF SERVICES

Internationalisation is both a process and a strategy. Trans-border flows of business travellers, foreign currency transactions, electronic information and data exchange involved in service, manufacturing and government transactions have underpinned the extension of corporate activities into international markets. Domestic regulations restricting services trade and the growing acceptance of, and rise in, international lending have promoted strategic expansion of multinational enterprises (MNEs) and their service affiliates. Traded services such as accounting, advertising, insurance or engineering consultancies have therefore engaged in merger/takeovers or organic growth to deliver services 'tailored' to markets outside the national context.

Deployment of internationalisation as a strategy is strongest amongst business services (Kromenacher 1984; Nusbaumer 1987) trading in information that is particularly amenable to the use of telecommunications and related technology. Such trade takes place both between and within firms (Markusen 1986; Enderwick 1989). Schwamm and Merciai (1985) enumerate five ways in which services can be provided internationally:

1 exchange of data, images or people between countries;
2 granting licensing contracts to suppliers in overseas markets;
3 consumers can travel to another country to purchase/benefit from, a service;
4 service producers travel to another country;
5 sale of services through a foreign affiliate.

Whichever approach is used (and more than one may be employed by the same organisation) it is evident that while a manufacturer can export a product without necessarily being directly represented in the purchasing country, this is not the case with services. Most white-collar services are intangible (and are not consumed on a once-and-for-all basis at a point in time) and cannot be effectively supplied without the physical presence of the producer or an agent/ representative. In addition, legislative and regulatory environments in individual countries often discourage or prevent cross-border transactions which can only be circumvented by direct representation. Finally, successful marketing of a service often requires adequate proximity to prospective and existing clients if a supplier is to command an increasing share of a market. Localisation has therefore become a crucial part of the globalisation strategy of many large corporations.

Edvinsson and Edvardsson (1989) show that the internationalisation of knowledge-intensive service companies requires considerable reorientation, refocusing and 'jumps' in corporate perceptions. They suggest a new paradigm for internationalisation (Table 1) which recognises some fundamental differences between the relevant foci for manufacturing and for service corporations. Indeed, empirical evidence collected from seven Swedish

Table 1 A new paradigm for internationalisation of knowledge-intensive services

New focus	Traditional focus
Infrastructure	Infrastructure
Information and skill	Raw material/products
Shrinking the world/global	Export
Social innovations	Technological innovation
Information technology	Production technology
Softronics	Economics
Evolving marketing/spiral	Distribution and sales
Leverage/scaling up	After sales service
Customer integration	Manufacturing integration
Mental management	Activity management
Creativity mix	Marketing mix
Unbundling	Standardisation
Networking/twinning/alliance	Subsidiaries
Infopreneurs	Product managers/producer
Thoughtware/know-how value adding	Production
Value added	Margin
Time	Assets
Lateral	Vertical
Globalisation	Export

Source: Edvinsson and Edvardsson (1989, Fig. 1, p. 6).

service companies suggests that internationalisation can be divided into four phases (all corporations need not go through all these stages in chronological order). These might be useful for the purpose of analysing the dynamic of the internationalisation process.

The four phases are: the prospecting phase (open searching and learning strategy); the introduction phase (organisation arranges its activities in a more systematic/goal-oriented manner); the establishment phase (establishes position in market and becomes more effective); and the further development phase (company adjusts itself to the different conditions for each market, local position consolidated by networking development through alliances or joint ventures). Therefore, in the early stages of internationalisation companies need a perceptive and flexible organisational format; in the later stages local adjustment to each market is crucial. It is at this stage that flexible specialisation using networking for marketing and delivery of services is the key to success. Telecommunications would therefore seem to be important during the later phases of internationalisation rather than during the early stages.

World trade in services

The growth of world trade since 1945 has been accompanied by much greater global economic interdependence. It has been substantively reinforced in recent years by a widespread relaxation of the constraints on capital flows, deregulation of various national exchanges and the dramatic developments in communications, computers and electronics that have created a global market for financial and other advanced services (Sauvant, 1987; US Government 1983; OECD 1983; 1984). It has been estimated, using IMF statistics, that global service exports in 1984 accounted for some 20 per cent of world trade valued at 375 billion dollars (UNCTAD 1989). The United Kingdom (29 billion dollars) ranked third behind the United States (45 billion dollars) and France (39 billion dollars) as the leading exporter of services, followed by West Germany, Japan and Italy. The pattern of trade in services is partly explicable in terms of national comparative advantage (Sapir 1982; Richardson 1987) although for intra-firm trade, micro-economic or locational priorities may be more important (Harrington 1989).

It remains extremely difficult, however, to measure the share of business services in national exports; one US study quoted by Noyelle and Dutka (1987) estimates foreign revenue from business services at 25 per cent with about half coming from the sales of advertising, management consultancy, accountancy and legal services. Only some 10.4 per cent of Canadian Current Account receipts in 1984 were contributed by services (Seigel 1987) largely composed of trade with the US. An improvement may follow ratification of the US–Canada Free Trade Agreement in 1988 (effective from 1 January 1989). The agreement, the first to include comprehensive treatment of services between the world's two largest trading partners, will ensure that each side will provide treatment to each other's citizens that is no less favourable than that granted to its own with respect to all new measures affecting services (Harrington 1989). Financial institutions in each country will be able to compete with each other, there will be fewer restrictions on cross-border investments and steps will be taken to develop an open and competitive telecommunication and computer services market.

The United States hopes that ratification of this agreement will lend more weight to its efforts to obtain worldwide liberalisation of trade in services. Such trade is not included in the General Agreement on Tariffs and Trade (GATT) (Richardson 1988; Schott 1989). International provision of services is a dynamic process involving both trade (even though services are often thought of as untradeable) and foreign direct investment (FDI) (Noyelle 1987). Air transport, shipping and related travel are predominantly trade-oriented, while producer services such as banking, other financial services, professional services and telecommunications are largely oriented towards FDI as the preferred method of international provision. The latter is encouraged by the tight domestic regulation of many services which have important social and political roles in national economies. Thus, the services' share of FDI out-flows from the United Kingdom rose from 41 per cent in 1970–71 to 49 per cent in 1971–80, and in Japan from 20 per cent in 1975 to 67 per cent in 1984 (United Nations 1983). Producer services' contribution to foreign FDI is not easy to quantify but seems to range between 25 and 50 per cent (OECD 1981b).

The growth of MNEs has also encouraged international trade. These have developed to overcome international transaction costs (the legal and other impediments in the way of individuals and corporations crossing frontiers to provide services) (Rugman 1981; Caves 1982). The structure of an MNE permits control of overseas subsidiaries which produce and distribute a service which it owns while still retaining ownership of any proprietary information (Dunning & Norman 1987). Successful MNEs have an organisational structure that permits quick adoption to changes in consumer requirements or the identification and occupation of market niches; economies of scope are much more important than economies of scale.

It is likely that the majority of international trade in services is currently conducted by MNEs (Stern 1985; Markusen 1989) or transnational corpora-tions (TNCs) (Clairmonte & Cavanagh 1984). TNCs can be further subdivided into transnational service conglomerates (TSCs) that operate in two or more service sectors and transnational integral conglomerates (TICs) which cover industrial and service sectors (e.g. Lonrho plc). During the last decade a number of major firms in accountancy and advertising, for example, have become TSCs through merger or takeover of overseas firms or through the establishment of agency or representative offices at offshore locations (see, for example, Leyshon *et al.* 1987a). Control of these conglomerates remains highly centralised with respect to administration, finance or corporate planning but is combined with a decentralised system of service distribution to clients throughout the world. Telecommunications are clearly vital for sustaining such networks, ensuring effective two-way exchanges of information relating to many aspects of conglomerate business activity (Feketekuty 1985). TICs are, in many respects, even more significant than the TSCs and their predecessors, the manufacturing conglomerates. They permit vertical integration in the production process: from design through to assembly of a product, to marketing and promotion for sale to a consumer or client. As a result the 'internationalisation of services is being prodigiously speeded up' (Clairmonte & Cavanagh 1984, p. 217).

SIGNIFICANCE OF TECHNOLOGY

The information technology industry is itself becoming more international through cross-border joint ventures, minority stakes in companies with strong local market positions or cooperative research and development projects. Again, the sudden globalisation of world markets has provided the trigger (Noyelle 1986). In the public switch market, most of the large telecommunications equipment manufacturers were secure in their own home markets until the development of digital equipment; such is the cost of continuously enhancing the efficiency of the present range of products and services using this equipment that domestic markets are inadequate. Convergence of telecommunications and computer technology has been encouraged by user firms in financial services, for example, who no longer want data processed on computers in different locations, often thousands of miles apart, treated in isolation. By networking remotely located computers, printers or files, primarily a telecommunications task (see, fof example, Marshall & Bachtler 1984; Hepworth 1986; Holly 1987), information is exchanged more rapidly, client services are improved and costs more readily monitored and controlled. Telecommunications companies are themselves identifying network possibilities for computer users as a way of offering a complete package of services to their customers. IBM, for instance, has links with MCI, a long-distance telecommunications carrier, and with Rolm, a manufacturer in private telephone exchanges. Some companies are forming alliances with overseas partners as a swift way of filling gaps in their own products and services, e.g. British Telecom's takeover of Mitel (Canada) or its recent announcement that it intends to acquire the network systems and applications business of McDonnel Douglas Corporation. If approved by US regulatory bodies it will allow British Telecom to take advantage of the US value-added telecommunications market as well as an international market (served by Tymnet) which links eleven countries in Europe and the Pacific to 750 stations in the United States. Cable and Wireless, historically an operator with lines linked to British overseas interests, has recently completed a number of overseas arrangements that will allow its 'global highway' concept based on a fibre-optic cable network from western Europe to North America and on to Japan to be realised.

The impact of telecommunications on the spatial development of services is inextricably intertwined with public policy. The public service monopoly that has long dominated telecommunications services in many parts of the world has become much more vulnerable since governments have begun to question its efficiency. Deregulation is seen as a way of increasing competition and will likely bring costs down for users. This will encourage service businesses to make full use of the power of telecommunications in their global strategies. It does remain to be seen, however, whether deregulation will actually mean that customers receive better services from a tightly organised monopoly or a free-reigned competitive system. Indeed, the European Commission is more interested in re-regulation. A directive (Open Network Provision, THELIA) is about to be brought before the Council of Ministers for final approval. This proposes liberalisation of telecommunications services rather than of networks. Hence, public operators will maintain a monopoly in constructing and generating the telecommunications infrastructure but will be required to open up their networks to rival private service providers. The aim is to boost competition in the fast-growing data communications markets such as electronic mail, electronic trading and electronic banking. The European Commission is keen to make life easier for telecommunications users who have businesses in several European countries. At present, Europe's telecommunications operators offer services with widely different tariff structures and technologies that do not interconnect properly. This organisation of telecommunications services prevents users from effectively interlinking operations spread throughout the European Community. The great variety of services, equipment and suppliers now available, for example, possibly causes confusion amongst businesses trying to identify the most suitable services for their needs.

There is another dimension to the impact of new technology on producer services. In addition to being major adopters, they are also increasingly engaged in the development and marketing of new services using the new technology. Specialist software packages for accountancy, banking or broking are marketed by the organisations initially responsible for creating the demand for them. Some firms also trade or sell access to their own databases. Other specialist services market information that is updated daily (if not hourly in some cases) on, for example, financial market information, currency prices, property deals, the firms most likely to be seeking additional office floor space, the locations likely to be required and so on. Value added network services (VANs) have enabled companies to save on the capital and staff they would otherwise need to provide the same services in-house. Small companies can start their own VANs for a small start-up cost by 'piggybacking' them on to established systems. Furthermore, international telephone lines make it easy to develop international VANs such as EDINET which carries documents across the North Atlantic in a joint operation between British Telecom and McDonnell Douglas. Such services tend to be expensive; only large companies (able to spread the costs and benefits as widely as possible) can afford either to purchase them, or to set them up. It is not surprising that the major users and suppliers are multinational service firms, especially in financial and business services.

There is therefore a massive market for computer systems and office and communications equipment, much of it attributable to business services (*Economist* 1987). It has been estimated, for example, that 5650 firms in banking and finance in Britain had over 2 billion dollars of installed computer equipment at the end of 1983 and that this would increase to 3.7 billion dollars by 1988. Equivalent figures for insurance are 1.5 billion dollars in 1983, rising to 2.8 billion dollars by the end of the five-year period to 1988. With expenditure per employee averaging some 1400 dollars in 1984, British service firms would seem to be heavily committed to information technology but expenditure per head compares unfavourably with US firms which averaged 3000 to 4000 dollars per employee. This is still less than the average for French or West German firms (*Economist* 1985). Indeed, cost has become a major issue for major users of technology (together with the control and regulation of the new electronic delivery mechanisms). Recent figures for US banks, for example, show that the largest spend more than 200 million dollars on information technology and Barclays in the United Kingdom is spending more than 300 million dollars on its IT budget. This is leading to increasing polarisation between the super-players (the biggest banks) and the middle-sized and smaller banks with less ambitious IT funding programs. About 40 per cent (6.5 billion dollars) of total bank spending in the United States in 1990 will be made by just seven banks (McKinsey & Co. 1987). This will enable these banks to derive enormous competitive advantage since electronic technology not only reduces by one-fourth to one-third the costs of displaced paper technologies, it also establishes great economies of scale and virtually insurmountable barriers to entry.

The symbiosis between information technology and producer services operating at the global scale has been demonstrated by Langdale (1984; 1985). Internationalisation of financial services, for example, has stimulated demand for electronic funds transfer systems. Three groups of telecommunications services used by banks and other financial institutions have been noted: public switched services (telephone, telex, data transmission), international leased communications networks, and cooperative systems such as SWIFT (Society of World Interbank Financial Telecommunications) for inter-bank transactions (Langdale 1984). Many users prefer to operate private leased networks which offer greater security, reliability, flat-rate charges allowing a higher volume of use, links tailored to specialist requirements between offices and an ability to piggyback information services on their network of leased lines.

Computer switching and data processing centres are crucial to the operation of leased networks. Typically, these are located in key financial centres. Singapore, for example, is the switching centre for Citibank offices in Australia, New Zealand, Sri Lanka, Indonesia, Malaysia and Thailand (Langdale 1984; see also Langdale 1987). Indeed, telecommunications now ranks third after salaries and accommodation in the operating overheads of major MNEs such as Citicorp (Moss 1988). The Hong Kong and Shangai

Banking Corporation has an extensive leased network covering more than 100 offices in sixty countries organised around six switching centres in, amongst others, the United States, Sydney and Brussels. SWIFT involves more than 1000 banks in a comprehensive system for foreign exchange confirmations, bank transfers and transmission of statements but not payments which still rely on linkages through correspondence. The SWIFT network is dominated by United States and European Banks (well over 50 per cent of the membership) who also account for a large proportion of the traffic.

Thus, a large proportion of the expenditures by services on technology is made in the information-intensive corporate complexes such as London, New York, Chicago or Toronto. This could be interpreted as giving a competitive edge to the firms in these high-spending locations. A recent survey of telecommunications (*Economist* 1987, p. 1) notes that there are 'more telephones in New York than the whole of Black Africa' and that the waiting list for telephones in India is close to the one million mark. But if technology is a necessary condition for success in the global marketplace, it is not, on its own, a precondition. Much depends on the way it is used, for what purposes, and the human resources deployed to make decisions using the large volumes of detailed information available at high speed in fast moving markets (Stonier *et al.* 1989). The hardware is becoming cheaper as user volumes increase but the software requirements are becoming more sophisticated and demanding; the cost of the human resources to produce the software is therefore rising. The problems are compounded by the need to link the word processors, facsimile machines, personal/mainframe computers and telex machines in order to derive maximum benefit from using them.

In summary, information technology has given rise to a variety of new service industries. It has greatly enhanced the output and productivity of other economic activities. It has made it possible to transfer large amounts of information through interacting telecommunications channels in an economic and time-efficient fashion. Technology has therefore dramatically enhanced the tradeability of services such as accountancy, advertising, engineering consultancy, computer consultancy or legal services, without the need for producer and consumer to be in the same geographical location. Services such as shipping and tourism have also been affected because of the increased tradeability of the information available and therefore the competitiveness of different locations. For many services, the telecommunications infrastructure provides a single distribution system; thus competitiveness is determined by access to a suitable system. This affects both individual firms and individual metropolitan areas. Finally, technology has lowered the barriers to market entry especially where access to, and the cost of, network use is shared by all the users. Thus, it would seem that the configuration of spatial telecommunications systems necessary to increase the productivity of services and their distribution in domestic and world markets is a vital development discriminant.

SERVICES, TECHNOLOGY AND METROPOLITAN DEVELOPMENT

Service businesses can no longer view information technology as a mere adjunct to the conduct of their activities; they must consciously allow for it in their corporate strategies. Some firms not only rely on major telecommunications carriers, but are also involved in developing leased systems that synchronise with their corporate strategy. But deregulation (as in the United States) or privatisation and deregulation (as in Britain) are not a panaceas for improving access; if anything, telecommunications infrastructure is increasingly focused on existing information processing complexes in major metropolitan areas since these represent the major market (although not necessarily the only one). Thus, the development of Mercury's fibre-optic network in Britain is predicated on the assumption that the bulk of the traffic handled will be generated by the major cities linked by a network sharing the same routes as those used by the railways linking the same cities. Another reason for the disproportionate focus of advanced telecommunications on information-intensive environments is the removal, following deregulation, of the extensive cross-subsidies used to standardise prices across a state or country irrespective of variations in user density and the costs of linking users to the system (rural costs per installed unit being clearly much higher when compared with urban areas). This is increasingly underpinned by a move away from universal provision and costing of telecommunications services (whereby urban users subsidise rural users and business users subsidise residential users) towards user-related rates and investment.

These circumstances are 'creating a new urban hierarchy, in which certain cities will function as international information capitals, with the most extensive electronic infrastructure and richest opportunity for economic interaction' (Moss 1986, p. 35; see also Moss 1987a). In other words, the 'emerging telecommunications infrastructure is an overwhelmingly urban-based phenomenon' (Moss 1986, p. 37). The disparity between large cities and smaller cities is being reinforced rather than ameliorated. The former act as control points dependent on telecommunications for extending the geographical limits of firms headquartered there. But the growth associated with such expansion (employment, incomes, expenditure on retail services) is not as dispersed as the global markets being created. As Castells (1985, p. 18) has observed, 'new technologies also enhance, simultaneously, the importance of a few places as locations of those activities that cannot easily be transformed into flows and that still require spatial continuity'. The recent expansion of professional producer services both within and between countries seems to accord well with this prognosis (Leyshon *et al.* 1987a; 1987b).

There is a paradox. Enhancement of personal interaction using a variety of communication channels from the telephone to the video-conference, has been paralleled by the continuing importance of direct face-to-face interaction in, for example, the dealing rooms of securities firms, on the floor of commodity or futures exchanges, in the offices of major insurance under-writers such as Lloyds of London, in the offices of international legal firms or between corporate headquarters and their specialist advisers. Technology has also been responsible for modifying the human resource inputs to the production of services. Specialisation and diversification of occupations (many of which are technology-derived) has discouraged the widespread spatial distribution of all but routine back-office functions (which require a high degree of technology input but a relatively limited range of occupa-tional skills, some of which can be temporarily transferred from other parts of the organisation if required). The purchase of the information/knowledge possessed by personnel is almost more important than the physical input which they represent. The widespread use of 'golden hellos' and numerous fringe benefits to make new securities firms competitive following the 'Big Bang' in London is an example. Employers' awareness of their needs and opportunities in such competitive labour markets depends on direct represent-ation even when the services of professional recruitment agencies are readily available. Employees with high value added are unlikely to be persuaded to abandon major corporate complexes, even if technology permits, because their future value may be down-rated in less dynamic or innovative labour markets.

Is there any empirical support for these interpretations of the relationship between technology and the location of services? It is possible to chart the growth of certain services in particular metropolitan areas (o'hUallachain 1988; Beyers 1989), to outline the characteristics of recent development in telecommunications services and, conversely, to trace the internationalisation of producer services headquartered in countries such as Britain or the United States (Leyshon *et al.* 1987a; 1987b). The expansion of international banking in London between 1975 and 1985 (Lamb 1986) provides an example of the impact of internationalisation on a major financial centre, but it also under-lines the contribution of historical factors to contemporary patterns of pro-ducer service location. London was already a key centre for international banking by the 1870s. Lending was largely linked to financing overseas trade. The governments of Russia, Chile, Spain and Sweden (amongst others) were already issuing securities on the London market by 1875 (Lamb 1986, after Jenks 1971). Since that time, London's historical importance, a tradition of creating the conditions conducive to international banking activities, and its cultural and political stability has sustained its attractiveness for foreign service firms (see also Dunning & Norman 1987). Just three major centres, New York, London and Tokyo, accommodated almost 50 per cent of all international banking activity in 1985 and had the largest capitalised stock markets in the world (Price 1986). Each acts as a regional financial centre, but their global status emanates from their strategic position within different time zones (Clarke 1986). Transactions can take place throughout the working day in each centre by passing on deals from one market to the next. Telecommunications permit a London-based foreign exchange dealer who starts work at 6.00 a.m. to catch the end of trading on the Tokyo exchange, to trade all day in London and to catch four to five hours on the New York exchange, depending on when the decision is taken to cease trading for the day. Only foreign exchange dealing currently operates on this basis but other markets in Eurobonds and international futures are beginning to function in the same way.

The confidence derived from geographical proximity and the scope for face-to-face interaction for negotiations encourages locational convergence. Telecommunications permit cross-border transactions or transfers of foreign currency to head, branch or subsidiary offices in parent countries or elsewhere. Technology and the dominance of inter-bank transactions might therefore be interpreted as reinforcing the comparative advantage of London and Tokyo. But deregulation or the plan to create a single European market by 1992 may modify these established relationships. In this context, technology will be just one part of a business environment characterised by fierce competition, shifting patterns of demand and quickly evolving government policies. There is a proposal, for example, to permit freedom of intra-EC trade in financial services. Presently, markets are very regimented due to national rules and restrictions; the removal of these will expose London, for example, to greater competition from Amsterdam or Paris provided that the national governments dismantle existing restrictions in line with EC directives. In Italy, non-national organisations in securities can undertake unlimited activities but cannot execute transactions in exchanges; in the Netherlands, Germany and France they are unlimited.

We should not lose sight of the importance of other factors for sustaining the dominance of metropolitan areas on the location of producer services. Agglomeration economies undoubtedly exist and are important, otherwise why would MNEs and the supporting complexes of business and other advanced services accept the high accommodation, staffing and related costs of operating from large metropolitan areas? (Sassen 1988; Harrison & Kleuwer 1989). It may also be the case that the corporate resources present in large cities are actually more productive: one estimate suggests that productivity (value added per worker) for services rises by 10 per cent as city sizes are doubled (Henderson 1986). Specialised labour requirements are increasingly important for successful producer services and the possibilities for obtaining such labour are most numerous around the largest corporate complexes (Vernon 1963). Agglomeration not only makes investment in the most advanced telecommunications infrastructure attractive, it also makes public sector investment in highways or rapid transit, for example, both necessary and feasible. This provides indirect subsidies for the operations of firms within the agglomeration. Goldberg *et al.* (1987) also suggest that investment decisions by financial services reinforce the status of the major cities. The risks in investment projects in large cities are lower because the default value of diverse but immobile assets is higher. The expected value of office development investment projects, for example, rises with city size and this will have a diversionary effect on the allocation of capital. Large metropolitan areas will benefit disproportionately and will tend to be the most stable part of the urban system.

CONCLUSION

International markets for producer services will continue to expand. Firstly, expansion will be into new geographical areas, primarily outside Europe and North America where market consolidation is already taking place. Some areas such as the Middle East or Latin America are unlikely to be attractive (stability, scale of existing debts), but the newly industrialising countries (NICs) such as Singapore, Hong Kong, Malaysia or South Korea do offer largely undeveloped market opportunities. Secondly, growth will continue as producer service firms devise new services in response to customer demand and their own identification of market needs and opportunities. The major accountancy conglomerates have been particularly effective at diversifying into services that allow them to provide clients with a fully comprehensive 'bundle'; property consultants, advertising services and legal firms are adopting similar strategies.

Technology will undoubtedly be a key intermediary in this growth process and in the degree to which it affects the relative performance of metropolitan areas. But there are other factors. For example, the overseas expansion of any business requires the deployment of special expertise in the new markets in ways that do not fit easily into existing practices and regulations. Noyelle and Dutka (1987) identified several types of restrictions encountered by multi-national business service firms when trying to extend the geographical range of their markets: on the mobility of professional personnel, on international payments, on technology and information transfers, on market access through local procurement policy and on the business scope of firms. From a metropolitan perspective, a number of key issues, in addition to the significance of investment in telecommunications, have been identified at a recent (and ongoing) Workshop on Tertiary Industries conducted for the World Association of the Major Metropolises (Daniels 1989). Metropolitan scale is a major determinant of the way in which the factors affecting the growth of the tertiary sector operate. Internationalisation of services is the driving force for growth and change in New York or in London but in second-tier cities such as Melbourne, Barcelona or Vancouver, the links between manufacturing and the tertiary sector are highly significant. In third-tier (smaller) metropolitan areas such as Seville, the manufacturing/tertiary sector link is still important but there are also important interland resource-related factors sustaining the tertiary sector in such cities. Investment in infrastructure and other telecommunications is crucial for maintaining the current level of service activity as well as stimulating conditional growth. New York and London, for example, have the most advanced tertiary sector economies but have invested least in new transport infrastructure (apart perhaps from investment in international airports) during the last twenty-five years. All the cities in the Workshop refer to the need to invest in their human capital. The specialisations/ diversification of producer services has raised the overall level of skill required by new entrants to the labour force. Differences between the human resource characteristics of cities could be just as vital for service sector development as differences in the quality and quantity of the telecommunications infrastructure. A growing number of cities are also actively considering, or have already introduced economic development initiatives for achieving objectives for service industry growth (as well as location). It is too soon to assess their value for stimulating service industry development or attracting inward investment and, in any event, it will be difficult to separate their effects from regional and national fiscal and other policies.

It is increasingly recognised that these and other issues all affect the ability of individual metropolitan areas to attract their share of growth associated with the growing internationalisation of many service activities. Clearly there are links between macro-scale factors, such as internationalisation of services or national fiscal policies, and more local strategic/infrastructural factors affecting their location within metropolitan areas. There may be sufficient inertia in the system for cities like New York and London to overcome the fact that in certain respects they are first-world cities with fourth-world infrastructure. Yet they cannot be complacent, second-level cities are clearly sharpening up their strategies and development policies for service industries. Information technology may allow them to compete more vigorously for the spin-offs from service industry growth while major changes in the business environment, such as the internal European Market from 1992 or the US–Canada Free-Trade Agreement, offer new opportunities for large cities in and around the regions affected.

15

THE NEW TECHNOLOGY CITY: INFRASTRUCTURE FOR THE FUTURE COMMUNITY

Edward Blakely

INTRODUCTION

Cities are molded by the requirements they serve. Over the last two centuries, cities have emerged to service goods production or distribution. As we enter a new century, a new set of economic and social needs have arisen that are reshaping existing cities or totally altering the urban development landscape. In each of the major economic eras that characterised the last two hundred years, the city has developed several features that we now assume to be essential. First, we think of most cities as places that are identified with specific sets of industrial and commercial activities. This ranges from considering New York as a financial centre to Rotterdam as a shipping terminal. Almost every major city in the world has served the agricultural era as a major transportation hub and the industrial era as a large-scale production or distribution centre. Second, we think of cities as business districts or market centres. The central business district emerged from the open-air market in the agricultural era and subsequently as the central area for commercial and professional services.

We are now faced with major sociotechnology trends that alter the nature and purpose of the city. The city is now a point in the flow of information rather than the flow of goods. As a result, the basic conceptualisation of the city must now be reconsidered and the support systems upon which it is based need to be re-examined. In fact, the agri-industrial city we know, with its high density, its web of interconnections and its socioeconomic pattern, may become as extinct an urban form as the horse is as a means of transportation today.

THE BASIS FOR RECONSIDERING THE CITY SYSTEM

Clearly, there is too much futurist hype regarding the shape of the future city. Some futurologists '...have created such a ridiculous atmosphere of science fiction scenarios', as Castells (1984) states, 'that we have to produce analysis based on fact not fiction'. The basic facts that need to be considered in the development of the city are the implications of the changed and accelerating economic system that is already in place. The configuration of any city will have to be based on several increasingly important economic factors, as follows.

Information as a basic resource

It is very clear that flows of data and information will play a larger role than the flow of goods or capital. Cities that are the transmission points and the control centres for information systems will play an increasingly important role in shaping the world. It is for this reason that many cities are attempting to develop teleports and similar information infrastructure irrespective of their actual utility in the transmission and reception of data. The real race is over the control of information, not the use. As Rothenberg (1982) points out, 'our largest social problem with new communications technologies is that... we create socioeconomic classes, namely those that are communications rich and the communications poor'. What is true for individuals is even more true of cities. The cities that are information-rich, as Moss (1987b) suggests, are becoming the central nervous system for the international economic system. In essence, telecommunications infrastructure is analogous to the ship or rail terminal of the industrial era.

Knowledge as a product

The next century economy is already well developed. Irrespective of whether we call it the post-industrial, advanced industrial, technology- or knowledge-intensive, the basic notion is very clear. It is the quality and availability of selected human resources that are the engine for economic development. Innovation is no longer the servant of industrial growth. Innovation and new techniques are now the basis for economic wealth creation. In essence, the development of new products and services now surpasses the actual production of the goods that result. As Castells (1984, p. 37) states, 'the very special content of the new industries [whose main product is information rather than the material that embodies it] introduces a basic dichotomy between general and spatial diffusiveness of the final product and highly specific space conception'. This transformation in the economic system has dramatic impacts for the economy as a whole, individual firms and the shape of communities. Table 1 shows how dramatic this reshaping of human resources will be over the next several decades.

Table 1 US workforce distribution (%)

	1920	1955	1975	2000 (est.)
Agriculture and extractive	50	28	14	4
Manufacturing, commerce, industry	36	53	37	29
Other services	12	10	20	17
Information, knowledge, education	2	9	29	50

Source: Cleveland (1987, p. 49)

These data indicate one overwhelming direction for the shape of cities. Cities must become knowledge-dense. That is, a city that will participate in the future will base its strategic importance on the configuration of knowledge institutions such as universities and colleges, and knowledge transfer and information centres. The learning and human resource system of the new city will be far more complete than our current schooling arrangements. The home, work and even leisure activities will become increasingly knowledge-dense. Home-based information systems are already being implemented. These systems allow people to use their homes as communication hubs for business services and personal development. Knowledge, as Drucker (1980) puts it so clearly, is now a city's 'crucial resource'.

This pattern is already very clear. The rich research milieu of Silicon Valley, Route 128 and the North Carolina Triangle are illustrative of this pattern in the United States. While there may be many variables associated with the economic resurgence of the New England (Boston) region, one of the most important has been the growth of its knowledge centres and their ability to generate new wealth in the community.

The quality of educational systems and educational resources is an increasingly important discriminator in locational choice for several reasons. Educational institutions are no longer adjuncts to the wealth generating process. They are now central to it. Universities are spawning new enterprises and revitalising old ones in ways that no one could have perceived only two decades ago. At major universities, like MIT, the annual job formation rate according to David Birch[1] is equivalent to the total new job production of whole nations such as West Germany.

Education as a stimulator for innovation is very important to firms irrespective of whether they are engaged in new or old technologies. The key to profitability is increasingly based on the innovative capacity of the workforce. As Magda McHale (1984) puts it, 'in the new knowledge environment, civilisation will be built around communities of *people*, and less around communities of *place*'. There is little doubt that new firm start-ups and the location of high-tech employment is directly related to the density of knowledge institutions in the community and not cheap labour (Blakely 1987).

Amenity as infrastructure

Increasingly the social environment is becoming the central force in determining the physical geometry of places. Communities are recognising that the best attribute a community can offer is the 'quality of life'. This is an elusive concept to demonstrate empirically. Yet, there are very obvious illustrations of how important it is in determining a community's destiny. Quality of life dimensions include an entire range of attributes ranging from personal safety to the presence of a wide range of cultural facilities. This 'soft infrastructure', as I have termed it elsewhere (Blakey 1987), is increasingly important in city building. The critical elements of soft infrastructure include both tangible items like conference and meeting facilities along with less tangible items like an active informal network of scientists and engineers in the community through associations and organisations.

The work of Richard Gordon and Linda Kimbell (1987) has suggested for some time that the networks are more important than any other factor in determining the development of high technology places and other non-market considerations. In support of this contention, interview research conducted by the University of California at Berkeley's Institute of Urban and Regional Development on the emergence of software firms, indicates 'lifestyle...and a creative atmosphere' as the major locational choice factor (Hall 1983). While lifestyle means different things to different people, there are several important coincidental ingredients in communities ranging from Seattle to Los Angeles. These factors include relatively easy access to preferred recreational areas, good housing and school choices, cultural diversity and an active community social life. In essence, the community presents a milieu that is attractive for a lifelong experience and not merely for work. The new city will merge those things that modern life has split apart – work, play, shopping, education and leisure. In essence, the physical zoning of the past and current regulatory system will be rethought to provide a more homogeneous environment that allows functional rather than territorial discrimination.

The notion of planning a city as a social experience rather than to accommodate business activities is not well developed in the professional planning literature. There are some refreshing starts at developing this concept more fully in the contemporary sense, reflected in the work of Michael Southworth and Peter Bosslemann of the University of California at Berkeley and Peter Droege of MIT.

Technology image as technology reality

While academic researchers and professional planners pan the notion that an image of technological sophistication can be developed, state and local policy makers defy these data. American states are convinced of the efficacy of technology image development on the basis of the North Carolina Triangle experience of two decades ago and the more recent Texas strategy. Europeans are impressed with the apparent success of Sophia Antipolis (France), Cambridge (United Kingdom), Uppsala (Sweden) and other areas, while the Japanese technopolis dominates the thinking of Asian nations with respect to high technology image development. Not all image seeking has been successful, however, there seems to be real substance to the basic concept. In those communities where significant resources have been devoted to creating the basic technology framework as well as developing the appropriate image, the results have been both real and substantial. In earlier research on this topic, I pointed out that a technology image is based on the presence of two critical factors: the presence of a 'super centre' specialising in an advanced technology; and 'magnet facilities' that are designed to support technologies associated with the super centre[2]. For example, the presence of the Lawrence Berkeley Laboratories, the world-class biological science teaching and research programs of the University of California at Berkeley combined with the University of California at San Francisco research and clinical facilities, provide an enormously rich set of facilities for the development of biotechnology. Of course, the world's densest set of biotech firms have emerged in this milieu.

George Kometsky of the University of Texas has examined the tangibles and intangibles of a technology emphasis, and his research clearly indicates that a 'single high tech industry strategy offers more benefits to most communities and states than does a more generic high tech approach' (Kometsky 1987).

The research park or science park is a component of the image-producing structure. The park, in the case of Stanford and North Carolina, represents the magnet facilities. However, in too many instances, the research park is considered the totality of the image system. The park is only symbolic of a deeper infrastructure and a creative atmosphere. The park does not generate the firms. It is the combination of other factors such as the quality of the basic science system and the capacity of the intellectual environment to facilitate new ideas into the commercial marketplace.

THE TRANSITION TO THE NEW TECHNOLOGY CITY

The new technology city will be a city that exhibits the characteristics described above not in unidimensional form but in multidimensional ways. We can already see the illustrative new community systems that can be used as illustrations of the new pattern, however, we have not been able to understand them in totality. In fact, our current research on technology and community overemphasises one of the dimensions of the technology base. For example, some researchers emphasise the lifestyle dimensions of the new technology city. Other researchers place more importance on factors like universities and research parks. All of these perspectives have some validity. However, it is by placing them within a total context that we can begin to sketch the basic dimensions of the community of the future. The real problem in actualising these dimensions is in trying to forge the basis for a new city based on ideas and flows rather than a city as functions.

THE DIMENSIONS OF THE NEW TECHNOLOGY CITY

The basic dimensions of the new technology city involve three interrelated areas – technology-environment-humanity. Incorporating these dimensions into a city or urban system has been attempted by the Japanese with their technopolis programs and the development of the Science City, Tsukuba. The most recent attempt to design clearly a city with all of these dimensions is the new Australian multi-function polis. This new civic system incorporates all of these dimensions into a single framework, as illustrated in Figure 1.

These components create a community that alters our perspective on the city in three major ways. First, the city as a technopolis becomes part of the worldwide interconnectivity. The city will not serve its hinterland, rather the city is part of a global network. City connectivity provides a new logic in the design of the community. The city becomes more of an open than a closed design. The fortress-style model gives way to a wider space concept with settlement systems developed in a hub with transnational satellite arrangements that build on communication networks and rely less on the centrality of place and the hierarchy of city systems. According to Gillespie and Hepworth (1987), 'the future prospects for individual cities and regions will, therefore, depend on the spatial transformation of this network economy'.

Within the new city system all of the components can serve interdependent functions that provide the urban feel without the urban congestion and lack of human interconnections. Major technology and technology development will be incorporated into the city structure and not separated in parks or special technology enclaves. Electronic zoning will take the place of physical zoning. That is, the flows of information and data will determine location rather than physical space predetermination. This will allow separation of uses over time in a far more orderly process than can occur today.

Second, the new city will have environmental management as central to its development. The environment has been the victim of development rather than the goal for development. As a result, communities are a jumble of unrelated functions that cannot function harmoniously. The new city will be designed as self-sufficient and self-sustaining as well as environmentally sound. Community design will not be oriented toward mitigating the damages to the physical, social and human systems but enhancing them. This system will attempt to balance the agricultural, open space, energy and transportation systems into small village-like units. In this way, each segment of the community will act as a complete human experience rather than be divided into fragmented and disconnected living units.

Finally, the new city will represent the best in human spirit in a truly renaissance environment. The arts will be central to the development of the community and education will be open entry and open access. Education by

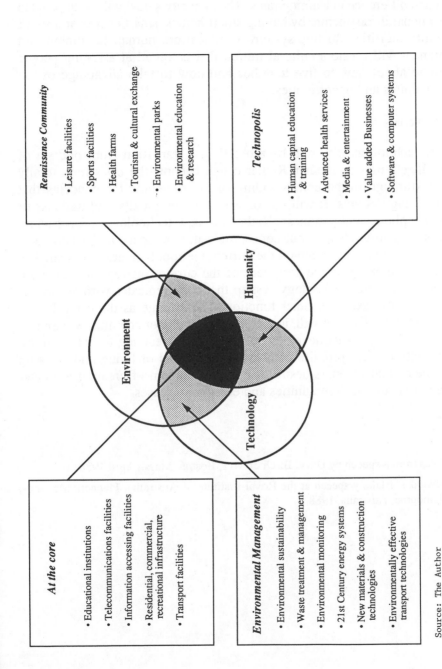

Renaissance Community

- Leisure facilities
- Sports facilities
- Health farms
- Tourism & cultural exchange
- Environmental parks
- Environmental education & research

Technopolis

- Human capital education & training
- Advanced health services
- Media & entertainment
- Value added Businesses
- Software & computer systems

At the core

- Educational institutions
- Telecommunications facilities
- Information accessing facilities
- Residential, commercial, recreational infrastructure
- Transport facilities

Environmental Management

- Environmental sustainability
- Waste treatment & management
- Environmental monitoring
- 21st Century energy systems
- New materials & construction technologies
- Environmentally effective transport technologies

Environment

Humanity

Technology

Figure 1 Synergies for the new technology city.

Source: The Author

demand rather than by mandate will be the main vehicle to develop the community. This form of education will cater to abilities over time as well as interest and difference in learning rates. The new city's goal will be to provide an educational infrastructure by having smart homes, smart offices and smart community facilities. In this system of education, human fulfilment and development will create a cultural milieu that is aimed at assisting people learn more about how to live together and how to take advantage of the world's cultures and opportunities.

CONCLUSIONS

The new technology city will be more than a transition from one set of functional activities to another. Rather it will become the basis for a totally new breakthrough in the understanding of the roots and the concepts that underlie living systems. It will not be urban in complexity and ugliness or rural in simplicity and plainness. Rather the new technology infrastructure will cause a quantum leap in our conceptualisation of space in the same way the auto and airplane have altered the current metropolitan environment. The new city will emerge on the periphery of the current metropolitan areas. It will begin with a rich technology system that communicates with the world. It will gradually take over other functions and emerge as the central node away from the old CBD. It will, in fact, become a city or community based on the notion of shaping its development rather than reacting to externalities. The new city has the promise of providing the kind of living and working environments that planners desire. It has the problem of creating a greater differentiation among communities and economic classes.

NOTES

1.   Notes from a speech by David Birch of MIT, Boston, Mass., April 1988.

2.   Edward J. Blakely speech at the Royal Institute of Australian Planners Meetings, Melbourne, Australia, 1988.

16

THE MULTI-FUNCTION POLIS – AN INFORMATION AGE INSTITUTION

Thomas Mandeville

BACKGROUND

When the multi-function polis (MFP) idea was first mooted early in 1987, many observers did not take it seriously. The Japanese Ministry of International Trade and Industry (MITI) (1987a) suggested that Japan and Australia should cooperate to build on Australian soil a new, futuristic city that could become a forum for international technological and cultural exchange in the Pacific Rim region, as well as a model for twenty-first century industries and life-styles. The multi-functions, envisaged then, included:

* high technology industry, and research and development activities;
* recurrent adult education associated with new lifestyle patterns of work, education and leisure;
* resort and leisure activities; and
* cultural exchange.

By 1989, the MFP idea had already become a highly complex institution, although it was still only at the conceptualising and planning, and feasibility study stage. Organisations involved in funding and carrying out the MFP feasibility study included the Japanese and Australian governments, six State governments in Australia, 170 Australian and Japanese business firms, various consultants, and a Secretriat attempting to coordinate it all.

The MFP has partly become a catalytic process for the Australian community by stimulating discussion about where Australia is going with Japan, with the Asia/Pacific region, and with the future twenty-first century information society. New business opportunities that can come from collaboration with other organisations are on the agenda. Indeed, the MFP idea has already opened up new business communication channels between the 170 firms in Australia and Japan involved in the feasibility study. This may only be the beginning for the MFP as a truly Australia-wide and Pacific interchange.

ANTECEDENTS TO THE MFP

Perhaps not surprisingly, many people have difficulty coming to grips with just what an MFP is. Like most ideas, it didn't come out of nowhere, but had a number of antecedents, forerunners, or prior influences leading up to it.

Technopolis

An important forerunner is the Japanese technopolis experience (Mandeville 1988). Indeed, when the MFP idea was first raised in Australia, some observers referred to it as an 'offshore technopolis'. The ambitious Japanese Technopolis Program began with MITI posing a question back in 1979. Could the creative, entrepreneurial, innovative and successful phenomenon found in California's Silicon Valley somehow be recreated or cloned in Japan?

The answer was the Technopolis Program, consisting of about nineteen designated high technology regions scattered throughout non-metropolitan Japan. Each technopolis region aims to organically integrate three formerly diverse elements: high technology industry, science, and a comfortable life environment.

It is too early to assess whether the Technopolis Program is, or will be, a success, but there are three aspects about the way the program is being implemented that deserve comment. They are worth noting because they are consistent with the way the innovation process works in the emerging information era, and with the way the MFP in Australia might work.

1 Emphasis on 'bottom up' initiative rather than 'top down' planning. Local area industry, government and universities have come together to initiate and carry out regional technological development strategies.
2 Emphasis on soft infrastructure of people, information networks, financing, services, new ventures and innovation processes – rather than bricks and mortar.
3 Aspatial: technopolises are region-wide, utilising resources from all over each region.

Other forerunners

As well as technopolis, there are a number of other forerunners to the MFP idea. The utopian element comes through strongly in MITI's MFP documents (1987a; 1987b). Thus, utopias are a forerunner (Masuda 1985). So are new towns and cities such as Brazillia, Canberra and Tsukuba Science City. Other forerunners include world expos, international education and research institutes, and technology parks.

TRENDS IN THE GLOBAL INFORMATION ECONOMY

A number of trends in the global information economy can be related to the MFP. The MFP is an information age idea that is becoming an international institution. Thus, the increasing information intensity of economic activity which, in its international dimension, is ushering in the integrated global information economy (Mandeville 1985), is concomitant to the MFP idea.

Flows of information through the planetary circuits have indeed brought about McLuhun's global village. This international dimension of the information society has a number of facets that are highly relevant to the MFP. First, there has been a rise in the number of supernational organisations and institutions since the information society began to take off in the 1950s.

Second, Japan, perhaps the most successful country in the information era, has become fascinated by what it calls 'internationalisation' (NIRA 1988). This involves moves to become both a more open society, and to assume a greater role on the world stage. The MFP could facilitate this process.

Third is the recent upsurge in international technological collaboration amongst large firms – the formation of so-called 'strategic alliances'. This is what the MFP could partly be about – enhanced opportunities for international organisational and technological collaboration: or knowledge creation, communication and utilisation. International technological collaboration is becoming an important corporate strategy of large multinational firms (Vickery 1986). Of course, the Japanese have cooperated for years at home with large consortia of firms involved in joint R&D in technologically promising areas, for example, colour television, VLSI microchips, and fifth generation computers. Now they are seeking to form strategic international technological alliances abroad to stay at the forefront of developments. The MFP based in Australia could provide neutral ground for such arrangements.

International technological collaboration is consistent with the realities of the deepening information era and the economic characteristics of information – information can be easily shared, information builds on information synergistically, and the cost of production of information is independent of the scale of use. These characteristics in turn imply that it can pay to use and share information within as wide a net as possible. This is especially so for technological information.

ALTERNATIVE MFP CONCEPTS

To date, the MFP idea has yet to be fashioned into a workable concept that most can agree on, although there are a number of preliminary concepts. More progress has been made on what the MFP is meant to achieve, at least officially. At its April 1989 meeting in Tokyo, the feasibility study Joint Steering Committee established the common objectives of the MFP (MFP Joint Secretariat, personal communication May 1989). Apart from 'motherhood' statements, these include the following.

It is meant 'to establish a strategic role for Australia in the Asia/Pacific growth economy', and 'to establish a basis for economic cooperation and clarify Japan's role in the developing Pacific Region'. Thus, it is about the Pacific Rim economy and the enhancement of Australian and Japanese roles within that economy.

It is also about economic restructuring, business internationalisation and enhanced opportunities for technological development. It is meant to help restructure the Australian economy by fostering the 'increasing international-isation of Australian business'; the 'development of international trading positions in value-added manufacturing and science'; and a 'stronger con-nection between research and development and downstream markets'. For Japan it is meant 'to develop ways of advancing the internationalisation of Japanese companies, people and systems', and 'to establish a foundation for basic research, skill development and technical cooperation in order to develop industries central to the future'.

Presently, there are three articulated preliminary concepts of the MFP. These are the initial MITI concept, the preliminary Queensland concept, and the 'pilot concept' produced by the consultants to the feasibility study (MFP Briefing 1989). The latter remains vague about the spatial dimension, but envisages an MFP which would link three elements: a 'biosphere' which may become a hub for an international environmental management industry; a 'technopolis' which could focus on agricultural technology, biotechnology, information technology and new materials; and a 'renaissance city' which could provide health and education services, sport, tourism and convention facilities. While reaction to this concept has been mixed, particularly with respect to a biosphere focus for the MFP, it has been officially adopted by the feasibility study.

In terms of its spatial configuration, there are at least three options for the MFP. These are not mutually exclusive, nor are they precisely correlated with the above three preliminary MFP concepts. They are:
- a new city project;
- a distributed, networked MFP with sites around Australia and the Pacific Rim;
- a regional concept.

The initial MITI (1987a; 1987b) concept was a new utopian city on a single site. This new 'city of the fifth sphere' would require a huge investment. They regard the MFP as a leap to the 'fifth space' where living, leisure and work spaces are arranged in close proximity, and urban structures are 'humanistic'. Emphasis in the MITI discussion is on the resort and medical functions, and hardware aspects of buildings and amenities, computers and communications that would be required.

The preliminary Queensland concept came mainly from the Premier's Department (1987a; 1987b; 1988a; 1988b) in that State and included their own internally produced work, as well as work carried out by the Information Research Unit at the University of Queensland (Mandeville & Lamberton 1988; Mandeville 1989). This concept of the MFP regards it as more of an umbrella network process, as distinct from a specific project in a place. In other words, the MFP is a program not a place. It is still a polis – a city – but it is an invisible city. This proposed MFP is an informational organisation. Its functions would be knowledge production, dissemination and coordination, with networking being the key element (Lamberton 1989). This preliminary MFP concept emphasises the three features of technopolises mentioned previously: bottom up initiative, soft infrastructure, and aspatial configuration.

The latter aspect, perhaps, requires more elaboration. The MFP may have a core facility that could simply be an office block, a new town development, or a region within Australia. But the core facility (or hub) would coordinate a dispersed network (or spokes) of research and business ventures that would be the real strength of the MFP. Nodes in this network, linked by the latest transport and communication facilities, could be located anywhere in Australia, Japan or the Pacific Rim region. This is another feature of the preliminary Queensland concept. It would seek to internationalise the MFP – bring in other nations as well as Australia and Japan. The major players, MITI and the Australian Department of Industry, Technology and Commerce (DITAC), now seem to be in agreement on this point.

Where should the core facility housing the coordination and strategic management function of the MFP be located? It should be in an accessible place in Australia, but more importantly it should be in a place where the spirit of the future won't be swamped by the institutions of the past. A place where Australia is going in the twenty-first century, not where it has been.

There are a number of advantages of the preliminary Queensland network concept over the new city concept. Generally, it is more consistent with the realities of the emerging information society – new cities are a late nineteenth century idea; new organisational and electronic networks are a late twentieth century idea that is changing the nature and role of the city (Hepworth 1987b). Distance is a great constraint in Australia; the same could be said for the Pacific Rim region. A network can potentially mobilise resources anywhere in Australia, Japan or the Pacific Rim. State conflicts over MFP location may be reconciled by a distributed MFP. Furthermore, a dispersed MFP is not so likely to attract the public resentment that a new Japanese city well might. Finally, the preliminary Queensland concept will not only be a stimulus to telecommunications developments, but will also help insure reciprocity of people movement to Japan and other countries.

However, a basic difficulty with the aspatial, network concept, is that hardly anyone understands it in the familiar way that everyone understands bricks and mortar. Thus, a third possible spatial configuration for the MFP is a region. This offers a compromise between a too-focused city and a too-diffuse network. The ideal spatial dimension for the MFP initially may be a region – an offshore technopolis. It is ideal partly because it does not rule out the potential development of the other two spatial dimensions as the MFP evolves. A new town development could be built on a greenfield site within the MFP region, and affiliated facilities could arise outside the designated region.

An MFP region could draw from the outset on existing transport, service, academic, research, housing, convention and resort facilities in the designated area. Thus, it would not involve the huge investment, long gestation period, and white elephant potential that a new city necessarily would.

While the regional, offshore technopolis MFP concept would have the advantage of building on the Japanese technopolis experience, it would differ from the Japanese technopolises in a number of ways. First, it would accommodate cultural as well as technological exchange. Second, it would be more future-oriented. Third, it would face additional problems of organisation and communication associated with the need to accommodate and integrate different cultural perspectives.

In the information era, inventing the future involves inventing new forms of organisation as well as new technologies. The MFP may become an important example of such new organisations.

POSTSCRIPT

In 1990 the Federal Government decided that the MFP should occupy a single site. Of the States competing to host the development (New South Wales, Victoria, Queensland, South Australia), Adelaide in South Australia was selected as the metropolitan site to proceed with a planning study, to be undertaken during 1991. (First choice for the MFP site was the Gold Coast, Queensland. The government of that State was required to default, however, when the specified land could not be secured for development within a prescribed period of time.)

17

EXPORTING CITIES TO THE WESTERN PACIFIC RIM: THE ART OF THE JAPANESE PACKAGE

Peter Rimmer

In the past, when heavy chemicals were a leading industry, 'new industrial cities' were the focus of development. The nucleus of today's ultramodern industries is the 'technopolis' which is expected to be the trump card of regional economic activation.

Shotaro Ishinomori
(1988, p. 140)

INTRODUCTION

Japanese urban and regional planners have been active mapping the likely contours of their country's information-oriented society during the early years of the twenty-first century. The expected rapid transformation, coupled with the development of the associated computer and communications technology, has been responsible for the creation of a new information 'network' involving the diminution of time and space, spatial reorganisation and far-reaching impacts on regional systems. Specifically, attention has focused on the evolution of 'new media' promoted by the liberalisation of telecommunications circuits; the diffusion of cable television and its impact on local communities; the concentration of central administrative functions in Tokyo's inner city wards orchestrating the information-oriented society; and the estimation of regional disparities in the new society (Terasaka *et al.* 1988). Attempts have also been made to package these new developments into futuristic cities.

Little consideration has been given to the international implications and repercussions of these developments. Yet innovations in electronics, biotechnology and new materials are international in scope and related to the projection of Japan as the hegemonic power of the early twenty-first century. Indeed, there is evidence that Japanese planning ideas have followed the penetration of trade from Korea in an arc along the western Pacific Rim to Australia and New Zealand. Before getting involved with the western Pacific Rim, however, we should ask how Japanese planners have incorporated the new technological developments into futuristic cities. We are then in a position to explore how these cities have been prepackaged for export to corridors in eastern China, south-east Asia and eastern Australia. Finally, we need to contemplate the likely implications of the Japanese thrust.

As some of the implications have been discussed elsewhere (Rimmer, 1989a; 1989b; 1989c), attention is centred on the key innovations, technology and spatial impact involved in the creation of Japan's information-oriented society and the way in which they have been packaged into high-tech cities. With this background, detailed plans for prepackaging high-tech cities for export to eastern China, south-east Asia and eastern Australia are explored. Then an examination is made of the wider repercussions of these 'new city' developments.

PACKAGING HIGH-TECH CITIES IN JAPAN

In discussing the packaging of computers and communications into futuristic cities in Japan, attention is centred on a selective review of a monograph compiled by the National Land Agency entitled *Land and Informisation in the Twenty-first Century* (Kokudocho keikaku 1985). This survey and research into the likely impact of trends in technological innovations and information flows on people and land use in the twenty-first century, begins by focusing on the 'oil shock' of 1973 which marked the shift from heavy to light industries, notably electronics, and precision instruments, and the creation of integrated regional areas aimed at resuscitating regional activities. Simultaneously, individual industries decreased their proportion of investment in products and increased it in knowledge and services (i.e. 'non-products'). These far-reaching changes have required private business to seek closer connections with public producers of scientific information; improved contacts between manufacturers and 'stiletto' markets for customised products; and the development of a market for information. This 'softening' of individual industries and the economy as a whole was reflected in the Fourth National Plan which charted new fields of endeavour for small and medium-size enterprises in pioneering venture businesses (Kanayasu 1987). In the process, new urban and regional forms are emerging to accommodate an information-oriented society, and existing settlements are being reshaped or discarded as artefacts of the heavy industrial era. It was these new urban forms that the National Land Agency set out to chart (Kokudocho keikaku 1985).

Land and 'informisation' in the twenty-first century

The National Land Agency examined the prospects for the twenty-first century in terms of such trends as technological innovations, internationalisation and the problems of an aging population. Specifically, its survey and research examines: (a) key developments in computerised telecommunications; and (b) their impact on national land use, and urban and regional development.

Innovation and informisation trends

The National Land Agency surveyed technological innovations and new informisation trends, such as the computerised disposition of data, telecommunications and satellite transmission (i.e. the new media), which are permeating both industries and homes. It focused attention on developments in computerised telecommunications that have arisen from the convergence of the telephone and the computer in the office automation market (e.g. on-line railway ticketing systems and mechanisation of banks) to create the 'information processing industry' – the infrastructure of an informised society (Kobayashi 1987).

In particular, the Agency has focused on the feasibility of using the Nippon Telegraph and Telephone Corporation (NTT) information network system (INS) which links telecommunications and computers. An oft-quoted experiment by NTT with a model INS system in Tokyo's Mitaka-Musashino areas between 1984 and 1987 was based on the installation of machines in industrial enterprises, municipal offices and private homes (Terasaka *et al.* 1988). Equipped with optic-fibre cables, these digital communications facilities made high-speed transmission of visual patterns feasible. When the machines were hooked into the existing communications services, new types of services were possible, such as digital telephones, and visual, facsimile and video-tech communications, which made tele-conferencing, electronic newspapers, centralised control of home appliances and security, and computer shopping conceivable. Although the experiment revealed both resistance among participants in accepting the new media, and the high cost and time involved in expanding these services throughout the country, the national INS system was initiated – the main trunk fibre-optic cable running from Hokkaido to southern Kyushu (completed 1985) being connected progressively to branches in regional cities.

According to the National Land Agency, the growth rate in supplying INS terminals to both industrial enterprises and homes will parallel the spread of personal computers and reach a saturation point in the year 2010. A complementary development within households is the anticipated spread of Community Antenna Television (CATV) as a means of integrating local communities and advancing local areas. Initially introduced as a means of overcoming poor television reception in remote areas during 1955, CATV has spread to local cities, rural areas, housing estates and new towns, and metropolitan areas. Originally, its presence in the metropolitan areas was to cope with airwaves obstructed by high-rise buildings, but an urban CATV has evolved as the forerunner of a pay-television system (though progress has been slow compared with the United States). Incorporating two-way communications, CATV together with INS, will provide the social infrastructure of the advanced information society of the twenty-first century. Already these twin developments have been incorporated in the Ministry of Posts and Telecommunications' (1987) plans for sixty-three 'teletopias' and the new media concept promoted by the MITI as a means of revitalising provincial areas. In 1995, the global integrated services digital network (ISDN) will be introduced which will trigger the real explosion in telecommunications. It will be able to handle all kinds of services that can be transmitted in digital form – voice, data, facsimile and moving pictures (see Kobayashi 1987). The ultimate aim of ISDN is to permit simultaneous telephone and non-telephone services and the portability of terminals. As a result of privatisation, this infrastructure will be organised on competitive lines. Having identified the key innovations and trends in information technologies, the National Land Agency proceeded to outline the land-use plan for Japan's 'informised society'.

Spatial impacts

In detailing the national land-use plan for the twenty-first century, the National Land Agency categorised common issues in terms of their geographical focus: national; urban (large metropolitan areas and pivotal regional centres); rural; and urban-rural. In outlining the policy response, however, the Agency concentrated on specifying the strategy, its contents, the appropriate information facility and necessary information base in terms of revitalising metropolitan and local (i.e. non-metropolitan) enterprises.

   Within metropolitan areas, the Agency focused its attention on developing policies for the heart of the city, inner city and suburbs. As outlined in Table 1, the National Land Agency sought to rehabilitate the city's core; redistribute central functions from the Capital Region; improve international communications; develop 'better towns' in the suburbs; and encourage the creation of research and educational 'cities' in the suburbs and other areas. In pursuing the research and educational cities idea, for example, the content of the Agency's plan focused on developing a university and associated research facilities; accelerating the location of groups of R&D enterprises; and creating a congenial research environment. Institutional support will include an academic exchange centre, international conference venue, joint research facilities and automated academic research library. The information base will be provided by an area-based integrated network system (INS) and local area network (LAN), an academic and research-oriented database, cable television and videotext.

Table 1 Countermeasures for restructuring metropolitan areas and extending information communications

Strategy	Content	Facility	Information base
City core			
Rehabilitation of city core	• CBD street revitalisation • Inner city redevelopment through the attraction of city-style info. industries • Multistorey housing redevelopment	• Office street info. centre • General purpose interactive DB • Community info. centre	• Business street INS, CATV • DB for city-style area info. centre • Area VAN • CATV, satellite transmitter
City core/most important city			
Revise central functions in capital region	• Relocate Tokyo HQs to core cities • Divide & transfer HQ functions • Move government offices • Relocate small & medium enterprises • Locational restraint on local HQ and offices in Tokyo	• Inc.use of Tokyo's transport & comm. • Office street • INS building • Int'l conf. centre • Int'l tourist hotel • Int'l relations zone • Meeting place in prototypical city • Int'l exchange exchange centre • Start-up building	• INS, VAN, • DB, area info. centre • Area INS, area VAN • Area DB, CATV
Revitalising international interaction	• Developing int'l community base • Int'l DB promotion & exchange • Int'l conf. organisation	• Int'l conf./trade zone • Meeting place at prototypical city	• Fibre-optics reception • Broadcasting satellite • Int'l TV conf. network • Int'l VAN
Suburbs/other areas			
'Better town' redevelopment	• Dormitory development in large city suburbs • Promotion of satellite offices	• CATV centre • Satellite office	• Interactive CATV, security system • Data reception
Research & educational 'cities'	• University/other research facilities • Promotion of R&D sector • Creating a congenial environment for researchers	• Info. exchange • Int'l conf. venue • Joint laboratory facilities • Automated research library	• Area INS, LAN • Academic & research database • CATV • Videotext

Source: Kokudocho keikaku 1985

In the non-metropolitan areas, the National Land Agency discusses its plans for the twenty-first century in terms of rehabilitating local industry, restructuring settlement patterns and extending the use of information-communications. As shown in Table 2, the key regional issues involve the felt need to promote the growth of stagnating industries, local industry and agriculture, 'footloose' enterprises and those in competition with metropolitan firms. In addition, is is essential to develop specific local industry, encourage foreign industry and attract particular industrial plants. In restructuring settlement patterns, both educational standards and health care require improvement.

Table 2 Countermeasures for rehabilitating local industry, restructuring settlement patterns and extending use of information communications

Strategy	Content	Facility	Information base
Development of local industry			
Promotion of 'stagnating' industries	• Vocational schools (farming, forestry) • Open-air theatre • Int'l tourist resort • Convention centre (nature seminar park) • Development of regional industry & services • Natural resort centre	• Increased use of large city's transport & comm. • Incr. hotels/shopping • Incr. tourist facilities (e.g. resorts, sports & conventions) • Int'l PR centre	• International network, satellite transmission VAN • Area INS, VAN, DB • CATV, CAI • Public VTX • Comm. centre
Promotion of local industry/agriculture	• Processing of unique local commodity • Development of local crafts & opening up markets • Vocational training • Int'l delivery centre	• Incr. use of large city's transport & comm. • Exhibition centre • CATV • Area information	• Int'l VAN • Area INS, VAN, DB (for PR use), VTX
Promotion of footloose enterprises	• Promotion of advanced industry (e.g. software house, info. processing centre to promote footloose industry)	• Incr. use of large city's transport & comm. • Training centre • DB centre, satellite transmission • Leisure centre	• Int'l network, satellite transmission, VAN • Area INS, VAN, DB VAN • CAI, CATV
Promotion of industries competitive with metropolitan firms	• Attraction of R&D-type secondary industry (e.g high-tech firms within technopolises)	• Incr. use of large city's transport & comm. • High-tech industrial parks • Science & technology universities, high-tech info. centre • Int'l exchange centre • Highway, airport satellite comm.	• National network • Int'l VAN • Area INS, VAN, DB (for PR use) • Area technology, VTX, CATV • Area info. centre

Table 2 continued

Strategy	Content	Facility	Information base
Development of specific local industry	• Incr. standards of tech. inputs & management of specific local industry	• Increased use of large city's transport & communications	• Int'l network, VAN • Area INS, VAN, DB, VTX
Development of specific information centre	• Information, training, technology development centre for specific local industry • Transport centre	• CATV	• Area information centre for local industries
Attraction of foreign industry	• Attraction of foreign plants & research institutes not requiring metropolitan location	• Incr. use of large city's transport & comm. • Int'l R&D park, int'l exchange centre • Expressway, airport	• Int'l network, satellite transmission, VAN DB • Area INS, VAN
Attraction of plant	• Improve level of automation, personnel control, encourage development of industrial sites & employment, & absorb unskilled labour • Start new industrial design concept	• Incr. use of large city's transport & comm. • Industrial estate delivery centre • Satellite comm. • Highway development	• International network, VAN • Area INS, VAN • CATV
Restructuring settlement patterns			
Improvement of educational standards	• Improvement of local educational environment & level through changes in location & improvement in school environment	• Regional education information centre • University • Regional education institutions	• Int'l education network, library network, TV training system • Area INS, CAI, training system • Educational VTX, • VRS • Technical education DB
Health care	• Improvement of local health care level through establishing info. network within metropolitan health care centre • Revision of local health care facilities	• Regional health care centres • University hospital • Regional health care info. system • Development of health care facilities • Automated diagnosis	• Establishment of info. networks between large hospitals • Regional health care info. systems, first-aid health care, regional health care system

Source: Kokudo keikaku 1985, pp. 16–7

The key elements in the plan for stimulating the growth of local industry and agriculture, for example, are focused on the processing and development of 'unique' local commodities and local crafts. As in all non-metropolitan strategies, the main instrument is the increased use of the region's transport and communications facilities hubbing on its metropolitan city. Also, in this particular instance, more attention has to be given to the establishment of training and exhibition centres, vocational institutes and an international cargo delivery centre. The required information base would require access to an international communications network, international and regional value-added network, regional INS, database and videotext, cable television and a regional information centre.

In restructuring non-metropolitan settlement patterns, the aim is to improve educational and health care standards. The educational strategy, for instance, focuses on restructuring and relocating educational institutions and their associated information systems. A regional information centre, university and regional education institution have been identified as the main instruments to realise this policy. According to the Agency, they will be underpinned by an educational information base that is international in scope and supported by a regional INS and cable instruction, educational videotext, video response system (VRS) and a technical education database.

The National Land Agency has translated the information base needs of metropolitan and regional areas into an integrated telecommunications-land use plan for the twenty-first century. As shown in Figure 1, this basic plan comprises international value-added networks and self-operating domestic satellites – a main trunk, optic-fibre cable linking city and regional cores from which minor connections emanate. Other activities in the metropolitan area include an information centre, company value-added and LANS, office automation, family information terminal, CATV, cable instruction television, area and large-scale databases, and an INS building. A more or less parallel set of activities is envisaged within the region. They feature automatic health diagnosis and information collection centres, CATV, videotext using CAPTAIN (character and pattern telephone information access), cable instruction, agricultural and regional databases, and an INS building. The main difference between the two areas is the greater emphasis on value-added networks within the metropolitan areas.

A critical element in both the metropolitan and regional areas is the teleport (Sakashita 1987). Basically, it is a ground base for handling expanding international and domestic satellite communications through telecommunications facilities housed in a well-equipped 'intelligent building' (Telecom Centre) that is linked to other cities by optical fibres and other access circuits (submarine connections are not shown). The earth station is also linked to information networks such as LANs – the link terminals, mainframes, minicomputers and personal computers. New services such as wide area networks (WANs) and cable television (CATV) will then be possible. The teleport is expected to attract heavy users of

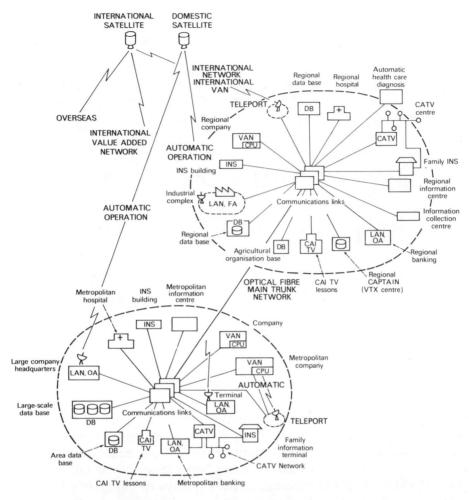

Figure 1   *A schematic diagram showing the key communications features in an idealised city and region (source: Kokudocho keikaku 1985, p. 292).*

Acronyms: CAPTAIN character and pattern telephone information access network; CATV community antenna television; CAITV cable instruction television; CPU central processing unit; D domestic; DB database; FA factory automation; I international; INS integrated network services; LAN local area network; OA office automation; VAN value-added network; VTX videotext.

telecommunications such as financial institutions, insurance companies, software development firms and information processing services. This need for a subcentre equipped with advanced telecommunications facilities and an 'intelligent' business centre prompted the Agency to accord the teleport a pivotal position when they represented the key features of the information-oriented city and region of the twenty-first century linked to the outside world by a communications satellite.

The teleport, as shown in Figure 2, is associated with the large city's international information exchange centre. In turn, it is connected to all

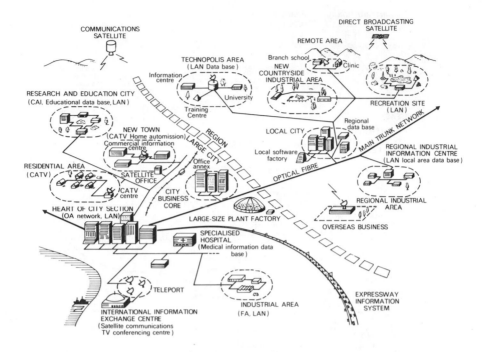

*Figure 2 The informised city and region of the twenty-first century
(source: Kokudocho keikaku 1985, p. 20). Acronyms as for Figure 1.*

other parts of the city and region. It is located near to an industrial area
(with factory automation and LAN), a specialised hospital with its own
medical diagnosis database and, most importantly, is connected to the so-
called 'heart of the city' which possesses both office automation and LAN.
Attention should also be directed to the expressway transport information
system and the large-scale factory nurturing plants for sale. North of the
heart of the city there are communication connections to residential areas
with cable television, the 'research and educational city' with cable
instruction, a new town with a home cable television network and
community information centre, and a satellite office. A free-standing city
business core, with an office annex and access to a commuter railway, is
connected to the main trunk, optic-fibre network. The latter links city and
region together – the region is also presided over by a broadcasting satellite.
   Within the region, south of the main trunk, optic-fibre network there is an
industrial information centre and a free-standing, overseas business
enterprise with its own satellite connections. North of the main trunk there
is a local city with a regional databank; a local software factory; a recreation
base; a new countryside industrial area; and a technopolis area with a
university, training centre and information centre. This technopolis area has
been at the forefront of moves to prepackage these futuristic, information-
oriented cities and regions for export.

PREPACKAGING HIGH-TECH CITIES FOR EXPORT

Much has already been written in a book (Tatsuno 1986) and a spate of papers about Japanese technopolises (Fujita forthcoming; Glasmeier 1988; JETRO 1983; Mandeville 1987; Morris-Suzuki 1988; Smilor *et al*. 1988; Tatsuno 1988). Attention is, therefore, focused on highlighting aspects of Mitsubishi Electric Corporation's (1985) review undertaken by PADECO (Pan Development Consultants). Although this study was commissioned by a private firm, its chairperson, Sandakazu Shindo, also chaired the Technopolis Committee, a private organisation established by the MITI to oversee policy development (Fujita forthcoming). Mitsubishi's report: (a) explored its export potential for newly-industrialising countries; (b) raised the concept of 'upmarket' technopolis sites; and (c) provided detailed site designs.

Exporting prepackaged technopolises to south-east Asia

Mitsubishi Electric Corporation's (1985) feasibility study proposes to extend the technopolis concept to industrialising countries on the western Pacific Rim. The proponent argues that it will help these countries develop production engineering, project execution, capital goods manufacture and research and development; facilitate the transfer of technology; create a high-quality environment to stimulate foreign investment (including Japanese domestic production dispersed abroad); and avoid the problems of fragmented and unproductive investment in research and education. In particular, the industrialising countries would be able to capitalise on the footloose nature of airfreight-oriented industries with their high value to weight ratios, small to medium-sized plants and interchangeable intermediate products. These are critical considerations to newly industrialising countries faced with diminishing labour cost advantages; accelerating rates of technological change; rising costs of entry into new technology markets; and major economies accruing to the innovating countries. Indeed, the technopolis concept is seen as being particularly apposite for industrialising east and south-east Asian countries with high levels of capital formation and gross domestic product.

Two major corridor areas have been identified by Mitsubishi Electric Corporation (1985) as ideal situations in which technopolises can be located (Figure 3). An eastern China corridor running from Hong Kong/Canton (Guangzhou) via Taipei to Seoul, encompassing the revitalised coastal cities of eastern China, which could be extended into Vietnam, and a south-east Asian corridor running from Chiang Mai in northern Thailand through Bangkok, Penang, Kuala Lumpur, Singapore and Jakarta to Bali. Although Brunei and the Philippines fall outside the eastern China and south-east Asian corridors, they are situated on international routes linking the world cities of Tokyo, Sydney and Singapore. The focus on the eastern China corridor had been heightened by the former General-Secretary of the Communist Party's (Zhao Ziyang) belief that computerised telecommunications would 'Toffler-

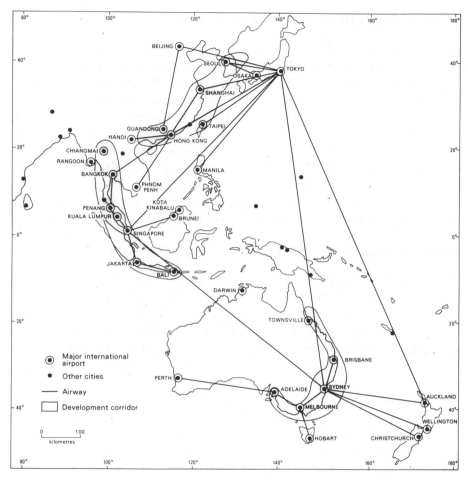

Figure 3 Development corridors within the western Pacific Rim
(source: Rimmer 1989a).

like' galvanise small and dispersed enterprises into efficient production
groups. This strategy was part of an intended general 'renaissance' of coastal
China orchestrated by Guangzhou and Shanghai respectively and focused on
the Special Economics Zones and fast-urbanising 'rural counties' (Fincher
1988; Chung Tong Wu 1987). Similarly, the emphasis on the south-east Asian
corridor is not surprising given the strong presence of Japanese trading
companies, manufacturing firms and construction corporations in the
Association of Southeast Asian Nations (ASEAN) and the opportunities
offered by local technopolis sites (e.g. Penang, Malaysia) for propelling
existing activities beyond the semi-conductor industry into higher-valued
production (Rasiah 1988; and forthcoming).

A step beyond the original Mitsubishi Electric Corporation's scheme is to
identify an eastern Australia corridor running from Cairns through Brisbane,
Sydney, Adelaide, Canberra and Melbourne to Adelaide. Although the
eastern China and south-east Asian corridors are likely to specialise on

intermediate technologies, the eastern Australia corridor would seem to offer the prospect of more advanced production and processing in biotechnology, new materials and mechatronics, possibly in joint ventures between government, private enterprises and academic institutions. All three corridors, together with the San Francisco–Los Angeles–San Diego corridor, would seem to be prime targets for developing Shinkansen-style high-speed surface transport (HSST) – a feasibility study is in progress into a Very Fast Train in Australia that would link Sydney and Melbourne.

As the cost of infrastructure for multiple sites is prohibitive it is likely that only two or three will be considered in the eastern China and south-east Asian corridors – the original proposal in Japan. A similar proposition is warranted in Australia as reflected in Japan's Ministry of International Trade and Industry's plans to build an 'upmarket' technopolis in Australian – the multi-function polis (MFP). The concept has captured the Australian imagination. As it forced planners to contemplate for the first time the urban and regional contours of the information-oriented society of the twenty-first century much has already been written about this intended 'hothouse' for development (Langdale 1988; McCormack 1989; Mandeville 1988; Menadue 1988; Morris-Suzuki 1988). Rather than repeat this material, attention here is focused on tying the proposition to its Japanese antecedents – the National Land Agency's plans for the twenty-first century and Mitsubishi Electric Corporation's scheme for exporting technopolises to industrialising countries.

Multi-function polis

The MFP proposal was more akin to the Tsukuba scientopolis-technopolis in scale. Nevertheless, the Ministry of International Trade and Development's proposal had its roots in the concept of exporting technopolises. Aimed at integrating work and leisure, this new proposition envisages an urban complex as a forum for industrial, technological, scientific and cultural exchange. Development of the futuristic city will centre on high-tech industries and services, research and development activities, and advanced educational, health and leisure facilities and services. The city is intended to be a joint effort between Japan and the host country and involves Japanese being residents for periods of a few months in the case of tourists to several years for scientific researchers. At the time it was regarded as a resurrection of the MITI's cheap 'Silver Columbia' proposal for retirement overseas of aged and non-productive Japanese people to Australia. Although this proposal was rejected by Australia's Federal Government, concerns about the retirement village concept still permeated a series of documents produced by Japan's Ministry of International Trade and Industry (1987a; 1987b; 1987c; 1987d).

First came a discussion paper, produced in February 1987, which outlined the background of the MFP concept, major functions, location and steering formula. Next was a report for the First Planning Committee in August 1987 that reiterated the background, surveyed Australia's current economic position, elaborated the MFP concept and detailed procedures for a feasibility study of a single site. Finally, a two volume report was produced in September 1987 on the basic concepts underlying the MFP, including supporting reference material which again restated the proposal's background but discussed the industrial potential, infrastructure and future issues in more detail (MITI 1987a; 1987b). Most attention has been focused on the last report, as it incorporated not only previous but additional material on the R&D, industrial and high technology components, presumably provided by the MITI's consultants in response to the Australian Government's comments on the original proposal.

As outlined in the final report, the underlying rationale of the MFP concept is to cater for the new urban lifestyle of the twenty-first century by accommodating the worldwide trends of internationalisation, technological innovation and aging populations. Drawing inspiration from Japan's Tsukuba Science City, South Carolina's Science Triangle and France's Science Resort City in Languedoc-Rousillon, the objective of the MFP is to incorporate home, work, recreation and short-stay vacations within a single city that offers: (a) a human-scale settlement encompassing high-level international, business, research and development and information supply functions; (b) new 'soft' infrastructure covering medical and health care systems featuring sports medicine, educational and training facilities for all ages; (c) transport, including the possibility of HSST using a linear motor to travel at speeds of between 300 and 500 kilometres per hour; and (d) new information systems. Key industries will include high-tech industries geared to export, such as biotechnology computer software and communications equipment, and to the future, such as new materials (polymers, non-ferrous metals and new ceramics), new energy and research and development into the oceans and space. Attention will also be paid to 'high touch' activities such as conventions and resorts with an associated academy to train their workers. Reportedly, these activities have been incorporated by the project's consultants, a consortium led by Arthur Andersen & Co., into three basic groups: biosphere (international environmental management); technopolis (R&D into agricultural technology, information technology and new materials); and renaissance city (leisure, health and tourism) (Roberts 1989).

As the MITI has only offered token finance and Australia's Federal Government is reluctant to provide place-specific subsidies, the viability of the project will depend on commercial developers and joint venturers seeing adequate potential return from their investment. Indeed, the feasibility study is being underwritten by eighty-three Japanese and eight-three Australian firms (as at October 1988). An analysis of their major activities shows the Japanese firms to be heavily represented in the banking sector, whereas Australian representatives are strongest among the research institutes and government sector (Seisan kozoka 1988). Surprisingly, there are few high-tech Japanese firms involved. Although there is almost a parity in the construction sector, the Japanese companies are also well-known as urban developers. Both countries are heavily represented in the communications sector, as without commitment to advanced telecommunications, the MFP will be little more than another 'science city' dependent upon a new contract between academia, business and government.

A major problem in evaluating the MFP proposal is that it still lacks substance. At the time of writing no firm site has been fixed. Most Australian States have established their own MFP committees and have one or more sites in mind (Queensland Premier's Department 1987a; 1988a; 1988b). Further, the original assumption that the concept must take the form of an isolated single city has been relaxed – the way is open for one or more cities; a truly 'invisible' city comprising units linked by computerised telecommunications; or a hub and spokes with activities distributed along high-speed transport and communications networks linking major Australian cities. As the 'invisible' city concept is unlikely to be adopted, MFP planners will be able to draw on Mitsubishi Electric Corporation's strategy for a London Docklands-style Development Corporation to design and run the new city.

Mitsubishi's prepackaged blueprints

Recognising that the eastern China, south-east Asia and eastern Australia corridors would not have the benefit of Japan's close collaboration between government, business and education, Mitsubishi Electric Corporation provided a primer for developing new cities as a means of unifying and concentrating the processes of industrial development, research training and education. The primer established: (a) a remit for the Development Corporation covering its aims, scope and timescale; (b) a design strategy; and (c) a modular design concept.

Remit

The basic remit for government, business and academic communities involved tying the new cities into the national development strategy by commissioning three independent studies: a survey of existing development plans of research, university and training centres to pinpoint those which could be incorporated in the new area; a review of industrial location policy as a means of specifying target activities; and preparation of the outline structure plans for one existing community and two greenfield sites. After the completion of these studies, it was intended that the results should be pooled and preliminary construction schedules created for existing and greenfield sites. While the former has the advantage of being brought on stream more quickly and at a lower cost, this does not necessarily negate the planning and environmental advantages of an independent site.

Design strategy

As outlined by the Mitsubishi Electric Corporation (1985), the new city concept could be conceived as the Toyama-Takaoka association of industrial estates and research and development, or a fully-fledged Tsukuba-style scientopolis-technopolis. Ideally, western Pacific Rim countries should avoid the proliferation of sites that occurred in Japan and concentrate their efforts on a limited number in concert with the host government's agreed economic and regional planning goals. Nevertheless, the host countries should be able to experiment with a variety of configurations to promote interaction between facilities – a task involving the judicious use of transport and communications, architectural design and micro-land use planning. A high premium will have to be placed by the Development Corporation on providing an attractive habitat and recreational facilities, paying particular attention to the need to provide uninterrupted power and water supplies, access to major transport routes and, above all, high-quality telecommunications connections. When the infrastructure is in place the basic modules that comprise the technopolis can be plugged into power, water, transport and communications.

Modular design concept

Mitsubishi Electric Corporation (1985) identified six sub-modules as the basic building blocks of the new city. Each of these components was designed to demanding specifications, though the emphasis on the associated ground transport would be of an advanced, but not necessarily new, design – the stress being on proven efficiency. As the new city developed, additional sub-modules could be aggregated to the structure. Although circular and rectangular structures were possible, Mitsubishi preferred the hexagonal form as it was suited to diverse topographical conditions. Within temperate climates each edge of the hexagon is expected to be 500 metres which is considered to be an acceptable walking distance – the total area enclosed being sixty-five hectares. Assuming neighbourhood populations of 5000, the housing mode for a technopolis of 50 000 would have nine contiguous sub-modules with another being devoted to campus accommodation. Where an existing area is involved, a circular form with the hexagonal telecommunications module as its central feature is inappropriate. As shown in Figure 4, the telecommunications facility has to be housed in the industrial complex module.

If a greenfield site was being developed, it would be most convenient to house telecommunications facilities in an engineering module. As reflected in Figure 5, this module would be linked by transport and communications to industrial, educational and housing modules laid out around the circumference of a circle to prevent ribbon development. Particular attention has to be paid to the layout of the areas' recreational amenities and access to a large airport. Although airport access is deemed desirable,

EXISTING SITE

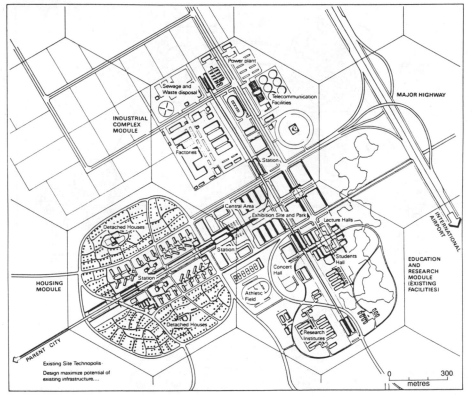

*Figure 4 Modular configuration of an existing technopolis site
(source: Mitsubishi Electric Corporation 1985, p. 49).*

though not essential, people living in the technopolis are expected to be frequent international travellers. Consequently, they would need sixty-minute access time to a local airport and ninety minutes to direct international services. Besides, a good-sized airport is important for marketing and distributing the products of high-tech industries.

Further, the original assumption that the concept must take the form of a separate city located in one place has been relaxed – the way is open for one or more cities; a truly 'invisible' city comprising units linked by computerised telecommunications; or a hub with spokes with activities distributed along high-speed transport and communciations networks linking major Australian and overseas cities.

Irrespective of the design chosen, the proposals on new hubs – technopolis or MFP – have driven home to people in eastern China, south-east Asia and Australia that urban and regional transport-telecommunications-land use developments within their major corridors must be seen within a western Pacific Rim context. Above all, they must be conscious of planning trends in Japan and the way in which cities are being prepackaged for export.

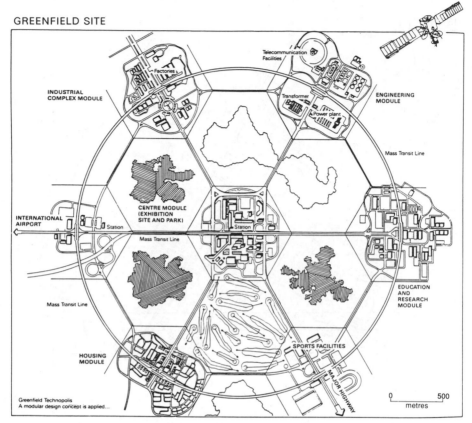

GREENFIELD SITE

Figure 5 Modular configuration of a greenfield site
(source: Mitsubishi Electric Corporation 1985).

CONCLUSION

This study has sought to unpack Japanese ideas on futuristic cities in the twenty-first century and their potential for export to the western Pacific Rim. Drawing on Japanese materials, it has linked together seemingly disparate reports to emphasise the underlying consistency of the Japanese package. First, it highlighted aspects of the National Land Agency's survey (Kokudocho keikaku 1985) to demonstrate how innovations in information technology were being packaged into futuristic cities within Japan. Then it examined Mitsubishi Electric Corporation's (1985) report to highlight not only how the technopolis concept has been used as a tool for 'regional activation' within Japan but its export potential. In particular, the MFP concept was examined to show that it was not an independent international initiative for Australian consumption but that it had much in common with the technopolis (albeit a deluxe version) which, in turn, was a component of the futuristic city discussed at the outset. Clearly, Japanese planners are developing a long-term strategy for 'supra-regional activation' within the western Pacific Rim as a whole.

As Japanese planners are now operating outside the country's national boundaries, there is a pressing need to be more conscious of the roots of their ideas about future economic and social development. In particular, the bureaucratic essays generated by the 'ideas men' in Japanese Government 'think tanks' have to be tracked. Specifically, we have to become attuned to their careful choice of words, deliberate vagueness and political neutrality – the art of avoiding coming to a firm conclusion. Their penchant for inventing and creating new English-type words in katakana, such as cosmopolis, technopolis, scientopolis and multi-function polis, has to be appreciated. The resultant reports are to generate discussion and gain a political advantage. As the Japanese government ministries are frugal with their resources, the emphasis is on private enterprises to establish these new information-oriented urban and regional forms.

There is little doubt that these Japanese communications-based investments in new cities will yield net benefits to western Pacific Rim economies and societies provided they are not subsidised, directly or indirectly, by government. The real problem for western Pacific governments, however, is not to overestimate Japan's economic clout and to appreciate that other factors may override commitment to new city development. Nevertheless, the packaging of computerised telecommunications into prototypical futuristic cities by Japanese planners may be more significant than has been appreciated in a global context.

Japan still lags behind the United States in computerised telecommunications but is catching up in some areas, drawing level in others and is ahead in opto-electronics. Making use of the speedier movement of light rather than electricity, these innovations in opto-electronics, supplemented by satellite and cellular transmission, are providing the infrastructure of the cities planned for the twenty-first century. Indeed, the Japanese package embodying advanced computerised telecommunications technology may be the most important innovation of all in terms of its spatial impact – a model of an advanced 'informised' society and a barometer of social development for the western Pacific Rim.

PART IV

NEW TECHNOLOGY INDUSTRY AND POLICY

18

LOCAL DYNAMISM, MILIEU AND INNOVATIVE ENTERPRISES

Denis Maillat

INTRODUCTION

For some time now, discussion of the mechanisms and origin of regional development has been evolving considerably. The usual models (polarisation, spatial division of labour, endogenous development, etc.) have lost part of their ability to explain phenomena. The trend is increasingly towards a theory of milieu-initiated dynamisms which combine internal regional impulses and external impulses.

This development is, of course, due to the modification of the predominant paradigms and the role the small and medium-sized enterprises (SMEs) have regained. Indeed, today the Fordian paradigm is opposed by the flexible production paradigm. The research conducted in the 1960s stressed the predominant role of the large company and the multinational groups in the functioning of the industrial countries' economies. The emphasis was placed on the Fordian organisation of labour, the spatial division of functions and the opposition between central and peripheral regions. Since the end of the 1970s, the increase in the number of small businesses, the manifestations of their creativity and their ability to innovate have led to a revival of the discussion of new forms of production organisation and regional development mechanisms.

This development has pinpointed the two fundamental logics that influence regional development. The functional logic of the large company, which led to the spatial fragmentation of production and to the spatial division of labour; and the territorial logic, which involves regional interdependences. The functional logic is characterised by the fact that large companies maintain highly asymmetrical relations with the territory in which they are located and only rarely become locally integrated. SMEs, on the other hand, develop a logic involving exchanges with the areas in which they are located. To the extent that the territories supply logistic support essential to their development (externalities, proximity effects, etc.), it is in their interest to rely on integration and enrichment of their local environment. In all these problems, the important element is not SMEs as such but all the networks which they constitute at the territorial level. Numerous examples testify to this dynamic today (Maillat 1988).

The territorial logic is thus able to account for the development certain regions are undergoing thanks to the dynamism generated by the milieu, since their territorial structures have been remodelled not from outside but from within. The model of innovation stemming from outside and disseminated by the major companies is being replaced today by a model in which the regions no longer appear as passive suppliers of locations for innovative companies but as active milieus capable of generating innovation. Large companies are thus no longer regarded as the only genuine and independent protagonists of the innovation process. Indeed, in the territorial logic, innovation results from enhancing the value of know-how and a technical culture, historically formed thanks to an internal dynamic (Maillat *et al.* 1988; Crevoisier 1988). In fact, local dynamism does not result from the action of a single firm but from an overall behaviour pattern resulting from a network of interdependences. 'The central concern of the local environment-based approach is to understand the firm in its local and regional context, and to ascertain what conditions external to the enterprise are necessary both for the creation of new firms and the adoption of innovations by existing ones. The firm, and the innovating firm, are not viewed as pre-existing in or separate from the local environment, but as being a product of it. Local milieus are regarded as the nurseries, the incubators, of innovation and innovative firms…The historical evolution and characteristics of particular areas, their social and economic organisation, their collective behaviour, the degree of consensus or conflict which characterises local society and economy, these are the major components of innovative behaviour…This approach implies that innovative behaviour is as much dependent on variables defined at the local and regional level as on national scale influences. Access to technological know-how, the availability of local industrial linkages and inputs, the impact of close market proximity, the existence of a pool of qualified labour – these are the innovation factors which will determine areas of greater or lesser innovative activity within national space' (Aydalot & Keeble 1988a).

In this chapter, I intend to propose an operational definition of the milieu and to highlight its role in the innovation process. To do so, we will have to identify the links which the firm forges with the milieu during this process.

The analysis will be based mainly on the work undertaken by the GREMI (European Research Group on Innovative Milieus) (Aydalot 1986; Aydalot & Keeble 1988a; Maillat & Perrin, in press). Various surveys were conducted to assess how local milieus stimulate or generate innovation.

The regions surveyed belong to three main groups: slightly industrialised (Nice, Ticino, Poitou-Charente); industrialised (Bergamo, the Jura Arc,

Wallonia) and metropolitan (southern Ile-de-France, Aix-en-Provence in the Marseilles metropolitan area, Silicon Valley and the north of the Milan area). In some cases the region is relatively autonomous (the Jura Arc, Ticino, Wallonia, Silicon Valley); in others, it is part of a more integrated territorial complex (in the case of the metropolitan areas). This diversity of the zones studied has revealed multiple and varied relations between innovative firms and their environments. It should be pointed out that in the surveys only the companies which have made product innovations have been selected.

THE INNOVATIVE PROCESS: THE INTERNAL/EXTERNAL DYNAMIC

Innovation is a complex process which presupposes collaboration between and linkage of complementary functions: fundamental research, applied research, development, preparation of prototypes, industrial investments, putting into production, marketing and adaptation of production to the market (Planque & Py 1986). Of course it is not a matter of claiming that innovation takes place linearly from upstream to downstream, but of stressing that the process encompasses several aspects, several stages and thus multiple entry points. The factor triggering innovation may appear at any stage (Maillat *et al.* 1988).

Whichever stage is selected, the motivation which leads to innovation incorporates elements which derive from within (internal component) and from outside the firm (external component). The enterprise is, in fact, an organisation which is open to its environment. As innovation strengthens this tendency, the nature of the links it maintains with that environment is exposed.

The internal component aims to enhance the value of the firm's specific knowledge: its know-how, its R&D capacities and its desire to keep pace with technology. The external component comprises the elements which help to trigger innovation from outside the firm (customers, suppliers, consultants, specialised journals, research laboratories, etc.).

As a general rule, taking all stages of the innovative process together, the internal component appears to be fundamental. The know-how acquired by the enterprise or entrepreneur in the course of time is one of the crucial determining factors of innovation. This fact confirms that technological knowledge cannot be transferred in the absence of a specific organisation within the company (Foray 1988).

The importance of the internal component naturally varies according to the different stages of the innovative process. Its role may be said to be more important in the upstream stages than in the downstream stages. This is particularly the case during the stages of product design and development and preparation of the prototype.

The external contributions are more frequently to be found in the downstream stages of the innovation process. In general, customers, suppliers and competitors play a decisive role.

However, we should certainly avoid getting caught up in a dichotomous interpretation of innovation according to which the latter would originate either from the firm's technical abilities (supply logic) or from market signals (demand logic). In reality, innovation results from the combination and inter-action of the two components. In particular, an idea elaborated and managed technically by the firm or by its research departments is nurtured by more or less direct and informal stimuli from the market (Camagni & Rabellotti 1988). According to Quévit and Bodson (1988), the triad of company-customer-supplier is one of the main vectors of the corporate innovation process. It is the strategic location at which the innovation process operates. In fact, innovation does not chiefly originate from the sphere of knowledge and gradually work its way into the sphere of industrial exploitation and the market.

Although it is possible to distinguish two main groups of companies – those which derive ideas and suggestions from their market relations, and those which find design and production elements within their firm – it is nevertheless true that in most cases innovation is the result of a dynamic which is both internal and external, as a firm adapts its own resources and know-how to external requirements, in conjunction with its market (Senn & Bramanti 1988).

The enterprise cannot therefore dominate all the stages of the innovative process. A strong internal component assures it control of its specific know-how. But in view of the speed and complexity of development, it has to rely, at all stages of the innovative process, on outside skills. The external component thus enables a link to be forged between the company and its environment and the influence of the latter on the innovative process to be understood. Indeed, the company is not an isolated unit; it has links with the outside environment which can be close-knit and frequent. It is through this external component that the role of the milieu can be analysed.

THE NOTION OF MILIEU

The literature on regional economic studies makes increasingly frequent use of notions such as the 'local industrial fabric' (Mifsud 1987; Thomas 1987), the 'localised ecosystem' (Planque 1983; Pecqueur 1987), the 'local industrial system' (Brun 1985), the 'territorial complex' (Stöhr 1986), the 'milieu' (Aydalot 1986a; Hansen 1989; Maillat 1988; Perrin 1986; Scott 1988a) to describe regional phenomena.

The abundance of new words entitles one to assume that there is still a poorly defined level of analysis which hardly corresponds to traditional analysis: it is trans-sectoral, does not regroup a well-defined category of agents and does not have precise geographical limits, but refers to notions of territorial interdependences and proximity.

The milieu may be defined as a coherent area organised around its physical structures (territorial production system, regional labour market, regional scientific institutes) and around its non-material structures (culture and technical culture, and representation system –, the collective way of perceiving events and reacting to them). The coherence between the various protagonists lies in a common way of understanding situations, problems and opportunities. The spirit of enterprise, organisational practices, corporate behaviour patterns, the manner of utilising technology, understanding the market and know-how are all elements which are both an integral and constitutive part of the milieu. Conceived in such terms, the milieu is a process of continual perception, understanding and actions. This process implies that the various protagonists differentiate between the elements they have 'appropriated' and integrated into their representation systems and the extraneous elements (Maillat *et al.* 1988).

The milieu is thus an area integrated with elements, in particular resources; the environment, on the other hand, is a disparate complex from which elements have to be derived which are likely to enrich the milieu.

Physical structures

The territorial production system is organised around three domains between which flows pass (Maillat & Vasserot 1986; 1988).

1 The territorial production system. This is formed by the firms, their characteristics and the relations they maintain with each other. In many regions firms have links with each other. Consequently a certain coherence appears, which may take the form of subcontracting relations (either trivial or specialised), relations based on complementarity, competition, interdependence, partnership, etc. The result is certain configurations of firms (networks, etc.)

2 The labour market. This exerts a structuring influence on the milieu. If the jobs offered by firms are not organised in chains of mobility, it will not be possible to retain, and consequently to train, labour. It is thus essential that structured chains of mobility ensure employees' mobility and the know-how they convey (Maillat 1984) .

3 The scientific institutions. These comprise all the milieu's training and research institutions. These complexes are important for passing on skills and know-how and, above all, for updating them and keeping them abreast of technological development and market requirements. Today the emphasis is placed on regional science policies. In fact, it is not necessary for a milieu to practice high technology to be dynamic: it is just as important for it to know how to capture and develop technology and tailor it to its requirements.

Non-material structures

1 The regional technical culture. The culture, particularly the technical culture, influences a milieu's mentalities and creativity. It consists of practices, know-how, standards and values that are linked to the transmission and accumulation of this knowledge:

- knowledge and know-how in direct contact with production (these may be used by firms directly);
- general scientific and technical knowledge taught by technical vocational schools and universities (this is academic knowledge);
- vocational knowledge which is available in professional circles and may concern all areas of firms' activity (technology, management, markets, networks of skills, etc.).

2 The territorial dynamic develops on the basis of the technical culture, and more particularly on the know-how which is the practical means of expressing the technical culture. It is this know-how which allows the production system to adjust to scientific and technological developments, to changes in markets, etc., and which forms one of the fundamental elements of a milieu's specificity.

3 Representations. For all the individuals living in a milieu, there are certain ways of looking at things, understanding their close and distant environment and of positioning themselves, with their collective culture, in this environment. In general, individuals belonging to an area seek, as a community, to preserve their representation system. However, when the environment changes, when new technologies appear and cultural changes occur, the protagonists belonging to an environment may be required to modify their behaviour, depending on a more or less selective 'reading' of events. Thus, they may reposition themselves in relation to the old representation systems. The protagonists' changes of behaviour are therefore conditioned by the development of their representation systems. In general, reformulation of old representations takes place in a process of break-dependence which ensures continuity between the old and new situations.

LINKS BETWEEN FIRMS AND THE MILIEU

On the basis of the aforementioned methodological considerations, a survey was conducted in the Jura Arc (Switzerland) in the context of the GREMI studies. In the course of the innovative process, the firm maintains, as we have seen, links with the outside environment. It is necessary to specify the nature and intensity of the links with the outside world: some have a fundamental influence on the innovative process, whereas others are merely trivial flows of exchanges. In general, partnership-type cooperation relations may be regarded as determining, whereas subcontracting links of the 'customer' type are trivial (Figure 1). It is obvious that some links may be both trivial and determining, depending on the manner in which they influence the innovative process. In this analysis, I propose to emphasise the determining links, because it is through them that the milieu is structured. The milieu is in fact characterised not only by the nature of the interdependences but also by their qualities (partnership versus trivial subcontracting).

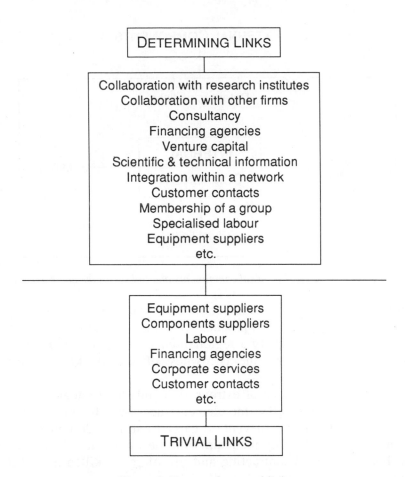

Figure 1 Nature of external links.

On the basis of this distinction, it is possible to examine whether the determining links are maintained with the milieu or, on the contrary, whether they do not belong to the milieu under consideration (Figure 2). It is also possible to shed light on the way the milieu is organised and its role in the innovative process.

1 Firms with a high degree of extroversion. These are firms belonging to a multinational group which only perceive the milieu from the angle of a location presenting a certain number of advantages (taxation, unskilled labour, etc.) which are not connected with innovation. These firms, whose markets are international, have no or only very few links with the milieu. They may sometimes introduce an innovation there. But in that case the determining elements of the innovation stem mainly from the network of international relations and an internal component connected with the firms' management strategy. These firms may be regarded as not belonging to the milieu.

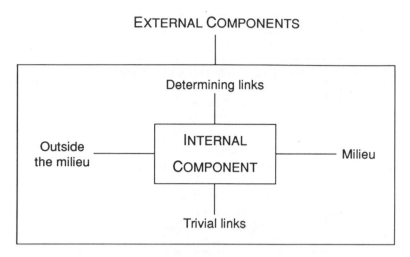

Figure 2 Internal and external components and links with the environment.

2 Firms with a high degree of integration into the milieu. These are locally
   based firms: they create new products in relation to the milieu's technology
   and are designed to satisfy a regional/domestic market. For this reason
   they fairly soon find that the narrowness of local markets constitutes a
   handicap.

3 Firms with a high degree of extroversion and slight integration into the
   milieu. These firms derive the elements necessary for innovation from
   outside the milieu (use of venture capital and outside consultants, for
   example). The links they maintain with the milieu are essentially ones
   involving trivial subcontracting and use of semi-skilled and unskilled
   labour.

4 Firms with a high degree of extroversion and high integration into the
   milieu. These are large companies belonging to high-tech sectors (electronics, microelectronics, etc.) with an international market. To innovate
   they have strong links both with the outside environment and within the
   milieu. These links are, above all, scientific and technical in nature (collaboration with research institutes and technical schools). These companies
   have an international market. Collaboration with their clientele is very
   important and most of their products have been developed with the end
   user. These firms use highly-skilled labour which they recruit partly from
   within the milieu and partly from outside. They generate spin-offs by
   encouraging some of their engineers to set up new businesses in related
   or complementary fields.

5 Firms with a low degree of extroversion and high integration into the milieu.
   These are SMEs belonging to high-tech sectors (electronics, machine
   construction, etc.) and originating from the milieu (the head of the company
   comes from the region, their registered office is in the region, etc.). They
   do not maintain any scientific links with research institutes. On the other
   hand, they collaborate closely with other local firms (suppliers and

customers) and use local consultants to solve specific problems. They are sensitive to the training environment provided by the local authorities. They look to the milieu for resources to finance their innovation by using private capital and/or local venture capital. Most of these SMEs have an international market, export a very large proportion of their production and enjoy privileged relations with their customers. Heads of such firms stress the importance of having commercial partners (e.g. distributors) outside the milieu.

6 Firms with a low degree of extroversion, slight integration into the milieu but with a strong internal component. These are firms which are constantly developing new products based on the specific know-how acquired by the head of the company or his staff after many years' experience. This know-how is very closely linked to the structure of the regional industrial fabric and to the resulting trades, but during the innovation process these firms have few links with outside establishments.

These results show that the degree of integration of innovative firms in a milieu varies and that they may very well innovate without using the milieu's resources. However, it should be pointed out that more than three-quarters of the innovative firms surveyed in the sample do have strong regional integration and that they are accompanied by significant links with the outside environment (Maillat *et al.* 1988). These are the firms which help to make a milieu dynamic.

Each group maintains different relations with the milieu. Consequently, the simultaneous existence of several types of corporate links with the milieu indicates that it is essential to identify clearly the nature of the relations that a firm maintains with its environment during the innovative process if one wishes to reveal the role of the milieu.

In the literature on the external links that a firm needs to innovate, it appears in general that the proximity-based links are vague or even unimportant. It follows that the territorial environment as a vector of innovation seems to be weak. Several surveys carried out by GREMI arrive at similar results. However, quite apart from global assessments and depending on the interpretation used, it is possible to establish different degrees of the role played by the territorial environment, and consequently by the external contributions of proximity. For example, it is possible to show that the links with the local environment are related to the degree of innovation characterising the new products. The least innovative firms (those which come up with incremental-type product innovations) have few links with the local environment, whereas the other categories have more (Senn & Bramanti 1988). In fact, my analysis shows that relations with the milieu do not depend on the type of innovation but on the nature and intensity of the interdependences which firms establish between each other at the territorial level. To arrive at conclusions about the role of the milieu, it should not merely be regarded as a warehouse from which the firm obtains supplies. The milieu should be viewed as a constituted whole, a complex system made up of economic, technological and cultural interdependences.

CONCLUSION: ORGANISATION OF THE INNOVATIVE MILIEU

The foregoing results would tend to prove that two characteristics determine the ability of a milieu to strengthen itself and to innovate: the interdependence of the elements located in it and the degree of extroversion. The interdependence of the elements of the milieu favours the formation of a coherent whole. In fact, the similarity of the representation systems makes for better communication between the protagonists because the approach to the problems is done in a similar manner. The result is an increase in the intensity of the relations and complementarities. Formal and informal networks take shape and/or become closer-knit and influence the milieu's dynamism by the synergetic effects which they stimulate (particularly by stimulating the spirit of enterprise, the dissemination of ideas and technologies, and partnership). The interdependence phenomena and the resulting networks assume a certain specificity which allows a milieu to be distinguished from other areas. This specificity implies an organisation with a certain independence.

This differentiation, which generally creates comparative advantages, is not in itself sufficient to ensure the milieu's dynamic. Indeed, it may give rise to the preservation of obsolete skills.

If innovation is to manifest itself in a milieu, the latter must incorporate or furnish determining information or resources. It is through the representations which it will have generated that the milieu will be able to understand and filter the information and put it in touch with its resources.

In order to stimulate innovation, the milieu must comprise two non-antagonistic characteristics of extroversion and strong integration within the milieu. It even appears that the more a milieu is characterised by a strong degree of openness, the more a strong local interdependence and integration between firms is necessary. The milieu is open to 'circulating' information on, in particular, scientific and technical knowledge, and to market-related information, which in today's world is often international. Without being open to the outside world from which the milieu and the firms draw fresh energy and information, the milieu and the firms cannot exist or at least they cannot develop. But at the same time the milieu is closed to 'structural information' in the sense that it is a coherent sphere organised around its material and non-material structures (Matteaccioli & Peyrache 1989).

Innovation is thus conditioned by the characteristics of the milieu, that is, the degrees of extroversion and of integration within the milieu. When the milieu succeeds in reconciling openness (acceptance of new ideas which trigger innovation) and closure (coherence of the socioeconomic fabric), it is able to stimulate and support the creativity of firms and, in return, to be enriched by the innovation they achieve. If it is too open it shatters or disintegrates; if it is too integrated it becomes too inward-looking and loses its competitiveness.

19

LOCAL AREA NETWORKS: INDUSTRIAL ADAPTION IN SILICON VALLEY

AnnaLee Saxenian

INTRODUCTION

During the 1970s, the rapid growth, technological vitality and entrepreneurial culture of Silicon Valley captured the imagination of policy makers and scholars around the world. This enchantment waned during the 1980s, however, as intensified Japanese competition left the region's leading semiconductor producers saddled with massive overcapacity and declining profits. Between 1984 and 1986, local chip makers' sales plunged 35 per cent, forcing them to lay off more than 7000 employees, while linked sectors eliminated another 20 000 jobs in the region ('The chips are down', *San Jose Mercury News* 1 Dec. 1986). Observers – drawing parallels with Detroit and Pittsburgh – were quick to predict the demise of Silicon Valley.

Despite this battering, more than eighty new semiconductor firms have been started in Silicon Valley during the past decade. This wave of new chip makers represents the state-of-the art in semiconductor design and product innovation and has generated some 25 000 jobs and more than two billion dollars in annual sales (Dataquest 1988; 'Largest 25 semiconductor companies in Santa Clara County', *The San Jose Business Journal* 13 Feb. 13, 1989). While the region's established producers struggle to stay in the black, several of these start-ups boast growth rates of 45 to 50 per cent a year and only a handful have failed. Firms in linked sectors – from computer systems and software, to disk drives and other peripherals – are flourishing as well.

The dynamics of Silicon Valley's revitalisation are reflected in the new wave of semiconductor start-ups. These firms, together with hundreds of neighbouring technology firms, are forging a flexible new model of production in the region. By building on the dense networks of social and professional relations which were created and then abandoned by the established semiconductor firms, these small and medium-sized enterprises are pioneering a new Silicon Valley – one which fosters collaborative manufacturing and reciprocal innovation among networks of specialist producers.

REINTERPRETING SILICON VALLEY

The experience of Silicon Valley suggests that the current debate over the future of America's high technology industry is miscast. Although public attention is currently focused on trade policy, Sematech, and high definition television, the resilience of the Silicon Valley economy underscores the importance of regional economies to industrial competitiveness and the need for explicitly regional institutions and policy in the 1990s.

Both advocates of national support for strategic industries, such as MIT's Charles Ferguson, and their free market adversaries, led by George Gilder, attribute the early growth of the American semiconductor industry to the individual entrepreneurs and small enterprises of Silicon Valley. They disagree only on the viability of such market-led growth in the 1980s – with the latter (Gilder 1988; 1989) glorifying it and the former (Ferguson 1988) viewing it as inappropriate, even 'pathological'.

For free marketeers such as Gilder, Silicon Valley's dynamism confirms the neoclassical vision of competitive markets as efficient and self-reproducing. These observers see entrepreneurship as the solution to America's industrial woes. Yet they conveniently ignore the role of military procurement in supporting the region's early entrepreneurs, and they cannot account for the current weakness of US semiconductor firms relative to the giant government-supported Japanese producers. Nor can they explain the failure of regions around the world to replicate the Silicon Valley experience, even after insuring unfettered flows of capital, skilled labour and technology.[1]

National policy advocates such as Ferguson, by contrast, invoke the crisis of the semiconductor industry to argue that Silicon Valley's small and medium-sized enterprises are no longer appropriate to the dictates of global competition. Claiming that the fragmented structures of competitive capitalism are no match for the institutionalised coordination of America's industrial adversaries (such as Japan and Korea), these analysts advocate government support and consolidation of key technology sectors. Yet the resurgence of the Silicon Valley economy – particularly the flourishing of the 1980s start-ups – casts doubt on this approach as well.

Despite their differences, these opposing approaches regard individual firms and national governments as the only relevant units of analysis. As a result, neither can account for the striking resilience of the Silicon Valley economy: it is neither a market nor a state-led phenomenon. A more fruitful approach begins with the region itself and the relationship between its productive organisation and social and institutional environment.

A growing literature compares Silicon Valley to the technologically dynamic industrial districts of Europe where innovative producers successfully export a shifting combination of high value-added products to global markets.[2] These regions are distinguished by industrial decentralisation and vertical and horizontal linkages among specialist producers of all sizes. In these districts, external economies replace internal economies of scale, cooperation complements competition, and the region replaces the firm as the locus of production; the result is a networked system which is more flexible than the traditional vertically integrated corporation.

By focusing on the organisation of the regional economy, these analysts are better able to explain the development of Silicon Valley, yet they cannot account for the crisis of the large semiconductor producers any better than the free marketeers. Much of this literature implies that productive decentralisation and spatial proximity alone will generate a virtuous cycle of regional advance (see, for example, Scott 1988c; Scott & Angel 1987).

The experience of Silicon Valley during the 1980s demonstrates, by contrast, that industrial districts are not self-reproducing. It suggests instead that they can be quite vulnerable, and provides insights into the social and institutional conditions needed to sustain such decentralised productive systems.[3] In particular, it highlights the importance of inter-firm cooperation and the need for regional institutions to coordinate the activities of firms in these flexible systems.

The first section of this chapter argues that Silicon Valley's new wave of semiconductor start-ups is creating a flexible model of production which is the inverse of the mass production model of the region's established chip makers. Section two describes how these specialist producers are rejecting the autarchic approach which led their predecessors into crisis, and formalising collaborative relationships with customers and suppliers. The third section argues that computer systems firms, which now dominate the Silicon Valley economy, are also collaborating with suppliers to create inter-industry production networks.[4] These network relationships are as important as the individual firms to sustaining the technological dynamism of the region.

Yet Silicon Valley remains vulnerable. The new wave of start-ups are better adapted to respond to today's volatile markets and technologies than their predecessors, yet they too have failed to recognise the collective sources of their own dynamism. The conclusion suggests a need for regional institutions which ensure the technological position and coordinate the activities of the firms in this decentralised productive system.

THE NEW WAVE OF SEMICONDUCTOR START-UPS

The wave of semiconductor start-ups in the 1980s represented a collective revolt by Silicon Valley engineers against the established semiconductor firms.[5] Successful entrepreneurs like Cypress Semiconductors' T.J. Rogers and Chips & Technologies' Gordon Campbell quit jobs at the large semiconductor firms in frustration with their employers' growing isolation from customers and unwillingness to pursue promising technical leads. Complaining that the big firms had lost the agility which made Silicon Valley famous, these engineers 'voted with their feet' and exposed the rigidities of the established semiconductor firms even before Japan did so (see, for example, Rogers 1988; Rice 1987). They also created the largest wave of new start-ups in the industry's history (see Figure 1).

These start-ups have pioneered a flexible approach to semiconductor production – one which appears well adapted to the market conditions of the 1980s. By unbundling production, these new firms have spread the costs and risks of developing state-of-the-art semiconductors, and by adopting flexible design and manufacturing technologies they have remained highly focused and responsive while avoiding the price wars which accompany commodity production.

While established firms like Advanced Micro Devices (AMD) and National Semiconductor (NS) mass produced general-purpose semiconductors such as commodity memories and microprocessors, the newcomers specialise in short runs of high value-added components, including semi-custom and custom chips as well as standard parts targeted at niche markets. Cypress Semiconductor, for example, manufactures more than seventy-five specialised, high-performance products on a single flexible manufacturing line. While few of these individual application niches are large or stable enough to attract a major competitor, they collectively represent a 1.4 billion dollar market – comparable to the market for 256K DRAMS. Specialist producers like Cypress emphasise product design, quality and high levels of customer service, not simply low cost.

The new firms have achieved flexibility in manufacturing by avoiding the dedicated high-volume production lines of their predecessors. In a move reminiscent of the mini-mills of the US steel industry, they have pioneered the use of 'mini-fabs' which process short runs (small wafer lots) of many different designs quickly and with high yields. And while the traditional 'mega fab' – optimised for very high throughput of a single design – costs 250 million dollars and takes two to three years to build, a 'mini fab' can be built in six months for only 20 to 50 million dollars.[6]

Developments in electronic design automation – which combine advances in computer-aided design (CAD), engineering (CAE), and testing – enable these start-ups to be still more responsive. Chip and systems designers are increasingly able to implement their ideas directly onto silicon; and it now takes weeks rather than months to design custom and semi-custom integrated circuits, while complex niche products at the very large-scale integration (VLSI) level are being developed in months rather than years.

Finally, by unbundling the production process, these start-ups have spread the prohibitive costs of chip making. While the established firms designed, manufactured and assembled integrated circuits in-house (and occasionally even ventured into systems production), the new firms tend to be highly focused. Many, such as Weitek and Altera, specialise exclusively in chip design and subcontract manufacturing, while others, including Cypress and

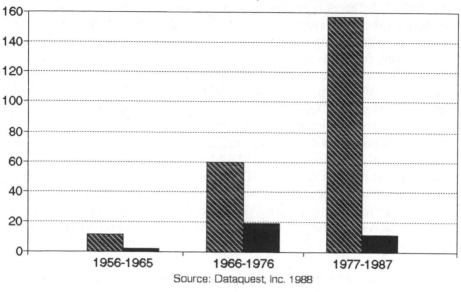

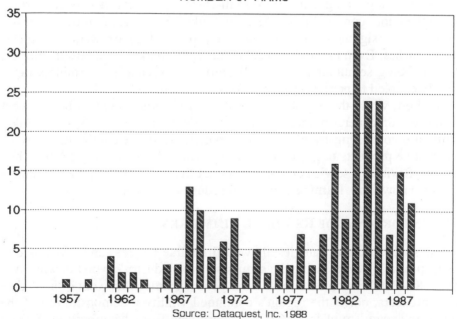

Figure 1 US semiconductor start-ups and closings.

Integrated Device Technology (IDT), specialise in leading-edge process technologies. Application-specific integrated circuit (ASIC) producers LSI Logic and VLSI Technology provide software and assistance to systems firms designing semi-custom chips which they then manufacture, while still others, like Orbit Semiconductor, serve solely as quick turnaround, high-performance manufacturing foundries for chip and system houses.

Unbundling allows each of these highly focused firms to remain at the leading edge of their particular technical expertise. It also dramatically reduces the investment required to produce state-of-the-art semiconductors: Sun Microsystems, for example, developed its Sparc microprocessor for less than 25 million dollars ('Computer maker aims to transform industry and become a giant', *Wall Street Journal* 18 March 1988). The continued success of small firms such as Cypress, IDT, Altera, and Chips & Technologies demonstrates that neither scale nor vertical integration are necessary to survive in the increasingly capital-intensive semiconductor industry. By focusing and relying on networks of specialised suppliers, Silicon Valley's small firms introduce state-of-the-art products faster than their more integrated competitors.[7]

As they continue to introduce differentiated new products, these specialist producers are fragmenting mass markets for semiconductors – forcing the established producers to become more flexible. In the words of John Rizzo, Weitek's vice-president of marketing: 'You've got to keep subdividing the market and making the niches smaller and smaller. A $1.5 billion market is not one product, it's one hundred products'.

And as fast growing demand for semi-custom products such as gate arrays turns them into commodities, ASIC firms like LSI Logic are moving further up-market, designing higher performance products for narrower, more specialised niches. Even the prototypical commodity market, standard memories, is now being segmented by a proliferation of specialised products more tightly coupled to particular applications or systems (Cole 1988).

In short, while the region's established producers sought to be low-cost producers of general-purpose, commodity devices, the new Silicon Valley firms are competing by getting to market first with a continuing flow of innovative products targeted at highly specialised needs (Cole 1989). They rely on flexibility, service and variety rather than on achieving high volumes to move down the 'learning curve' and reduce unit costs.

THE IMPORTANCE OF REGIONAL NETWORKS

These specialisation strategies allowed firms like Cypress and LSI Logic to grow profitably even during the semiconductor industry's worst downturn in 1985–86. But the success of these start-ups is not simply the work of individual entrepreneurs, nor is the region's continued vitality a demonstration of the intrinsic dynamism of free markets. These new firms have built on Silicon Valley's dense networks of social and professional relationships, and their successes – like those of their predecessors – are inseparable from an environment rich in skill and know-how where engineers are often more loyal to the industry and to advancing technology than to any individual firm.

The region's established producers created this culture during the 1950s and 1960s; but they abandoned it in the 1970s as they shifted to high-volume production. Viewing regional traditions of informal collaboration and net-working as attributes of immaturity rather than sources of dynamism, they standardised products and processes and distanced themselves from customers and suppliers. The 1980s start-ups, by contrast, are not simply building on, but also formalising their relationships with customers and suppliers both within and outside of the region.

Building on informal networks

When Wilf Corrigan left Fairchild Semiconductor in 1979, he sounded out former customers and colleagues on the potential market for semi-custom integrated circuits. He encountered a former employee, Robert Walker, who had recently completed research for an article on the custom chip business. Walker joined Corrigan to write a business plan for a firm called LSI Logic Corporation and they secured financing from a handful of Silicon Valley's leading venture capital firms, including former colleagues at Kleiner Perkins.

The two then recruited a team of engineers Walker had worked with on CAD and custom chips at Fairchild during the 1960s. This reunited group referred to themselves as the 'over-the-hill gang', reflecting the distinctive loyalty and solidarity among the region's engineers. The start-up in turn gained technical support from local trade associations, market research firms, and public relations specialists. By 1985 when LSI Logic went public (in one of the largest initial public offerings in the industry's history), it had created a burgeoning market for ASICs.[8]

Similar entrepreneurial histories are commonplace in Silicon Valley, where the region's networks and institutions foster the continual recombination of skill and technology into new enterprises. More than 100 new technology firms were started in 1988 alone; and most of these new enterprises have succeeded. A recent study found that while only 75 per cent of US manufac-turing start-ups survive their first two years, 90 per cent of Silicon Valley start-ups survive their first six.[9]

It is not simply the concentration of skilled labour and suppliers and the externalities they generate that distinguish the region (as many economic accounts would have it) (see, for example, David & Rosenbloom 1987). Equally important to Silicon Valley's dynamism are the dense networks of social relationships and the trust that develops with shared professional experiences, repeated interaction and geographic proximity. A variety of regional institutions – from business organisations, trade associations and universities, to public relations, consulting, market research and venture capital firms – provide services to the region's small and medium-sized firms. They also promote the informal cooperation, the continual interaction, and the pervasive information sharing which allow local firms to respond rapidly to emerging technologies and market opportunities.

And while legendary rates of inter-firm mobility may mean losses for individual firms, intangible skills and know-how, which can be gained only through experience with particular machines and processes, spreads primarily through the movement of people or hands-on learning. This tacit knowledge is key to innovation, particularly in the complex process of semiconductor production (for recent economic literature on the importance of tacit knowledge to innovation, see Dosi (1988) and Nelson and Winter (1982)). The region as a whole thus benefits from an ongoing process of experimentation and adaptation as new ideas are recombined with existing skills and know-how.[10]

'Outgrowing' the networks

The value of these relationships is demonstrated by the competitive difficulties of the region's established semiconductor producers – the 'fathers' of Silicon Valley – as they abandoned the networks. The companies which had made Silicon Valley famous for their responsiveness and innovation abandoned specialty production during the 1970s.[11] Faced with the growing threat of low-cost Japanese products, they invested heavily in dedicated, high-volume fab lines and facilities in order to reduce unit costs.[12] Not surprisingly, they quickly grew from the small, flexible enterprises which had made Silicon Valley famous, into large, commodity-oriented corporations. Most predicted an end to entrepreneurial start-ups in the semiconductor industry (Robinson 1980).

Rather than recognising the importance of the region to their responsiveness and ability to continually innovate, the merchant semiconductor firms chose an autarchic approach to mass production. As they standardised products and processes to achieve high-volume output, they saw little need for the inter-active relationships with customers which had characterised specialty production.

Intel co-founder and industry leader, Andrew Grove, announced in 1979, for example, that the task for the 1980s was to 'market prefabricated mass produced solutions to users' (cited in *San Jose Mercury News* 4 May 1980). The customer thus soon became, in the words of another executive, 'a distant entity' to the merchant semiconductor producers.[13] As a result, firms like NS, AMD and Intel missed a series of key technical and market opportunities, including the development of the CMOS process and the emergence of markets for ASICs and chip sets.

Not only did the large chip makers distance themselves from their customers, but they also antagonised their equipment suppliers – which tended to be small, undercapitalised firms.[14] As they geared up for volume production, the merchants sought to shift the burden of increasingly severe business cycles onto their suppliers by double ordering during boom times and cancelling orders abruptly during downturns. Forced to minimise costs, they distanced themselves from key vendors, playing them off against one another for price reductions. This reinforced the tendency of the financially weak equipment makers to ship products which were not fully debugged, contributed to the growing climate of distrust and eliminated any possibility of jointly refining the sophisticated and complex process of manufacturing semiconductors. The inferior quality and lower yields of US semiconductor manufacturers relative to their Japanese competitors was the direct result of this arm's-length relationship.

Even the informal cooperative practices of the 1960s and 1970s – including cross-licensing and second sourcing – were largely abandoned. Conveniently ignoring their own genesis, the merchants initiated lawsuits against former cross-licensees, suspected imitators and employees who left to start their own firms.

Finally, driven by the pressures of commodity production to minimise costs, Silicon Valley's merchants shifted manufacturing out of the region to lower cost locations, both in the United States and overseas. While semiconductor assembly and test operations were shifted to Asia during the 1960s to exploit substantial wage differentials, during the late 1970s the merchant producers began to relocate wafer fabrication facilities to lower cost areas within the United States (see Saxenian (1980) and Scott and Angel (1987) for documentation of this process). Only high level research, design and prototype production remained in the high-cost Silicon Valley. This spatial separation of design, manufacturing and assembly further undermined the ability of local semiconductor firms to improve products or to respond rapidly to market changes (see, for example, Markides & Berg 1988).

By pursuing this autarchic version of mass production, Silicon Valley's leading chipmakers abandoned the flexibility and dynamism which had distinguished them in the past.[15] In the words of one Intel Vice-president (cited in M. Schrage, 'Hard times descend on Silicon Valley', *Washington Post* 28 April 1985):

Remember what Silicon Valley companies were good at to begin with: sensing new market opportunities, new market development, and prototype product development... Until recently, the GNP of Silicon Valley was all new products. Silicon Valley simply hasn't been well positioned to handle the commodity market.

This is not to suggest that the shift to mass production was a mistake. Silicon Valley's producers could have pursued a successful mass production strategy without abandoning their customers and suppliers: this would have looked far more like the Japanese model, where learning from customers and suppliers is built into the industry structure, and where product development, manufacturing, and assembly remained spatially proximate (see Haas 1987; Stowsky 1987). By adopting an autarchic version of mass production just as the Japanese were refining a more highly integrated approach, however, Silicon Valley's established merchant producers lagged in manufacturing improvements and product quality, and quickly lost market share to Japanese competition.

Formalising the networks

Silicon Valley's 1980s start-ups, by contrast, are not simply building on the region's social networks, they are formalising them. Rejecting the arm's-length relations of the commodity producers, these newcomers are forging partnerships with customers and suppliers in order to monitor changing markets and jointly redefine products and manufacturing processes. Some of the most successful firms have maintained manufacturing as well as design and development activities within Silicon Valley.

The proliferation of strategic alliances is one indication of this reorientation. The new start-ups have forged more than 350 alliances since 1979, mostly focused in semi-custom and specialty production, and involving either the subcontracting of advanced fab facilities or technology sharing and joint product development (Dataquest 1988). Some involve collaboration with other local start-ups, such as the alliance between Cypress and Altera, to develop jointly electronically-programmable logic devices; while others involve established firms, as in the technology licensing and manufacturing agreement between Seeq Technology and National Semiconductor for high density Flash EEPROMs (electronically erasable and programmable read-only memories).

Engineers characterise these relationships as partnerships distinguished by a mutual commitment not to abandon each other during downturns or exploit advantages during upturns. With time, the best evolve into highly interactive, trust-based relationships involving technology sharing and joint product design and problem solving. Vice-president, Jeffrey Miller, at Silicon Valley start-up Adaptec reports, for example, that: 'We have a closer relationship with our fab at International Microelectronic Products than I had with the in-house foundry when I worked at Intel'.[16]

Such collaboration is not limited to small firms. Hewlett-Packard, for example, has opened up its state-of-the-art foundry for design specialist Weitek to manufacture a high-speed data-crunching chip. As a result, H-P now differentiates its workstations with a faster chip than it could have bought or designed in-house, while Weitek sells this more sophisticated chip to other systems makers. Both see the relationship as the basis for future collaboration.

Explicitly rejecting the distrustful, arm's-length relations between the merchant chip makers and their equipment vendors, engineers at LSI Logic, Seeq and Cypress underscore the importance of continuous interaction with their equipment suppliers to refine complex manufacturing processes.[17] They are, for example, collaborating with suppliers of equipment such as wafer steppers and automated test equipment to design and debug products which allow for rapid product change and reduced equipment set-up times.[18]

The new chip makers are building partnerships with customers as well in order to accommodate the accelerating pace of new product introductions. ASIC producers like LSI Logic and VLSI Technology interact continuously with systems firms and other customers in order to assist them in designing chips for highly specialised applications. Not surprisingly, this involves extensive sharing of proprietary information, and LSI engineers report developing very close relationships with their customer's engineers.[19]

Specialist firms such as Cypress and IDT similarly treat customers as an extension of their organisations. These firms need a detailed understanding of systems trends in order to define and design products for highly-focused niche-narrow markets. Larry Jordan, IDT's marketing director, reports that the firm has chosen to ally itself closely with approximately ten fast growing, small to medium-sized systems firms which it sees as future trendsetters. By building close, trust-based relationships with companies like Sun Microsystems and Silicon Graphics, that are introducing new technologies and architectures, IDT keeps apprised of the details of fast changing systems requirements and market trends.

Design specialist Weitek is so committed to building close ties with customers that it maintains one applications engineer for every field salesman – compared with an engineer for every sixteen salesmen at a traditional firm. Weitek's marketing vice-president, Rizzo, tries to 'create an intangible bond and loyalty between ourselves and the customer. Those intangible bonds are the hardest thing for a competitor to break'.

Of course all of these relationships are not within the region – or even within the United States. Hundreds of alliances have been formed between domestic and foreign technology firms. One of Weitek's closest relationships is with Texas-based Compaq; Chips & Technologies and relies heavily on foundries in Japan as well as Silicon Valley; and H-P is jointly developing its RISC microprocessor with Hitachi.[20] The remarkable fact, however, is that competitive pressures for rapid and frequent new product introductions place a growing premium on collaborative supplier relations – which confers an advantage to local suppliers of critical inputs (or non-local suppliers with a local facility). Thus, new and established semiconductor firms alike continue to locate in Silicon Valley, in spite of exorbitant housing prices and high labour costs.

THE CREATION OF REGIONAL PRODUCTION NETWORKS

This search for flexibility and focus is not limited to Silicon Valley's chip makers. During the past decade, the region has seen hundreds of new start-ups in sectors ranging from disk drives to electronic design automation, from networking software to test equipment. In fact, systems firms, not semiconductor manufacturers, are now at the centre of the emerging production networks in Silicon Valley. Start-ups like Silicon Graphics, Pyramid Technology, Mips Computers and Sun Microsystems are using ASICs and new generations of specialty chips to fragment systems markets with three-dimensional graphics supercomputers, super-minicomputers, high-performance engineering workstations, and the like (see McKenna (1989) on the fragmentation of the computer industry).

By building long-term, collaborative relations with specialised contract manufacturers and suppliers of software, microprocessors, disk drives and network hardware, Silicon Valley systems firms are spreading the costs and risks of new product design and production, dramatically reducing their time to market, and increasing the frequency of new product introductions. Sun Microsystems, for example, introduced four major product generations in its first five years of business. This in turn has forced the region's large systems producers such as Apple and Hewlett-Packard to become more flexible.

Sun is representative of this new wave of systems firms: Sun does only product design, software, prototyping and final assembly in-house, subcontracting the rest of its inputs – from microprocessors to disk drives to terminals – from the rich infrastructure of suppliers in the valley and elsewhere. Not only does this spread costs, but it allows the firm to innovate jointly with its suppliers. And when Sun involves its contract manufacturer Solectron in the process of designing as well as producing the central processing units and peripherals for its workstations, or when a team of Sun and Cypress engineers collaborate in a shared facility to develop a high-performance version of Sun's Sparc microprocessor, the boundaries of these firms begin to blur.

Despite this blurring, however, both customers and suppliers make an explicit effort to preserve each other's autonomy. Most companies prefer that no customer, itself included, account for more than 20 per cent of a supplier's output and many take steps to ensure that their suppliers survive hard times. When several of Adaptec's major customers went out of business simultaneously, for example, a key supplier extended credit to the firm, enabling it to stay in business. Other firms have gone out of their way to identify and develop new customers to help their suppliers through tough periods or to help them diversify their markets. The relations between customers and suppliers are thus increasingly those of equals – horizontal rather than vertical relationships.

Apple's purchasing director, Jim Bilodeau, claims that good partnerships with key vendors involve not simply on-time delivery and quality control but continual extension of the relationship to new areas. He suggests that joint investment in new capital equipment, joint product development and technology exchanges, or shared funding of key engineering talent are all ways to 'build suppliers that you can keep healthy and they in turn will keep you healthy...The more you can get your vendors to think about you when building new products the better'.

In short, the process of solving technical problems and charting future directions in a technologically volatile environment is increasingly a collaborative effort by a network of closely linked firms.

As collaboration extends to a wider circle of firms, it generates a process of complementary innovation between these autonomous but interdependent producers. Suppliers spread the experience and know-how gained from serving a customer in one sector to customers in other industries. This preserves the technological vitality of the region and insures that, in the words of Sun's purchasing director, Jim Metcalf, 'the world's best suppliers are in Silicon Valley'.

This process of reciprocal technological upgrading is clear in the transformation of the local contract manufacturing industry. Flextronics, one of the region's largest contract manufacturers, grew explosively during the 1980s as it shifted from being a consignment assembler (the classic job shop) to a full turnkey assembler with responsibility for selecting suppliers as well as assembling and testing printed circuit boards.[21] The business is changing from low-skill, low-tech assembly into high-skill, capital-intensive manufacturing – particularly as firms like Flextronics and Solectron invest in such sophisticated new technologies as surface-mount technology. By focusing and serving a range of customers in different businesses, they have achieved a level of manufacturing expertise which surpasses that of most of the region's systems firms.

Collaborative manufacturing is by no means limited to Silicon Valley firms, yet there is little doubt that geographic proximity fosters the frequent interaction and personal trust needed to maintain these relationships.[22] Robert Todd, chief executive pfficer of Flextronics, claims that, in his business, close and collaborative relationships cannot survive over great distances for long. As a result, Flextronics has built regional centres around the United States to serve localised clusters of customers. As Apple's Bilodeau notes ('How Apple buys electronics', *Electronics Purchasing* Nov. 1986):

> Our purchasing strategy is that our vendor base is close to where we're doing business. We like them to be next door. If they can't, they need to be able to project an image like they are next door.

The need for continual interaction with and access to the region's accumulation of skills and know-how – particularly in a period of market volatility and rapid new product introduction – thus motivates firms to continue clustering in Silicon Valley.

CONCLUSION

Silicon Valley's networks promote innovation because they foster collective problem solving among specialist firms and the continual recombination of skill and technical resources. Local firms are organising themselves to learn with their customers, suppliers, and competitors about what to make next and how to make it.[23] The informal networks which promoted the diffusion of skill and technology in the region in the 1960s and 1970s are being formalised in the 1980s and 1990s.

As a result, Silicon Valley is now flourishing, despite the ongoing crisis of the commodity chip makers.[24] Local firms generated more new jobs between 1980 and 1986 than those in other leading high-tech centres such as Boston's Route 128, southern California's Orange County and North Carolina's Research Triangle.[25] And as the region continues to spawn new firms and technological advances, its geographic boundaries continue to expand beyond Santa Clara

County. High-tech activity has now spilled north into San Mateo County, east to Alameda County, and south to Santa Cruz.

Nevertheless, the region remains vulnerable. Local firms continue to externalise their activities and the boundaries between firms continue to blur, yet there is no mechanism for regulating this decentralised productive system. The coordinating functions accomplished by corporate hierarchies in the vertically integrated firm are achieved only through an unstructured system of collaborative supplier relationships and informal social networks and associations.

The competitive difficulties of the semiconductor equipment industry are indicative of the need for institutions to assist local firms responding to the immense uncertainty and rapid pace of technological change in the industry. These institutions could provide long-term research, training and management education, export assistance, and other services which the region's entrepreneurial and often undercapitalised firms typically cannot provide themselves. Once established, they would provide a forum to coordinate collective responses to such external threats as technological advances from outside the region.

Such institutions can only be created through public action. Not only must engineers and managers in Silicon Valley overcome their deep-seated distrust of the public sector, but they must also recognise and articulate the social basis of their successes. As long as engineers believe that the region's dynamism is a product of inspired individual entrepreneurs, they will overlook the importance of the region and its relationships. The real challenge facing Silicon Valley entrepreneurs is to transcend the individualistic categories of American social science and business in order to recognise the need for forums to both build a consensus and establish explicitly regional institutions which cut across individual firms and sectors.

The infrastructure for more effective regional institutions already exists. The American Electronics Association (AEA) – which until the late 1970s was primarily a regional organisation supporting the development of small firms in Silicon Valley – remains an important focal points for information exchange among local producers.[26] As the only cross-cutting industry association in the region today, it is well positioned to serve the shared interests of firms in electronics-related industries by providing the collective services that most cannot support on their own. This would involve expanding services the AEA already provides, such as training and management education, and initiating others, such as long-term research and development and technical support.

An AEA with a broader mandate would be only a start. It, in turn, would need to encourage the creation of a wider range of institutions in Silicon Valley, institutions to coordinate cooperation among the region's firms and the local public sector, and to ensure the continued diffusion of technology and skill – thus preserving the flexibility and technological dynamism of its networks of specialist producers.[27] But first a public debate must begin.

NOTES

1 See Saxenian (1989a) for a discussion of the failure of this 'high-tech recipe'.

2 These regions are modern counterparts of the nineteenth century industrial districts described by Alfred Marshall (see Goodman *et al.* 1989; Storper 1989; Storper & Scott 1988; Scott 1988c; Sabel & Zeitlin 1985; Piore & Sabel 1984).

3 This approach builds on the theoretical lead of such scholars as Sabel (1989), Granovetter (1985) and Herrigel (1988).

4 A growing literature describes network forms of organisation, yet there is little discussion of the conditions needed to establish and maintain these forms. Scholars stress vertical disaggregation and the redefinition of supplier relations between complementary producers in this hybrid model, which falls between Williamson's ideal types of market exchange and bureaucratically administered hierarchy; and all agree that such networks provide the flexibility and responsiveness which are critical to the new competitive environment (see Miles & Snow 1986; Johnston & Lawrence 1988; Powell 1987; Johanson & Mattson 1987).

    The case of Silicon Valley suggests that geographic proximity fosters the trust and reciprocity which are crucial to the sustained viability of production networks.

5 The research for this project was based on more than fifty open-ended interviews with Silicon Valley executives, managers, engineers, and venture capitalists conducted between 1986 and 1988. Complete listing of the interviewees and a more complete discussion of the methodology and findings of this research appear in Saxenian (1989b).

6 The start-ups typically produce 100 to 200 different types of chips on the same line, with production runs of between ten and 10 000 units. The established US producers, by contrast, produce ten to twenty different commodity memory or logic devices on a line, with runs exceeding a millions units (Mehler 1987; Borrus 1988).

7 In fact, Cypress has chosen to support spin-offs as independent start-ups rather than attempt to grow internally and lose focus. The firm provided 7.4 million dollars to fund start-up Aspen Semiconductor and one million dollars to Multichip Technology Corporation, both of which are located in Silicon Valley.

8 Analysts predict that by 1992 ASIC devices will account for 24 per cent of integrated circuit sales (Cole 1987).

9 These are the results of a study of more than 400 Silicon Valley companies over a twenty-year period (1967 to 1987) conducted by Professor Albert V. Bruno, University of Santa Clara School of Business (cited in the *New York Times* 7 March 1988).

10 Many Silicon Valley firms recognise the benefits of this process, and actively support it. Amdahl Computers, for example, supported the formation of Saratoga Semiconductor in 1985 by a team of eight of its engineers: Amdahl offered the new firm advice on financial planning, arranged venture capital financing for it, and gave Saratoga first options on its used equipment. Apple is also well known for its support of spin-outs in linked sectors.

11 The flexibility of Silicon Valley semiconductor firms in the 1960s and 1970s came primarily from their small size and lack of automation. These firms avoided automation because the rapid pace of change in products and processes meant that investments in automation would be obsolete before costs were recovered. This contrasts with the flexibility of the 1980's start-ups, which lies in the adoption of flexible design and manufacturing technology.

The early history of the industry reflected a recurrent tension between strategies of product specialisation to serve particular applications and standardisation to achieve scale economies. As late as the early 1970s, the general consensus of the industry was that the future lay in customisation of large-scale integrated circuits and that the role of standard products would be small. The history is detailed in Wilson *et al.* (1980).

12   Between 1978 and 1980 alone, domestic semiconductor manufacturing capacity doubled, and capital expenditures increased from eight to 20 per cent of sales. In 1980, the top seven merchants spent over one billion dollars on plant and equipment – which represented a 51 per cent increase over 1979, which in turn was 63 per cent higher than in 1978 (*Business Week* 21 July 1980).

13   H. Jarrat, 'A look at the semiconductor industry in the 1990s', speech presented to Robertson, Coleman and Stephens at the 1990 Semiconductor Conference, San Francisco, Calif., 23 September 1987.

14   This section draws on Stowsky's (1987) insightful analysis of the semiconductor equipment industry.

15   This is ironic, since during the 1970s, the US auto industry – prototype for America's autarchic (Fordist) model of mass production – was being outdone by the more flexible approach pioneered by Japan's auto producers (see Abernathy *et al.* 1983). In both autos and semiconductors, it is less Japan's low costs and domestic protection than its superior product quality and manufacturing capability which account for their victory over US producers. For documentation of the merchants' crisis, see Borrus (1988).

16   This illustrates the limits of Williamson's (1975) markets-hierarchies dichotomy. If an external contracting relationship is closer than an internal one, internalisation is no longer the most efficient way to deal with the costs of uncertainty, small numbers bargaining and asset specificity.

17   A Cypress engineer claims, for example, that it is critical that their supplier of ion implanters has a facility located just across the parking lot because it allows them to confer easily and frequently.

18   LSI Logic, for example, joined with local IC production test equipment manufacturer Asix Systems to develop software for automatic test equipment for ASICs.

19   Such relationships require geographic proximity, hence ASIC firms like LSI Logic and VTI have design centres near their main customer bases around the world. It also accounts for the continued strength of US producers in ASICs, as domestic systems firms are hesitant to share their new product design specifications with Japanese competitors.

20   There is concern among some analysts that the reliance of design specialists on Asian foundries will lead to a net transfer of US technology (as happened with memory chips, for example). However this overlooks the difference between semi-custom and specialty products and commodity devices. On one hand, we have seen that semi-custom and specialty chip makers build very close relations with their customers which helps to protect them from imitators. On the other hand, these specialist producers are continually introducing new designs so that by the time an imitation is completed, the design is often obsolete.

Moreover, some of the most successful design firms, such as Weitek and Altera, use domestic foundries – and firms like IDT, Cypress, Saratoga and Performance Semiconductor have located fabrication facilities in the United States (largely within Silicon Valley) to ensure rapid and frequent feedback between design and production.

21   Contract manufacturers are getting involved in the early design process by not only manufacturing the boards, but also assembling them into finished systems.

22   Hence the geographic clustering of firms in Silicon Valley is not driven simply by the desire to reduce transaction costs through proximity, as Scott and Angel (1987) assert, but involves the creation of trust and goodwill which cannot be easily captured by analysis of costs.

23   These firms are also learning from their employees – a key element in these collaborative relationships which is not discussed here. The 'H-P way', which accords substantial autonomy and responsibility to employees has been adopted by some of the most successful firms in the region. In addition, new firms like Cypress, IDT and Sun are deliberately organised to promote cross-functional interchange and horizontal flows of information.

24   Of the big three in Silicon Valley, only Intel – which has capitalised on its design expertise and on its control of the proprietary personal computer market for micro-processors – is doing well. AMD and National Semiconductor remain in weak competitive positions despite horizontal consolidation (AMD acquired Monolithic Memories and National Semiconductor acquired Fairchild). All three have sought to become more flexible and move into new markets such as ASICs, with only limited success.

25   More than 18 000 high-tech jobs were created in the region in the twelve months between June 1987 and 1988 alone, and employment surpassed pre-1985 levels (*San Jose Mercury News* 11 July 1988; comparative data from Grubb & Ellis 1987).

26   During its first several decades, the AEA was not at all like the traditional American trade association, which focuses on lobbying Washington for beneficial legislation. The AEA grew by creating bottom-up regional councils based in high-tech centres around the country, in order to promote grassroots mobilisation and networking. In fact, the AEA only opened a Washington office in 1984.

27   There are models for such institutions in US experience. AT&T's Bell Labs served as a 'national applied research and development laboratory' in the 1950s and 1960s by openly diffusing leading-edge semiconductor research and personnel (Borrus 1988). At the regional level, the programs being pioneered by the Michigan Modernization Service are instructive (Russell 1986).

20

INFORMATION TECHNOLOGY AND THE MANAGEMENT OF TERRITORY BY FIRMS

Howard Williams and John Taylor

INTRODUCTION

The purpose of this chapter is twofold. First, it is to examine the interrelationships between the firm, its business activities, its spatial development, and the adoption of ICTs, particularly computer networks. Secondly, it is to explore how these interrelationships give rise to, and require, the management of territory. The perspective adopted is to build from micro-theorising and the evidence of case studies. As argued by Nelson and Winter (1982, p. 52), 'modelling at an industry- or an economy-wide level ought to be guided and constrained by a plausible theory of firm capabilities and behaviour that is consistent with the microcosmic evidence'.

THE NATURE OF THE FIRM

The conceptual framework developed here and used to analyse the relationships between the firm, ICTs, and the management of territory, stems primarily from economic theories of evolutionary change (Nelson & Winter 1982). Importantly, however, this chapter seeks to extend the analytical power of these concepts by their application to the space-economy of the firm. That is, to apply concepts which were aspatial in their origin to the geography of the economic activity of firms.

The basic model developed and deployed here interprets the firm as existing in an uncertain environment and in a complex set of intra- and inter-organisational relationships. The model seeks to explain the behaviour of the firm in terms of evolutionary developments, in which the existing activities and capabilities of the firm have their antecedents in its historic activities, and the future development of the firm is both constrained and made possible by its existing repertories of activities and capabilities (Teece 1985). Furthermore, it is assumed that the activities of the firm and its behaviour are designed to gain, with greater or lesser success, relative control over its environment thereby minimising uncertainty and reducing risk. Thus, the behaviour of the firm is not defined by reference to some optimising behavioural norm but rather in terms of its attempts to reduce uncertainties and exposure to risk.

The firm does not relate to markets solely as mechanisms for resource allocation, but as one of a range of phenomena which it faces which encapsulates, to a greater or lesser extent, risk and uncertainty. Moreover, and paradoxically, the market is interpreted not simply as an unstable threat but also as a prospective stabiliser for the firm (Encaoua *et al.* 1986, p. 55):

> In the struggle to create, maintain and expand favourable market positions, firms' actions are intended not only to affect the current conduct of rivals directly, but also to have an indirect effect by altering market structure in a way which constrains the rivals subsequent actions. In this dynamic process, market strategies or conduct interact with market structure; and current conduct can become embedded in future market structure through strategic investments made by firms to bar entry and reduce intra-industry mobility.

This evolutionary perspective on the nature of the firm brings into sharp focus the question of the relationship between market signals and the firm. Perceiving the market as a resource allocation mechanism carries with it an assumption that, without imperfections, the information it provides to economic agents through price signals accommodates discounted 'contingencies for future states of the world to which probabilities can notionally be attached' (Dosi *et al.* 1988, p. 18). However, the relationship between the market and the firm, seen from a perspective that focuses on responses to uncertainty and risk, is one that is more complex, for the information provided by the market cannot consistently incorporate or 'discount the possibility of future states of the world whose occurrence is, to different degrees, the unintentional result of present decisions taken by heterogeneous agents characterised by different competences, beliefs and expectations' (Dosi *et al.* 1988, p. 18). Thus, the firm, using the market as a means to offset uncertainty and risk, will instigate behaviour, the outcome of which is shaped unpredictably through the market presence of other firms. This relationship between the firm and the market is inherently based on gathering information to minimise uncertainties and risk.

Furthermore, the firm has an imperfect ability to process information deriving from the market, and this imperfect decision-making ability is not evenly distributed amongst firms (see, for example, Heiner 1988). Imperfections, both of decision-making capability and of the information itself, limit the 'competence' of the firm to make decisions and give rise to the so-called competence-decision making, or C-D, gap.

The C-D gap emerges from the relaxation of the 'extreme' assumptions in standard choice theory, for example that there are no errors in the decision-making process and that information is used perfectly. With the relaxation of this assumption, the nature of decision-making competence within the firm becomes an issue that needs to be understood in relationship to the nature of the decision being taken. It is assumed that the greater the difficulty of the decision the greater the C-D gap and, as a result, economic agents 'become progressively worse at imitating optimal decision rules' (Heiner 1988, p. 148).

These difficulties not only exist in the relationship between firms and markets but also within the firm where there are information uncertainties and imperfections, especially in the case of large and complex firms. These internal information problems conjoin with those derived from the relationship between the firm and its external environment, and thereby compound the C-D gap. These internal informational difficulties are a fundamental consequence, particularly in large and complex organisations, of the necessary interactions of organisational divisions and sub-units engaged in processes of both strategic and operational policy formulation, interpretation and delivery.

The existence of both internal and external informational uncertainties and asymmetries and their influence on the C-D gap is perhaps well illustrated in differentiating the responses to uncertainty of large and small firms. In essence, a simple paradox in the situation of large and small firms can be hypothesised. For the large and complex organisation, the influence of external informational difficulties upon the C-D gap is likely to be relatively small, whilst the influence of informational uncertainties with respect to the internal capabilities of the organisation is likely to be relatively large. The converse would be the case for small firms.

The chief source of external and strategic information for the small firm derives from its own operational interactions with buyers and sellers (Williams & Charles 1986). Sophisticated market and product information is unlikely to be used by small organisations not least because of the cost involved with its acquisition and processing. The small firm may well be relatively ignorant of its external world therefore. However, the same firm can be seen as having relatively full knowledge of its internal capabilities and relationships. For example, the small jobbing manufacturer may well have detailed and relatively complete information about its production capabilities, and thus be able to operate as a least-cost producer. However, its knowledge of changes in production processes and, more fundamentally, in terms of changes in products, including materials and quality, will be comparatively weaker.

By contrast, the large and complex firm invests in research and development, and 'watching and monitoring' activities such as market analysis, government relations and strategic planning. These activities can be hypothesised as enabling the firm to minimise informational difficulties in respect of the external world and thereby helping to narrow the C-D gap. Yet the large and complex organisation faces widening informational difficulties in respect of knowledge of internal capabilities and relationships, thus exacerbating the C-D gap.

THE SPATIAL DEVELOPMENT OF THE FIRM

Specific geographical developments of the firm can be seen in part as attempts by the firm to enhance its information and information flows related to both the external environment and its own internal capabilities. In the first instance, for example, through investments in the 'watching and monitoring' of the external environment, individual firms are better able to assess the behaviour and outcomes of changes in the external environment at both the operational and strategic level. Significantly, the firm can use this assessment in terms if its own functional and spatial development. In the second instance, the firm, through enhanced information and information flows, can better monitor its own internal performances, again both functionally and spatially. Thus the firm is better able to define the parameters within which it can operate.

The locational strategy of a firm can be seen as contingent upon the inter-play between information and information flows, the market, the technical foundations of production, and the nature of the organisation. It might be hypothesised, therefore, that a firm will tend to colocate all its activities in situations where opportunities for the realisation of economies of scale and scope are circumscribed by market conditions, such as a high degree of pro-duct specificity, short production runs together with a market bias or policy towards local procurement. In this instance, the co-location of investment in production, sales and marketing, as well as other functions, is seen as axio-matic to the minimisation of uncertainty and the reduction of risk.

The consequence of this strategy is that the expansion of the firm is dependent on the spatial duplication of the company. Unless the firm specific-ally addresses the informational difficulties attendant upon the expansion into spatially differentiated markets, the informational uncertainties deriving from its new external relationships grow prohibitively large. Without specific informational and organisational responses to the increasing geographical spread of its activities, the firm will remain trapped in its pre-existing space.

If a firm secures a geographical expansion of its activities through processes of spatial duplication, then questions of coordination and its cost arise. Though coordination costs are not insignificant in a spatially duplicated enterprise, the level of these costs is relatively small, for each establishment remains, to a large extent, ring-fenced.

What this argument begins to raise is that the relationship between the firm and place is more fully understood at the level of territory rather than that of 'geography'. The notion of territory as employed here involves a claim being made by the firm upon a particular geography, and it represents therefore more than the mere presence of an organisation in a particular space of an organisation. As observed by Sack (1984, p. 34), territoriality is the 'assertion by an organisation, or an individual in the name of the organisation, that an area of geographic space is under its influence or control'. Within the analytical framework of the firm deployed here, the basis of territorial claims rests on the firm's information creation use and analysis in the context of the desire to reduce uncertainty and minimise risk.

The notion that firms operate through territorial management introduces the firm as operating in a set of relationships with other firms and organisations. The firm pursues its territorial claims through defensive and aggressive strategies in respect to other firms and organisations which are simultaneously making territorial claims.

The notion of territoriality thus brings into question the role of markets, for, when defined geographically, they come to be conceptualised by the firm as the focus of territorial claims as well as resource allocating mechanisms. Thus the market as an object of territorial management has in effect become endogenous to the firm.

The definition and the subsequent strengths of the firms claim on territory are the outcome of an informational analysis of the economic and social geography of particular places. The creation of territory from the informational analysis of place is integral to the firm's strategy to minimise uncertainties and reduce risk. Through the informational analysis of geographically differentiated resources, the firm is able to select those which enable it to minimise uncertainties and reduce risks.

The strength of specific territorial claims will be shaped by this informational analysis and its degree of integration with the uncertainty-reducing and risk-minimising strategies of the firm. Further, it can be anticipated that a change in the nature of the territorial claim by a firm will emanate from either a deepening of its informational analysis of a particular place, or from its response to a change in the territorial claims and management strategies of other firms.

Different firms will define places differently reflecting the nature of their informational analysis. Furthermore, a single place may well be the subject of a multitude of territorial claims and management strategies which will be prosecuted with differing intensities by different firms. For example, a specific location may well appear to have economic potential significant to a number of individual firms. However, this potential will not necessarily be of equal relevance and value to each of them. Different firms make their territorial claims with differing degrees of intensity.

THE FIRM AND THE ADOPTION OF ICTS

The conceptual view of the firm in which the C-D gap is created both from informational uncertainties within the firm, and between the firm and its external environment, provides a framework within which to understand the adoption and diffusion of ICTs, particularly computer networks. From such an analysis it follows that the strategic response of the firm to an uncertain environment is centred on the collection, storage, manipulation and transmission of information. For example, as argued by Willinger and Zuscovitch (1988, p. 246) the firm can be seen to operate an 'information intensive production system' in which it seeks to coordinate inputs and outputs through network management:

The firm is increasingly trying to match the variety of properties demanded by the user with its own technological 'data-base'...The definition of the product can no longer be made without the active cooperation of the user...

In consequence, firms face increasing information costs. In order to reduce these information costs the firm may well respond through the codification and routinisation of decision-making procedures, thereby simplifying internal operations, and through the development of greater coordination skills. These responses are facilitated by the adoption of ICTs, in particular computer networks.

The coordination of the firm is achieved by a complex fabric of information flows. Within a single establishment firm and/or even the spatially duplicated firm, the coordinative function remains largely unspecified and informal. Thus the activities that surround these information flows are likely to be relatively non-routinised. However, the implementation of a strategy which is based on the spatial fragmentation of functions necessarily focuses attention on the nature of coordination and how such activities can be formally specified.

Coordination activities can be seen to embrace a range of interwoven information flows – administrative, programming, planning and strategic (Capello 1988). The outcome of the process of spatial fragmentation and functional separation is determined by the extent to which the firm is able both to specify fully and separate out the different coordinative information flows, and to achieve their reconstruction into an effective system. Where the process of identification of different coordinative information flows is only partial, the implementation of the spatial fragmentation and functional separation of the firm is necessarily limited.

The type of coordinative information flows that can be formally specified and separated out is influenced by the nature of the communications technology adopted by the firm. Thus, for example, Thorngren (1970) argued that the telephone was only an effective mediator of coordinative information flows of the sort which could be reduced to routine transactions. As a technology, the telephone has facilitated the spatial distribution of functions which can be controlled through routinised information flows.

However, computer networks permit the capture, storage, manipulation and transmission of greater volumes of information and thus provide a further impetus to spatial fragmentation and functional separation. Such outcomes will only occur if these increased volumes of information and their communication correspond to those specific information flows central to and capable of reconstruction into the complex fabric of coordination management. For example, in some firms the use of computer networked information flows has permitted the coordination of spatially dispersed research and development functions. However, resonance between the nature of computer networked information flows and those information flows necessary for the coordination of spatially complex organisations, helps to define the trajectory of the spatial development of the firm.

Axiomatic to this strategy of spatial fragmentation and functional separation is the monitoring of internal activities in terms of their organisational costs as opposed to the per unit cost of output. This monitoring process therefore exposes an information axis, for example, to production both in terms of physical processes and the management of those processes. Investment in ICTs will enable the firm to enhance its collection, storage, manipulation and transmission of data and better facilitate the management of a strategy of spatial fragmentation and functional separation. For example, within an ICT investment will be focused on two main areas: the actual production processes, such as CNC machines and manufacturing LANs, and on management systems.

CASE STUDY EVIDENCE

In this section we will present an interpretation of a case study firm in the context of the preceding discussion. The case study firm is a manufacturer of cleaning products for the consumer market. The company was founded in the United Kingdom during the last century and was acquired by an American firm in the early part of this century. As a result, the United Kingdom operation is an integral element of an international company. It has commercial and production activities in almost all OECD countries, and research and development activities in several countries, including the United Kingdom.

The development of a national market for the firm's products in the 1920s and 1930s signalled the demise of markets which had been constructed regionally, largely served by regional companies. The development of a national market was the result of the competitive strategies of the major players who sought to exploit both technical innovations in products and economies of scale, in order to challenge the market position of the regional companies. The case study firm, when independent, was a victim of this strategy but on acquisition adopted new products from the parent company and implemented a national development strategy.

The development strategy of the parent company was based on securing a major market position in each national market. The company could therefore be seen as spatially duplicated, with each operating company providing its own objectives and product strategies with a relatively large degree of autonomy.

The ultimate outcome of this competitive process in the United Kingdom was, by the late 1950s, a duopoly of national manufacturers in a context in which the retailers (the customers) were fragmented and dependent on the manufacturers, for example, for market intelligence of consumer behaviour and retailing synergies. Moreover, the industrial suppliers of raw materials, who were a potential competitive threat, were not actually so because they were uninterested in what was seen as low volume and technically complex products unsuited to current manufacturing technologies, which were deployed to produce high volume, low value products.

The confluence of three key processes of change throughout the 1970s brought a profound challenge to the established practices of the dominant suppliers. The first of these sources of change was associated with the growing concentration of retailers and the development of their own centres of retailing expertise and analysis of consumer information. As a result, the retailers sought a partnership with the suppliers, including the case study firm, breaking away from the dependency they traditionally had on them as a supplier. Secondly, the basic technology that underpinned the development of the products underwent a period of profound change which restricted the product innovation capability of the case study firm unless it had the explicit support of the raw material suppliers. Again the result was a change in the relationship away from one based on the dominance of the case study firm and towards one based increasingly upon mutual dependency. Thirdly, and related to the growing authority of retailers and the increased involvement of the raw material suppliers in the production of these relatively high value, low volume products, an alternative source of product became available through third-party manufacturers supplying retailers with 'own-label' products.

The case study company has responded to these challenges by restructuring its businesses in three ways – through the spatial reorganisation of its activities, through the development of information flows upon which the organisation is able to coordinate its business, and through its redefinition and management of territorial claims.

In effect, the firm has sought to put in place two parallel organisational structures, the activities of which are coordinated through computer networked information flows. These parallel structures are concerned with organising the firm's activities around strategies designed to reduce and minimise uncertainty.

The first of these parallel structures is concerned with reducing uncertainty and risk which emerges from the external environment, through the development of enhanced information flows. The activities included in this structure are, for example, sales management, brand management, advertising, consumer research, and market and product analysis. This structure accounts for between 20 per cent and 40 per cent of product costs. In instances where the firm has relatively limited informational resources, the proportion of information costs associated with total product costs are greater. Thus, with new products, typically 40 per cent of costs are associated with the development of new information flows.

These new information flows through this first parallel structure are integral to the better specification of consumer requirements, the enhanced support of customers (the retailers) in terms of order handling, the definition of new product opportunities, the formal modelling of markets, the redefinition of sub-national markets, and the better definition of the retail environment, including product synergies and shelf displays. In effect this new structure seeks to provide information 'haloes' around the firm's existing products, and a catalytic informational basis from which to define both new products and territorial claims.

Significantly this first parallel structure is more properly understood as a constellation of regional and national agents within the firm, each of which is seeking to minimise its own uncertainties. Thus, within this structure are the national operating units, excluding manufacturing, and the emergent regional operating units. The significance of these regional units is that they represent a specific claim upon a territory based on an enhanced informational analysis of the location. Thus, for example, the company is attempting to understand the use of its products in different consumer environments through informational analysis which incorporates local cultural differences, regional and national differences in relevant regulatory regimes, and differences in specific physical environments.

In asserting these new territorial claims, the case study firm is raising the entry costs for potential competitors, and defining the terms of a new partnership with the retailers based on relatively better informational resources. Through this informational analysis, the company is creating new operational certainties paradoxically based on the rediscovery of territorial differences.

The second parallel structure is concerned with the procurement, manufacture and delivery of products. The scope of its activities accounts for about two-thirds of employment, and between 60 per cent and 80 per cent of total product costs. Thus, this second parallel structure contains a substantial element of the costs of the company, and their management and control is central to its viability. As opposed to the first parallel structure which at its most aggregated level remains national, this second parallel structure is designed to operate at the European level and can thus be seen as an integrated cross-national operating unit seeking to establish and implement homogeneous processes. In essence this parallel structure is concerned with the reduction of risk and minimisation of uncertainties at an international level.

Moreover, this procurement–manufacture–delivery organisation has sought to realign the activities and processes of its constituent departments. This is particularly so in, for example, manufacturing engineering where pre-existing engineering values led investment in manufacturing processes towards greater and greater efficiency measured in terms of output per unit of time. This performance measure had been promulgated without regard to broader questions such as the time taken to retool a production line or the difficulties experienced when, for example, differences in the manufacturing tolerances of different suppliers' raw materials caused the production line to be readjusted. An example of this is the detrimental impact of the different technical characteristics of a packing case upon the smooth operation of the production line. In many instances the production line operated on such fine tolerances that a change in packing cases stopped the line and necessitated its readjustment. This occurred despite the apparent identical specification of such packing cases.

As a result, the manufacturing activities of the firm became gradually distanced from its commercial activities, and what had historically been a key element of competitiveness had become a liability. The manufacturing investment program had become divorced from the commercial needs of the company. For example, in one case quoted, the advantages of two hours of production (at high speeds) were offset by the two shifts required to retool the line for a different product.

Similar issues were exposed in the procurement activities of the firm which had sought to buy the cheapest materials in markets defined nationally. Such a policy began to impose significant cost penalties on the organisation. For example, the suppliers of certain raw materials operated a de facto cartel across Europe which resulted in national prices being different, and all above world prices. Without any concentration of its buying power internationally, the case study firm was unable to confront the pricing agreements established between certain suppliers.

Furthermore, the policy of competitive tendering and the acceptance of the cheapest price led to formality and rigidity in the relationships between the case study firm and its suppliers. As a result, the case study firm found itself having to carry an increasing range and volume of raw material stocks in order to be able to guarantee the availability of materials for manufacturing, and to allow sufficient time to exercise its formal procurement procedures. In many cases, the firm was carrying as a minimum, three months' stock.

In the mid-1980s these rigidities were addressed through the following policies, the key elements of which laid the foundations of this second parallel structure. Specifically these were:
- the reorientation of engineering activities towards the profitability of the company through the introduction of new and different review processes for projects, and the linking of engineering activities to product ranges;
- a focus on the integration of materials, manufacturing, engineering, and distribution at the European and national level; and
- the integration of the 'production' activities of the firm with product design in order to minimise the mismatch between product and process technologies.

The integration of production processes within single plants, and thereby the increased utilisation of production resources, together with the integration of production between plants, has enabled the company to review its manufacturing facilities. In this review it was evident the traditional investment patterns, whilst consistent at the national scale, were idiosyncratic at a European level, resulting in the company carrying approximately 50 per cent excess capacity in some products. The result of the review was the closure of one-third of the manufacturing facilities.

Thus, the case study firm has sought to implement a new spatial division of production and a new spatial division of labour, but has done so within the envelope of existing establishments. The spatial reorganisation of the company has not resulted in the exploitation of new locations. The new spatial divisions of labour and production are being articulated in an established geography of the firm that had been determined by the needs of a different spatial division of labour and production.

This constraint on locational reorganisation of the company reflects the nature of the territorial claims made, which have been reinforced by the firm's long-established knowledge and experience of particular localities. Conversely, those new activities of the company designed to enhance its informational resources related to the external environment, have seen new spatial structures introduced.

The company also set about developing a real-time information system upon which the process of reorganisation has become increasingly dependent. Through the creation of this information system, the firm is able to manage its risk minimisation strategies and integrate the activities of the two parallel structures. The development of the information system has been conceptualised around a three-layer model. These layers are

- process control and optimisation within all activities;
- process integration on a product/category basis; and
- process and management systems integration at the corporate level.

The first two layers are primarily concerned with the reduction of risk through the better collection, storage, manipulation and transmission of information related to dominant cost structures of the firm. The third layer is concerned with the enhanced coordination of the company, and as such acts as a bridge between the two parallel structures that have been created to implement the distinct strategies of the minimisation of uncertainty and the reduction of risk.

CONCLUSIONS

This chapter has sought to examine the interrelationships between the spatial and functional development of the firm, its management of territory and the role played by information and information flows, particularly those mediated by computer networks, within each of these.

The perspective of this chapter has been to focus on the behaviour of the firm. The basic analytical framework stems primarily from economic theories of evolutionary change and development. In essence, such theorising focuses on the internal structures and activities of the firm, seeing them as both constrained by, and the outcome of, the previous structures and activities of the firm. Thus the firm is not a free agent able to restructure itself by reference solely to strategic criteria, but one whose future development is both defined and constrained by the repertoire of its current activities, and their antecedents.

The behaviour of the firm is seen, in abstract, to focus on the minimisation of uncertainties and the reduction of risk. The firm is seen as confronting two sources of uncertainty and risk, one associated with its information and knowledge of the external environment, and the second with respect to the firm's information and knowledge of its own internal capabilities. It is argued that the enhancement of information and information flows is critical to the reduction of risk and the minimisation of uncertainties. However, it is recognised that the firm confronts not only informational uncertainties which confound its formulation and delivery of policy, but also that the firm is unable to process perfectly the information available. Thus, a firm can be seen to possess a competence-decision, or C-D, gap which is exacerbated by the complexity, and the nature, of the information uncertainties which surround the decision being made.

Thus, the firm is seen to deploy those strategies which secure the minimisation of uncertainties and the reduction of risk. Of particular concern here are both the variety of organisational responses of the firm to an uncertain world in terms of its spatial structures and its management of territory, and its adoption of ICTs, particularly computer networks. It is argued that the information available to the firm and the flows of information within and between the firm and its external environment, are enhanced by the adoption of computer networks. Moreover, it is through the analysis of these enhanced informational resources that the firm is able to surround its existing products and territories with information 'haloes' and establish a catalytic informational basis from which to define both new products and territorial claims and their interrelationships.

Through the use of case study material, different organisational responses of the firm have been identified here, namely, spatial duplication and parallel structures. These structures can be seen as emerging from an interaction between the nature of the firm, the external world, the territorial claims and management strategies of the firm and, in the case of the parallel structure, its computer networked information flows.

In the case of spatial duplication, the firm is seeking to secure greater certainty and less risk through the functional and spatial integration of the firm, the articulation of multiple but independent territorial claims, and the development of information flows that are to a large extent specific to these territorial claims. Moreover, the products and activities of the firm are established in relationship to these specific territorial claims.

The development of a parallel structure within the firm, each element of which is focused on risk reduction and uncertainty minimisation, raises new issues about the spatial development of the firm, the nature of its territorial claims and the role played by ICTs, particularly computer networks. The development of parallel structures is more than the fragmentation of the firm into branch plants, administrative centres and the Head Office, or however else the corporate hierarchy might be expressed. The concept of parallel structures involves the functional separation and spatial fragmentation of the firm into a multitude of interdependent territories.

The development of the firm, however, is centred upon its 'virtual' coordination through the use of computer networked information flows. Furthermore, the firm brings to bear upon its development, not the simple aggregation of its territorial claims, but the consequences of their interrelationships and synergies. Thus, specific territorial developments pursued by the firm are surrounded, and secured, by the pre-existing territorial claims of the firm. The consequent space-economy of the firm represents a complex spatial system, which is itself underpinned by computer networked information flows.

The evolutionary nature of the firm, however, places a constraint upon it in terms of existing structures, activities and locations, as well as providing the framework for its development. The adoption of computer networks, and the enhanced information flows that come in their wake, introduces to the firm a new and further set of criteria by which it is able to conceptualise and implement change. Thus, although bounded by its antecedents, the firm is able to secure its development through the creation and management of territory by enhanced information flows.

21

TECHNOLOGICAL CHANGE, INDUSTRIAL ORGANISATION AND THE RESTRUCTURING OF UNITED STATES MANUFACTURING

Marshall Feldman

INTRODUCTION

In the middle of the 1970s, for the first time since the United States became a nation, the small business share of employment began to increase (*The State of Small Business* 1987). This event captured the attention, imagination and dollars of economic development agencies across the country. A host of small business-oriented economic development tools, such as small business incubators, enterprise zones and local venture capital funds was introduced. Today, it is virtually impossible to find an economic development plan in the United States without at least some component aimed at small businesses.

Associated with these tools, a new terminology and set of concepts have come to dominate the field. Instead of speaking of multipliers and export sectors, today planners talk about entrepreneurship, innovation and – most recently – flexibility. Implicit in these terms is an underlying theory, albeit rarely stated and developed with full rigour, that somehow sees a strategy based on small businesses as desirable in today's economy.

This chapter explores this issue by analysing national data on employment, location and industrial organisation over the period 1976 to 1984. The chapter's purpose is twofold. On one hand, it attempts to shed light on recent economic restructuring and the underlying theoretical issues. On the other hand, it is a first attempt at developing a methodology for examining such issues on a broad, national scale. The research at this point is therefore exploratory. As we will see, the issues are quite complex and require far richer data and methods than are ordinarily available.

SIZE OF FIRM AND REGIONAL CHANGE

How we interpret contemporary economic change, how we plan for the future, and what future we plan for all, hinges on our interpretation of broad historic changes. At one extreme we may be lulled into a sanguine state by a theory that sees such restructuring as the automatic self-adjustment of otherwise beneficial markets. Then, except perhaps where market 'imperfections' are at work, all we need do is stand back while markets do their magic. At the other extreme, we may be roused by a theory that sees restructuring as an episode in capitalism's historical drive to maintain class exploitation. Restructuring then presents the opportunity to plan a better world built around a kinder and gentler economic system.

There is no shortage of explanations for the spread and persistence of different sized firms (Averitt 1968; Gold 1981; Scherer *et al.* 1975; Steindl 1965), but explanations of broad historic periods characterised by particular patterns of size are relatively rare. In general, the few existing theories may be grouped under the headings: technological systems, accumulation regimes, and corporatism and monopoly capitalism.

Technological systems

The technological-systems approach is descendant from Kondratief and Schumpeter and emphasises clusters of technological innovations. In *Business Cycles,* Schumpeter (1939, p. 93) argues that innovations tend to cluster in time, space and industry. During economic upswings, innovations are inhibited by a resistant environment, uncertainty and lack of complementary goods. Innovations are therefore most likely during depressions, when low returns in established industries make the risks associated with innovation less onerous. When a successful innovation is new and has no competition, its owner enjoys a monopoly and captures technological rents. But these high returns spur other firms to imitate the innovator, so innovations come in spurts, in selected locations and in selected industries.[1]

If innovations come in waves and are situated mainly in small firms, then small firms prevail during periods of innovation. Schumpeter does not make this argument, but instead assumes major innovations require new plants and that new, but not necessarily small, firms are most prone to innovate. In fact, elsewhere Schumpeter (1942) argues that large corporations are increasingly the site for innovation. Stigler (1951) makes a parallel argument, stemming from Adam Smith, that scale economies foster increasing specialisation (vertical disintegration) as a market grows. Others argue the opposite, claiming bureaucracy in large firms stifles innovation (see Kamien & Schwartz 1982 for a review). This view is prevalent in the product cycle literature, which commonly sees firms growing as their markets mature (Abernathy & Utterback 1978; Hayes & Wheelwright 1979; Link 1980; Mueller 1972; Oakey 1984; Rothwell & Zegveld 1985; Vernon 1966).

When wedded with assumptions about the geography of labour markets, final demand and invention, the product cycle hypothesis becomes a theory of industrial location and regional growth and decline (Hall 1985; Markusen 1985; Miller & Côté 1987; Norton & Rees 1979; Thompson 1975; Vernon 1979). Innovations, particularly innovations in small firms, are thought to depend heavily on external urbanisation economies. Consequently, innovations come about in large metropolitan areas acting as 'seedbeds.' As a product matures it becomes standardised, its markets become mass, and it is mass produced by relatively low-skill labour. This, together with the bunching of innovations in small firms, sets in motion a geographic dynamic as waves of new, small firms grow in large urban areas, mature, and then establish production facilities at low-cost peripheral sites.[2]

Product-cycle theory has been criticised for relying on biological metaphor, for projecting historical patterns as essential features of all periods, for being technologically deterministic, and for ignoring the diversity of actual historical experience (Scott 1988a; Storper 1985; Walker 1985). Some of these limitations are overcome by abandoning the product-cycle model while still accepting Schumpeter's thesis on technological clustering. Each cluster of innovations involves a closely interrelated set of technologies that constitutes a 'technological system' with its own unique 'technological trajectory' (Freeman *et al.* 1982; Nelson & Winter 1977; Perez 1985). Such systems also involve their own economic practices, and together these practices and technologies constitute a 'technoeconomic paradigm'. Transitions between paradigms usually involve crisis and social upheaval because paradigms interface with socio-institutional structures, and as new technologies mature a 'mismatch' develops between the existing socio-institutional structure and the technoeconomic paradigm (Perez 1985).

In fact, it is plausible that today's new technologies are encouraging a shift to small firms. Small batch technologies are becoming cost-competitive with mass production and offer small and medium-sized firms the opportunity to enter markets previously dominated by large firms (Bollard 1983).[3] New technologies based on microelectronics and robotics allow even small firms to offer a variety of semi-customised goods and rapidly switch between products (Cohen & Zysman 1987, ch. 10; Perez 1985). Advances in telecommunications allow entire factories and even complex, multi-establishment production systems to respond to almost instantaneous feedback from 'point-of-sale' systems at warehouses and retail outlets, so manufacturers can adjust their operations on a day-to-day basis. These technologies are affecting both 'immature' and 'mature' industries, and even making some industries, such as automobiles, undergo 'dematuration' (Abernathy *et al.* 1983).

Accumulation regimes

The technological-systems approach is highly reminiscent of the 'social structure of accumulation' (SSA) or 'regulation' theory of political economy.[4]

Regulation theory's central proposition is that capitalism cannot maintain itself through market mechanisms alone. Competition, accumulation, class struggle and technological change continually transform capitalist societies, but sustained growth requires relatively stable patterns of social reproduction and allocation of net product between investment and consumption. Market mechanisms do not ensure stability or balance in these patterns, so capitalist economies contain a variety of extra market institutions and social practices. During periods of growth, these elements have a certain internal coherence and integrity, but during periods of crisis they come increasingly into contradiction with one another. This allows one to view capitalism's history as one of construction and breakdown of successive 'accumulation regimes'.

Most regulation theorists characterise the postwar US political economy as a regime of 'Fordism'. Under Fordism, mass production is articulated to mass consumption so that productivity growth is absorbed by increasing effective demand. Starting in the late 1960s, Fordism entered a period of crisis as economic turbulence increased dramatically. This was due to several reasons, some exogenous and some internal to Fordism itself. First, a series of political events (the OPEC oil embargo, the Vietnam war, etc.) rocked an increasingly integrated international economy. Second, after two decades of growth, markets in industrial countries became saturated. Third, international competition increased as western European and Japanese economies recovered from the Second World War. Adding to this, several third-world countries went into debt to finance development strategies based on low-cost, mass produced exports. Fourth, labour and popular movements developed considerable strength in the advanced capitalist countries and pressed demands for wages, business regulation and social legislation that cushioned the impact of job loss. The latter enabled labour to resist management attempts at increasing productivity, and combined with the other demands to impinge on already stagnating profits. Fifth, in response to the crisis, neo-conservative regimes in the United States, Britain and elsewhere added to the instability by dismantling Keynesian mechanisms for economic stabilisation and by privatising and deregulating certain activities. Sixth, business tried to re-establish profitability by restructuring, and the resulting spatial and economic change made the economy even more volatile.

Many believe the 1980s marked the beginning of a new regime of 'flexible accumulation' (Harvey 1987; 1988; Lash & Urry 1987; Piore & Sabel 1984; Scott & Storper 1988; Storper & Scott 1988; Swyngedouw 1989; Tolliday & Zeitlin 1987). In response to fierce international competition and cost-cutting, firms differentiated their products to attract customers, and so mass production lost much of its advantage. Stable markets had allowed firms to realise the scale economies of mass production, but economic instability put large capital investments at risk. Consequently, businesses adopted small-scale, flexible production methods that lowered risk and allowed rapid response to changing economic conditions (Piore & Sabel 1984).

Perhaps even more important were new strategies for competition. In Japan, Germany and elsewhere, the state became an active partner with business. This was partly accomplished through corporatist policies that gave workers stable, long-term employment. Consequently, firms invested heavily in training and gained enormous flexibility in assigning work assignments. The Japanese in particular used a strategy combining continual process innovation, product innovation and market segmentation (Kenney & Florida 1987). The Japanese achieved these results primarily in large firms which orchestrate the operations of tight confederations of independent suppliers (Dohse *et al.* 1985; Tolliday & Zeitlin 1987).

Flexibility is commonly associated with vertical disintegration, and this is why many authors speak of growing 'flexible specialisation.' Irregular product markets, competition through rapid product innovation, technologies favouring varied scales in different phases of production, capital shortages, the drive to lower labour costs and re-establish control over labour, the drive to circumvent restrictive union contracts, and the need to overcome sporadic labour shortages – in short, the feature of recent economic change – all favour vertical disintegration (Holmes 1986).

In turn, vertical disintegration implies a specific spatial pattern. Vertically disintegrated firms rely on 'external economies of scope' achieved by producing multiple products in a single location (Scott 1983a; 1986; 1988a; Goldstein & Gronberg 1984). Such firms therefore cluster in space, and agglomeration takes on increased significance. There are two models of spatial organisation under flexible specialisation (Scott 1986, p. 224). In the firm-based model, a large firm creates a network of specialised suppliers located near, or even in, the main plant. Inventories are minimised and flexibility increased by just-in-time (*kamban*) delivery systems. Since suppliers are linked to a single customer, this requires long-term, cooperative arrangements and implies relatively stable linkages. In the industrial-district model, flexibly specialised firms are typically small, rely on a wide range of suppliers, and sell to numerous customers. These linkages are inherently unstable, and resulting fluctuations in labour demand implies that firms have access to substantial pools of labour.

Agglomerations of flexible specialists tend to be in 'newer' areas because older cities (Storper & Scott 1988):

constitute difficult environments for flexible production...[because of] the rigidification of labor relations and...unionisation. Some of the consequences of this are...ossified work rules and job demarcation, limitations on managerial discretion, high wages and fringe benefits, and...additional costs and restrictions through local government planning and legislation.

Flexible specialists therefore locate in (a) suburban peripheries of established metropolitan areas, (b) pre-existing districts formed by industries that relied on flexible production in an earlier time period, and (c) cities, such as those of the US sunbelt, with relatively limited histories of industrialisation (Sabel 1989). Firms are often active participants in this and actively create these complexes (Storper & Walker 1983). In time, the process accelerates through a Verdoorn effect as agglomeration and vertical disintegration feed back on each other (Scott 1986; Scott & Angel 1987).

Corporatism and monopoly capitalism

Given that such notable thinkers as Marx, Schumpeter, Sweezy and Galbraith have argued capitalism inherently tends towards increasing size and economic concentration, it is understandable that the idea of a new epoch of flexibility built around vertically disintegrated, small firms has attracted some criticism. Flexibility does not solve the problem of stagnant demand and may in fact exacerbate the problem by polarising income, so there is little ground for believing a new boom based solely on flexibility is possible (Mahon 1987; Solo 1985). Furthermore, flexible production is hardly new and has existed historically side-by-side with mass production, sometimes even within individual sectors (Feldman & Mullin 1989; Gertler, forthcoming). Indeed, it is questionable that mass production or flexible specialisation can by themselves constitute production systems (Williams *et al.* 1987).

Marx (1967, p. 626), Schumpeter (1942, p. 140) and Galbraith (1978, ch. 2) use scale economies to explain the secular trend towards big firms. Marx adds a second argument in that firms surviving economic crises take over the assets of firms that fail. For Marx, crises are a corrective that restore profit ability by devaluing capital. Schumpeter also sees crises as a self-corrective mechanism, but for him innovation, rather than devaluation, rescues capitalism. Baran and Sweezy (1966), in contrast, argue modern capitalism inherently tends to stagnate, but accidental, exogenous events (wars, epochmaking innovations, etc.) and intervention by the state have so far held off the inevitable.

Despite appearances, these theories do not imply that a shift towards small size is impossible.[5] They do, however, contradict some recent interpretations of this shift. Corporatist and monopoly capital theories maintain that capital, not necessarily employment, tends to concentrate. Although small business' share of employment has increased, in other areas, such as gross product originating, its share has declined (*The State of Small Business* 1987). Furthermore, imprecise treatment of vertical disintegration in the literature on flexibility has created considerable confusion. While industrial organisation theory usually applies this term to enterprises, the logic of the flexibility argument primarily applies to establishments (Feldman 1989). Further, the shift to small businesses partly reflects a shift from manufacturing to services, and small firms dominate the latter while large firms dominate the former. This may in fact be vertical disintegration, with manufacturing firms purchasing services externally, but it does not imply large firms' dominance is declining. Multinational corporations purchase many business services, and the growth of business services reflects the growth of giant firms (Hymer 1972). Baran and Sweezy themselves note that large corporations rely on small firms to pioneer new products. Also, as mentioned above, external purchasing is used to break unions and to lower labour costs. Dislocated workers may find service employment preferable to unemployment, as selling apples was during the Great Depression, but this does not mean either services or small businesses are the foundation for a new economic age.

Corporatist and monopoly capital theories do not contradict technological systems or regulation theories in general, but they do have different economic and spatial implications than versions of technological systems and regulation theory that see small, flexible firms as the hallmark of a new era. International competition intensified during recent years, but this may subside as firms lose out in the competition and are bought up. The end result may be monopoly capitalism on a world scale. Given the Japanese effectiveness, corporatism, rather than flexibility, may be the wave of the future. A plausible scenario pits a few corporatist blocs against each other, with oligopolistic arrangements negotiated by firms and national governments. Presently industrialised countries that do not make the transition to corporatism would lose market share and become clients to those that do. Mass production could make a comeback, if in fact it ever declined, particularly if NICs establish mass domestic markets while overcoming income distribution and environmental problems.

Spatial patterns under this scenario also differ from those under industrial-district flexible accumulation. A new international division of labour would take shape, with finance and management concentrated in a few world centres, manufacturing located in a new periphery comprised of NICs and selected areas in the advanced capitalist countries, and relative stagnation in other formerly industrialised regions (the region as reservation). With Japan as a model, more firm-based flexible agglomerations would take shape, but not, as Sabel (1989) suggests, more industrial districts. The state would take on a new role, as a proactive partner in the corporatist countries and as a supplicant in the client countries. Given the multinationals' economic power and mobility, firm-based agglomerations would grow where governments offer the best deals and tailor local conditions to the multinationals' desires.

EMPIRICAL EXPLORATIONS

This discussion presents a rich tapestry of empirical issues. To date, virtually all empirical studies of flexible specialisation have been place-specific industry case studies (Barff 1987; Scott 1983b; Scott & Angel 1987; 1988; Storper & Christopherson 1987; Swyngedouw 1989) and, as such, are prone to the usual drawbacks of case studies. The industries and locations studies may be unrepresentative, so generalising beyond the original industry or area is dangerous. More importantly, there is no way to judge how widespread the phenomenon is, how it is changing the economy as a whole, or how it interacts with other processes. Consequently, more sweeping claims about flexibility remain largely unexamined.

Hypotheses

The remainder of this chapter is devoted to a study of such issues. In particular, each of the foregoing perspectives implies different hypotheses about industrial organisation and industrial performance. The technological systems perspective implies that innovation is centred in small firms. Other things being equal, during a period of restructuring, industries with small firms will perform better than industries with large firms. Regulation theory implies that restructuring will generally lead to a new pattern of business organisation, but there exists no general tendency towards any one pattern. The small-scale flexibility version of regulation theory suggests that in the current restructuring an industry's performance depends on how innovative and flexible it is: those that have been quick to adjust and make the transition to small, flexible firms will be most successful. Unlike the technological systems hypothesis, this hypothesis emphasises change in firm size over time rather than size at any one point. In other words, vertical disintegration is treated as a process, whereas the technological systems hypothesis treats it as a state (see Feldman 1989 for further discussion of this distinction).

In contrast to these two hypotheses, the corporatism/monopoly capital perspective predicts growing concentration and centralisation. A particularly simple and naive version of this implies that integration and size of plant tend to grow in successful industries. Also, since large firms have an advantage over small, integration is treated as both a process and a state. Several qualifications to this interpretation are necessary. The theory implies that state intervention is even more important than industrial organisation. Furthermore, industries with large firms are likely to stagnate during a crisis caused by lack of investment outlets. Therefore, an alternate version of this hypothesis implies no clear-cut relation between industry performance and size of firm.

The Data

Data for this study are from the Small Business Data Base (SBDB) developed by the US Small Business Administration (SBA). These are the only comprehensive spatial, time-series data on US establishments and their parent enterprises. The SBDB is a highly refined version of Dun and Bradstreet's Duns Market Identifier (DMI) data and has the major advantage of being 'cleaned' with (a) imputed values to correct for inconsistencies in the raw data and (b) estimated weights to correct for sampling bias in the data (Armington & Odle 1981; Harris 1983; Odle & Armington 1983; Applied Systems Institute 1987). Comparisons with tax data indicate the SBDB is a reasonably complete census of full-time businesses with employees (*The State of Small Business* 1984, pp. 7–8, 416–8).

The SBDB contains the name, address, industry, employment, annual sales and parent company for close to five million establishments at two-year intervals. Because of the amount of data and a non-disclosure agreement between SBA and Dun and Bradstreet, the data used here are an aggregated version of the SBDB covering the period between 1976 and 1984. Each aggregated record has a unique combination of nine categorical variables. The number of categories for each variable is given in parentheses[6]: state (50), metropolitan area (380), four-digit industry code (451), enterprise employment size (6), establishment employment size (7), establishment function (3), enterprise spatial organisation (6), enterprise industrial organisation (5), and enterprise sales size (8). Every record contains totals for establishments and employment at two-year intervals.

Establishment spatial organisation (ESTSPATL) distinguishes establishments by the spatial organisation of their parent enterprise. This variable measures an enterprise's spatial complexity and integration. It is defined as follows:

Independents – single-establishment enterprises.

Locals – multi-establishment enterprises whose branches are all in a single metropolitan area and state; multi-establishment firms located outside metropolitan areas are considered 'locals' if their operations are entirely within the non-metropolitan area of a single state.

States – multi-establishment enterprises whose branches are located in two or more metropolitan areas and a single state.

Tristates – enterprises with branches in two or three states. This category is included because doing business in more than one state is much more complex than doing business in a single state.

Regionals – enterprises with branches in more than three states but a single census region.

Nationals – enterprises with branches in more than one census region.

Similarly, enterprise industrial organisation (ENTINORG) measures specialisation and is based on four-digit SIC codes:

Specialists – operations of the parent enterprise and its branches are in a single four-digit detailed industry.

Industrials – operations of the parent enterprise and its branches are in two or more four-digit industries within a single three-digit industry subgroup.

Sectorals – operations of the parent enterprise and its branches are in a single two-digit major group but more than one three-digit subgroup.

Diversifiers – operations of the parent enterprise and its branches are in a single industrial division but more than one two-digit major group.

Conglomerates – the parent enterprise has operations in more than one two-digit major group.

Measuring relative change

Common measures of change are subject to several well-known problems (Markus 1979; Plewis 1985; Rummel 1970). A variable's change between time 1 and time 2 depends on its magnitude: between two times, Asia's population will change more than Greenland's. If we use ratios such as growth rates, the variable's magnitude at time 1 enters the denominator, yielding slow rates for large units and fast rates for small: other things being equal, Greenland will change by a larger percentage than Asia. Furthermore, the value for any individual case will necessarily tend to regress towards the mean between two points in time.

A deviational measure overcomes these difficulties (Rummel 1970, p. 239; McClelland 1976, p. 88). Suppose we measure employment change. To control for initial employment, we fit a regression line between the initial value and the incremental change. Assuming a linear relation between the change and the initial value, the residual from the regression's predicted value is change independent of initial employment. Because incremental change equals employment at time 2 minus employment at time 1 and the latter is the independent variable, this procedure is equivalent to regressing the variable at time 2 against itself at time 1. The latter approach is preferable because the increment combines values for two time periods and more information is retained if only the value at time 2 is the dependent variable (Markus 1979).[7]

A further complication arises with proportions. Changes in proportions are bounded. This means industries with high initial proportions cannot show much upward change and industries with low initial proportions cannot show much downward change. This difficulty is overcome by fitting a logit model between the proportion at time 2 and time 1. The residual between the actual and predicted logits is then used as the measure of change.

Since the regression estimates are crucial to the analysis, several steps were taken to satisfy ordinary least squares assumptions. Various transformations were tried until normally distributed residuals were obtained. In general, this yielded logarithms of the odds ratios for proportions and logarithms for whole numbers. Then, weighted least squares (WLS) regression was used to correct for hetroskedasticity. Following Hanushek and Jackson (1977), the number of establishments was used to weight each industry when the variable in question was a whole number, and the binomial estimate of the variance was used for proportions. Given that the data were originally collected to check on individual firms' credit-worthiness, unequal error variances across industries most likely reflect other variables, such as size of enterprise and rate of growth, which are imperfectly correlated with the number of establishments in each industry. For this reason, a maximum likelihood procedure was used to set exponents for the correction weights. Using these weights, the WLS regression was repeated, this time without industries whose residuals from the first estimate were greater than three standard deviations. The final residuals were computed from this last regression and used in the analysis.

Variables

The SBDB was used to construct several variables as measures of industry –
performance, integration/disintegration and specialisation.

Performance

Industry performance is usually measured in terms of sales, domestically
produced share of sales, or employment (Little 1989; Bluestone *et al.* 1984).
Sales reflects changes in demand and therefore is not strictly a measure of
performance. Moreover, preliminary investigations indicated sales data in
the SBDB are somewhat unreliable. Since international competition plays a
major role in the three theories, domestically produced share of sales is perhaps
the best indicator. Unfortunately, reliable data on total size of market and
sales were unavailable, so this measure could not be used.

Therefore, two employment-based measures were used: industry share of
total employment (EMPSHR) and industry employment (EMPLOY). These
measures are not perfect. Employment reflects a variety of factors besides
industry performance: total size of market, productivity, hours worked, etc.
Nonetheless, employment and employment share are common measures of
economic performance and would have to be taken into account in any case.

Vertical disintegration

There is no generally accepted measure of vertical disintegration (see Feldman
(1989) for a review and elaboration on the points made here). This partly
reflects the conceptual ambiguity surrounding the term. Vertical disintegration
commonly refers to disintegration within and across enterprises, but the
spatial literature implies disintegration across establishments. Vertical
disintegration is also a very complex concept and difficult to measure. Even
sophisticated measures based on input-output tables use relative prices and,
if integration (aggregation) alters relative prices, are prone to the problem
that integration itself can alter the metric being used to measure integration.

In the absence of a precise measure based on an invariant underlying
metric, vertical integration was measured by employment per establishment
(EMPEST) and by enterprise spatial organisation. As a measure of vertical
disintegration, employment per establishment assumes constant productivity
under varying patterns of integration and that the number of operations in a
production process is proportional to the number of workers involved in it.
Piore and Sabel's (1984) argument implies employees per establishment is a
valid measure. If an uncertain economic environment makes capital investments risky, much smaller capital investments will occur. This might result
in lower labour productivity and therefore more workers per unit output, but
it seems unlikely that this would compensate for the overall reduction in size.
Furthermore, the technologies identified as encouraging vertical disintegration
are thought to do so because they increase productivity and make smaller

scales competitive. Certainly the argument that vertical disintegration is the basis for industrial district agglomeration implicitly assumes vertical disintegration involves establishments with relatively fewer employees.

Enterprise spatial organisation can also be interpreted as partly measuring vertical integration. The assumption here is that multi-location enterprises very likely produce intermediate goods for themselves, so the complexity of an enterprise's spatial organisation is partly a reflection of the complexity of its productive organisation. Two proportions are used to measure this spatial organisation: independent establishments as a proportion of all establishments in the industry (PINDEST) and metropolitan establishments as a proportion of all establishments in the industry (PMETEST). Alternatively, the proportion of employment in independent and metropolitan establishments could have been used, but these variables are correlated with the establishment-based variables, so only the latter were used.

Specialisation

Specialisation is measured by the industrial organisation categories based on SIC codes described above. In particular, the proportion of establishments in an industry that are specialists or industrials are measures of specialisation in that industry. The proportion of specialists is highly correlated with the proportion of independents, so only the proportion of industrials (PINDUS) was used.

Testing the hypotheses

In order to test the hypotheses concerning industry performance and industrial organisation, two regression equations were estimated:

1 $\text{DEMPSHR} = b_0 + b_1 \text{EMPEST}_1 + b_2 \text{PINDEST}_1 + b_2 \text{PMETEST}_1 + b_3 \text{PINDUS}_1$
$$+ b_4 \text{DEMPEST} + b_5 \text{DINDEST} + b_6 \text{DMETEST} + b_7 \text{DINDUS}$$

2 $\text{DEMPLOY} = b_0 + b_1 \text{EMPEST}_1 + b_2 \text{PINDEST}_1 + b_2 \text{PMETEST}_1 + b_3 \text{PINDUS}_1$
$$+ b_4 \text{DEMPEST} + b_5 \text{DINDEST} + b_6 \text{DMETEST} + b_7 \text{DINDUS}$$

where the subscripted variables are the values of the respective variables in 1976 and DEMPEST, DINDEST, DMETEST and DINDUS are the deviational changes in these variables measured as described above. Table 1 summarises these variables and gives their means and standard deviations.

To make the test more stringent, only manufacturing industries are used in the analysis. Thus, any relation between industry performance and industrial organisation is not merely an artifact of the growth of service employment relative to manufacturing. Since scale economies are most often associated with manufacturing, a relationship between vertical disintegration and performance among manufacturing industries is particularly strong evidence for growing importance of vertical disintegration.

Table 1 **Means and standard deviations of variables used in regression equation**

Variable	Description	Mean	Standard deviation
DEMPLOY	Deviational change in employment, 1976–84	0.00	0.15
DEMPSHR	Deviational change in employment share, 1976–84	–0.02	0.34
$EMPEST_1$	Employees per establishment, 1976	79.06	86.23
$PINDEST_1$	Proportion of establishments that are independents, 1976	0.58	0.16
$PMETEST_1$	Proportion of establishments that are metropolitans, 1976	0.08	0.16
$PINDUS_1$	Proportion of establishments that are industrials, 1976	0.04	0.04
DEMPEST	Deviational change in employees per establishment, 1976–84	0.01	0.11
DINDEST	Deviational change in proportion of establishments that are independents, 1976–84	0.03	0.29
DMETEST	Deviational change in proportion of establishments that are metropolitans, 1976–84	–0.09	0.60
DINDUS	Deviational change in proportion of establishments that are industrials, 1976–84	–0.04	0.64

RESULTS

The regression results are presented in Table 2. The most striking result is the similarity of the two regressions. This is most likely an artifact of the dependent variables, industries that gained employment also increased their shares of employment. The second striking characteristic is the uniform significance of the process variables and the insignificance of the state variables. The process variables as a group are significant at the 0.01 level using a multivariate F-test, while the state variables are not. On the surface this seems to be strong evidence for the regulation-restructuring hypothesis.

Table 2 Regression results (beta weights) for deviational change in total employment and in employment per establishment

Independent variable	Dependent variable	
	DEMPLOY	DEMPSHR
Constant	0.00	–0.00
	(0.08)	(–0.02)
EMPEST$_1$	–0.05	–0.04
	(–1.35)	(–1.12)
PINDEST$_1$	0.06	0.06
	(1.46)	(1.55)
PMETEST$_1$	–0.06	–0.06
	(–1.70)	(–1.67)
PINDUS$_1$	–0.05	–0.05
	(–1.35)	(–1.44)
DEMPEST	0.68	0.68
	(18.47)*	(18.32)*
DINDEST	0.16	0.16
	(4.19)*	(4.10)*
DMETEST	0.62	0.62
	(16.97)*	(16.99)*
DINDUS	–0.12	–0.12
	(–3.50)*	(–3.50)*
Adjusted R^2	0.63*	0.62*

* Significant at the 0.01 level (one-tailed test).

However, the signs of the variables are not as the small-scale flexibility thesis would predict. Those industries that increased average employment per establishment also increased total employment and their share of employment. On the other hand, vertical disintegration does seem to account for performance. Industries in which the share of locally oriented establishments – independent firms and multi-establishment firms contained entirely within metropolitan areas – also improved their employment performance. Finally, employment declined in industries that saw an increase in the proportion of establishments belonging to firms with operations in a few related industries. If DINDEST is interpreted as a measure of specialisation, we can infer that very narrow specialisation was associated with relative employment growth. Economic restructuring does appear to have been the order of the day, and, at least in terms of employment, there does appear to have been a shift towards specialisation but not necessarily small establishments.

There is little evidence for the naive monopoly-capital hypothesis. Perhaps this is because we should not be so naive. An examination of residuals reveals that the industry that gained employment above what would be predicted by the regression line was SIC 3761 – Guided Missiles and Space Vehicles!

CONCLUSION

These results are preliminary and should be viewed with caution. The next step is to use a more meaningful measure of economic performance, such as import penetration. Furthermore, it is possible to refine the independent variables to get a clearer picture of vertical disintegration and specialisation. Once these technical details are out of the way, an examination of spatial patterns will allow us to test some of the geographic elements of the flexibility thesis.

Nonetheless, these preliminary results are quite rewarding. We have found little evidence that small is beautiful: during the study period, industries that increased their average size of plant also gained employment. This may simply reflect capital intensity, and we will know more by looking at import penetration data. Neither did we find much evidence of increasing concentration and centralisation of capital. On the other hand, we do see strong evidence of economic restructuring, with a tendency towards specialisation and vertical disintegration, albeit with increasing plant size. If the hallmark of Fordism is large-scale manufacturing, notice of Fordism's demise may have been premature.

ACKNOWLEDGMENT

Contribution #2539 of the College of Resource Development, University of Rhode Island, with support from Rhode Island Agricultural Experiment Station. Additional support for this research was provided by the University of Rhode Island Council on Research and the Northeast Center for Rural Development. The author wishes to thank Richard Florida, Bennett Harrison, Michael Storper and Richard Walker for their comments on this and related research.

NOTES

1 There is considerable debate over the empirical evidence for the temporal bunching of innovations (see Mensch 1979; Rosenberg & Frischtak 1983; Freeman *et al.* 1982).

2 There are variations. For example, Norton and Rees (1979) believe older metropolitan areas in the northern United States have lost their seedbed role to newer cities in the south and west.

3 Cohen and Zysman (1987) estimate as much as 75 per cent of all US manufacturing is already batch production.

4 See Kotz (1987) and Noël (1987) for summaries. The differences between SSA and regulation approaches are, in my opinion, largely stylistic. I therefore treat them as a single, combined approach which I refer to as 'regulation theory', but see Coriat (1989) and Walker (1989) for elaborations on some points of difference.

5 Kotz (1987) reconciles Baran and Sweezy with regulation theory by arguing the former's 'exogenous' events are actually systematic outcomes of restructuring brought on by the failure of an accumulation regime. This functionalist argument should be rejected. While a crisis may set off a scramble to restructure, restructuring need not result in a

non-capitalist economic organisation. A long 'dark age' is also a possibility. There is no automatic mechanism that invariably restores capitalism to a major period of growth.

6 A complete description of the data is available from the author.

7 It can be shown that residuals computed from the two regression methods are identical. When used to measure exogenous variables, this approach assumes the change accounted for by the regression is purely an artifact of initial size (Plewis 1985, ch. 4).

22

REGIONAL TECHNOLOGY POLICIES: THE DEVELOPMENT OF REGIONAL TECHNOLOGY TRANSFER INFRASTRUCTURES

Roy Rothwell and Mark Dodgson

INTRODUCTION

Traditionally, in most advanced market economies, regional policies have been exogenous in nature. There are two aspects to this: in the first place, regional policies were generally formulated and implemented by national authorities; secondly, they were largely oriented towards attracting branch plants of both national and foreign companies to locate in designated development areas. Under these policies, overall financial allocations were made by central governments. Administrative structures, of course, vary considerably from country to country, ranging from strong central government in the United Kingdom to the federal systems prevailing in the United States and West Germany. This means that the degree of local or regional autonomy in formulating, funding and administering regional development policies also varies considerably between countries.

During the high economic growth, high employment 1960s, exogenous regional policies were effective in reducing employment bottlenecks in the developed regions and in creating employment – albeit mainly low level, blue collar job – in the less-developed regions. During the structural economic crisis of the 1970s, however, the appropriateness of such policies was seriously questioned. They did little to enhance the technological potential of the development regions. Branch plants were amongst the first to close and the largely traditional industries in the development regions increasingly suffered through low-cost competition from newly developing countries. Newly emerging technologies were introduced first in the relatively R&D-rich developed regions, and regional disparities in economic growth rates and unemployment both increased (Thwaites 1982).

From the mid to late 1970s onwards, at least within Europe, there has been a general trend towards increased regional autonomy with respect to economic and industrial development. For example, in Sweden a number of regional development companies were established, and in the United Kingdom three regional development agencies were created. In France, where perhaps the trend away from strong central control and towards regional devolution has been most marked, a number of new regional initiatives have been undertaken in parallel with the decentralisation of notional bodies such as ANVAR (Agence Nationale pour la Valorisation de la Recherche) and the CNRS (Centre Nationale de la Recherche Scientifique).

During the 1980s this trend has intensified specifically with respect to technology or innovation policies, which has marked a dramatic shift from the old exogenous policies of the 1960s to the strongly endogenous policies of the 1980s. Endogenous policies focus on the mobilisation and enhancement of regional technological and industrial resources and often are targeted on assisting small and medium-sized firms and on creating new technology-based small firms.

Perhaps the most marked trend in regional technology policy has been the creation and enhancement of regional technology transfer infrastructures (Rothwell *et al.* 1989). In some countries, such as France and West Germany, central governments have played a significant direct role in this process; in other countries, such as the United States and the United Kingdom, the direct role played by central governments has been relatively minor.

A major purpose of these regional technology transfer infrastructures is providing support for technology-based small and medium-sized firms (SMFs). These firms are believed to be important means for technological development, employment generation and wealth creation. Technology-based SMFs face particular problems when compared with traditional firms. To overcome these problems such firms may require technological support and advice, financial support (to cover the high costs of R&D), managerial support (to assist business and project planning) and support to employ or access specialist staff. As we shall see in the subsequent description of some of the major infrastructural organisations in France, Germany and the United Kingdom, these problems are often the target of the technology transfer organisations.

FRANCE

Background

The French Government has long adopted the view that it has a central role to play in directly influencing the rate and direction of industrial technological change (Rothwell & Zegveld 1981). Some significant features of industrial R&D in France in the 1980s were: heavy concentration of R&D in the top 100 companies; high level of public financing of R&D (65 per cent of the total in 1985); nationalised companies' high share in R&D expenditure (more than 50 per cent); and high concentration of R&D (about 75 per cent) in six industrial sectors (automobiles, aerospace, electronics, pharmaceuticals, energy and chemicals).

Despite the dominant role of public R&D expenditures and nationalised industries in R&D in France, since the end of the 1970s there has been a significant movement towards decentralisation in the provision of services via publically funded R&D institutions (e.g. ANVAR, CNRS). During the 1980s in particular, the French Government has laid considerable emphasis on developing regional technology policies and on policies towards SMFs. This process has been described by Sunman (1986, p. 93–4) as follows:

> It is in the context of increasing concentration of research activity in state-owned companies that the government has introduced policies which have a strong impact on technopole development. One is an emphasis on SMFs as a vehicle for growth, and another is a shift towards decentralisation within a coherent regional technology and research policy...the Ministry of Research and Technology is encouraging state-owned industrial enterprises to make some of their research and development capabilities available to small and medium-sized enterprises...In view of the general truth that the most efficient form of technology transfer is achieved through the transfer of skilled staff, the nationalised industries have been asked to distribute widely amongst their personnel the legal provisions concerning leave of absence for the creation of enterprises – a particularly creative move by government. In addition, arrangements for aiding spin-offs are progressively being put in place...Various regional organizations encourage linkage, cooperation and decentralisation by promoting collaboration between research organisations, advanced teaching establishments and large enterprises.

A number of administrative and infrastructural developments which were undertaken during the 1980s for the implementation of regional technology policy in France are described briefly below. More comprehensive information on these developments can be found in the detailed reports of Sunman (1986) and Sweeney (1985).

DATAR

The Delegation a l'Amanagement du Territoire et a l'Action Regionale (DATAR) was established in 1983 under the direct authority of the Prime Minister. DATAR prepares the agenda for the inter-ministerial committee on regional development (CIAT), which makes the major decisions on regional policy. Since the mid-1970s funds have increasingly been used for decentralisation and are channelled through the 'contrats de Plan' mechanism. DATAR also has a network of offices in major countries for the attraction of foreign direct investment to France.

CRITT

The Centres Régionaux d'Innovations et de Transfer de Technologies (CRITT) began from the early 1980s onwards. They were designed to facilitate technology transfer from public R&D institutions to industry and to assist the product and process innovation activities of SMFs. CRITT generally specialises in a narrow field of technology which reflects the distinctive industrial and technological competence of the region in which it is located. In 1983, fifteen CRITT were in place; by 1986 there were forty.

Technopoles (science parks)

A key element in French regional technology policy has been the development of the so-called technopoles. Technopoles are rather grandiose developments whose conception owes more to the areas of technological concentration in Japan than to the more limited American concept of the science park. They bring together strong concentrations of scientific and technological activity, linking public and private R&D organisations, training institutions and high technology companies. Initially started with large R&D-performing companies, they have subsequently emphasised SMFs and new technology-based firm start-ups.

Most of the infrastructure financing of technopoles has derived from public sector sources. Up to 1980, public sector finance for the three established technopoles was about 643 million francs. Direct public sector investment since 1980 has totalled over 1400 million francs.

Between 1972 and 1980, three technopoles had been established; a further five were established between 1980 and 1985, and in 1986 a further eight were in the late planning or early start-up phase. By early 1986 there were 400 establishments on the eight most advanced parks employing between them 10 000 people.

WEST GERMANY

Background

For many years, public policy in West Germany has emphasised the importance of technology transfer from infrastructural institutions to industrial companies. This is at least partly the result of the perceived importance of the small firm sector in German manufacturing. According to Meyer-Krahmer (1985), for example, approximately 40 000 manufacturing companies employing less than 1000 employees accounted for about two-thirds of the industrial workforce. However, only between 10 and 15 per cent of these firms performed R&D, primarily development work, and often only on a sporadic basis.

In addition to long-standing policies to support small and medium-sized engineering firms, during the 1980s there has been enhanced federal and regional support for centres that perform industrially relevant R&D on the one hand, and for mechanisms that convey appropriate know-how to potential industrial end users on the other. The network that is being publically supported is aimed not only at the more traditional medium-sized engineering firms and, to a lesser extent at large companies, but increasingly towards creating an appropriate environment for new technology-based start-ups.

Some of the technology transfer structures, which have arisen as the result of a series of publically funded pilot projects, are (Meyer-Krahmer 1985):
* Technology transfer offices attached to large federal research establishments, which previously were not seen to have much relevance to their intended industrial targets due to the nature of the services (big science) that they attempted to disseminate.
* Technology transfer centres attached to applied research institutes.
* Administrative support units established for the promotion of federal technology programs.
* Rationalisation Board, Chambers of Industry and Commerce and freelance consultants.

Both the technology transfer centres and the administrative support units have been aimed primarily at SMFs, offering consultancy, training and testing services, particularly in fields such as CAD/CAM, robotics and microelectronics applications.

An important aspect of regional technology policy has been the encouragement of linkages between academic institutions and industry, a process which appears to be intensifying. As far back as the mid-1970s, the Federal Ministry of Research and Technology (BMFT) and the Federal Ministry of Education and Science (BMBW) initiated several programs to install technology transfer units at various levels within technical schools and universities.
* 'General information transfer units', with a staff of one to four people, were installed alongside the administrative staffs of various universities and colleges.
* 'Technology transfer offices' were installed at colleges without a technology transfer centre. By mid-1987, twenty-five of the fifty-six universities and technical universities had installed transfer offices.
* 'Regional technology transfer institutions', e.g. those established by the states of Baden–Wurttenberg and North Rhine–Westphalia. These, with financial assistance from their regional Ministries of Commerce, are able to subsidise the first two or three consultations by small firms to scientists and engineers based within technical colleges.

The increased pressure to increase university/industry technology transfers has resulted in the implementation of several new initiatives.
* Joint research programs: an initiative was established in 1984 to promote club-type research projects between groups of firms and publically financed research institutes, including universities. The initiative was developed by the BMFT and subsequently consumed nearly 60 per cent of its budget for the promotion of R&D projects in industry. Three 'Verbundtorschungsprogrammes' were in operation by 1987, in the fields of information technology, environmental technology and production engineering.
* Personnel transfer: it was recognised that the temporary transfer of technical personnel between universities, research institutions and industry can be a potent means of technology transfer to local companies.

- Transfer research institutes: since 1981 there have been attempts by both Federal and Länder governments to reduce legislative 'demotivation' in the whole area of university-industry technology transfer. An example is the 'Arbeitnehemererfindergesetz', which is a federal law favouring university scientists by denying universities automatic intellectual property rights over their inventions. Since 1982 several important institutions dedicated to providing solutions to firms' perceived technological problems have been established. One example is the Informatik Research Centre at the Technische Hochschule Karlsruhe, which is expected to finance itself through contract research and which has won substantial contracts for IBM (Schimank & Scholz 1987).

To summarise, a complex web of interface organisations and mechanisms exist in West Germany for the encouragement of technology transfer, particularly for the benefit of SMFs. A term commonly employed in the German policy literature is that of the 'network' (Hemer 1984):

> Since the seventies a more or less dense network of agencies have been built up by the Federal Republic and West Berlin, which offer to the manufacturing industries technology or innovation consultancy and technology or information transfer respectively, supported by the government.

The network is aimed primarily at supporting SMFs.

Before proceeding to a description of the development of science/technology parks and innovation centres in West Germany, it is worthwhile describing one national technology transfer institution which has strong regional representation, the Fraunhofer Society.

The thirty or so institutions of the Fraunhofer Society (FhG) are located throughout Germany. Their main functions are to perform contract research for industry and government and to act as a primary mechanism for bridging the gap between scientific research and industry. Clients range from small firms to groupings of firms, government departments and multinationals. Contracts vary in size from tens of thousands of deutschmark to millions of deutschmark. Contract research income is matched deutschmark for deutschmark with a government subsidy to cover infrastructural maintenance and development.

In addition to the general subsidy, additional aid is available for small firms from the Federal Government. Amounting to 40 per cent of the costs of projects they commission, it is to help them break through what is considered to be an 'entry barrier' to the services of a Fraunhofer institute. Between 1976 and 1982, the percentage of FhG income from industry doubled from about 15 per cent to about 30 per cent. Although the FhG institutes employ only about one per cent of Germany's total R&D staff, by nature of their proximity to industry their contribution to successful innovation within the economy is considered to be far greater. One factor that may account for the FhG's success is the specialisation by institutes in strategically important areas of science and technology, e.g. microelectronics, micro-optics, sensors, data processing, manufacturing and office automation, laser technology, materials science and biotechnology. The FhG also has an important licensing role.

Finally, the Max-Plank Society, comprising fifty-two widely distributed institutes, and which concentrates on publically funded basic research, is also involved in transferring research results to industrial applications.

Innovation centres and science/technology parks

As in other western European countries, there has been a rapid growth in West Germany in the number of initiatives to create science/technology parks and innovation centres. For example, in excess of 100 million dollars is estimated to have been invested in innovation centres between 1981 and 1985. Within this period, nineteen centres were established, another fourteen were close to being established and forty more were said to be in the pipeline. Those established housed over 300 high tech companies which had a combined employment of 3000. Forty million dollars of the funding has been in the Berlin Innovation Centre and the associated Technology Innovation Park. Over 80 per cent of all other funding has been by regional and local governments. German innovation centres have mainly been created by rehabilitating existing buildings and the expressed aim is generally to nurture the development of technology-based firms. The development of these various initiatives, which tend to be called technology or innovation centres, is closely tied to regional and local government priorities.

Beyond public funds for start-up costs, many of the centres benefit from additional financial support. Examples include the subsidising of operating losses by the State government, and direct rent subsidises for those wishing to locate within an innovation centre. An alternative used by some local governments is to charge the innovation centre a low rent. Public funding has been an essential ingredient for most of Germany's technology and innovation centres, for everything from start-up and equipments costs to ongoing operational subsidies.

Of the various federal schemes designed to nurture the country's base of technology-based firms, the most important to the technology and innovation centres has been the TOU (technology-oriented enterprise) program, which began in 1983 and had a budget of 325 million deutschmark. The TOU program was aimed at technology-based new businesses throughout Germany, offering grants, loans and guarantees. It also offered access to a variety of managerial advisory support mechanisms.

TOU was discontinued in 1989, and evaluations of the program have yet to be completed. It has been found, however, that the generous level of grants encouraged R&D-undertaking SMFs to considerably increase their R&D expenditure.

German innovation centres are highly dependent upon public subsidy. Their primary usefulness, at least initially, appears to have been as symbols of a new enterprise spirit: a signal to would-be entrepreneurs that from now on their efforts will be encouraged rather than frowned upon. Most German innovation centres still are relatively young and they have much to learn, and possibly, also, to prove. Indicators of their success or failure must be treated with caution since, although centre-based firms are said to be more successful than average, they have greater opportunities for subsidy and, to be accepted on to parks, they have often had to endure a rigorous application procedure. Added to this is the fact that once located on a centre, companies tend to find venture finance from various financial institutions rather more accessible. Finally, one major issue of current concern is the growing number of technology and innovation centres in the pipeline; there are strong fears that the quality of applicants for location on these centres will be diluted.

THE UNITED KINGDOM

Background

Public policy in the United Kingdom is aimed largely at creating the appropriate overall climate for industry to operate effectively. At various times during the past decade, instruments have been in place to improve the nation's base of technical skills, to provide inputs to assist firms' innovatory activities and to improve manufacturing efficiency, product design and product quality. Significant policy emphasis has been placed by the current administration on the small firm sector, on stimulating collaboration between firms and on creating new technology-based firms through the development of a dynamic and fast growing venture capital industry. It is becoming apparent, however, that this industry is not catering for innovative small firms (Dodgson & Rothwell 1989).

In 1983, for the first time since the beginning of the industrial revolution, the United Kingdom suffered a negative balance in trade in manufactures. This decline in international competitiveness in manufactures has persisted, reaching record levels in recent years. The overall decline in UK trade performance has been magnified in the development regions of Wales, Scotland and the north-east of England, which are strongly characterised by traditional industries (steel, mining, shipbuilding, textiles, metalworking) and branch plant economies. If the economies of the development regions are to be revitalised, considerable structural industrial change is required to shift output to higher value added, more knowledge-intensive product groups.

Location in an R&D-rich environment is clearly an advantage to firms of all sizes, but particularly to SMFs since physical promixity reduces the costs of access to, and increased awareness of, external technology. There exists considerable evidence to show, however, that the external environment facing firms in the peripheral regions in the United Kingdom is considerably less rich than that facing their counterparts in the economically advanced regions. This pattern was emphasised in two studies undertaken for the STRIDE Committee of the European Commission (Rothwell & Beesley 1987; NBST 1987), which showed that:

- the main R&D concentrations are in the south, especially the south-east. The south-east region dominates the regional distribution of employment in technology-based industry with 37 per cent of total high tech employment;
- in 1983, 45.5 per cent of industrial firms' R&D units were in the south-east;
- in 1984, 51 per cent of professional engineers and scientists in the engineering industries were employed in the south-east;
- the two southern regions outrank all others in terms of productivity and R&D capacity;
- government funded research facilities, both military and civilian, are concentrated largely in the south-east; and
- Ministry of Defence development contracts go mainly to firms located in the south.

This paints a picture of structural regional inequalities in technological potential, with public sector R&D expenditure mainly favouring the R&D-rich southern regions of the country, with their already high concentrations of technologically innovative firms.

Despite the pattern of uneven geographical distribution in R&D capacity, regional development policy in the United Kingdom has, in the main, under-valued technology as a developmental tool, although some of the limited number of centrally administered technology development and transfer programs have, of course, had some regional impacts. During the 1980s, however, the three regional development agencies have played an increasingly important role in stimulating technological development; there has been rapid growth in the number of science parks and innovation centres; and the government undertook an initiative to establish a number of regional technology centres. These initiatives are described briefly below; they should be viewed in the light of the total national system of technology transfer in the United Kingdom.

Regional development agencies

The three main regional development agencies in the United Kingdom are the Scottish Development Agency (SDA), the Welsh Development Agency (WDA) and the Industrial Development Board of Northern Ireland (IDB) – previously the Northern Ireland Development Agency. These agencies were established by Act of Parliament and have, as their primary task, the economic and industrial renewal of their respective areas. They are funded by central government, but all enjoy a high degree of automony in pursuing their development aims.

While the development agencies intervene in economic and industrial development in a variety of ways – e.g. providing industrial premises, land reclamation and environmental improvement, marketing and promotion, attracting incoming industries, offering advice and assistance to small firms – stimulating technological development and technology transfer has become a major feature of their activities. Increasingly this has involved attempts to stimulate indigenous technological capabilities through developing the small firm sector, including new technology-based start-ups.

For example in 1976, following a report commissioned from a leading UK consultancy organisation, the WDA set up WINtech (Wales Innovation and Technology); the major aims of WINtech, as outlined in the report, were to:

- act in a dynamic, catalytic way to stimulate technological advance within existing industry;
- help translate new ideas, products and processes into commercial reality;
- act as a channel of information and advice on technological matters for companies and individuals;
- forge links between industry and university colleges in Wales carrying out vital research work; and
- present Wales as a 'technology friendly' country to encourage new business development.

The WDA also played an important catalytic role in the creation of the Welsh Venture Capital Fund in 1984. During 1984/85, the WVCF raised 5.6 million pounds for investment in new projects and firms and growth businesses. Fifty per cent of the fund's capital derived from City sources and, of the remainder, 1.4 million pounds was provided by the WDA. The fund invests in amounts of up to 500 000 pounds in unquoted companies ranging from 'greenfield' start-ups to established enterprises.

In Northern Ireland, the Department of Economic Development (DED) undertakes functions in the Province broadly corresponding to those undertaken in Great Britain by the Department of Trade and Industry, the Department of Employment, the Department of Energy. the Training Agency, and the Health and Safety Executive.

The Department has the strategic aims of strengthening the Northern Irish economy to provide self-sustaining employment, and of supporting existing employment where it is cost-effective to do so. The Department also provides the institutional and infrastructural services essential to the Province's economic development. Northern Ireland now has its own Chief Engineer and Scientist, a post equivalent to the corresponding position in the DTI, London.

Two industrial development agencies operate under the aegis of DED:

1 The Industrial Development Board (IDB), which replaced the Northern Ireland Development Agency in 1982, has the remit of encouraging the development of the manufacturing and tradeable services sector of the economy; establishing and expanding companies with over fifty employees; and attracting new inward investment.
2 The Local Enterprise Development Unit (LEDU) carries responsibility for sponsoring the creation and development of small companies of less than fifty employees.

The IDB promotes national Department of Trade and Industry schemes. In most cases, schemes run within Northern Ireland are more generous than their mainland counterparts. As well as being more generous, the Northern Ireland Schemes are not constrained by rigid cash limits as they are on the mainland, so that all eligible firms can be funded.

In Scotland, the main aims of the Scottish Development Agency (SDA) are to:

- encourage the innovative and high technology sectors;
- strengthen the technology base of companies in Scotland;
- promote Scotland internationally as a base for manufacturing and service initiatives through Locate in Scotland;
- support joint ventures between Scottish and overseas companies and the transfer of technology;
- invest directly in viable business enterprises both large and small;
- provide expert advice on all aspects of company performance;
- build industrial and commercial premises to meet the business needs of today;
- identify growth potential within the Scottish economy such as the service sector, and implement strategies to release such potential;
- take special initiatives to develop Scotland's services and amenities such as the Scottish Exhibition Centre and the 1988 Glasgow Garden Festival;
- offer professional help to small business in the areas of finance, marketing and production;
- improve the environment in town and country through land clearance and renewal programs throughout Scotland;
- stimulate the development of local economies by initiating and coordinating area-based projects; and
- act as a central point of business information and advice in Scotland.

An important aspect of the SDA's industrial policy is the renewal of existing sectors, and the SDA sees its role in this process as being catalytic. SDA surveys of indigenous Scottish companies have confirmed the Agency's belief that their primary need is for assistance in the general area of business development, and to this end the Industry Services Division's services were, in 1984, grouped together under Business Development: Scotland.

The SDA recognised at an early stage that industrial renewal and technological development involve considerably more than simply the supply of technology. It is for this reason that the emphasis is very firmly on business development, and the Agency, having identified specific opportunities – in collaboration with the target company – aims to offer a package of assistance which might include technology transfer, product/market planning, market information and finance.

Amongst the main objectives of the SDA is 'the encouragement of entrepreneurial initiatives and viable enterprises'. To this end the Agency provides a wide range of advisory, investment and instructional services with, in all cases, an emphasis on stimulating ongoing personal contacts with client companies. Among the services available are:

- Finance support: SDA loan and equity investments; and loans from the European Coal and Steel Community and the European Investment Bank; special schemes of finance and assistance are also available to craft workers.
- Management support: advice is available on all managerial aspects of running a successful business.
- Marketing support: advice is available on planning marketing policy and in specific aspects of selling both at home and overseas; advice and help is also available for companies seeking to exhibit at trade fairs and related events.
- Counselling services: advice is provided throughout Scotland by a team of professional and experienced retired businessmen.
- Technical services: expert help is available on all aspects of production, factory planning and the working environment.

In recent years, the SDA's Technology Transfer and Training Division has grown considerably in terms of members of staff and areas of responsibility. Some more recent technology transfer and related activities undertaken by the SDA are:

- The SDA provided managerial and financial support to two universities to assist the development of viable business plans for establishing two new centres: the Institute for Computer Integrated Manufacture and the Institute for Computer Aided Engineering and Management.
- The Technology Transfer Division has assisted a number of Scottish companies to acquire new technology via inward licensing in order to enable them to diversify their product/market base.
- In the field of academic/industry liaison, the SDA provides finance and management for venture capital funds which support the early commercialisation of new university products and processes. A technology-based area strategically targeted by the SDA is biotechnology in health care. Biotechnology in health care has been identified as a worldwide market area with exceptionally high growth potential. In developing this sector, the SDA is focusing heavily on Scotland's long-established traditions of research excellence in its university medical schools. The major aim of the Agency's Health Care and Biotechnology Unit is to develop this indigenous expertise commercially and to enhance the technological capabilities of, and the technological infrastructure available to, existing companies. Since health care and biotechnology do not enjoy the advantage of large-scale inward investment and are highly diverse areas of activity, the SDA's emphasis is on capitalising on indigenous strengths through promoting the university/industry interface and encouraging and supporting new start-up.

Enterprise agencies

Local enterprise agencies or trusts are organisations established by local government and/or business and/or financial institutions to improve the support facilities available to small firms. There is now reported to be about 300 enterprise agencies in the United Kingdom. An illustrative example is the Clydebank Enterprise Trust (CET) in Glasgow, Scotland. The CET, which is associated with the Clydebank Task Force and the Clydebank Business Park, is a joint venture between the Scottish Development Agency (SDA) and the Bank of Scotland, both of whom initially committed 250 000 pounds to the Trust.

While the Trust is directed towards new ventures, it does not preclude established small businesses seeking finance for new projects. To be eligible, applicants must demonstrate that sufficient funding is not available from normal commercial sources and be prepared to bank with the Bank of Scotland. Typically the Trust seeks to provide pre-venture funding, i.e. it aims to close the 'equity gap' faced by many new starters, by providing loans up to 25 000 pounds at 5 per cent interest (the SDA covers the subsidy element). However, additional finance up to 50 000 pounds is also available. The loans are unsecured and aim to provide the entrepreneur with medium-term working capital or funds for long-term capital investment.

To qualify for government assistance under Section 11 of the Industrial Development Act of 1982, 'an organisation needs to demonstrate that the area in which it is located has special features which inhibit its start-up or development'. Financial assistance is provided on a pump-priming basis to get the organisation established and is normally given for a period of one to three years.

REGIONAL TECHNOLOGY CENTRES NETWORK

Under the Local Collaborative Projects (LCP) program, of the DTI, a number of Regional Technology Centres have been created with the purpose of forming a network to assist the process of technology transfer:

The overall aim of the RTC Network is to:
- Establish a system of collaborative centres both in the sense of individual groupings or consortia and throughout the Network itself.
- Offer a range of technology transfer services based on training and related delivery mechanisms on a self-financing basis.
- Create a highly flexible and responsive initiative that will develop on the basis of experience.

The functions of Centres in such a Network could be to:
- Ensure that they have easy access to information about the latest technological discoveries and innovations both in their own establishments and elsewhere including not only those concerned with production processes but also new materials and technological advances which could be relevant to management, marketing, financial control, storage, etc.
- Disseminate information about those developments in the form most acceptable to industry. This might include awareness-raising courses directed at decision takers, more detailed courses for those concerned with

developments themselves who can be assumed to have a body of background knowledge, courses for 'trainers', i.e. who have the function of disseminating information within their firms. In all cases, 'courses' is used in its widest sense and is intended to include one-off lectures, seminars, distance learning (print and/or audio or audio-visual materials) as well as more traditional courses of varying length.
- Provide a training consultancy service for the introduction of new technology or, where it is thought more appropriate, to provide a referral service for other consultancy services. This would involve ensuring the fully-expert staff were employed for this purpose.
- Offer training to employees arising from the introduction of new technology, at full-cost fees.

About fourteen Centres have been, or are in the process, of being approved.

Science parks

In a highly detailed report, *Science Parks in Britain*, Currie (1985) defines science parks as 'real estate developments associated with a university or other higher educational institution with a major objective of facilitating the transfer of technology between academic bodies and operational business'. According to Currie, while in 1980 only three science parks (broadly defined) were in operation in the United Kingdom, by 1985, 'twenty ventures were either functioning or under construction. At least ten other schemes were in advanced stages of planning'.

In her study, Currie included innovation centres (five), science parks (eleven) and research parks (four). Innovation centres were defined as 'developments within a restricted space intended primarily for small newly established companies'; science parks were defined as 'larger areas of land suitable for knowledge-based firms of different sizes and stages of development, usually, though not necessarily in landscaped surroundings. The planning permission should be sufficiently flexible to permit light manufacturing'; research parks were defined as being 'similar to science parks but the planning permission is more rigid, permitting only prototype manufacture'.

In 1988, Monck *et al.* reported thirty-three science parks in the United Kingdom with a further three under construction. While science parks in the 1970s were funded mainly by academic institutions, local authorities and development agencies have subsequently played a dominant role in the provision of finance, eighteen parks having been initiated by development agencies (English Estates, nine; WDA, three; SDA, four; IDB, one; Mid-Wales Developments, one). During this period most science parks were established in the less developed regions (Monck *et al.* 1988, p. 81).

> By the end of 1986, a total of £153 million had been committed to Science Park developments. Some £92 million had been spent on completed parks, £46 million for expansion on existing schemes; and £15 million is being invested in seven new schemes due for completion.

The institutional sources of the 153 million pounds, according to Monck *et al.* were as follows:

Development agencies	£31m
Local authorities	£35m
Universities	£29m
Tenant companies	£44m
Private sector institutions	£14m

The development of science parks in the United Kingdom had little to do with explicit policy initiatives on the part of central government, although some stimulus – if in a sense an unwelcome one – was provided during the 1980s when government cutbacks on university funding forced academics to seek new employment and funding activities.

Monck *et al.* (1988) identified 346 businesses located on UK science parks at the end of 1986. Of these

- 28 per cent were less than four years old,
- 35 per cent were between four and nine years old, and
- 26 per cent were between ten and twenty-five years old.

In addition,

- 26.2 per cent had activities in hardware and systems,
- 15.3 per cent had activities in software,
- 9.8 per cent had activities in microelectronics,
- 14.2 per cent were involved in analysis and testing, and
- 4.9 per cent offered financial and business services.

According to Quintas (1987), research into UK science parks suggests that firms located on them are unlikely to build significantly greater ties with higher education institutions (HEIs) than they would do situated elsewhere. His research involved a sample of science park based high-tech companies and a control group of similar high-tech non-science park-based companies. Informal links with HEIs were found in 60 per cent of the science park-based sample and 44 per cent of the control. This difference could easily be accounted for by straightforward geography. Surprisingly only 28 per cent of science park-based companies were found to have formal links with HEIs; exactly the same percentage as with the control group. The importance of informal linkages has been stressed elsewhere (Rothwell 1989).

CONCLUSIONS

By examining some of the major infrastructural organisations designed to stimulate technology transfer in France, Germany and the United Kingdom, we have seen both similarities and differences in approach. In each of these countries there has been a recent growth in the number of agencies designed to encourage regional technological development. In all these countries budgetary constraints have been important in limiting the extent to which the technology transfer mechanisms have been implemented. There generally appears, however, to have been an increase in the priority given by these agencies to encourage the formation and growth of technology-based SMFs, comparative to their other functions of encouraging both traditional sectors and inward investment. One manifestation of this priority has been the growth in science parks and innovation centres.

Regional technology transfer agencies offer various forms of support to technology-based SMFs. These include financial provision, technological assistance, and managerial support, often in conjunction with national schemes. There are broad differences in the form of national assistance available, and this relates to the political structure and individual philosophy of ruling governments. The French government has placed considerable emphasis on decentralising its technology support agencies, and the German Federal political structure ensures strong regional concern for regional technology bases. Both are 'interventionist' in the sense that they offer a range of support mechanisms designed directly to assist technology transfer. The UK government has not in the past placed great emphasis on technology as a regional development tool, although its three individual Development Agencies do encourage regional technology transfer. However, compared with France and Germany, the United Kingdom offers very little in the way of national support mechanisms for technology transfer into SMFs. With the exception of one small scheme, the UK government, unlike the French and German, do not offer direct grant assistance to individual firms wishing to innovate.

23

WHAT PRICE KNOWLEDGE IN THE ELECTRONIC AGE?

Britton Harris

INTRODUCTION

I begin this chapter with a few fictitious news stories, intended to illustrate from a popular point of view the nature of the problems which we will discuss.

**Distinguished Cambridge Professor Seeks
Legal Protection for His Methods**

London, 23 September 1695. The well-known Cambridge University don, Sir Isaac Newton, today filed suit in London and Geneva, petitioning for a restraining order against the German philosopher and mathematician Gottfried Wilhelm von Leibniz in the use of certain calculational methods, and the publication of works based on them. He also sought punitive damages for what he called 'thievery of ideas'.

Professor Newton's case has a long history in the courts. Originally, he sought letters patent for both his theory of gravity and planetary motion, and for new methods of calculating these motions, which he called the 'method of fluxions'. The outcome of administrative rulings and prolonged litigation was that the courts denied a patent on the theory, but granted one on the method of calculation. They argued that planetary motion was a natural phenomenon and that an explanation of it was not patentable. The method of fluxions, however, was a practical device intended to assist calculations, and therefore patentable.

Doctor Leibniz has published a calculation method which he claims is identical in effect to that of Newton, superior to it in concept, and prior in point of discovery. Newton claims that his method is prior to that of Leibniz, and is protected by his patent, which Leibniz has infringed by copying the 'look and feel' of the method of fluxions – regardless of whether he uses identical methods. The courts are thus being asked to determine the priority of Newton's method and the extent to which it is protected by his patent.

AT&T Acts to Protect Its Rights in
Long-distance Calling Codes and Methods

New York, 27 August 1989. The nation's largest long-distance carrier, AT&T, today announced a dramatic move to tighten its hold on its long-distance business and make the conduct of such business more difficult for its competitors.

The company has copyrighted the system of area codes which direct the routing of calls across the nation, the definitions of the areas to which they refer, and the whole method of identifying and directing these calls. It intends to license the use of this system, and has announced that it will 'prosecute to the fullest extent of the law' companies which use the system without prepaid licenses. The company has also copyrighted several scores of possible names for area codes, such as 'calling areas' and 'region codes', to make it harder for competitors to set up new systems.

The president of US Sprint met this announcement with scorn. 'AT&T can sue all they like', he said, 'but they will be laughed out of court. What right have they to define areas like the state of Delaware or Rhode Island, which are now long-distance dialling areas? Anyhow, the numbers assigned to them are there for anyone to use!'

The Federal Communications Commission announced that it had started an investigation of this issue, and would make a ruling after it receives the results of the study. Asked when this would be, a spokesman stated that 'we expect results in one or two years – say at least by late 1991'.

Calling All Flies:
Near a Frog? Don't Move!

Woods Hole, 1 April 1989. It may sound like an April Fool's Day story, but scientists at the Woods Hole Oceanographic Institute have figured out how frogs detect motion, so that they can quickly snap up tasty bugs which fly past. (They capture the bugs using a sticky tongue which is hinged at the front.) The discovery of this neurological trick has also led the scientists to patent an electronic device which serves the same purpose of motion detection, and which may have many military and civilian applications.

It is said that both the frog's eye and the patented device have an array of tiny light sensors. When one of these is switched on or off by a change in the environment, all of the adjacent cells are put in a 'ready' condition which will amplify a similar change when and if it occurs. If no change occurs, the ready signal dies out – but if a change does occur, the amplification is extended. By activating several successive receptors, a moving object triggers a high level of response which tells the frog (or an alarm system) that motion has been detected.

Experts on patent law question whether this patent will survive a court test, since it is based on a natural phenomenon.

We may note that the first two stories are wholly fictitious, but that there is an element of truth in the last one. A patent on this device has actually been granted, but the inventors have not tested the hypothesis that this is how frogs detect motion. One wonders what the state of affairs would be if, after the inventors had collected millions of dollars in profits and royalties, the patent office discovered that biologists had confirmed this as the real mechanism. Is it possible to patent a speculation about natural law?

Exploring the background of these and many similar but true stories which have already appeared in the press will require us to examine more closely the social nature of knowledge, the existence or non-existence of property rights in knowledge, and the changes which have occurred in these characteristics of knowledge in the electronic age. These explorations are intended to be indicative rather than conclusive: the social issues which surround them are much too important and complex to unravel in a short chapter and without the participation of a much larger community of scholars and other citizens, and even lawyers.

To an extent, the chapter directs attention away from the main theme of this volume, which is concerned with the impact of the electronics age on the spatial organisation of human society. Both that organisation and research into its characteristics depend heavily on technology, whose dissemination is the general subject of my discussion. The research itself depends heavily not only on material technology, but on computer software, which is a form of realised theoretical and algorithmic knowledge. With many of my colleagues, I have been concerned with the fate of my own ideas, and have had at least a certain *amour-propre* with respect to them, if not an *amour-proprietaire*. Perhaps we have a somewhat relaxed attitude toward our own 'intellectual property' because we are led in these respects by the academic tradition of open dissemination of ideas, or perhaps we have not hit on ideas whose high value suggests that we make property of them.

KNOWLEDGE, 'INTELLECTUAL PROPERTY' AND SOCIETY

It is tempting to start this discussion with the flat claim that the common phrase 'intellectual property' is an oxymoron – a contradiction in terms. But since this is not immediately obvious, we will explore the matter in some depth.

At the outset, we recognise that knowledge is a social phenomenon, and in two senses. It is generally accepted, if not immediately obvious, that non-trivial knowledge has social utility. But more important for our present purposes, the generation of knowledge and its dissemination proceed in a matrix of social relations. It originates in an environment of social institutions – universities, research institutes and corporate activities. It is recognised by society as providing the conceptual basis for progress in the exploitation of nature, the increase of productivity and well-being, and the potential improvement of social relations. Because of its special role, it has received special consideration. The dissemination of knowledge is, to some extent, a protected activity – protected by guarantees of freedom of speech, by the organisation of scientific publication, by the establishment of public libraries, and by scores of other subtle social rules and arrangements.

Of course, it is recognised that 'knowledge is power', but in fact the ultimate power is monetary or political, and rests on force. Thus, more exactly, we can say that the capacity to sequester knowledge provides the holder with a potential advantage over others who do not possess the same access. This advantage is often short-lived and time-bound, and is frequently condemned; current American examples include insider trading on the stock market, and insider betting on baseball games. In the final analysis, society anticipates that most knowledge, and especially the findings of science, cannot be kept secret and will in due time be revealed – particularly because most knowledge is based on the realities of nature, which we believe are not susceptible to change. Often, as in the case of the hydrogen bomb, being assured that a scientific fact or a technology exists is enough to make possible its rediscovery.

Between the perishable knowledge of the insider, and the more nearly perpetually durable knowledge of the scientist, there is a wide range of types of knowledge whose possessor can gain a temporary but non-trivial advantage by secrecy. The most notorious early example of this was the invention of the obstetrical forceps, and its preservation as a trade secret by several generations of doctors. (This example is well-preserved in the folklore of sociology because of its force as a morality fable.) Such a temporary advantage leads to the rise of so-called proprietary knowledge, which suffers from two great social disadvantages. First, being withheld from a wider public, it becomes less knowledge than property; and second, the withholding of information and the means used to enforce its privacy turn out to be socially divisive.

Thus, in the final analysis, society (acting by means of national legislation and international agreements) has been led to grant temporary monopolies on proprietary knowledge in return for its disclosure. Typically, these monopolies take the form of patents, but in recent years the use of copyrights to protect proprietary knowledge has grown rapidly. We will discuss some aspects of this shift at a later point.

Now we can take a wider view of the concept of 'intellectual property'. No one would seriously argue that the laws of gravity and planetary motion were ever the property of Isaac Newton, in the sense that he owned or controlled them and could in fact destroy them (although some property like slaves cannot be freely destroyed by its owner, and some like land is inherently incapable of destruction). The right of controlling access, which belongs to the owner of indestructible land, is intrinsically contradictory with respect to an accepted natural law. Indeed, once the full nature of these ideas was known to even a handful of others, or to one person, Newton no longer controlled them and they were no longer his property if they ever had been. In the case of knowledge of this type, which has no immediate and direct application, the idea of 'owning' the knowledge is inherently paradoxical or oxymoronic – because if it is not communicated it barely exists, and if it is communicated it cannot be controlled.

The possessor of proprietary knowledge is in much the same predicament, except that his possession at once leads to applications which convey benefit. Access to these benefits is protected, while the knowledge is added to the social pool, by the granting of a patent or copyright. However, in the ordinary event, the granting of a patent does not change the facts of ownership, or rather of lack of ownership. The patent does not give the inventor title to the idea, or knowledge, but rather a temporary right to the use of its applications. By instituting patents, society has created a property right in the use of certain knowledge, in return for its disclosure – that is, in return for giving up any pretense of ownership. Thus, even the idea of intellectual property of a practical nature is an oxymoron.

PATENTS AND COPYRIGHTS

The historic distinction between a patent and a copyright has been implied in the foregoing discussion. As the name implies, the latter form of protection covers the right to duplicate or reproduce – that is, copy – a work which is essentially the product of intellectual activity. The utility of such a work lies in its possession, and not in its application. Having a copy of a book or a drawing gives the holder a source of amusement or instruction; he does not usually employ it to drive nails. Following the instructions in a copyrighted manual is not a violation of the copyright. In opposition to the idea of a copyright, the idea of a patent is that having a copy of a patented machine gives the holder a useful tool, which he can use to do new things, or to do old things better, quicker or cheaper.

The developments of the last four decades (based on the invention of the electronic computer and the transistor) have blurred the distinction between text and tool. A patent might describe a process (say to refine sugar or spin yarn) somewhat independently of the equipment used, but the patent does not forbid its own reproduction – only the use of the process. However, the instructions for the performance of a particular task by an electronic computer are a text in themselves, and a tool, once put into the computer. For this reason, a copyright which prohibits the reproduction of the text also prohibits the duplication of the tool.

The use of copyrights to protect computer software (programs) has several important consequences. The life of a copyright is several times the life of a patent. Copyright protection, if it does not extend to the source code, which may be proprietary, fails to provide for the wide dissemination and examination of the scientific content of the invention. And current interpretations (not yet fully tested in the courts) suggest that the coverage provided by copyright goes beyond the process which a program text produces, to the appearance of the outcomes of that process.

This last protection, which has many potentially pernicious effects, has been granted, at least for the present, to the 'look and feel' of the spreadsheet calculations performed by the most popular and profitable software ever created – Lotus 1-2-3. Similar copyright wars are about to be waged over the look and feel of graphic user interfaces in personal computers. This type of interface originated in the Palo Alto laboratories of the Xerox Corporation about two decades ago, and the results were in part licensed to the Apple Computer Corporation. Apple in turn extended some of its rights to the

Microsoft Corporation, but later brought suit on the grounds that more was taken than had been granted. Meanwhile, the success of this user interface (largely popularised by Apple) has led to a psychological and technical revolution in computer control systems, as evidenced in products like Microsoft Windows, X-Windows (used in networked computer systems under Unix), the IBM Presentation Manager, and many less widely promoted types of software.

It remains to be seen whether copyrights in this domain will be used to fragment and disrupt the standardisation of software which is beginning to characterise the microcomputer field and to exert an influence on the use of larger computers. This endangered prospect is of great importance in freeing computer users from the domination of hardware suppliers, system managers and computer programmers.

SCIENCE IN THE ELECTRONIC AGE

The influence of the electronic revolution on scientific investigation and the dissemination of scientific ideas is much broader than the embodiment of processes in texts, which we have just discussed. In this section we suggest some of the scope of other influences which appear to be important today.

The wide use of computers for a variety of purposes (in conjunction with the intellectual curiosity which they have stimulated) has led to the need for scientific understanding of computer function, and thus to the establishment of computer science as a theoretical and applied discipline. Computer science has been very influential in the expansion of mathematics, and their conjunction has led to the discovery of many new algorithms or procedures for solving problems. Many such procedures can be derived scientifically or shown rigorously to have certain characteristics. Others are 'heuristic' in nature and typify a serendipitous approach to the development of methods. Methods of both types have been patented, but few such patents have been tested in the courts, where it may be ruled that selected methods are in the nature of scientific discoveries which are excluded from patent protection.

An unfortunate by-product of the supposed patentability of algorithms arises when research is conducted for profit; this is common in the corporate world, is increasingly evident in universities, and is not unheard of in the attitudes of individuals. Under these conditions, the publication of scientific ideas may be delayed during the patenting process, and the final revelation may be incomplete.

For example, several years ago a new method for solving problems in linear programming, the Karmarkar algorithm, was announced by AT&T and the author. For many months, applied mathematicians were frustrated and defeated in their efforts to understand the algorithm. Finally, it was announced that some parts of the procedure had originally been suppressed pending the completion of the patent application review. The full scientific content of the work has now been put in the public domain, but it is not known whether this description plus the patent will make the process understandable, whether other workers will be able to make use of the scientific ideas, and whether the patent will be upheld in the courts. (In a prior similar case, when the courts required the Eastman Kodak Company to license its patents for colour film processing, competing users were unable to produce the proper results because some key information had been withheld.)

In another well-known case, the publication of results of experiments aimed at producing fusion in a beaker was undertaken prematurely for reasons of scientific priority. At the same time, the withholding of information while filing for a patent resulted in endless confusion and dispute, as the importance of the discovery was potentially much greater than in the Karmarkar case.

Frequently the computer, through simulations or other uses, is a major tool of scientific research, and the computer codes which are used in this process are auxiliary tools. Examples include the programmed search over cases in proving the four-colour theorem of mapping, the computation of millions of digits of pi, the factorisation of large numbers which are the product of two large primes, simulating astrophysical events, simulating quantum-mechanical chemical reactions and the folding of large molecules, and simulating the weather. In some cases, the practical applications of these methods are obvious, and in others not: for example, factorisation is important for the encryption and decryption of secret messages and for computer security codes. Regardless of immediate applications, it is generally true that the exchange of these codes is important for scientific progress, and for testing the results of other scientists' experiments. Meanwhile, the commercial value of the codes may restrict their circulation and, if they are patented or copyrighted, their use.

Still further, the results of scientific research could consist of large masses of information which, if copyrighted by their discoverer, might be unusable by other researchers. Probably the best example of this would be the genetic sequencing of a large part of the chromosomal information for any species, but especially for humans, for micro-organisms causing disease, and for species of economic value. Biogenetic information is increasingly important as a basis for profitable enterprise, and at least one species of genetically engineered animal has been patented. Locking up this information through copyrights would weaken the force of traditional rules for the dissemination of scientific results, and could paralyse all but the most economically powerful sectors of the research community.

Many other tools of scientific research are electronic in nature; this is most obviously evident in medical affairs, where such large instruments as CAT scanners and machines for electromagnetic resonance are increasingly important. In the past it has been quite clear that one of the tenets of scientific openness is the sharing of methods and even of research materials. This form of openness is in danger. Not only is the cost of sharing such methods increasing with the complexity and sophistication of science, so that 'small' science becomes more and more difficult in relation to 'big' science, but the scientific community may be increasingly at the mercy of the producers and suppliers of equipment and materials, much of which will be patented.

The publication of scientific results is yet another area in which the rapid growth of scientific activity may be in conflict with commercial acquisitiveness coupled with the effect of copyright laws. In recent years there has been a proliferation of new scientific journals, often oriented to new subdisciplines of science, and almost invariably sponsored by commercial publishers rather than by professional organisations. The monopoly conveyed by copyright laws permits these publishers to segment the market, charging much higher prices to research libraries than to individual subscribers, and often prices which yield monopoly profits. For research libraries this has been a budgetary disaster, and some are beginning to strike back by selectively cancelling their subscriptions to the less valuable journals. Meanwhile the scientists are at risk in trying to copy the material of these journals and circulate it to their students (whenever it is valuable), because the limits of the doctrine of 'fair use' have not been adequately explored.

In short, it is clear that science (which has never actually been the property of isolated thinkers) is becoming more unified and more deeply embedded in a complex technological and social matrix. As we will briefly explore, the protection which is offered by copyrights and patents in this matrix may have the effect of raising the price of knowledge, without necessarily affecting its rate of production or its cogency. It is time to consider knowledge in a narrower, but in some ways revealing, economic context.

PRICE, COST AND VALUE – KNOWLEDGE AS A PUBLIC GOOD

Knowledge availability is a pure public good in the sense that there is no increase in its cost of production resulting from an increase in the number of users. The classic illustration is radio or television broadcasting, whose cost is not affected by the number of listeners.

Of course the listener to broadcasting incurs his own costs in listening: the purchase of a receiver, its consumption of power and its maintenance. So also the user of knowledge may incur costs of putting the knowledge in place: borrowing or subscribing to printed matter, duplicating material through a photocopier, copying a diskette, or downloading information from a public source. The marginal cost of acquiring a broadcast or a form of knowledge is usually very small, even in the case of a printed book or a magazine (and especially if we examine the cost of the text, not the advertising).

However, the price of receiving a broadcast or acquiring knowledge is usually much higher than its very small marginal cost. The discrepancy between price and cost is maintained by a monopoly of some sort.

In England and other countries (and for certain US 'cable' broadcasts) the receiver must be licensed for a fee. Similarly, the licensing of broadcasters confers a monopoly over a small part of the electromagnetic spectrum, and the nature of the broadcast material establishes a partial monopoly (imperfect competition in the economic sense) over the attention of the listening public. In the United States, the enjoyment of these monopolies is sold to advertisers – usually for more than the cost of production of the broadcast.

Copyrights and patents restrict the right to the acquisition of available knowledge whenever it is embodied in some identifiable and controllable form. The reproduction or dissemination of that knowledge is a decreasing cost activity because the major cost is the original production of the knowledge – possibly including the cost of a master from which it can be reproduced, such as the plates for book production or a movie negative. Decreasing cost industries, even without protection, tend toward competitiveness and then toward monopoly, as the economies of scale and large runs are realised by a few industry leaders. The success of block-buster books and dominant magazines like *Time* rests on capturing just this economy of scale, while the current rash of mergers and takeovers in the publishing industry shows the past, present and anticipated effects of monopoly profits on the valuation of the equity in large publishing corporations.

There are thus two problems with respect to decreasing costs in the various knowledge industries. On the one hand, the existence of monopolies and prices which exceed marginal costs encourages the phenomenon of the free rider, or the person given to the illicit evasion of monopoly prices. On the other hand, monopolies which are adequately enforced may generate excess profits, and may impede various forms of social progress in ways which we have already outlined.

The greater the discrepancy between price and marginal cost, the greater the temptation to the potential free rider. A computer software package which costs from 500 to 1000 dollars can be duplicated in secret for as little as twenty dollars. The duplication of a manual is more difficult and more exposed. The user of this pirated software must also forego any support services which are offered by the producer. But customer pressure has caused most software producers to eliminate copy protection, leaving them with no easy way to prevent or police copyright violations. Of particular concern is the invasive nature of the enforcement of copyright protection: the pirated software can be found only by direct inspection of the user's files and computer storage, because the nature of duplication has shifted the focus of concern away from producers and toward consumers. Access to potentially pirated material is difficult, and the inspection process exposes the user's other and more private files to outside investigators. There are, however, in addition to the social costs of copyrights, some social benefits which are sacrificed with widespread disregard of their legal force. (In this discussion we will assume that the same problems – *mutatis mutandis* – can be identified for other patents and copyrights besides computer software.)

Of primary concern is the economic necessity for recovering long-run marginal costs. These are the costs of production of the protected material in the first place, spread over the life of the discovery and the number of users. No anticipatory pricing scheme can exactly cover these costs. If low prices reduce revenue or high prices sufficiently discourage demand, then costs will not be recovered and the producer will face losses which may put him out of business. If demand at the given price is sufficient, the producer may secure monopoly profits. These may be socially acceptable if the copyright does not absolutely foreclose competition, and particularly if the producer uses some of the profits to create new products. This problem has now arisen in acute form with regard to cable television in the United States. Like electric power and other utilities, this service is often intrinsically non-competitive. Rate of return regulation has not been acceptable, and the enforcement of community social conditions have not proved practical. Changing technology can change the terms of reference for such regulation, and the anticipation of change is a destablising factor in the development of suitable community policies.

In considering industries which produce or disseminate knowledge, there is another powerful consideration which goes beyond economics and urges widespread legitimate circulation of materials. Science is, as we have seen, a collective effort in the social sense, because the dissemination of results brings a larger community into contact with new ideas and new tools. Not only does a limitation of access reduce the audience, but stigmatising some kinds of access reduces the feedback from this wider audience. One acquaintance has argued that he need not publish in journals, because he can reach everyone he needs to reach with a limited circulation of preprints; but clearly, he does not know whom he should reach amongst scores of potential readers who might absorb, use and react to his ideas. Our view of the importance of wide interchange of ideas is even more powerful amongst the community of users and potential users of computer software. Correspondence, publication and the use of the providers' consulting services provide a kind of feedback in which the user becomes a participating scientist in the process of software invention and development. At the same time, two of the most fertile fields for this participation are amongst the most prone to piracy: these are college campuses and third-world countries.

Most societies have provided some institutional recognition both of the need to recover the long-run marginal costs of the development of knowledge, and the cultural imperative for wide participation in this development. University research, libraries, public education and other measures like agricultural research and extension are socially subsidised by governments, philanthropies, religions and other groups. Such social support can be invaluable, and indeed imperative wherever the return on investment is uncertain, very long-term or widely diffused – but potentially socially important.

It seems unlikely, however, that these sources will provide funding at the levels recently seen in various branches of the 'knowledge industry', and especially its computer- and electronically-based branches. Public institutions are sometimes risk-averse and often subject to political intervention. Most important, applied knowledge is in contention with academic basic research, even though it often leads research by finding new results which are incompletely understood and inadequately generalised. At the same time, public institutions are held to a certain kind of financial accountability which entrepreneurs escape almost by definition. Thus, universities, research institutes and governments alike tend to fail as active investors in the application of knowledge, which is an essential component in its generation and improvement.

It is evident, as we proceed further into the current scientific revolution (based largely but not entirely on the electronic revolution), that these distinctions are beginning to blur. The cycle of research and applications becomes ever shorter. Entrepreneurs become more dependent on science and researchers more dependent on technological applications – for both the experience and the financial support which they can provide. Not despite, but because of, this convergence, the issues of cost recovery, monopoly and regulation which we have just discussed are constantly becoming more acute. We cannot expect to propose any definitive solution. Nevertheless, having explored the issues in a limited way, we may also explore some of the measures which can be used for their resolution, in the same way.

POLICIES FOR THE TRANSFER OF KNOWLEDGE

Because there is a prospect of constant technical advance in the transfer of information and knowledge, and of a constant decline in the costs associated with these transfers, there is a romanticised prospect of the free flow and costless acquisition of knowledge. The possibility of such an electronic enlightenment, resulting perhaps from the marriage of the encyclopaedists with IBM, is tempting but not wholly realistic. In an effort to speed this revolution through the provision of modest protection to invention and disclosure, society has brought into sharp focus the contradictions inherent in the increase and dissemination of knowledge. The development of social, customary and legal policy must aim to facilitate a progressive and healthy resolution of these contradictions.

In this section, I will discuss some of these policy issues largely from the point of view of computer software, which is an area familiar to those who do research in urban, regional and other spatial development problems. Since software is one of the most important tools in wide use in the electronic age, and since it is a bridge between the computer technician and the user (specialised in other fields, or unspecialised), this topic will touch the concerns of a large audience, and may point the way to policy in other fields as well. This brief survey will only open up many issues which will require much further study and discussion.

There is a strong feeling among some computer programmers and users that software, like the circulation of library materials, should be free. The idea of free software has to depend in part on the attitudes of those individuals and groups who are themselves committed to the production of software (often of very high quality) but who do not depend on this production for their economic support. This idea can be extended to many aspects of scientific productivity, and it often turns out that the support of the producers is decoupled from specific products but not from their activity in general. To develop this type of scientific activity in a beneficial way requires first that there be a way to judge the potential productivity of individuals and groups, and second that there should be a form of rewards, and a source for them, which is not conditioned on specific outputs. This provides a public good which cannot recover its costs directly, and which therefore requires social intervention in the process of scientific management.

The judgmental aspects of this process may of course, even though realistic, turn out to be anathema to the advocates of scientific freedom. These may consent at least to the idea that the disbursement of limited resources will have to be controlled by some form of scientific peer organisation, but such scientific control through the judgment of peers is far from the reality with respect to both public and corporate allocations for science. A well-rounded policy, however, must take into account the existence and the vitality of this viewpoint, and provide for the existence of activities which are *pro bono publico*, and which are not forced to fit the Procrustean bed of political management or competitive free enterprise.

In a larger economic setting, the objective of policy should be to narrow the gaps between the short-run marginal cost of knowledge, its long-run marginal cost, and a monopoly price which may exploit its value to the user.

Wherever the fixed cost of production of knowledge is low, or where that cost is spread over a very large number of users, long-run costs begin to approach short-run costs. Long-run costs may be considered to be very low whenever the production of knowledge is a by-product of an activity which is in the first instance supported for some other purpose. This is true when software is produced to help the sales of computers, when research institutions support studies which incidentally produce software, and when data is collected for governmental or private purposes but can be placed in the public domain.

Many instances of these phenomena are well-known. The study of computer science and of many substantive disciplines – well-supported by many corporations and universities – creates software which is sometimes widely circulated. The mechanisms for establishing standards and facilitating such circulation need to be strengthened. Similarly, local and national governments acquire a great deal of data for many purposes: the census is a periodic assessment of national resources and socioeconomic conditions which in some places is designed to serve a variety of private as well as public purposes; meteorological, hydrologic and geodetic data serve a multitude of purposes and are now collected in prolific detail by satellite; agencies conduct massive special studies (such as transportation surveys) which turn out to have manifold other important applications; and local government at various levels maintains extensive administrative and land-use data which are now beginning to become available for wider use.

Proliferation of knowledge of these types has begun to uncover a number of fundamental problems.

A major issue which we can only touch on here is the preservation of confidentiality and privacy; this is a political, social and cultural issue whose treatment varies widely. For instance, in Scandinavia and the Netherlands, the census is maintained on a perpetual basis, with registration of each change of residence, and the records are in the public domain. In the United States, strong rules of confidentiality prevail, partly because a fear of disclosure would degrade the quality of information from the respondents. Because of this confidentiality, several companies in the private sector collect similar information (and update it more frequently) so as to provide services and information for mail advertising, locational planning and the like. One might question whether such information is any less controversial in private rather than public data files.

Another problem arises out of the shortage of government and research funds in many countries, which has led to a major emphasis on cost recovery in the distribution of data and methods. This issue leads to endless debate as to the role of government and universities, to a failure to evaluate the need for the data for some function which precedes wider distribution, and to the consequent confusion between average and marginal costs as the basis for pricing. Indeed, there is a tendency to consider charging 'what the traffic will bear' because of the monopoly which intrinsically surrounds the collection of data and the invention of methods. These difficulties are compounded in many cases where there is drive toward privatisation, and the monopoly is transferred to a private concern, often for political considerations; then the desire to realise excess profits is not tempered by considerations of public welfare.

Narrowing the gap between marginal and average cost, and between marginal cost and price has the effect of widening the market, and widening it in several different ways. First, there is the normal operation of demand, which generally increases when price declines – for the existing structure of the market. Second, in a dynamic industry like computing and software, lower prices and the anticipation of lower prices stimulate the invention of new applications and the substitution of these products for older ones; thus the demand curve is shifted upward over time. Finally, in a market where the piracy and bootlegging of products, and their imitation, is prevalent – closing this gap tends to reduce the incentive for evading controls.

This last effect is important for several aspects of public morality and for world development. College students are notorious for evading copyrights and patents, and as leading figures in the future knowledge professions they may carry this morality with them. In the third world, piracy is rife – and small wonder. A legitimate copy of Lotus 1-2-3 (or of many other kinds of software costing upward from 400 dollars) takes the equivalent of a year's family income in Bangladesh, and foreign exchange for the purchase is likely to be unavailable in most of the developing world. This habit of piracy disrupts the development of a market for internally produced knowledge, and makes it more difficult to create a world community in knowledge.

High prices for the use of knowledge are regressive, creating more difficulties for poorer individuals and for small establishments in business, education and government than for the more advantaged. These difficulties can dull the edge of entrepreneurial creativity, which is widely regarded as important in the development of knowledge, and which is probably inversely related to size and wealth.

The creation of standards in the transfer of knowledge through the use of software and data will reduce the possibility of making users captive to a single brand or style of operation. Such captivity reduces competition by restricting entry into the market, and thus helps to maintain excessive prices. Standardisation will ultimately lead to the invention and wider use of more efficient methods for creating software and other forms of knowledge. This will further reduce the fixed costs of knowledge and the gap between average costs and marginal costs. There is a danger here that the wide acceptance of standards will, in the end, block the introduction of some major innovation which is not now even foreseen.

In the final analysis, the best guarantee of lowering the prices governing the transfer of knowledge is competition. The competition will be between nations, between industries, between the public and private sectors, and between firms and individuals. The competition should be buttressed by ease of entry into the activity, and by regulation against the use of monopoly power to restrict entry and to exact undue profits from the exploitation of public goods. Means by which knowledge can be cooperatively produced and freely transferred should be encouraged. The principal instruments for creating a monopoly product and intellectual property – patents and copyrights – should be carefully tuned to the needs of society. The components of natural phenomena and pure science which cannot and should not be protected may need to be redefined, and the use of copyrights to protect technology may need to be restricted.

In the development of the needed policies to foster competition and stimulate the creation and dissemination of knowledge, the basic contradiction which has animated this entire discussion will continue to exist. The knowledge industry intrinsically resists regulation and responds badly to it. At the same time, it needs support of many different kinds, some of which give it powers which virtually demand regulation. The proliferation of the consequences of this dilemma will test the creativity of public policy making for many years to come.

24

A DUAL APPROACH TO
TECHNOLOGY POLICY

Keith Newton

INTRODUCTION

There is widespread conviction that science and technology in general, and information technologies (IT) in particular, hold the key to productivity and competitiveness in fiercely contested global markets of the next century. Such conviction is illustrated in Canada by the Science Council's designation of IT, biotechnology and advanced materials as the 'strategic' or 'enabling' technologies that will shape Canada's future comparative advantage (Science Council of Canada 1989, p. 11).[1]

At the same time, however, there are frequent lamentations that Canada is failing to keep up in the international technology race so that the country's overall prosperity – as well as its equitable regional distribution – may be jeopardised. Such concerns lead, in turn, to strident calls for a more concerted national strategy for science and technology to encourage more and better research and development, innovation, and rapid diffusion of new technologies such as IT.

Some observers (Kenney-Wallace & Mustard 1988) contend that important changes are underway – changes that signal a new approach to science and technology policy. Indeed, there are *some* signs of gathering momentum, public profile, coordination and even political will in governments' approach to science and technology policy in Canada. And there are encouraging indications of private (or public-private) sector initiatives.[2] They are necessary and should be encouraged.

This paper argues, however, that a truly comprehensive – and, above all, realistic and effective – national science and technology strategy to promote the development and use of new technologies must be one that is broad enough to consider their role in a more general process of social change (OECD 1988a).

Specifically, such a strategy must regard human resource development as a necessary, synergistic accompaniment of technological progress.

This argument is based on the findings of a large-scale project of empirical research that examined a variety of dimensions of the labour market impacts of technological change, including impacts on the level and distribution of employment, skill content, work organisation, industrial relations, and the employment of particular groups such as women, youth, older workers and the disabled. Those findings clearly point to the need for innovation on two fronts. That is, policies to promote rapid diffusion of technological innovations manifested in new products and new production processes must be accompanied by policies to promote innovations in the organisation of work, education and training, and labour force adjustment.

The reasons for such a dual strategy are clear. First, the process of technological change is inevitably uneven in its effects: various sectors, occupations and regions are affected in different ways and to varying degrees. Change creates winners and losers.

In the context of the Canadian labour market, this concern may be illustrated by the regional dimension. There are fears that major, and growing, disparities in income and employment could be exacerbated by the forces of technological change. Hence there is an equity rationale for a technology strategy that includes human resource development.

Secondly, there are sound efficiency reasons for such an approach. The willingness of the work force to embrace new technologies will be enhanced by policies that promise equitable distribution of their benefits and costs. And the ability of the work force to fully exploit the potential of the new technologies depends critically on a solid basis of skill formation. Such a dual strategy may thus represent one instance in which the simultaneous pursuit of both equity and efficiency objectives (traditionally a frustrating trade-off to the economist) may be a synergistic one.

TECHNOLOGY POLICY UNDER SCRUTINY: NEED FOR NEW DIRECTIONS

In a context of globalisation fuelled by rapid technological progress, Canada faces fierce competition not only from the United States (heightened by the recent Free Trade Agreement), Japan and Europe, but also increasingly from 'newly-industrialised' countries such as the 'little dragons' of South-East Asia – Korea, Taiwan, Singapore and Hong Kong. To many observers, technological progress is a global race, and one in which Canada is lagging behind. The evidence for this position derives from a number of observations.

First, Canada's performance with respect to a number of science and technology performance indicators looks rather poor in comparison to that of other major industrial countries. As Table 1 indicates, Canada ranks low in several measures of R&D expenditures as a proportion of gross domestic product, for example. Although her R&D spending in government laboratories appears to be in the middle ranks of comparable countries, some analysts such as NABST (1988) argue that the work of Canadian government laboratories is transformed only slowly and inefficiently (if at all) into industrial applications. Furthermore, Canada's industrial R&D spending is highly concentrated: the top four firms account for almost one-third of the total.

Table 1 Canada's science and technology performance

Measure of science and technology competitiveness	Canada's ranking among eight comparable countries*
Gross R&D expenditures as per cent of GDP	Lowest
Industry-funded R&D/GDP	Lowest
Government-funded R&D/GDP	2nd lowest
Government-performed R&D/GDP	Middle
Higher education R&D/GDP	2nd lowest
Domestic patents granted per 10 000 inhabitants	2nd lowest
International patents granted (by population)	Lowest
Advanced degrees awarded (by population)	Middle
Scientists and engineers in labour force (by population)	Lowest
Number of technology-intensive industries with positive trade balance	Lowest

* Canada, United States, Germany, France, Sweden, United Kingdom, Netherlands, Japan.
Source: Kenney-Wallace and Mustard (1988).

Second, measures of technological intensity in 1000 private sector establishments led the Economic Council of Canada (1987, ch. 6) to conclude that Canada lags behind most other advanced economies in the use of various information technologies. A recent paper by Newton (1988) shows Canada trailing the international field in the use of robots, CAD-CAM systems and flexible manufacturing systems.

Third, as shown by Table 2, Canada's international ranking is no better than modest on the basis of additional indicators of technological performance. Canada stands lower than not only the United States (which itself performs only moderately) and highly-ranked Japan, but also well below Sweden, a medium-sized, open economy with which Canada is often compared.

The concern expressed over such indicators of technological performance stems ultimately, of course, from their corollary – namely, that the productivity and competitiveness required for future economic prosperity may not be up to the task. An examination of Figure 1 clearly shows that, until the late 1970s, Canada was closing the productivity gap vis-a-vis her major trading partner, the United States. In the 1980s, however, that gap again widened. Moreover, the productivity performance of certain other countries, such as Germany, France and Italy, has now surpassed that of Canada.

**Table 2 Technological performance indicators: Canada's ranking
among twenty-two industrialised countries**

Indicator	Rank			
	Canada	US	Japan	Sweden
Extent to which labour force willingly accepts new technology	14	9	1	2
How much and how well automation is utilised in major industry sectors	14	11	3	1
Efficiency of companies in scanning new technologies worldwide and commercially exploiting them to create new processes/products	10	7	1	5

Source: World Economic Forum, Geneva, June 1987.

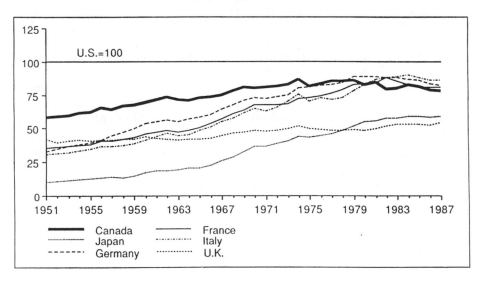

*Figure 1 Canadian manufacturing labour productivity level (output per hour)
relative to the other G–7 countries, 1951–87 (source: Statistics Canada;
US Bureau of Labour Statistics).*

Not surprisingly, given such facts and figures, there have been frequent
calls for renewed efforts by both the public and private sectors to improve
Canada's technological performance. Two particularly influential authors, who
are chairman of the Science Council, and head of the Canadian Institute for
Advanced Research, respectively, have persuasively argued the need for a
cultural change in Canadian science and technology that would encourage

long-term, industry-based applied research. Specifically, they argue that a country or region wanting to be an effective competitor in the global economy must (Kenney-Wallace & Mustard 1988, p. 208):

* establish an effective science-based innovation capability;
* create an effective global marketing capability;
* develop mechanisms for financing high-risk, long-term research and development equivalent to what is done in other regions;
* establish institutional arrangements to mobilise the scarce high-quality resources necessary to be effective in all aspects of the innovation process, including people and money; and
* establish an effective consensus mechanism between the private sector and government to develop appropriate strategies.

While these are undoubtedly essential components of a strategy to promote innovation and competitiveness, we would argue that greater emphasis should be placed on the human resource dimension of innovation and technological progress. This conviction derives from empirical studies of the labour market impacts of new information technologies. Some major results of those studies are contained in the following section.

THE NEED FOR A DUAL STRATEGY

Labour market impacts of technological change

One of the most contentious issues concerning IT is its impact on jobs and skills. Some analysts contend that new technologies are essentially labour-displacing and skill-eroding so that, understandably, the work force and its union representatives have not always welcomed them with unsullied joy. On the whole it seems fair to say that the empirical evidence from North America, Europe and Japan is rather mixed about the impacts on jobs and skills. Not surprisingly, there is evidence of job loss and job gain, skill erosion and skill enhancement due to technological change (Mowery 1988).

As far as employment effects are concerned, the consensus appears to be that major, widespread and lasting unemployment is unlikely to result from the introduction of new technologies (Mowery 1988). What is most important, however, is that while net displacement of jobs may be small, it is the occupational, industrial and regional composition of employment change that is problematic.

Canada provides a good illustration of this point. A recent macro-econometric modelling exercise called MESIM (micro-electronic simulation model), constructed for the Economic Council of Canada by McCurdy (1988), shows that the impact of computer-based automation is extremely uneven across occupational groups. Taking into account both initial displacement effects and potential indirect employment generation from productivity pay-offs, net employment impacts were calculated for some seventy-six occupations as well as for more aggregated occupational groupings. The most important conclusion, however, resides not just in the magnitude of individual results, but in their direction. Certain occupational groupings, such as 'clerical' and 'machining and related', show large negative net employment impacts when projections to 1995 are compared with the 1981 census employment levels. For other major groups, such as 'professional' and 'sales', the net impact is positive. The conclusion is clear: unevenness is a principal characteristic of the labour market impacts of computer-based technologies.

The policy implications of these findings are also clear. New technologies have the potential to create both winners and losers. The process of technological change is, therefore, simultaneously a process of labour market adjustment in which the objectives of both efficiency and equity – to maximise benefits, minimise costs and fairly distribute each – must both be pursued.

Additional evidence supports the case for this emphasis on labour market adjustment. A reflection of shifts in the occupational structure of employment and in the skill content of jobs is a change in income distribution. While new technologies may not cause the extreme polarisation of skills and incomes hypothesised in Kuttner's (1983) 'declining middle', they are one of the factors (along with the shift from goods to service production and shift in family composition, for example) underlying the observed decline in the proportion of middle-class incomes in Canada in recent years (Wolfson & Leckie 1988). Furthermore, results of a nationwide survey of innovations, and a set of case studies, indicate that technological change is typically accompanied by innovations in the design of work, workplace communications, and decision making, industrial relations, and compensation schemes (see Betcherman & McMullen 1986; Betcherman *et al*. 1989).

The regional dimension

These observations about the need to promote technological diffusion and labour market adjustment together are reinforced when one examines the regional characteristics of the Canadian economy. Despite a variety of federal and provincial government initiatives, there is significant inequality across and within Canada's regions with respect to unemployment and several other socioeconomic indicators, including income, educational attainment and the percentage of families living below the poverty level. For example, Table 3 shows that disparities in regional unemployment rates have persisted since the early 1970s. The Atlantic region's unemployment rate in 1988 was more than twice that of Ontario, for example. And the income data of Table 4 show equally disturbing disparities.

The debate about the role of IT in Canadian regional development is fractious and, as yet, inconclusive, as the recent work of Britten (1986) and Lesser (1987) illustrates. In the context of our principal theme, however, a few observations are in order. First, there are clear regional differences in the private sector's uptake of computer-based technologies (CBT). Survey results show that on three measures of 'technological intensity' – the proportion of establishments that had introduced CBT in 1980–85, the proportion of

Table 3 Relative unemployment rates in the Canadian regions: Canada = 100

Year	Atlantic	Quebec	Ontario	Prairies
1969	138.2	137.3	72.4	46.2
1970	107.2	122.8	77.2	53.6
1971	112.9	117.6	87.2	51.1
1972	124.1	120.1	80.3	52.0
1973	140.6	122.0	77.4	50.7
1974	158.3	123.3	83.3	38.1
1975	142.3	116.6	91.8	34.4
1976	152.3	121.7	86.5	35.3
1977	154.7	127.3	86.3	36.5
1978	148.8	130.2	86.6	38.0
1979	157.0	128.7	87.6	35.6
1980	147.5	131.8	91.4	35.1
1981	152.6	136.8	87.0	36.3
1982	128.7	125.0	89.3	42.4
1983	126.3	117.2	87.0	50.5
1984	136.4	113.5	80.3	53.8
1985	151.2	112.7	76.4	53.5
1986	158.4	114.9	72.7	56.7
1987	158.8	115.9	68.7	58.7
1988	160.2	118.4	63.3	98.7

Source: Statistics Canada, *The Labour Force*, cat. 71–007.

Table 4 Average family income in Canada, 1979 and 1987

	1987 $	1979 $	1987 Canada = 100	1979 Canada = 100	Change 1987–79
Canada	35 965	20 164	100.0	100.0	0.0
Atlantic	30 627	16 616	85.2	82.4	2.8
NF	30 365	16 885	84.4	83.7	0.7
PEI	28 617	16 023	79.6	79.5	0.1
NS	31 681	16 482	88.1	81.7	6.3
NB	29 818	16 701	82.9	82.8	0.1
Quebec	33 409	19 750	92.9	97.9	−5.1
Ontario	40 326	21 089	112.1	104.6	7.5
Prairies	34 524	19 881	96.0	98.6	−2.6
MAN	32 556	17 848	90.5	88.5	2.0
SASK	32 093	18 377	89.2	91.1	−1.9
ALB	36 392	21 597	101.2	107.1	−5.9
British Columbia	33 998	21 106	94.5	104.7	−10.1

Source: Statistics Canada, cat. 13–207.

employees working with CBT in 1985, and expenditures on CBT as a proportion of sales – the Atlantic provinces ranked considerably lower than other regions (Economic Council of Canada 1987). Second, notwithstanding the lack of consensus on whether or not IT can alleviate regional disparities, there is agreement that shortages of skilled labour, and the lower levels of educational attainment of less developed regions, could markedly limit their ability to exploit the potential of new technologies (see, for example, Brodhead *et al.* 1989).

The dual approach

The evidence set out in the second section of this chapter suggests that Canada, as yet, lacks an explicit national commitment to new technologies and the cohesive policy framework needed to accompany that commitment. We argue that such a framework must rest on two foundations. The first is rapid diffusion of new technologies. There is no alternative. It is a matter of economic survival: if Canada does not embrace the new technologies its trading partners surely will, and jobs will be lost as a result. The second is a cohesive program of labour market adjustment and organisational change that will develop a committed and well-trained work force that can fully, rapidly and fairly realise the potential of technological progress.

The two dimensions of this dual approach, illustrated in Figure 2, are clearly mutually supportive. On the one hand, labour market and adjustment policies and programs, public and private, at all levels, can help ensure that individuals are protected from the disruptions that inevitably accompany a process of rapid change. On the other, it seems reasonable to assume that programs that adequately prepare people for such change and lessen the pain of transition will enhance the acceptability of new technologies and hasten their adoption. In such a context, equity and efficiency may therefore be synergistic goals.

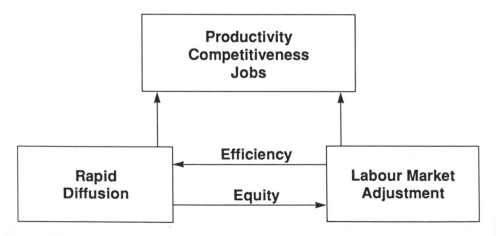

Figure 2 Strategic policy framework.

RECENT INITIATIVES

Following the October 1986 Speech from the Throne, which explicitly recognised the crucial importance of science and technology to Canadian economic and social development, the Prime Minister announced the establishment of the National Advisory Board on Science and Technology (NABST). Composed of prominent and influential representatives of business, labour, government and the academic and research communities, NABST was given additional profile and prestige by the Prime Minister's chairmanship. Its recognition of the human dimension of the technological change process is exemplified by the report of its industry subcommittee (NABST 1988) which devotes half of its text to a discussion of 'technological advance and social change', which covers such topics as education, training, the impact of new technologies on women and special labour force groups, industrial relations and workplace innovation.

Such coverage is also found in the documents of the federal-provincial Council of Science and Technology Ministers, established in 1987 in an effort to promote a more coordinated approach to the formulation of a national science and technology strategy. Furthermore, the newly-reorganised federal department known as Industry, Science and Technology Canada (ISTC) recently released a discussion paper on the 'human dimension of competitiveness' (ISTC 1989) that suggests, at least implicitly, that the federal government's science and technology policy should embrace such issues as labour force training, the quality of the education system and management training. And the Canadian Workplace Automation Research Centre, set up in 1985, has already produced several in-depth studies of the implementation of IT in Canadian organisations.

Such federal initiatives are, of course, welcome in themselves, in that a clearly-enunciated expression of concern for the human side of the change equation represents a step forward. What is needed, however, is recognition that the very word 'innovation' means not just advances in machinery and equipment, in products and processes, but, most importantly, in workplace design, the development of human resources, communication and decision making, remuneration and industrial relations. It is true that the initiatives we have described place emphasis on education and training, but we would argue that there is little evidence of understanding (or acceptance, perhaps?) of a crucial symbiotic relationship between technological and organisational change.

One hears much about 'globalisation' and competitiveness these days – frequently in the same breath as R&D, science and technology, IT and so on. But rarely is organisational change accorded the same status as technological change in the rhetoric of national debate or in the formulation of government policy.[3] What, then, of the private sector?

While there are clear exceptions – Northern Telecom is the outstanding example – the record of Canadian firms is unimpressive. The survey of 1000 private sector establishments referred to by Betcherman and McMullen (1986) revealed that while most firms that had introduced CBT in 1980–85 had introduced some form of organisational change, the take-up of individual programs was somewhat low. Quality circles (which flooded the North American management science literature in the late 1970s and 1980s), for example, were reported in only 13 per cent of the sample.

Mansell's (1987) tour d'horizon of workplace innovation in Canada clearly indicates that the incorporation of the concept of organisational change into technology policy at the micro level is beset by a number of problems. These include not only the deeply inherent risk-averse conservatism of Canadian management, but, in addition, the acute suspicion of many Canadian trade unionists that organisational change is merely a thinly-veiled ploy to undermine union influence and effectiveness. In-depth case studies (in addition to Mansell 1987; see Betcherman *et al.* 1989) confirm this view. Celebrated examples of sociotechnical design at the Shell Canada plant in Sarnia, Ontario, and General Electric in Bromont, Quebec, have gained worldwide attention. But the overall record suggests that innovations in organisational design and human resource development have not matched even the modest advances in computer- based technology.

CONCLUDING COMMENTS

It is clear that new technologies such as IT hold the key to productivity and to competitiveness in the global economy. This conviction has led to numerous and varied initiatives by the public and private sectors in most industrialised countries to encourage technological progress. In many countries, including Canada, this has involved much agonising over the concept of science and technology policy. In this context, a particularly disturbing fact has, until recently, received surprisingly little attention. It is that, since the early 1970s most industrialised countries have shown a marked slowing in their rates of growth of productivity. In other words, in precisely the period when IT and the 'micro-electronic revolution' were transforming, the global economy productivity growth declined. Why?

A recent international seminar at the OECD in Paris reviewed papers on this topic by experts from a number of countries. Various possible reasons for the failure of new technologies to boost productivity growth were considered, including the first OPEC oil stock, difficulties in measuring productivity in the burgeoning service sector and structural changes in the economic environment, such as tax regimes, the welfare state, and the size of the public sector. Not surprisingly, little consensus emerged.

However, considerable attention was devoted to an explanation which is consistent with the central tenet of this chapter – namely, that the full potential of the new technologies can only be realised when they are accompanied by organisational change and an innovative approach to human resource development.

Lindbeck (1989) characterised this explanation as 'the asserted deterioration of the internal organisation of firms – or possibly changes in either technologies or market conditions – that have made traditional hierarchical, centralised, command-oriented organisations of firms less conducive than before to efficient operations'. A more specific version of this notion is the hypothesis of increased obsolescence of 'Tayloristic' organisations because demand has shifted to more differentiated, high quality products, because modern technologies place human skills at a premium, and because highly educated people tend not to thrive in rigidly hierarchical organisations.

Such an interpretation lends support to the dual strategy advanced in this chapter. It also poses major challenges for the less developed regions of the country. Hypotheses concerning the opportunities to benefit from IT-based economic activities for such regions that do not rely on traditional spatial endowments of resources, have encountered empirical evidence that, even for IT, there still appear to be important agglomeration economies that favour the more prosperous growth poles.

But the double dilemma may be that, because of the critical importance of the human dimension of innovation, the inferior skill mix, educational preparation and organisational structure of firms in less advanced regions may in fact exacerbate existing disparities. From a policy perspective, this means that the various government initiatives to stimulate economic activity and technological advance in such regions must embrace the human dimension. Thus, a more integrated, 'horizontal' approach to program delivery – one that cuts across traditional, compartmentalised departmental lines – is required at the national level. At the regional level there must be explicit recognition of the need for human resource development and initiatives to encourage organisational change in order to promote the kind of environment in which IT can flourish.

NOTES

1   See also Economic Council of Canada (1987a), National Advisory Board on Science and Technology (NABST) (1988), and Canadian Chamber of Commerce (1988) for other examples of this conviction.

2   One such example is the involvement of government laboratories with new industrial research consortia such as PRECARN (the Pre-Competitive Applied Research Network, established in 1986 to stimulate industry to build a base of interactions focused on artificial intelligence and robots).

3   Nor can one claim that the situation is markedly better at the provincial level where two institutions devoted to the study and facilitation of technological and organisational change – the Ontario Quality of Work Life Centre and Manitoba's Workplace Innovation Centre – have recently closed.

25

CONCENTRATION OF NEW INFORMATION TECHNOLOGIES: ARE THERE SPATIAL POLICY CONCERNS?

Joanne Fox-Przeworski

INTRODUCTION

This chapter addresses some ramifications of the 'information society' on urban areas. The first part responds to the question: is there a spatial concentration of information-based activities and, if so, what is tending to concentrate, where and why? The discussion is supported by selected examples from telecommunications. The continuing attraction of major metropolitan areas is then considered. In the second part, the consequences of these developments on 'the meaning of space' are discussed. The conclusions in the third part touch on policy issues relevant to information and communication technology (ICT), urban planning and the functioning of local government.

GEOGRAPHY OF TECHNOLOGICAL CHANGE

New technologies offer enormous potential to deconcentrate economic activities involving the production and processing of information. The inherent capacity of telecommunications to transcend spatial constraints is evident. The simple installation of an earth station can bring a peripheral area of a country into a worldwide network. Yet these technologies are having a powerful centralising effect, reinforcing the functions of the principal cities within a country. The new technologies are being installed first and foremost in central locations. Thus, although the shift towards information-related occupations is occurring globally, it especially and first affects the labour force and economic structures of major metropolitan areas.

It must be added that contrary views, often imaginative scenarios, are set in terms of likelihoods and probabilities. Decentralisation of the information economy remains down the road, a medium- or long-range development perhaps parallelling the extension of telephone services, an analogy which may be weakened by negative regional effects of increased liberalisation and the growth of proprietary networks. Even the most footloose of the ICT industries, telecommunications using satellite capacity, are drawn to central urban locations. Eventually, as installation costs drop and the 'utility-penetration rate' (Abler & Falk 1981) drives up demand sufficiently, the new technologies will spread throughout the urban hierarchy. The time frame of this eventuality must be considered in light of the massive investment and organisational factors involved.

A number of cost and agglomeration factors mediate against large-scale dispersion in the near future to non-urban and peripheral areas. Cities at the top of the hierarchy will be the first to receive innovative applications (Abler 1987b). Moreover, geographically scattering back-office functions or production-related activities may not result in decentralisation of management and decision functions. On the contrary, it often leads to the reinforcing of control and functional dependencies (on IBM's hegemony, see Bakis 1980). Communication networks convey information both ways, of course, and the centralised control of a few firms can be greatly facilitated through satellite connections and cabling. Analyses of major international conglomerates have confirmed the regional market expansion that can be garnered by centrally located firms at the expense of provincial businesses (e.g. in accounting, advertising, and banking (Noyelle 1987b; P.W. Daniels 1987); in newspaper and advertising sectors (Hepworth 1986)).

High-tech industries and R&D activities tend to be overrepresented in a small number of conurbations or central areas. In Japan in 1983, the heavy concentration in three megalopoles of R&D laboratories (83 per cent), scientists (69 per cent) and computer experts (74 per cent), led the government to embark on its national strategy of deconcentration through technopoles (Kawashima & Stohr 1988; Toda 1987; Nishioka & Takeuchi, 1987). Public R&D grants in Europe tend to be distributed disproportionately to urban-based institutions and to a few, usually large, ICT firms, perhaps a further factor favouring the development of strongest firms in central locations (Richardson *et al.* 1984). Similarly, the financing of high-risk ideas and new technologies through venture capital funds, at least in the United States, is highly geographically concentrated in major cities (OECD 1985).

If these trends continue, not only will one or two principal cities of a nation be strengthened, it follows that the primacy of existing international centres will also be reinforced.

The tendency towards concentration of information-based activities can be illustrated by three developments in telecommunications: integrated networks, teleports and value-added network services (VANS).

Integration of digital networks/ISDN

Recent technological advances permit the upgrading of the digital/analogue network mix by shifting transmission from existing separate networks used to supply voice, data, text and image services to an integrated services digital network (ISDN). Without compatible digital networks, wide-band integrated systems based on cable and satellite connections are not possible.

Where and when ISDN will be installed have obvious implications for the nature of information flows and decision making. These technological changes are being overlaid on a system that has important national variations in the extent of digitalisation and switching capability, as well as sharp differentials among regions and cities within a country, e.g. in telephone penetration rates (OECD 1988b). These variations coupled with the already high concentration of communications traffic, both national and international, highlight the powerful role of telecommunications in economic competitiveness.

Teleports

Teleports provide integrated facilities that link a multitude of satellite and cable services via telephone, fibre-optic or microwave installations. The concept, which originated in the United States, refers to an earth station, often related to real estate, with a distribution network serving customers within a metropolitan or regional area. The teleports have the potential to be placed anywhere, but they are being installed in the largest cities; their effectiveness depends on an intricate and compatible computer architecture in the service area (Abler 1987b). Hence, the answer to the question 'where to put future teleports' is inextricably linked to the answer to 'who will use them?'. For example, of the forty operating teleports in the United States in 1987, twenty-seven are located in the seventeen largest metropolitan areas (populations of two million or more), another four in the next largest metropolitan areas (populations between one and two million).

These centralising tendencies could be reinforced through recent developments in transmission and earth station technology. Since the late 1980s, the use of higher frequency Ku-bands, which do not share space with earth systems, has assisted in removing problems of interference and increasing data transmission rates. Transmission can therefore be received even in heavily congested metropolitan areas through receivers on customer premises. Additional advances which tend to concentrate control in a large hub earth station are very small-aperture terminals (VSATs) and 'star' networks. A characteristic of this network is that the thousands of VSATs at remote locations can communicate only with the central station.

Value-added services

Value-added network services exploit the potential of the computer-telecommunications linkages by providing functions involving the electronic transfer of information and data. The pattern in Europe indicates the predominance of VANS consumers in major cities in 1979. The capitals of Belgium, France and the United Kingdom, for example, accounted for between 40 and

50 per cent of data network terminating points in 1979 in their respective countries (Gillespie *et al.* 1984).

With the rapid growth in communication-dependent services, the spread of computer networks will have a determining influence on the distribution of jobs, markets and decision-making power (Hepworth 1987). Indeed, the generation and diffusion of these networks already exert 'a clear spatial dimension which favours large urban centres and core regions' (Howells 1988, p. 177). A study of the spatial impact of computer culture in the United Kingdom, for example, indicates that 'post industrial Britain will be the Britain of the South' (Batty 1985, p. 36).

Telecommunications now provide the basic infrastructure for certain services, especially in banking, finance, tourism and the travel business. As a consequence, the nature of this infrastructure and its development will be important, if not the critical factors in determining the supply of these communication-intensive, high value-added activities. In the United Kingdom, the networks are serving to strengthen the market position of established industries, which are the main exporters of new as well as traditional information services to weaker or economically peripheral regions (Gillespie & Hepworth 1986). In 1985, of 164 companies registering under the VANS general license, 125 were located in London and the home counties, underscoring the 'pronounced core region and metropolitan bias' (Gillespie & Hepworth 1986, p. 98).

Whether or not these services, in terms of providers and users, will remain highly concentrated in core regions will also depend on the stimulation of demand, as illustrated by Minitel videotex in France, a telecommunications network-based service with public and private sector applications. Free availability of the Minitel terminal to telephone subscribers resulted in widespread use within a short period and rapid returns to scale (Bacle 1988; OECD 1988c). By contrast, a detailed study of telecommunications use in the north-east of England suggests that businesses, especially small firms in peripheral areas of the country, generally make only limited, traditional use of telecommunications (primarily telephony and telex) (Gillespie *et al.* 1989).

Thus, the centralisation problem needs to be examined not only in terms of physical placement of lines, main frames and networks. Inquiry must be made as to whether there is an existing market, and, if not, how demand can be stimulated. The answer in turn leads to the consideration of the type of network, whether open subscriber or private leased lines, and of the compatibility in both network and infrastructure as well as equipment. Access through an appropriate infrastructure and adequate demand are both essential to creating widely dispersed VANS which, in turn, will stimulate other economic activities and innovations. Given the initial directions of investment in telecommunications infrastructure and services that most countries seem to be taking, however, major metropolitan areas will continue to benefit at the cost of currently less-served areas.

Some explanations

Geographical concentration has traditionally been regarded as the effect of the pull of agglomeration factors that are clustered in metropolitan areas. Current analyses, although less conclusive than we might like, suggest that there are a number of good reasons why characteristics most often found in or near major cities – whether combined in 'an incubator profile' (Malecki & Nijkamp 1988), a 'milieu of innovation' (Castells 1987) or as factors of agglomeration – are and will continue to be important to locational decisions of ICT-based activities. External economies and social relationships are still generated in urban areas for information production just as they previously were for industrial production. Walker (1985, p. 256) reminds us that 'geography cannot be read off from technology', moreover that 'evidence does not sustain most prevailing theories of broad spatial patterning based on technological forces'.

People transacting business and research still need to, and apparently want to, get together on a personal basis: 'why can people be paying Manhattan or downtown Chicago rents for, if not for being near other people?' (Lucas 1988). Face-to-face negotiations are made possible and facilitated by an urban environment with easy access to a major airport. They remain important to firms whose activities are highly dependent on informal sources of information (Salomon 1988b). Conference calls and video-conferencing enhance the range of meetings but do not seem to have substantially diminished their number. The initial speculations of a transportation-telecommunications trade-off have thus far not been realised, the projections often based on technological determinism with insufficient attention to sociocultural and organisational factors (e.g. Koppelman & Salomon 1988; Olson 1987; Wigan 1985).

Urban areas usually maximise access to information because of the higher proportions of knowledge-based workers, an assembly of universities and research institutions, large numbers of related activities, options for job mobility, and amenities. As a consequence, cities with clusters of ICT activities are natural seedbeds of innovation and hence attractive to potential entrepreneurs. One has only to note the higher rates of innovation of larger enterprises in core regions of the United Kingdom (Harris 1988; Goddard 1984). Moreover, the image of an innovative environment has a 'positive feedback effect' (Brugger & Stuckey 1987; Castells 1987).

Advanced manufacturing industries using computer-assisted production methods also tend to be biased towards urban areas, especially those with a long-standing industrial tradition, the 'mechantronics connection'. For the most part, microelectronic applications are introduced in large establishments. For example, in France, Japan and the United Kingdom, more than 50 per cent of robots have been installed in plants with more than 1000 employees in a small group of industries. The highest uptake of these applications is in the automobile, metal and machinery industries (OECD 1989a). In the United

States, the traditional manufacturing belt remains strong in absolute numbers of high-tech jobs (Glasmeier 1985). Unlike previous decentralising tendencies during which manufacturing producers left the urban industrial centres in search of lower-cost labour, premises and transport, the pull of agglomeration factors may facilitate spatial reconcentration of skills and services integral to the organisation of flexible automation manufacturing and just-in-time production. The space-saving aspects of flexible manufacturing permit certain industries with expanding productivity to remain within cities. Related suppliers as well as information-based business services also seek proximity to major clients (and frequently to former parent companies). The growing importance of these intermediate inputs in the production process is noted in the United States, where between 1947 and 1985 business services grew from 27 to more than 40 per cent of the GNP (Noyelle 1987b). Thus, an additional attraction of metropolitan areas is the availability of a wide range of services in advertising, engineering, consulting, finance and accounting. (Daniels 1987; Noyelle 1987b; Batty 1985; Howells 1987). Also, more likely to be found in metropolitan locations are certain technologies that require multidisciplinary teams and special equipment, notably in the field of scientific and medical diagnosis.

This sketch of the geography of information technology underscores the present concentration of ICTs and raises questions about their spatial impacts.

RAMIFICATIONS OF ICT ON THE 'MEANING OF SPACE'

Some of the ramifications are touched on here in anticipation of basic policy questions they raise. The impacts are considered on the inter-urban level, both nationally and internationally, on the intra-urban scale, and on the home and personal lifestyles.

On inter-urban space

Diffusion and adoption obviously build on installed infrastructure and networks in place. The transformations of the communications systems are already bypassing less-endowed areas. A city's relative dominance of information sets its position in this infrastructure and determines, to a large extent, their comparative advantage in national and international trade (Hepworth & Dobilas 1985). In this sense, the linkages are 'creating a new urban hierarchy in which certain cities will function as international information capitals' (Moss 1988, p. 271). Moreover, the trend toward liberalisation and deregulation policies in the trade of information is likely to make one or a few major cities within a country 'national champions' with respect to foreign investment and advanced services (Howells 1988; Gillespie *et al.* 1987). It is not yet clear what effects the significant consolidation of economic power in a few world cities will have – not only on the economies of other metropolitan areas, but also on national economies as well as on governments and major corporations. Is it likely that Buenos Aires will be tied more closely to London than to Tucuman? Are the 'world cities' going to be 'talking to each other', quite literally, with ever more capital and jobs leaving national boundaries? (Manhattan already dominates an estimated 40 per cent of the world's international traffic (OECD 1988b, p. 48). Will the hegemony of a major world centre reach across national boundaries? Sydney, facilitated by locational freedom of ICT, is becoming in this sense the primary city of New Zealand, as well as of Australia.

Ultimately, the effects of these changes may be seen not in conventional locational terms but rather in divisions based on information-rich and information-poor areas. A pivotal question may be how to gain access to telecommunications services without direct investments. Transmission of certain information is over private networks with controlled entry. In the current climate of deregulation, a critical role may be played by 'information brokers' (Batty 1985) who will be instrumental in securing entry once the infrastructure is in place. Peripheral regions and cities will remain considerably disadvantaged unless appropriate policies are adopted that are concerned not only with universal service definition, quality and pricing of services, but also with organisational, cultural and less tangible market constraints that may be inhibiting diffusion. Moreover, if they are to have useful consequences, these policies will need to be tied to heavy investment commitments.

On intra-urban space

It is argued that the leading-edge technology exacts its own requirements on urban form – on the infrastructure that is part of the new built environment in world cities (Goddard & Hepworth 1988). The refurbishing of older structures and the new office space that will be required by users of information technologies must be functionally capable of integrating with local area networks (LANs) and metropolitan (wide area) networks (WANs). Limited experience with LAN technology users suggests that existing space is likely to become rapidly outmoded as information-based businesses tend to move to specially designed accommodations (see, for example, Hepworth & Dobilas 1985 on Toronto).

With a view to moving in this direction, so-called 'smart' or 'intelligent buildings' and even projected 'smart cities' are cropping up (Dutton *et al.* 1987) (see also Langdale 1988a; Mandeville 1987b on Australia's 'Multi-Function City of the 21st Century'). The buildings generally employ advanced information technologies in communication facilities, security systems, building automation and amenity features. With the intelligent city concept as the basis of planning the 'city of the future', the Japanese government is trying to ensure that certain conditions are met in terms of land use, renewal and public benefits from the installation of telecommunications networks (Kitamura 1987).

Urban economies are likely to be most deeply, and perhaps most immediately, affected by development of area-wide networks, both public and private. Less than 10 per cent of communication traffic extends beyond 500 miles and typically 60 per cent occurs within an office building or local complex. The subsequent interconnection of LANs with intercity or wide area systems (a growing proportion, e.g., in 1986 comprising about 15 per cent in France and Germany, 25 per cent in United Kingdom (OECD 1989b, p. 25) is viewed by city administrators as critical for integrating local economic activities with national and international economies (Hepworth 1987). Similarly, the new organisation of work is seen to offer promise in regenerating former industrial areas, as in the Boston area, Milano and the Detroit-Pontiac regions (Camagni 1987; Schoenberger 1987). Despite the perception of ICT as a tool for economic development, a recent survey of the use of information technology in the United Kingdom revealed local authorities were not paying much attention to basic infrastructural requirements (Hepworth *et al.* 1989).

New information technologies are providing the means to introduce flexibility in urban planning and to provide more efficient and socially beneficial services. The use of coordinated information systems, such as pioneered in Denmark, allows policy makers to respond more readily to changing demands. As a result, technological innovations which are applied to the running of cities and towns are leading to organisational as well as technical modifications to government operations. Indeed, the very nature of the role of local government may be in the process of changing. (Taylor & Williams 1988; Moskovitz & Mammon 1985). In light of these developments, the OECD Group on Urban Affairs initiated a survey of innovative uses of ICT in member countries to determine if and where policy interventions are appropriate (report expected 1991).

On the home and lifestyles

Housing will become an even more critical unit for planners. Even as the average household size has contracted dramatically in OECD countries, the home is taking on roles expanding well beyond providing physical shelter for the family. Through new communication linkages, a range of services previously unavailable can now be exploited comfortably from home (Miles 1988). Although telecommuting or home-based work via cabling hook-up has not become nearly as widespread as technology would permit (Korte *et al.* 1987; Olson 1987; Salomon 1985; 1986), the home is nonetheless still heralded as the future self-contained unit for work, entertainment, recreation, convalescence, aging in place, education, teleshopping and telebanking. New information technologies will no doubt also influence the way leisure time is spent and hence blur distinctions between work and leisure. Some brakes on this inevitable march of technology are examined through sociological analyses (e.g. Koppelman & Saloman 1988; Vitalari & Venkatesh 1987).

Taken together, these spatial and lifestyle changes would seem to have immense implications for urban planning which touch on legal, tax, zoning, education and social issues. What is worrisome for planners is that the policy areas affected and the changes that need to be considered are not well articulated.

CONCLUSIONS: LONG-TERM POLICY ISSUES

Fundamental technological mutations are occurring rapidly. Yet cities must repeatedly engage in policies which irreversibly commit large amounts of resources over long periods. The focal challenge for urban policy making is: How to plan for the long term under pervasive volatility and uncertainty? The key operational issue is what and who to plan for the long run, and what and how to leave open for contingencies. Long-term commitments that anticipate future transformations and short-term responses to already pressing problems, constitute alternative strategies for dealing with a changing environment. Each has advantages and each has costs, each offers promises and each runs the risk of failures. The central policy issue is to assess which type of response is appropriate given our current knowledge, priorities and resources?

In the case of technological change, its pace, both in terms of generating new products and new processes, is historically unprecedented and there is every reason to expect that these changes will continue at an ever-increasing rate and often in unpredictable directions. Moreover, a distinctive feature of the new technologies is that they also become obsolete at an increasing pace and in often unpredictable ways. Local governments' limited experiences in this area, for example with ambitious projects such as local television broadcasting using fibre optics have been for the most part scaled down or abandoned due to high investment costs (OECD 1988c, p. 16).

The scale and uncertainty of these developments pose a new challenge to urban policy makers. They raise two key questions:

1 How to plan irreversible commitments of large amounts of resources normally required by cities?
2 How to exploit the newly appearing technological opportunities?

These are distinct questions. The first concerns traditional subjects of urban planning, mainly infrastructure – embracing technical networks as well as facilities and public buildings. Cities continually invest in the infrastructure. They also mould urban form by regulatory policies, such as zoning, often through fiscal policies. Infrastructural investments tend to be indivisible, very expensive and interdependent. Their physical lifetime tends to be long. The volatility and the scale of recent demographic and technological changes means that the decisions to invest must be now made under increasing uncertainty and under the increasing cost of mistakes.

The second question concerns the rational use of the potential inherent in new technologies. These technologies offer opportunities for accelerating economic development, facilitating economic transactions, improving the quality of life, and establishing new patterns of social interaction. At the same time, they allow urban governments to develop new, more flexible services and to make more efficient the functioning of urban administration. Yet, to use new technologies, cities must again sink large amounts of resources into hardware, software and databases, as well as into infrastructural investments, such as cabling and interactive networks within and between buildings. Moreover, they must do so at a time when the benefits are not entirely apparent and under conditions when technologies become rapidly obsolete. Hence, on the one hand, city planners may be well advised to wait until they can be sure to distinguish temporary from enduring innovations, but, on the other, they would not want to delay harnessing the potential inherent in the new technologies.

Hence policy makers face a dilemma which does not have a general solution. The appropriate responses hinge to a large extent on the specifics of the various social and technical transformations discussed above. Hence the generic policy issue is: which transformations should cities anticipate by committing resources with a long-term perspective, and which changes should they respond to on a contingent and ex-post basis? This is why urban planners and government officials must rely on research concerning the spatial nature of these technological changes and their policy implications.

Public authorities will need to assess whether existing policy instruments respond to spatial impacts of sociotechnical change and capture the benefits of potential applications. They must consider whether new designs and standards are needed with regard to the urban infrastructure, public facilities, social housing, services, zoning, transportation and so on. Because of the complex interactions posed by new technologies, occupational structures and social-cultural factors, guidelines also are needed that would integrate urban policies with other policies that have distinctly urban impacts.

Despite the urgency and pervasiveness of these changes, however, most cities in OECD countries have yet to begin planning for their consequences.

NEGOTIATING THE TRANSITION TO ECUMENOPOLIS: ECOLOGICAL PLANNING FOR NEW URBAN GROWTH

Richard Meier

INTRODUCTION

Three years ago, I took up the puzzle of picturing the kind of urbanism that is evolving in the world today – the patterns that are allowed by the scarcity of global natural resources and the micro-vectors presented by the participating cultures and social units (Meier 1987). The projections took us three generations hence to Doxiadis' Ecumenopolis – the global city that comes into being as the metropolises and megalopolises of the world are knitted together by jet aircraft, telecommunications and shared images (Doxiadis & Papaioannou 1972).

My study introduced the world servers, a small but rapidly expanding stratum of the urban population dedicated to elaborating, managing, and sustaining world-scale activities. Their principal loyalties are to transnational institutions. It also introduced about a hundred or so agglomerations which are expected to receive the surplus people produced in the countryside, but unable to survive there. The metropolitan agglomerations are expected to transform them into a self-supporting population, the bulk of whom will be struggling to rise above bare subsistence – as has happened in the past century. The nuclei receiving these human flows already have names, so we can talk about the respective sites quite handily, and compare their progress and prospects.

Three generations hence, cities are expected to contain 7 to 8 billion people, as compared to the 2 to 2.5 billion occupying urban environments today. Presumably growth will have levelled off by then. However, some of the migrants will be moving on again to places that are more hospitable.

During the period that the birthrate comes into balance with the death rate, and total population stabilises, the bulk of the remaining fossil fuels will have been exhausted. Currently all cities depend on these sources of energy for their livelihood. On-site sunlight and wind power are too meagre in intensity to support human population densities greater than about 2000 persons per square kilometre, with the predominant majority of them consuming the minimum for survival. Efficiencies in the integration of human activities really only appear at densities of 5000 persons per square kilometre, and may be optimal around 10 000 (even more when imported energy is expensive, because energy is needed to overcome the friction of land surface). Thus this huge wave of human habitat transition is complicated by the simultaneous transition to alternative sources of energy.

Fortunately the earth receives enough energy from the sun to sustain civilisation at this scale. Measures made by scientists on photosynthesis have assured us of this about fifty years ago. The problem is to find the optimum technologies applicable to the respective sites and getting the energy processing equipment constructed and operating with the lest wrenching changes in the lives of the residents (Meier 1966).

Straightforward projections based on the mind-sets of the educated people today lead to universal death and misery. As is common with threats to societies, communities and individuals, the existence of the threat is initially rejected, although it may be buried in the subconscious. In any case, a kind of paralysis results, and no action is taken, or at best, just a token to assuage the worried minority.

In an ecosystem it is not uncommon for a population explosion to get under way after a period of conditions favourable for reproduction. Many textbook examples have been provided of such instances. When it happens to people, a Malthusian outcome ensues. Humans were once normally subject to famine one to three times in a full life, but two centuries ago they started drawing upon stocks of energy, first in forests and then underground, The Malthusian crises were once localised and of moderate scale, but postponements have raised it to a global crisis.

It has been stated paper that no body of knowledge can be found which can be applied to the situation in which virtually the whole of Africa finds itself now. No path can be suggested which would lead that continent to an urbanised sustainable state. Indeed, the statistics on human consumption arriving from Africa suggest that the suffering has already begun.

The Population Crisis Committee has constructed an International Human Suffering Index, based on aggregate data such as nutrition per capita, infant mortality, energy consumption, annual rate of inflation, etc. (Camp & Speidel 1987). It has then ranked these countries on a scale of 100. The worst in the world with their respective ratings were:

Mozambique	95
Angola	91
Afghanistan	88
Chad	88
Mali	88
Ghana	87

Somalia	87
Niger	85

For comparison, they put a few intermediate countries at:

Brazil	50
China	50
Mexico	47
USSR	19

At the same time the most developed and urbanised countries are, by these indicators, the most comfortable:

Switzerland	4
West Germany	5
Luxembourg	6
Netherlands	7
United States	8
Canada	9
Denmark	9
Belgium	9
Japan	11
Sweden	12
United Kingdom	12
France	14

The correlation of the human suffering index with population growth was 0.83, and every society with a growth rate above 2 per cent seemed to be losing ground.

The relative trends can be briefly summarised as follows:

Africans	now double in number in	20–22 years
Muslims	"	24–27 "
Hindus	"	40–50 "
Catholics (Latin)	"	45–70 "

Chinese (Han) should add at least 50 per cent and then level off.

Europeans, Russians, Americans and Japanese all are heading below the levels of needed replacement due to deaths, converging on 1.6 births per woman (Davis *et al.* 1987b).

However, the population that is really out of control is automotive passenger vehicles, which double in number in twelve to fourteen years.

The autos dwell mostly in and around cities, primarily in America, Europe and Japan, but are rapidly invading cities elsewhere. Their expansion in numbers is very serious, because it is occurring in the face of a declining stock of petroleum. We see that middle class suburbanites are multiply threatened; it is not only their mobility that is at stake but their preferred habitat and their freedom of choice in natural environments for leisure time activities that is being closed to them. Until now, suburbanites have refused to consider the threat, perhaps feeling that if they ignore it, the problem will go away.

These simple figures suggest that ecologically the urbanites who have designed suburbs so they could live comfortably with their automobiles are in greater risk of population overshoot and subsequent crash than even the Africans. Is the symbiosis so strong that *homo urbanus* will be pulled down into chaos as well? And what about the habitat that accommodates large free-standing houses with greenery and pets? Can it be sustained? Obviously we have identified in this crude calculation a mind-set that is suicidal over a three-generation span.

The mind-set of most Africans seems to be impervious to the incentives for family planning that are working elsewhere in the world (Caldwell & Caldwell 1987). Tribal outlooks reinforced for many centuries have reinforced high fertility rates without taking into account the huge drop in the death rate brought about by epidemic control. Anthropologists conjecture that the incentives may be acceptable only in the event of a conversion to a new religion (other than Islam, which is still gaining ground in Africa) or world-view. However, new belief systems are spread very slowly in a largely illiterate population, so the population expansion continues.

The preoccupations of the automobile operator appear to be equally intractable. Most drivers appreciate the environmentalist point of view, so they disapprove of the prevalence of automobiles, however even the most emphatic Greens have not divorced themselves from their cars. The relationship is a kind of addiction, but it is one that has cultural reinforcements, rather than physiological. Tobacco use is declining in suburban population, but not automotive attachment. It is true that the environmentalist belief system has made inroads on the talk and the diffusion of imagery, but actual behaviour reveals a large number of hypocrites.

ECUMENOPOLITANS: THE GLOBAL PLANNERS

Problems of overshoot like these require planning and coordinated action to overcome them. However, no precedents come to mind. There is no effective world government – no agency to take the problem in hand. Planning method is non-existent. Yet the growth of this new population of world servers offers grounds for hope, in part because they can more readily comprehend the worldwide implications.

Who are they, and what are their connections with each other? Table 1 presents an outline.

Whereas only tens of millions of people take on these part-time roles at the moment, their number is growing much faster than the world population. After looking at the expansions of international agencies, the multinational firms, the international voluntary agencies, long distance tourism, and the increased readership of scientific and other intellectual journals, it would appear that the growth rate is in the neighbourhood of 8 to 10 per cent per year. Given that membership is only for a few decades (one graduates into world server status most often after becoming a nation-serving or organisation-serving professional), the entry rate must be growing about 10 to 13 per cent per year, while 2 to 3 per cent are retiring from the fray or dying from stress-related diseases.

Table 1 The ecumenopolitans: the world-serving roles

---

1 United Nations organisation personnel
2 International governmental organisation representatives (common market, OECD, OAS, etc.)
3 International non-governmental organisation members (Red Cross, CARE, scientific societies, etc.)
4 International business organisation managers/professionals (IBM, EXXON, ICI, FIAT, AEG, etc.)
5 International Service Organisations (Peace Corps, Friends Service Committee, etc.)
6 International consultants (Scientific, technical, economic, legal, etc.)
7 Knowledge producers (researchers, university administrators, etc.)
8 Overseas tourists
9 Intellectuals' circles

These numbers suggest a doubling rate of seven to nine years, but this pace will slow down during a global depression or be stifled by the polarisation of a cold war. Thus, perhaps, a tenfold increase in numbers can be anticipated in the course of a human generation. Their influence should be much greater than the population dimensions suggest.

At the present time, the world servers are furiously forming networks, each of them a specialised circle, but some are networks of networks. Outside of the military (not all nation-serving), the most farflung network is managed by IBM, and the second by EXXON, with both organisations exceeding 100 000 stations, according to personal reports of specialised consultants. The retirees are kept organised by a 'seniors' net.

The networkers are in daily communication with each other, many times across international boundaries, so they are demolishing all attempts at national censorship.

Curiously, the creation of teleconferences on the net does not seem to reduce the attendance at international conferences. What it does do is make the agenda more up-to-date and relevant. The trend is to add local detail to whatever global problems become agenda items, so that exceptions to the widely believed rule are picked up, explanations are found, and the accuracy of the generalisations greatly improved. The discovery of a discriminable amount of global warming over the past century is illustrative of a process that is due to become routine (Powledge 1989).

The world servers do not have the power to change the direction that the world is going, but they do have rapidly increasing influence. If one of them has the ear of a decision maker, he can call upon the others for help. If consensus can be obtained, the facts will speak loudly. The action is then taken in communities, metropolitan regions, and organisations that separately make a small contribution to the global problem. Thus the resolution of some transnational problems is achieved incrementally.

An example of how this works is found in the program against tobacco addiction.

The national interests have always been in favour of tobacco, because the craving can be harnessed to become a major collector of revenue for the State. The tobacco growing interests were politically powerful in agricultural circles, and the companies were economically potent; both were willing to battle to maintain their position. However, the scientists, doctors and welfare workers first achieved consensus on the scale of the costs to society, then set up independent channels of persuasion – journalists, school teachers and the leading cliques among the high school students – and they designed social support groups for those smokers who quit 'cold turkey'. Progress is finally also appearing with respect to alcoholism, and it is hoped that other drug problems will follow as the consensus about tools improves. This was achieved by the link-up of world servers with dedicated community servers before the networks have come into play. The leverage will be greater in the future.

THE TRANSPORT ENERGY PROBLEM

How might the networks of world servers resolve the threat of the automobile population overshoot? Fortunately a few of the investigators, faced with portions of the global problem, have scoured the scientific literature in search of contributory clues and have sometimes arrived at comparisons of costs. We shall try to trace a path for sustainable development that leads to a stable state of the urban system. Because the world servers have no political power, that path must lead through intermediate states of increasing efficiency in the consumption of energy that require no reduction in quality of life, but have improved security over the previous trend, and therefore yield a small new improvement. Local policy makers can tolerate such advice. The consequences are illustrated in Figure 1.

The developed cities must greatly reduce their per capita consumption of fuels, and use their superior access to technical and social knowledge to improve noticeably the quality of life. The poor cities will, after some lag due to the need to digest large numbers of immigrants, start applying some of their own resource-conserving ideas for improvement. In this period some will make the transition to the developed category (Goldemberg *et al.* 1987).

It is perfectly natural to take on huge and complex problems in pieces that appear negotiable, and then go back to the holistic picture to see what else needs to be done. Identification of the overshoot in vehicle population allows us to explore first what can be done using the present body of knowledge, and then we can discover what these tentative solutions imply for the global system.

The public is aware that the stocks of liquid fuels are limited, that the search for new supplies is becoming increasingly expensive per unit discovered, and that the predominant proportion of those deposits held in reserve are located in parts of the world that are politically unstable. Therefore it is increasingly willing to consider, and even sponsor with subsidies, alternative sources of energy for propelling vehicles.

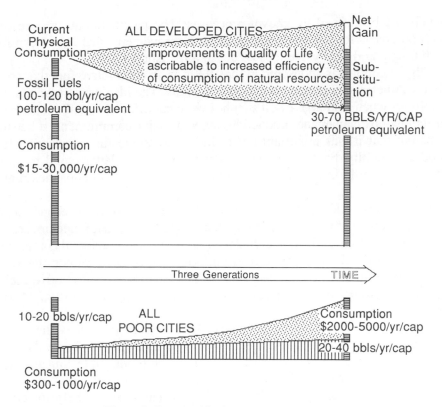

Figure 1 Sustainable development in cities.

The earliest of these was the use of electricity stored in batteries. It was pushed out of the market very early by the internal combustion engine, mainly because there were no substantial improvements in the storage efficiency of batteries that could be mass-produced. Over the past several decades quite a few incremental improvements have been offered, so that a review of the locales where electric cars have competitive advantage should be worthwhile. Electricity should regain a significant share of the market. In that case the transport fuel would become whatever energy sources are needed to quicken the metropolitan grids.

The chemists have been contributing to a long saga on the development of technologies for the conversion of oil shales and tar deposits into liquid products suited to existing refineries. Just about the time that the processes have become viable, complaints about the environmental impact have cast doubt on their desirability. The Canadians have launched a few multi-billion dollar enterprises which will test acceptability.

During the Second World War, the Germans converted lignite and low-grade coal into sufficient liquid fuel to keep their mechanised troops in the field. Those processes have been further developed. One family of them employs intermediate gasification and reformation into the molecular types desired, while another hydrogenates solid fuels to arrive at a petroleum-like product which can be refined by known processes. The patent literature is replete with proposals for alternatives and minor improvements that have been less well tested, and hardly ever costed out in a realistic way.

Ethyl alcohol was sponsored in the 1930s as an automotive fuel that could rid the American continent of the grain surplus. The idea was resuscitated in the 1970s when Middle East oil supplies were cut off, and Brazil, on the basis of its low-cost sugarcane production, made a major commitment. It became apparent that it was important not to link automotive fuel production to a food commodity, because world market prices in the latter could multiply three- to fivefold in a matter of months, making transport subsidies highly inflationary.

Methanol is no longer 'wood alcohol' because it can be made economically from any source of reduced carbon in manufacturing plants of medium scale – coal, natural gas, wood, tar, etc. It can be used in existing internal combustion engines with little or no modification, and it does not produce the smog associated with petroleum fuels. Thus, it may become the automotive fuel of choice for environmental reasons alone, in places like California, Mexico and Greece.

In a recent review of these issues, Sperling (1988) raises the strong possibility that hydrogen, the cleanest fuel of all, will overcome the risks presently associated with its distribution. It can be produced technically from any fossil fuel, from sunlight and from low-priced organic materials, and distributed by regional grid like natural gas. The cost is likely to remain relatively high in the foreseeable future, so quality of life justifications may be required to sustain its use in transport.

Another method of economising on fuel is to find methods of substituting a flow of information and knowledge, which have only trivial inputs of energy, as a substitute for trips and shipments. This substitution has already been underway in international trade, where it has been noted that energy required for transporting American international trade has declined 2.5 per cent per year over the last two decades, the real value has risen more than 5 per cent per year (Greenspan 1988). The energy cost per passenger mile on aircraft has shown a similar trend, while the engineering cost per vehicle has increased several fold. A major part of the conservation achieved since the onset of the energy crisis of 1973-74 may be ascribed to this substitution process.

The limits to this substitution process, as far as they can be foreseen, would be reached in an automotive vehicle with about twenty managing/ monitoring programmed subsystems that would be controlled by a computer cooperating with the operator. Many of the functions would be assigned to improve the safety of passengers and others, rather than strict economy. The cost for controls may be expected to be more than half the total for a vehicle considerably lighter than those on the road today.

Given the gestation period, production and sales time, and the active lifetime of new models, we cannot expect these super-economy vehicles to make a strong contribution for forty to fifty years. Beyond that, the world would have to institute some kind of birth control, or rationing, of the vehicles themselves, which is presently considered a truly drastic measure among the people we have identified as world servers, because 'my car' (to use a common Asian expression) is as much an addiction for them as others in their income class.

The overall most hopeful prospect that would fit the transition depicted in Figure 1 is summarised in Figure 2.

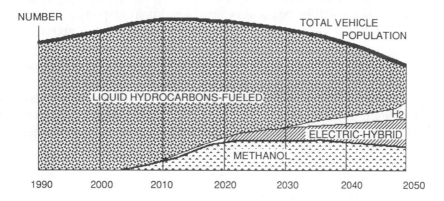

Figure 2 The transition to post-modern urban transportation – current prospects.

Developed countries are approaching the all-time peaks of their vehicle registration. Future vehicle populations will depend on expectations regarding fuels supply during the life cycle of the vehicle. After the year 2000 a large share should be capable of doing 30 km/litre in urban traffic, and more outside, so that almost half the fuel is saved as compared to current experience. Altogether it is anticipated that the demand for petroleum-type fuels will have been reduced by two-thirds in two human generations.

Because they were endowed with cheap fuels, sufficient to meet their needs until the 1970s, the North Americans developed appetites for energy that exceeded sustainability to a much greater degree than those found elsewhere. Addiction to automobiles and their peak performance is found in western Europe and Japan, and it is often expressed more strongly there (since authorities have not been able to repress speeding on the open road). European countries and Japan have reduced their vulnerability to shock (Hourcade 1988).

Scientists may be able to use the global warming threat as a means for gaining common global action. Once the impact of the phenomenon has been established, it may sound reasonable to place an escalating tax on the production of atmospheric carbon dioxide in the world. This would have a selective impact upon North American consumers and help keep automotive design in balance with the equipment using electric power.

At the moment it is estimated that the use of passenger cars in the United States (35 per cent of the world total) is indirectly subsidised at the level of

$3.50 per gallon, for which the purchaser pays less than $1.00 ($0.37 per litre) for production, distribution and road taxes (Renner 1989). That is what would be needed to repay the loss of land and crops, pay medical bills, and achieve the air quality standards already set. Alternatively, it would add $2400 to the cost of the average automobile.

In the United States, the use of the personal automobile is intimately tied to the predominance of the ownership of free-standing homes on larger lots, so the communities themselves will be forced to make major adjustments. These connections will generate very strong political responses on the part of householders with short-term interests, who constitute the majority. For example, it may wipe out the equity they hold in the house, so that 10% or more of the units may revert to the bank or the savings and loan company. A much smaller failure rate in mid-America caused a major financial crisis in 1988–89. Thus, a 'quick fix' in the petroleum fuels sector has such wide ramifications it appears necessary to move on many fronts simultaneously, each one calculated to reinforce the others. For that to happen we need to further develop the comprehensive ecosystems framework underlying sustainable development.

SUSTAINABLE DEVELOPMENT ELABORATED

Recently almost the whole of an issue of *Futures* (Pearce & Redclift 1988) was dedicated to this subject. All but two of the contributors were economists. They were all impressed with the inadequacy of contemporary economics to provide guidance, but they had nothing to put in its place. The same defects in the economic paradigm were revealed with documentation by Etzioni (1988), but for a different purpose. (He was, in effect, marshalling evidence and arguments for ethical consideration by the collectivity of world servers.) These critiques offer nothing new, since there is a long history of objections, but it is evident that a small minority is recruiting backers, and a need for consensus for an alternative is evident.

Everyone has been looking at the problem one aspect at a time, so there was no opportunity for a consensus until Kenneth Boulding's *Ecodynamics* (1978) came along. It is an outcome of General Systems thinking that started appearing two decades earlier. Even then, for professional investigators accustomed to plodding along a straight, narrow, highly disciplined path, it spread more confusion than light. His extension of that thinking in *The World as a Total System* added to consistency, but not to applicability to problem solving. His ecodynamics reduce economics to a special case – an achievement that was perhaps only possible for a recognised master of economics who had earlier written leading advanced texts.

Boulding's model (Figure 3) emphasises the primacy of energy and information as flows. These are far more measurable than labour and land inputs, and introduce a comprehensiveness previously not available. It fits the real and prospective world far more precisely than can be achieved at present..

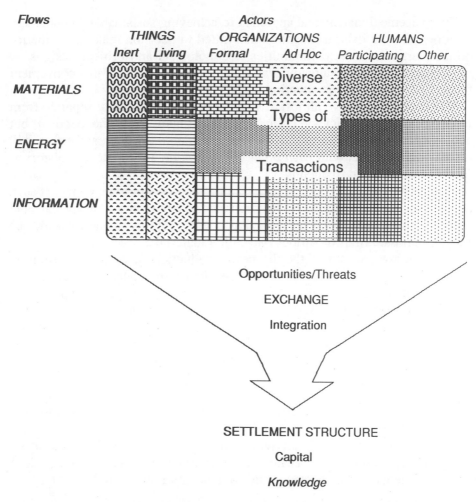

Figure 3 Boulding's ecodynamic system.

The better fit is achieved through the application of recent developments in information theory, network monitoring and social survey methods.

The real life in the ecosystem is found in the *Transactions*. The respective individuals participating in the community (ecology is often referred to as the 'science of communities') initiate transactions with each other, with things, and the environment in the hope of improving their state of being. When two individuals participate with this intention the outcome is likely to be win-win. Organisations are formed to expedite win-win transactions. A trip, a conversation, the notice of an image in the environment, a caress, a swim in the sea – all of these are transactions, and only a minority are market-related. In the absence of a real crisis, the greater the number and range of transactions, the greater is the stability of the system and the resultant quality of life for the dominant species – humans.

The piecemeal incremental approach to achieving sustainable development requires relevant data. It must be transmitted to decision makers for metropolises, organisations, communities, technologists and project designs. A very large share of it is already available, but not necessarily in a convenient form. The major shifts in attention to data can be outlined.

The energy data have almost always been kept completely separate from food, because the policies required are almost completely independent, but ecological thinking requires that they be considered together, since they will increasingly interact with each other (Brown *et al*. 1988). Recent history is likely to be repeated frequently.

Environmental authorities will be tracing the flows of toxic elements such as lead, mercury, radon, the toxins produced in nature and as by-products to manufacturing. They will be worrying about vitamins in the diet and the recycling possibilities of various packaging materials.

All of these are part of the the the new 'production function' according to Boulding. They can be measured independently of monetary value, so the vagaries of foreign exchange need not be a factor that gets in the way of evaluation. They make possible human activity in the global sense.

The outputs are outlined in a similar way in Figure 4. It serves as a means for reminding planners and decision makers of the full range of factors to be taken into account when committing scarce natural resources, including human time.

Work is obviously the most important activity in a city, even in the post-industrial society, but other uses of human time are gaining importance. They contribute to balance and to diversity, which are necessary features of sustainable development. They will increase also as the average age of the resident population rises, because the accumulation of experience adds to both experience and competence and sophistication in cultural activity.

SUSTAINABLE DESIGN FOR URBAN COMMUNITIES

The most difficult task is to find a sustainable design for Third World urban environments. However, that has been taken up elsewhere for the most challenging environments, such as estuarine wetland, Bangladesh, India and China (Meier 1987; Meir & Shen 1988; 1989). The readers of this report will be more interested in the prospects for metropolises in the most developed sectors of the world.

An early attempt was sponsored by the Sierra Club, a prominent environmentalist organisation in North America (Van der Ryn & Calthorpe 1986). The authors, who were architects, and their consultants, sensed the proper directions in which to push their designs (expedite public participation, openness, energy conservation through passive solar heating and removal of the need for air-conditioning, reduced dependence upon the automobile, densification, etc.), but the kinds of efficiencies in consumption implicit in their proposals went perhaps only a quarter of the way that is needed (Flavin

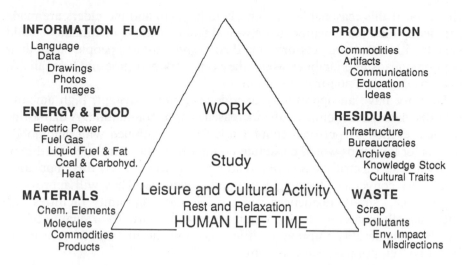

INFORMATION FLOW
Language
Data
Drawings
Photos
Images

PRODUCTION
Commodities
Artifacts
Communications
Education
Ideas

WORK

ENERGY & FOOD
Electric Power
Fuel Gas
Liquid Fuel & Fat
Coal & Carbohyd.
Heat

RESIDUAL
Infrastructure
Bureaucracies
Archives
Knowledge Stock
Cultural Traits

Study

MATERIALS
Chem. Elements
Molecules
Commodities
Products

Leisure and Cultural Activity
Rest and Relaxation
HUMAN LIFE TIME

WASTE
Scrap
Pollutants
Env. Impact
Misdirections

NOTE. The intention here is to recognize existing distinctions, hierarchies, databases, and paradigms while being more comprehensive than any predecessors. For any project not all the data should be collected, but we should know what has been omitted and why it is believed to be trivial.

Figure 4 Checklist for data collection when measuring for Boulding's ecological production function (to be applied to metropolitan regions, firms, NGOs, communities, technologies and projects.

& Durning 1988). What kinds of designs can be imagined that more closely approximate the economies that are required?

One obvious feature of cities a generation hence is that they will contain an extraordinary proportion of aging people due to the baby boom associated with the Second World War, and, due to improvements in medicine, the fraction will not decline much thereafter. Demographers often worry publicly about the small size of the work force which is expected, according to precedent, to support the elders in the community, but in only a very few instances is mention made that this new generation of elderly is better educated, more wealthy, and much less frequently disabled by illness. They have been dubbed the 'Yeepies' (Youthful, Energetic People Interested in Everything) in a newspaper report on a speech by gerontologist Stephen Golant (1984), whose work foreshadowed these outcomes. (The term 'Yeepie' is taken from a United Press International report of 17 February 1989, on a speech given in the University of Florida.) Perhaps half of that generation will have become computer-literate by the time they retire from their full-time position. This condition of life makes it possible to reverse the past in most instances. A new rule can be announced: *work at something until you drop!*

The elderly can be small-scale entrepreneurs in the provision of local services. Those that are less business-oriented can join people-helping-people organisations that are already linked to all hospitals and service centres.

However, if this reasonable outcome is to happen, and the elders are made happier by their participation, the physical facilities in the community should expedite it. Even more pressure should be exerted to force people out of their big homesteads into facilities where they can work part time and be available to help others in a non-trivial fashion.

Here we have an opportunity to redevelop some distant, high amenity suburbs made uneconomic by the increased cost of commuting. A dial-a-ride service reached by personal cellular telephone, combined with automobile rentals for long trips would constitute an improvement over the ownership of a private car. Electric carts have already been discovered by this population to be very convenient for neighbourhood movement. They will approve of barrier-free, 'smart' residences and commercial/community facilities that automatically conserve energy, water, space and effort. Their quality of life can be considerably improved while adjusting the metropolis to a much˙ lower consumption of scarce resources.

Similar results should be obtainable for highly networked households. They would have alternatives to routine trips to work and to schools. Cities could escape from the threat of gridlock by offering much more flexitime and totally new working arrangements.

The categories and lists in Figure 4 are intended to compile a comprehensive set of variables. These are the events that are countable and measurable by independent observers, and therefore can contribute to consensus. We have already argued that world servers need consensus before they can be influential.

A purist will argue that the list is not truly comprehensive, because important things happening in a community as a result of transactions are still left out. Among these are: (a) the shifts in emotional context (happy/sad, funny/serious, confident/worried, etc.); (b) resultant changes in the community power structure; (c) cultural patterns may emerge on a larger scale comprising many transactions; and (d) externalities from some kinds of transactions build up to create stress, so that a glut of win-win transactions can still lead to 'burnout' and breakdown.

Therefore the assessment of human well-being, or quality of life, must be undertaken at several levels. One that has already been explored quite thoroughly is the feeling of satisfaction with 'life-as-a-whole' and with specific features, like the neighbourhood environment and the government, that are known to contribute to it (Andrews & Withey 1976). Regular sample surveys will suggest whether any improvements have been made in the interim.

This approach is somewhat culture-bound, because it will, for example, work less well in Japan, where quality for the group is more important than for the individual. A person may participate in several groups, such as a firm, a neighbourhood, and a religion or hobby. Viable groups must continue to attract at least as many individuals as they lose. The measure of the relative quality of a community is the attractiveness for migrants. A survey at the community level would identify features that attract desirable immigrants.

These arguments suggest that quality of life information be collected at three levels if it is to be judged adequate for guiding sustainable development – individual or household, organisation or work, and community or metro region. Even that may not be enough, since certain cultures seem to be vulnerable to addictions, such as alcohol, drugs or autos, that cause a deterioration in the lives of others. Moral dimensions to behaviour are not readily counted or measured so that improvements can be noted. We can readily see that different kinds of moral codes will be emphasised among the family servers, the community servers, the organisation servers, and the nation servers. Some gaps that could be identified in a recent international conference (Kidder 1988) were:

• a child's bill of rights;
• educational curricula in community schools emphasising international interdependence;
• community service arrangements to expand a sense of caring and sharing; and
• codes of ethics for international business.

When consensus on such matters of personal obligation has been reached, it can be communicated to the next generation for internalisation – setting a gyroscope for guiding behaviour in synchrony with others so as to reduce the costs of conflict. These are the most subtle aspects of sustainable development.

CONCLUSIONS: A PROGRAM FOR PLANNING

Any promising path for sustainable development of urban settlement in the world (the present image of Doxiadis' ecumenopolis) must pay particular attention to the control of population overshoot. What is the anticipated impact of each of them? How soon will it be felt? What counterforces can be mobilised?

The principal populations out of control are discovered to be in the human population of Africa and the automobile populations of the most developed countries. No policy solution can be found for Africa as yet; there are no local successes to guide us. By introducing a comprehensive form of urban ecological analysis based upon Boulding's ecodynamics, a path could be found for dealing with the population explosion in automobiles. His proposals get beyond the limitations of economic analysis in programming change.

Identification of such a pathway for the control of automobile-human interdependency and similar addiction-like compulsions would be meaningless without an agency with global power. Since none exists, or is likely to come into existence soon, another means must be found for implementation. A world-serving stratum of professionals which is rapidly growing in number (perhaps tenfold in one human generation), and dedicated to the expansion of global institutions of all kinds, seems likely to be able to fill this role. At the moment they are using the new capacity in worldwide telecommunications to network and build up their influence. They can use their knowledge of local situations, together with their understanding of the technical opportunities and limits of the biosphere, to adapt available technologies and persuade local decision makers. Progress would be made in small steps on many fronts. Quality of life should improve perceptibly simultaneously.

Substitute fuels for automobiles must be given high priority, but they must be associated with a thorough redesign which can get up to three times as much service per energy unit. Telecommunications can, by indirect arrangements, become a partial substitute for 'my car'. Bicycles may help in a few places. Ultimately it appears that there must be a reduction in the number of automotive vehicles, despite further growth in world population. Therefore plans must be prepared for the densification of their 'habitat' – the suburbs. Fortunately a rapidly aging population can find good use for redeveloped high-amenity suburbs. A more compact urban settlement with efficient equipment could then survive on fuels of solar origin three generations or so hence.

EPILOGUE

If one had to specify the single factor with the greatest impact on urban society during the last fifty years, it would surely be the development and spread of information technology. Yet the effects have proved curiously difficult to forecast, even using the rather conservative conditional types of prediction which have traditionally been used for the purpose. Indeed, those who should have known best have made the most bizarre of predictions. In the early 1950s, IBM confidently predicted that the demand for computers would never exceed fifty machines; in the mid-1970s in Silicon Valley, those closest to the development of the integrated circuit and minicomputer failed entirely to anticipate the microcomputer. These stories are now legend; but they remind us that any exercise in forecasting, even in the short-term period up to a decade ahead, is fraught with hazard.

Yet the future is not entirely unknowable. Limited forays into predicting the form and structure of early twenty-first century cities are both possible and necessary. We can identify present trends, work them through to their 'logical' conclusions, and thus develop a framework within which we can anticipate problems and develop solutions for future cities. In their different ways, the chapters in this book – some more descriptive of present trends, some more theoretically general, some more speculative about the future – have demonstrated different aspects of this approach. They also show that there is no one agreed approach to assessing the impact of new information technologies on spatial form; rather, they demonstrate the value of pursuing many different methods, which individually may detect some facet of the urban future, and which complement each other in building up a synthetic picture of the twenty-first century city.

Although no single framework emerges from this symposium, it is useful to compare the contributions with those resulting from two earlier conferences whose proceedings were published in 1985 and 1987 (Brotchie, Newton, Hall & Nijkamp 1985; Brotchie, Hall & Newton 1987). The comparison shows that our thinking has progressed from 'speculative dreaming' to an approach which is more conservative in its explanation of how new technology affects the social and economic future of large cities. The present contributions also emphasise the need for detailed empirical work as a prelude to even the most narrow kind of forecasting. This is clearly evident from the fact that the circle of experts included in the project has expanded to include diverse theoretical and philosophical viewpoints. We think that these various approaches complement each other but clearly also have something to say about how we might best approach these complex issues. It seems likely that future conferences on this theme will be more specific in focus, narrowing down on better defined problems, and positively exploiting the differences between the various theoretical approaches.

In this epilogue, we do not wish to attempt any grand synthesis of the papers. Rather, we want to chart an emerging consensus concerning six major themes:

1 The new economics of information. It is already clear that the new technology, which makes information into one of the most valued commodities, is leading to a new economics of information, characterised by new types of market and new productive processes. As a result, we see the emergence of complex substitutions which are enabling new freedoms to be realised and new opportunities to be grasped.

The developed world at the end of the twentieth century is still in transition from an industrial to an information economy where information becomes the most important, indeed all-pervasive, commodity. This does not mean that manufacturing industry will atrophy or that the demand for goods will diminish; on the contrary, there will almost certainly be massive increases in demand for manufactured products. But it does mean that various complex substitutions will take place. One involves the introduction of ever more powerful information technology into the manufacturing process, hence the substitution of this technology – based on robotics and automation – for labour and traditional energy-intensive capital. Another is the substitution of knowledge and intelligence for some material and energy resources, thus achieving the more efficient design of products, greater knowledge of their markets, and tighter, more robust planning and operation of their production and distribution processes. These two changes are also facilitating the shift to increased quality, diversity, and 'personalisation' of the products involved.

2 Changing goods, changing markets. The mass markets of the industrial age are evolving into smaller, more specialist niche markets, offering the consumer specialised services and products which in the past were assumed to be totally inconsistent with traditional manufacturing.

As telecommunications, computers, and machine intelligence become integrated into production processes, major economic changes occur: higher quality goods and services can be produced, more personalised services become commercially viable, and information-based services – 'on-line' entertainment, education, shopping, banking and management advice – become increasingly available. The new information economy also facilitates increased home-based activities; intelligent home information systems are being developed to assist in these activities, while more routine tasks – meal preparation, maintenance of comfort and security in the home – are being automated with little difficulty and at low cost.

3 Changing work, changing location. These changes involve complex chains of cause and effect whose ultimate impact might seem remote from their origins. For example, one consequence of automation is a reduction of employment in manufacturing industries in favour of service industries, particularly information-based industries. These changes set off a reduction in arduous manual tasks, thus changing the work environment. And in turn these processes interact with social and demographic changes, producing increased female participation in the work force and the option of a longer working life. Further forces are driving more flexible working arrangements, including teleworking in some cases; and all these factors are changing the very nature of work and its relationship to other daily activities and behaviour patterns.

The shift to information-based industries is also facilitating much greater informality in the spatial organisation of activities, with the formation of multiple centres in metropolitan areas combined with greater spatial integration of commercial, residential and recreational activities. These, in turn, are motivated by the realisation of human potential and a better quality of life which are increasingly important in personal priorities. Much greater speeds and capacities for moving information, people and goods are allowing better coordination of commercial activities and greater integration of production, communication and information processing. This is leading to increasing integration of functions within the urban system, and to the development of efficient production systems from the local, through the regional to the global level. There is greater freedom in locational choice for individuals who seek urban, rural or recreational amenities; for some non-routine functions such as research, design and education, the locational sequence of cause and effect is being reversed, as jobs follow people into high amenity areas.

Yet the transition to an information economy also has its negative side. Greater income differentials, rising unemployment through the mismatch of jobs and skills, alienation in the workplace and in society generally, and other social problems in the community: all these bring inexorable demands for many more institutions and procedures to engender greater security and community support. Thus, as well as changing and ameliorating old urban problems, the transition is generating new ones.

4 Globalization and the locality. At the international level, telecommunication networks are facilitating the global organisation of industry, the rise of global markets for finance, securities and commodities, and the further growth of cities at the hubs of these information networks. These high-speed networks – consisting of both telecommunications and high-speed personal transportation – are becoming the new trade routes of the twenty-first century; resources are shifting to the information-based industries, which in turn are attracted to the global cities at their nodes. And, although the hierarchy of world cities is subtly changing, the traditional global trade centres – New York, London and Tokyo – have so far emerged as the most significant of these information exchanging nodes.

Another expression of this globalisation of networks is the concept of the new international 'designer city', deliberately developed for the sharing and development of new technologies. The multi-function polis is the urban embodiment of the trend towards the formation of alliances between firms at local and global levels, enabling them to realise agglomeration advantages in knowledge and technology in high-tech industries. And these processes are hugely stimulated by the reduction of economic barriers between nations, seen most dramatically within the European Economic Community, coupled with radical changes in political allegiance in major areas of the world such as eastern Europe.

5 The ecological priority. The transition to an information society is accompanied everywhere by a new concern for ecological balance, and this leads to complex interactions, especially in the political sphere. The present concerns for international cooperation spring from the contamination of our atmosphere, land and water by industrial and urban wastes, while their impacts on climate change are likely to prove even more significant. Urban activities involving transport, the heating and cooling of buildings, and the fuelling of production processes, are major contributors to this global warming or 'greenhouse' effect. The new networks linking the global information cities will, in turn, be affected by these impacts. City governments must expect to cope with significant changes in temperature, rainfall, sea level and with extreme climatic events; even sooner, they are likely to feel the impacts of national and international policy measures for environmental control. These may include regulatory constraints or pricing policies aimed at reducing energy use and promoting sustainable activities, which will have complex repercussions on urban societies entering the information age. Yet the new technologies also offer the potential for controlling the greenhouse effect: through new forms of emission control, the facilitating of shorter journeys to work and to shop, the substitution of more efficient transport and energy forms, the use of telecommunications to substitute for some travel, and the application of information systems to conserve materials and energy.

6 Increasing social complexity. Finally, there is the whole range of dilemmas posed by the fact that information technology tends to an ever-increasing complexity of the society it sustains. Thus, life in the twenty-first century can be expected to be longer (through better medical care and better conditions of work), richer in information and perhaps in knowledge, and more recreationally diverse. Travel will be faster yet more energy efficient; a wider range of lifestyles and living environments will become possible. Substantial changes in the balance and distribution of income among individuals, cities, regions and nations will occur, as more countries such as China and India progress along the development path. But resources – human as well as physical – will be more tightly stretched, as food and energy costs and constraints take effect, and as information and knowledge become increasingly important as factors of production.

Cities in the twenty-first century will be characterised by much greater rates of change, set in motion by the increasing speeds of development of new technologies and by their dispersion to the developing world. This dispersal process is likely to be assisted by the very nature of these technologies, but it must necessarily result in increased uncertainty and instability in urban life.

The Paradox of Forecasting

The urban future, therefore, contains a number of major paradoxes: increasing information but increasing uncertainty; increasing diversity of lifestyle but increasing differences in income and opportunity between the information-rich and the information-poor, both locally and globally; increasing efficiency and quality in production of goods and services but increasing constraints on energy and resources. There will be significant shifts in production and consumption between transport modes, between communication modes, between transport and communications, between regions and between energy sources.

Not all this is known, or can be known. Yet, though the prototypical twenty-first century city may be stranger than we can now imagine, many of the trends already identified in this volume will work themselves out in a reasonably predictable way. Our uncertainty largely concerns the subtle and unexpected interactions between these trends; particularly, those arising from the ever increasing complexity of computers and communications, and the novel ways in which human ingenuity might exploit them. As an immediate next priority for research into the future, we might usefully sit back and spend some time on devising better frameworks for ordering and synthesising the insights and speculations of our contributors, and those of countless other workers in the wider research community. In that way, we might produce at least a most-likely surprise-free urban future, and perhaps also some other less predictable outcomes.

John Brotchie
Michael Batty
Peter Hall
Peter Newton

ACKNOWLEDGMENTS

The editors are grateful to Dr Gyula Sebesteyen and the International Council for Building Research Studies and Documentation for convening and supporting these workshop studies and their publications. We are also grateful to CSIRO for its support, to the contributors, and to Cheryl McNamara, Cathy Bowditch, Rhyll Reed, Molly Athaide, Sandra Roberts and Anne Andress for their various roles in the organisation of the activities and information involved and its communication, copy editing and processing.

REFERENCES

Abernathy, W.J., Clark, K.B. & Kantrow, A.M. 1983, *Industrial Renaissance: Producing a Competitive Future for America*, Basic Books, New York.

Abernathy, W. J. & Utterback, J.M. 1978, 'Patterns of industrial innovation', *Technology Review*, **80**(7), 40–7.

Abler, R.F. 1987a, 'The geography of telecommunications in the United States: Local and regional research problems', *Le Bulletin de l'IDATE*, **26**, 120–5.

Abler, R.F. 1987b, What if somebody built a teleport and nobody called? Communications and regional development in the United States, Paper presented to the Government of Greece–OECD Seminar on Information and Telecommunications Technology for Regional Development, Athens, 7–9 December.

Abler, R.F. & Falk, T. 1981, 'Public information services and the changing role of distance in human affairs', *Economic Geography*, **57**, 10–22.

Alexy, R. 1987, 'The TRANSRAPID maglev system: Its application in the Rhein/Main–Rhein/Ruhr corridor', *Proceedings of the International Conference on Maglev & Linear Drives*, Institute of Electrical & Electronic Engineers, New York, 195–204.

Allen, T. 1979, *Managing the Flow of Technology*, MIT Press, Cambridge, Mass.

Andersson, Å.E. 1985a, 'Creativity and regional development', *Papers of the Regional Science Association*, **56**, 5–20.

Andersson, Å.E. 1985b, *Kreativitet: StorStadens Framtid*, Prisma, Stockholm.

Andersson, Å.E. & Batten, D.F. 1987, 'Creative nodes, logistical networks, and the future of the metropolis', *Transportation*, **14**, 281–93.

Andersson, Å.E. & Strömquist, U. 1988, *K-Samhällets Framtid*, Prisma, Stockholm.

Andrews, F.M. & Withey, S.B. 1976, *Social Indicators of Well-being*, Plenum, New York.

Anon. 1989a, 'Roissy et le Bocage de France, Porte d'Entrée franÿaise en Europe', *Cahiers de l'Institut de l'Aménagement et d'Urbanisme de la Région d'Ile-de-France*, **89**, 8–26.

Anon. 1989b, 'Un Pôle Européen à Massy', *Cahiers de l'Institut de l'Aménagement et d'Urbanisme de la Région d'Ile-de-France*, **89**, 32–48.

Applied Systems Institute 1987, *The USELM Development Process: From USEEM to USELM for 1976–1984, Documentation and Results*, Applied Systems Institute, Washington DC.

Armington, C. & Odle, M. 1981, 'Associating establishments into enterprises for a microdata file of the U.S. business population', in *Statistics of Income and Related Administrative Records Research*, US Internal Revenue Service, Statistics Division, October, Government Printing Office, Washington, DC.

Arnold, E. & Guy, K. 1986, *Parallel Convergence: National Strategies in Information Technology*, Frances Pinter, London.

Arrow, K.J. 1974, 'Limited knowledge and economic analysis', *American Economic Review*, **64**(1), 1–10.

Arrow, K.J. 1979, 'The property rights doctrine and demand revelation under incomplete information', in *Economics and Human Welfare*, ed. M. Boskin, Academic Press, New York.

Averitt, R.T. 1968, *The Dual Economy: The Dynamics of American Industry Structure*, Norton, New York.

Aydalot, P. (ed.) 1986a, *Milieux Innovateurs en Europe*, GREMI, Paris (privately printed).

Aydalot, P. 1986b, 'Trajectoires technologiques et milieux innovateurs', in *Milieux Innovateurs en Europe*, ed. P. Aydalot, GREMI, Paris, 345–61.

Aydalot, P. 1988, 'Technological trajectories and regional innovation in Europe', in *High Technology Industry and Innovative Environments: The European Experience*, eds P. Aydalot & D. Keeble, Routledge & Croom Helm, London, New York, 22–47.

Aydalot, P. & Keeble, D. (eds) 1988a, *High Technology Industry and Innovative Environments: The European Experience*, Routledge & Croom Helm, London, New York.

Aydalot, P. & Keeble, D. 1988b, 'High technology industry and innovative environments in Europe: An overview', in *High Technology Industry and Innovative Environments: The European Experience*, eds. P. Aydalot & D. Keeble, Routledge & Croom Helm, London, New York, 1–21.

Bacle, J.Y. 1988, Teletel still growing fast: Videotex and success, Paper presented to Teleview Conference, Comcentre, Singapore, 19–20 April.

Bakis, H. 1980, A case study of IBM's global data network, Paper presented to 24th International Geographical Congress, Tokyo, August.

Bar, F. 1987, *Business Users and the Emergence of the New Telecommunications Infrastructure: A Preliminary Framework of Analysis*, OECD-BRIE Telecom User Group Project, mimeo.

Bar, F. & Borrus, M. 1989, *Information Networks and Competitive Advantage. Vol. 1: Issues for Government Policy and Corporate Strategy Development*, OECD, Paris

Baran, P.A. & Sweezy, P.M. 1966, *Monopoly Capital: An Essay on the American Economic and Social Order*, Modern Reader, New York.

Barff, R.A. 1987, 'Industrial clustering and the organization of production: A point pattern analysis of manufacturing in Cincinnati, Ohio', *Annals of the Association of American Geographers*, 77(1), 89–103.

Barrett, R. & Farbrother, B.J. 1976, *FAX – A Study of Principles, Practice and Prospects for Facsimile Transmission in the U.K.*, British Library Research and Development Reports, 5257 HC, British Library Board, Boston Spa.

Batty, M. 1985, 'The spatial impact of computer culture', Paper in *Planning Research 91*, Department of Town Planning, University of Wales, Institute of Science and Technology, July.

Batty, M. 1987, 'The intelligent plaza is only the beginning', *The Guardian*, 17 Sept., p. 19.

Batty, M. 1988, 'Home computers and regional development: An exploratory analysis of the spatial market for home computers in Britain', in *Informatics and Regional Development*, eds M. Giaoutzi & P. Nijkamp, Avebury, Aldershot, 147–65.

Batty, M. 1989, 'Technology highs', *The Guardian*, 22 June, p. 29.

Batty, M. 1990, 'Intelligent cities: Using information networks to gain competitive advantage', *Environment and Planning B*, **17**, 247–56

Bell, D. 1973, *The Coming of Post-Industrial Society*, Basic Books, New York.

Bender, W.G. 1987, 'Switching: The future begins to emerge', *Spectrum*, Arthur D. Little Resources, September, 1–49/55.

Beniger, J.R. 1986, *The Control Revolution. Technological and Economic Origins of the Information Society*, Harvard University Press, Cambridge, Mass.

Berlioz, C. & Leboeuf, M. 1986, 'Les résultats du TGV Paris – Sud Est: Bilan a posteriori du TGV Sud-Est', *Révue Générale des Chemins de Fer*, **196**, 759–68.

Betcherman, G. & McMullen, K. 1986, *Working with Technology*, Economic Council of Canada, Ottawa.

Betcherman, G., Newton, K. & Godin, J. 1989, *Two Steps Forward: A Casebook on Technologial and Organizational Change*, Economic Council of Canada, Ottawa.

Beyers, W.B. 1989, *The Producer Services and Economic Development in the United States*, Final Report to US Department of Commerce, Economic Development, Administration, Technical Assistance and Research Division.

Blakely, E.J. 1987, 'Introducing high tech: Principles of designing support systems for the formation and attraction of advanced technology firms', *International Journal of Technology Management*, **2**(3).

Bluestone, B., Harrison, B. & Gorham, L. 1984, *Storm Clouds on the Horizon: Labour Market Crisis and Industrial Policy*, Economic Education Project Working Paper, Brookline, Mass.

Bollard, A. 1983, 'Technology, economic change, and small firms', *Lloyds Bank Review*, **147**, 42–56.

Bonnafous, A. 1987, 'The regional impact of the TGV', *Transportation*, **14**, 127–38.

Boon, C.J., Hayes, W.F., Schwier, C., Eastham, A.R., Campbell, T.I. & Dawson, G.E. 1987, 'High speed ground transportation technologies for the Las Vegas–Southern California corridor', *Proceedings of the International Conference on Maglev & Linear Drives*, Institute of Electrical & Electronic Engineers, 227–40.

Borrus, M. 1988, *Competing for Control*, Ballinger, New York.

Boulding, K.E. 1960, 'The present position of the theory of the firm', in *Linear Programming and the Theory of the Firm*, eds K.E. Boulding & W.A. Spivey, Macmillan, New York.

Boulding, K.E. 1978, *Ecodynamics*, Sage, Newbury Park, Calif.

Brand, S. 1987, *The Media Lab: Inventing the Future at MIT*, Penguin Books, New York.

Britten, J.N.H. 1986, 'A policy prospectus on regional economic development: The implications of technological change', in *Still Living Together: Recent Trends and Future Directions in Canadian Regional Development*, eds W.J. Coffey & M. Polèse, Institute for Research on Public Policy, Montreal.

Brock, G.W. 1980, *The Telecommunications Industry: The Dynamics of Market Structure*, Harvard University Press, Cambridge, Mass.

Brodhead, D., Lamontagne, F., & Peirce, J. 1989, *New Directions for Regional Development*, Economic Council of Canada, Ottawa.

Brotchie, J.F., Newton, P.W., Hall, P. & Nijkamp, P. (eds) 1985, *The Future of Urban Form: The Impact of New Technology*, Croom Helm & Nichols, London, Sydney, New York.

Brotchie, J.F., Hall, P. & Newton, P.W. (eds) 1987, *The Spatial Impact of Technological Change*, Croom Helm, London, New York, Sydney.

Brown, L.R. *et al.* 1988, *State of the World – 1988*, Worldwatch Institute, Washington.

Brugger, E.A. & Stuckey, B. 1987, 'Regional economic structure and innovative behavior in Switzerland', *Regional Studies*, **21**(3), 241–54.

Buchanan, J. 1962, *The Calculus of Consent*, University of Michigan Press, Ann Arbor.

Brun, R. 1985. 'Approche systémique, industrie et region', *Revue d'Economie Régionale et Urbaine*, **1**, 119–26.

Burmeister, W.J. 1985, 'Telephone operating company loop and exchange network technology', *Telephony*, **208**(5), 48–60.

Caldwell, P. & Cladwell, J.C. 1987, 'The cultural context of high fertility in sub-Saharan Africa', *Population and Development Review*, **13**(3), 409–37.

Camagni, R. 1987, Diffusion of flexible automation processes in the Lombardy region: Evidence and policy issues, Paper presented to the Conference on Automatisation Programmable et Conditions d'Usage du Travail, Paris, 2–4 April.

Camagni, R. & Rabellotti, R. 1988, 'Knowledge inputs and information channels in the innovation process: The case of Milan', in *Colloque GREMI II*, GREMI, Ascona.

Camp, S.L. & Speidel, J.J. 1987, *International Suffering Index*, Population Crisis Committee, Washington.

Canadian Chamber of Commerce 1988, *Focus 2000*, Report of the Task Force on Technology and Canadian Business, Ottawa.

Cane, A. 1989, 'A promise of big gains in productivity', *Financial Times*, 24 Nov.

Capello, R. 1988, *Telecommunications and the Spatial Organisation of Production*, Newcastle Series on the Information Economy Working Paper No. 10, Centre for Urban & Regional Development Studies, Newcastle-upon-Tyne.

Carrelli, C. & Decina, M. 1987, 'ISDN in Europe: Challenges and opportunities', *Telecommunications*, **21/10**, 63–70.

Castells, M. 1984, *Towards the Information City? High Technology, Economic Change, and Spatial Structure: Some Exploratory Hypotheses*, Institute of Urban & Regional Development Working Paper No. 430, University of California, Berkeley.

Castells, M. 1985, 'High technology, economic restructuring and the urban-regional process in the United States', in *High Technology, Space and Society*, ed. M. Castells, Sage, Beverley Hills, 1–18.

Castells, M. 1987, 'The new industrial space: Information technology manufacturing and spatial structure in the United States', in *America's New Market Geography: Nation, Region and Metropolis*, eds. G. Sternlieb & J.W. Hughes, Rutgers State University, New Jersey.

Caves, R.E. 1982, *Multinational Enterprise and Economic Analysis*, Cambridge University Press, Cambridge.

Cawkell, A.E. 1982, *An Investigation of Commercially Available Facsimile Systems*, British Library Research and Development Reports 5719, British Library Board, Boston Spa.

Cheshire, P.C. & Hay, D.G. 1988, *Urban Problems in Western Europe: An Economic Analysis*, Unwin Hyman, London.

Christopherson, S. 1989, 'Flexibility in the U.S. service economy and the emerging spatial division of labour', *Transactions, Institute of British Geographers*, **NS14**, 131–43.

Chung Tong Wu 1987, 'China's re-entry into the world system: regional impacts of foreign investment', in *Transnational Capital and Urbanization of the Pacific Rim*, eds M. Douglass and J. Friedmann, Center for Pacific Rim Studies, University of California, Los Angeles.

Clairmonte, F. & Cavanagh, J. 1984, 'Transnational corporations and services: The final frontier', *Trade and Development*, **5**, 215–73.

Clare, C.P. 1984, *A Guide to Data Communications*, Castle House, Tunbridge Wells.

Clark, G.L. (in press), 'Remaking the map of corporate capitalism: The arbitrage economy of the 1990s', *Environment & Planning A*.

Clarke, W.M. 1986, *How the City Works*, Waterloo, London.

Cleveland, H. 1987, 'The twilight of hierarchy: Speculations on a global society', *International Journal of Technology Management*, **2**(1), 45–66.

Coathup, P. 1988, 'Electronic data interchange', *Computer Bulletin* , June, 15–17.

Cohen, S.S. & Zysman, J. 1987, *Manufacturing Matters: The Myth of the Post-industrial Economy*, Basic Books, New York.

Cole, B. 1987, 'AISC houses revise their strategies', *Electronics*, 6 August, 73–6.

Cole, B. 1988, 'By the mid-90s the memory market will look like the logic business', *Electronics*, August.

Cole, B. 1989, 'Getting to the market on time', *Electronics*, April.

Commonwealth Department of Industry, Technology & Commerce 1988, *The Multifunction Polis Proposal: One Australian Perspective*, Commonwealth Department of Industry, Technology and Commerce, Canberra.

Connell, S. & Galbraith, I.A. 1980, *The Electronic Mail Handbook: A Revolution in Business Communications*, Century, London.

Coriat, B. 1989, Social structures of accumulation versus French 'Theorie de la Regulation', Paper presented to the International Symposium on Regulation, Innovation, and Spatial Development, University of Wales, Cardiff, UK, 13–15 September.

Costigan, D.M. 1971, *FAX: The Principles and Practice of Facsimile Communication*, Chilton Book Company, New York.

Cowan, P. & Fine, D. 1969, *The Office: A Facet of Urban Growth*, Elsevier Publishing Company, New York.

Crevoisier, O. 1988, 'The interconnection of local resources and external constraints in the regional milieu', in *Theories and Policies of Technological Development at the Local Level*, Regional Science Association, Arco, Italy.

Currie, J. 1985, *Science Parks in Britain – Their Role for the Late 1980s*, CSP Economic Publications, Cardiff, UK.

Daniels, P.W. 1985, *Service Industries: A Geographical Appraisal*, Methuen, London.

Daniels, P.W 1986, 'Producer services and the post-industrial space economy', in *The Geography of De-industrialisation*, eds R.L. Martin & R. Rowthorn, Macmillan, London, 291–321.

Daniels, P.W. 1987, Internationalization of producer services and metropolitan development, Paper presented to International Conference on the Future of the Metropolitan Economy: New Challenges for Policy and Policy-oriented Research, The Hague, 9–10 June.

Daniels, P.W. 1989. Moving out of metropolitan economic crisis: The role of tertiary industries, Paper presented to International Symposium on the Role of Services in Urban and Regional Development, Barcelona, 15-16 June.

Daniels, W.W. 1987, *Workplace Industrial Relations and Technical Change*, Frances Pinter, London.

Darmaros, T. 1989, *Beyond the Sales Pitch: Realising ISDN in the US, Japan and Europe*, Working Paper No. 5, Centre for Information and Communications Technologies, Science Policy Research Unit, University of Sussex.

Dataquest Inc. 1988, *Report on Start-ups in the US Semiconductor Industry*, Dataquest, Mountain View, Calif.

David, P. & Rosenbloom, J. 1987, *Marshallian Factor Market Externalities and the Dynamics of Industrial Localization*, Center for Economic Policy Research Publication No. 118, Stanford University.

Davidson, F.D. (ed.) 1987, *Tunnelling and Underground Transport*, Elsevier, New York.

Davis, K. *et al.* (eds) 1986, *Below Replacement Fertility in Industrial Societies*, Supplement to *Population and Development Review*, **12**.

Dean, R. 1987, 'Public e.mail services: Will they be allowed to survive X.400?', *Electronic Message Systems 87: Proceedings of the International Conference, London, November*, Online Publications, London, 207–13.

Diamond, D. & Spence, N. 1989, *Infrastructure and Industrial Costs in British Industry*, Department of Trade and Industry, HMSO, London.

Dizard, W. 1982, *The Coming Information Age*, Longman, London.

Dodgson, M. & Rothwell, R. 1989, Financing early-stage innovation, Paper presented to 'Enterprise, Innovation and 1992: Innovation Support Services in Europe' Conference, Nice, 26–27 October.

Dohse, K., Jürgens, U. & Malsch, T. 1985, 'From "Fordism" to "Toyotaism"? The social organization of the labor process in the Japanese automobile industry', *Politics and Society*, **14**(2), 114–44.

Dordick, H.S. & Kyrish, S. 1989, 'The emergence of ISDN in Pennsylvania: Speculations about ISDN in the United States', in *European Telecommunications Policy Research*, ed. N. Garnham, IOS, Amsterdam.

Dordick, H.S., Nanus, B. & Bradley, H. 1981, *The Emerging Network Marketplace*, Ablex, Norwood, New Jersey.

Dosi, G. 1988, 'Sources, procedures, and microeconomic effects of innovation', *Journal of Economic Literature*, **XXVI**, 1120–71.

Dosi, G., Freeman, C., Nelson, R., Silverberg, G. & Soete, L. 1988, *Technical Change and Economic Theory*, Frances Pinter, London.

Dosi, G. & Orsengio, L. 1988, 'Co-ordination and transformation: An overview of structures, behaviours and change in evolutionary environments', in *Technical Change and Economic Theory*, eds G. Dosi *et al.*, Frances Pinter, London.

Douglas, S. 1989, 'Why travel when you can call?', *Telephony*, **216**(14), 38–42.

Dowall, D.E. & Salkin, M. 1986, *Office Automation and the Implications for Office Development*, Institute of Urban & Regional Development Working Paper No. 447, University of California, Berkeley, April.

Doxiadis, C.A. & Papaioannou, J. 1972, *Ecumenopolis: The Inevitable City of the Future*, Athens Center for Ekistics, Athens.

Draper, J. 1988, 'Security, integrity and legality – barriers to EDI progress in Europe', *Trade Facilitation*, **2**(4), 160–8.

Drennan, M.P. 1989, 'Information intensive industries in the USA', *Environment & Planning A*, **21**, 1603–18.

Droege, P. 1988, 'Technology for people: A campus city guide', in *Information Systems for Government and Business: Trends, Issues, Challenges*, ed. H. Sazanami, United Nations Centre for Regional Development, Nagoya, Japan, 525–72.

Drucker, P. 1980, *Managing in Tubulent Times*, Harper & Row, New York.

DTI Communications Steering Group 1988, *The Infrastructure for Tomorrow* [The Macdonald Report], HMSO, London.

Duboff, R.B. 1983, 'The telegraph and the structure of markets in the United States, 1845–1890', *Research in Economic History*, **8**, 253–77.

Duffy, F. & Henney, A. 1989, *The Changing City*, Bulstrode Press Ltd, London.

Dufour, P. & Gingras, Y. 1988, 'Development of a Canadian science and technology policy', *Science and Public Policy*, February, 13–18.

Dunning, J.H. & Norman, G. 1987, 'The location choice of offices of international companies', *Environment & Planning A*, **19**, 613–31.

Dutton, W.H., Blumler, J.G., & Kraemer, K.L. 1987, *Wired Cities: Shaping the Future of Communications*, Annenberg School of Communications, G.K. Hall & Co., Boston, Mass.

Earl, M. & Runge, D.A. 1987, *Using Telecommunications-based Information Systems for Competitive Advantage*, Oxford Institute of Information Management Research and Discussion Paper 1987/1

Economic and Transport Planning Group 1989, *Telecommunications in Rural England*, Rural Development Commission Research Report No. 2, Rural Development Commission.

Economic Council of Canada 1987, *Innovation and Jobs in Canada*, Minister of Supply and Services Canada, Ottawa.

Economist 6 July 1985, 'City of London survey'.

Economist 17 October 1987, 'Telecommunications'.

Edgington, D. 1989, 'The consequences of economic restructuring for Melbourne's metropolitan policy', *Urban Policy and Research*, **7**(2), 51–9.

Edvinsson, L. & Edvardsson, B. 1989, Managing internationalization in knowledge-intensive service companies: A tentative frame of reference, Paper presented to 4th Nordic Conference on Service Management, Oslo, 27–28 April.

Encaoua, D., Geroski, P. & Jacquemin, A. 1988, 'Strategic competition and the persistence of dominant firms: A survey', in *New Developments in the Analysis of Market Structure*, eds J. Stiglitz & G. Mathewson, MacMillan Press, London.

Enderwick, P. (ed.) 1989, *Multinational Service Firms*, Routledge, London.

Engelbrecht, H.J. 1986, 'Analysis of structural change using an information sector perspective', *Asian Economies*, **58**, 22–46.

Etzioni, A. 1988, *The Moral Dimension*, The Free Press, New York.

Fairlamb, D. 1987, 'The New York connection', *The Banker*, **137**, 54–5.

Feeny, D.F. and Brownlee, C.G. 1986, *Competition in the Era of Interactive Network Services*, Oxford Institute of Information Management Research and Discussion Paper 1986/17, Templeton College, Oxford.

Feketekuty, G. 1985, 'Negotiating strategies for liberalizing trade and investment in services', in *Trade & Investment in Services*, ed. R.M. Stern, Ontario Economic Council, Toronto, 203–14.

Feldman, M.M.A. 1989, The flexibility thesis and vertical disintegration: Some issues, Paper presented to the 85th Annual Meeting of the Association of American Geographers, Baltimore, 19–22 March.

Feldman, M.M.A. & Mullin, J. 1989, *The Blackstone Valley and Its Recovery from the Waves of Creative Destruction*, Graduate Curriculum in Community Planning and Area Development Working Paper BV89-01, The University of Rhode Island, Kingston.

Ferguson, C.H. 1988, 'From the people who brought you voodoo economics', *Harvard Business Review*, May–June, 55–62.

Fincher, J. 1988, Rural bias and the contemporary renaissance of coastal China, Paper presented to the Workshop on the Spatial Development of China and Australia, Department of Human Geography, Research School of Pacific Studies, The Australian National University, Canberra, 30 September to 1 October.

Flamm, K. 1989, 'Technological advance and costs: Computers versus communications', in *Changing the Rules: Technological Change, International Competition, and Regulation in Communications*, eds R. Crandall & K. Flamm, The Brookings Institution, Washington DC.

Flavin, C. & Durning, A. 1988, *Building on Success: The Age of Energy Efficiency*, Worldwatch Institute Paper No. 82, Washington.

Foray, D. 1988, 'Industrial dynamics and technical research: Toward a new economic representation', in *Theories and Policies of Technological Development at the Local Level*, Regional Science Association, Arco, Italy.

Freeman, C. 1987, *Technology Policy and Economic Performance*, Frances Pinter, London.

Freeman, C., Clark J. & Soete, L. 1982, *Unemployment and Technical Innovation: A Study of Long Waves in Economic Development*, Frances Pinter, London.

Friedman, M. & Friedman, R. 1980, *Freedom to Choose*, Secker & Warburg, London.

Fujita Kuniko (forthcoming), *The Technopolis: High Technology and Regional Development in Japan'*, Department of Sociology, University of Michigan, East Lansing.

Galbraith, J.K. 1978, *The New Industrial State*, 3rd edn, New American Library, New York.

Garnham, N. 1989, 'Universal service in European telecommunications', in *European Telecommunications Policy Research*, ed. N. Garnham, IOS, Amsterdam.

Gerla, M. 1985, 'Packet, circuit and virtual circuit switching', in *Computer Communications. Vol. 2: Systems and Applications*, ed. W. Chou, Prentice-Hall, New Jersey.

Gershuny, J. & Miles, I. 1983, *The New Service Economy*, Frances Pinter, London.

Gertler, M.S. (forthcoming), 'The limits to flexibility: Comments on the post-Fordist vision of production and its geography', *Transactions, Institute of British Geographers*.

Gibbins, H. de B. 1901, *Economic and Industrial Progress of the Century*, The Linscott Publishing Company, London.

Gilder, G. 1988, 'The revitalization of everything: The law of the microcosm', *Harvard Business Review*, March–April, 49–61.

Gilder, G. 1989, *Microcosm*, Simon & Schuster, New York.

Gillespie, A.E. *et al.* 1984, 'The effects of new information technology on the less favoured regions of the community', *Regional Policy Studies*, No. 3, CEC, Brussels.

Gillespie, A.E., Goddard, J.B., Hepworth, M.E. & Williams, H. 1989, *Information and Communications Technology and Regional Development: An Information Technology Perspective*, STI Review No. 5, 85–111, OECD, Paris, April.

Gillespie, A.E., Goddard, J.B., Robinson, J.F., Smith, I.J. & Thwaites, A.R. 1987, 'Competition, internationalism and regions: The example of the information technology production industries in Europe', in *The Development of High Technology Industries: An International Survey*, eds M.J. Breheny & R.W. McQuaid, Croom Helm, London, New York, Sydney.

Gillespie, A.E. & Green, A.E. 1987, 'The changing geography of producer services employment in Britain', *Regional Studies*, **21**, 397–412.

Gillespie, A.E. & Hepworth, M.E. 1986, *Telecommunications and Regional Development in the Information Society'*, Newcastle Studies of the Information Economy Working Paper No. 1, Centre for Urban and Regional Development Studies, University of Newcastle-upon-Tyne, UK.

Gillespie, A.E. & Hepworth, M.E. 1987, 'Telecommunications and regional development in the network economy', in *Telecommunications: A Strategic Perspective on Regional Economic and Business Development*, eds M. Estabrook & H. Lamarche, The Canadian Institute for Research on Regional Development, Ottawa.

Gillespie, A.E. & Hepworth, M.E. 1988, *Telecommunications and Regional Development in the Information Economy: A Policy Perspective*, PICT Policy Research Papers No. 1, Programme on Information and Communications Technologies, ESRC, London.

Gillespie, A.E. & Robins, K. 1989, 'Geographical inequalities: The spatial bias of the new communications technologies', *Journal of Communications*, **39**(3), 7–18.

Gillespie, A.E. & Williams, H.P. 1988, 'Telecommunications and the reconstruction of regional comparative advantage', *Environment & Planning A*, **20**, 1311–21.

Gillespie, A.E. & Williams, H.P. 1989, 'The impact of telecommunications liberalisation upon small firms', in *European Telecommunications Policy Research*, ed. N. Garnham, IOS, Amsterdam.

Glasmeier, A.K. 1985, 'Innovative manufacturing industries: Spatial incidence in the United States', in *High Technology, Space and Society*, ed. M. Castells, *Urban Affairs Annual Reviews*, Vol. 28, Sage Publications, Beverley Hills, London, New Dehli.

Glasmeier, A.K. 1988, 'The Japanese technopolis programme: High tech developments or industry policy in disguise', *International Journal of Urban & Regional Research*, **12**(2), 268–84.

Goddard, J.B. 1978, 'Urban and regional systems' *Progress in Human Geography*, **1**, 309–17.

Goddard, J.B. 1984, *The Impact of New Information Technology on Urban Structure*, Centre for Urban and Regional Development Studies, University of Newcastle-upon-Tyne, UK.

Goddard, J.B. 1989, ' The city in the global information economy' in *The Rise and Fall of Great Cities*, ed. R. Lawton, Belhaven Press, London.

Goddard, J.B. & Gillespie, A.E. 1986, 'Advanced telecommunications and regional economic development', *Geographical Journal*, **152**(3), 383–97.

Goddard, J.B. & Gillespie, A.E. 1988, 'Advanced telecommunications and regional economic development', in *Informatics and Regional Development*, eds M. Giaoutzi & P. Nijkamp, Avebury, Aldershot, 121–46.

Goddard, J.B. & Hepworth, M.E. 1988, *Internationalisation of Information Technology*, Report of an Expert Meeting on Urban Developments and Impacts of Technological, Economic and Sociodemographic Changes, OECD, Paris.

Goddard, J.B. & Pye, R. 1977, 'Telecommunications and office location', *Regional Studies*, **11**, 19–30.

Golant, S.M. 1984, *A Place to Grow Old: The Meaning of Environment in Old Age*, Columbia University Press, New York.

Gold, B. 1981, 'Changing perspectives on size, scale, and returns: An interpretive survey', *Journal of Economic Literature*, **19**(1), 5–33.

Goldberg, M.A., Helsley, R.W. & Levi, M. 1987, *The Evolution of International Financial Centres*, Final Report to Ministry of Finance & Corporate Relations, University of British Columbia, Faculty of Commerce and Business Administration, Vancouver, mimeo.

Goldemberg, J., Johansson, Reddy & Williams 1987, *Energy for a Sustainable World*, World Resources Institute, Washington.

Goldstein, G.S. & Gronberg, T.J. 1984, 'Economies of scope and economies of agglomeration', *Journal of Urban Economics*, **16**(1), 91–104.

Goodman, E., Bamford, J. & Saynor, P. 1989, *Small Firms and Industrial Districts in Italy*, Routledge, New York.

Gordon, R. & Kimball, K.M. 1987, 'The impact of industrial structure on global high technology location', in *The Spatial Impact of Technological Change*, eds J.F. Brotchie, P. Hall & P.W. Newton, Croom Helm, London, New York, Sydney.

Gottmann, J. 1966, 'Why the skyscraper?', *The Geographical Review*, LVI(2), 190–212.

Gottmann, J. 1983, *The Coming of the Transactional City*, University of Maryland, Institute of Urban Studies.

Granovetter, M. 1985, 'Economic action and social structure: The problem of embeddedness' *American Journal of Sociology*, 91(3), 481–510.

Greenfield, H.I. 1966, *Manpower and the Growth of Producer Services*, Columbia University Press, New York.

Greenspan, A. 1988, 'Goods shrink, and trade grows', *Wall Street Journal*, 24 October.

Grewlich, K.W. 1989, 'HDTV: The struggle for telepresence', *Transnational Data & Communications Report*, 12(4), 17–23.

Grimshaw, D. & Haddad, A. 1988, 'Trends in the use of information technology in local government', *Local Government Studies*, July/August, 15–25.

Grubb & Ellis 1987, 'High tech America: Where it is, where it's going', *Market Trends*, Quarterly Newsletter of Commercial Real Estate Activity, August, 1–9.

Haas, E. 1987, 'Applying the lessons: Networking semiconductor companies', *Entrepreneurial Economy*, 6(1), 40–1.

Hall, P. 1985, 'The geography of the Fifth Kondratieff', in *Silicon Landscapes*, eds P. Hall & A. Markusen, Allen & Unwin, Boston, 1–19.

Hall, P. 1987a, 'The anatomy of job creation: Nations, regions and cities in the 1960s and 1970s', *Regional Studies*, 21, 95–106.

Hall, P. 1987b, 'Time to play the merger game', *Times Higher Education Supplement*, 15 May, p. 13.

Hall P. & Breheny, M. 1987, *Western Sunrise: The Genesis and Growth of Britain's Major High Tech Corridor*, Allen & Unwin, London.

Hall, P., Glasmeier, A.K. & Markusen, A. 1983, *The Computer Software Industry*, Institute of Urban & Regional Development Working Paper No. 410, University of California, Berkeley.

Hambleton, R. 1988, 'Consumerism, decentralisation and local democracy', *Public Administration*, 66, 125–47.

Hanneman, G.J. 1987, 'Telecommunications, teleports and the new urban infrastructure', in *Telecommunications: A Strategic Perspective on Regional, Economic and Business Development*, eds M.F. Estabrooks & R.H. Lamarche, Canadian Institute for Research on Regional Development, Moncton.

Hansen, N. 1989, *Innovative Regional Milieux, Small Firms, and Regional Development: Evidence from Mediterranean France*, Department of Ecomonics, University of Texas, Austin, Texas.

Hanushek, E.A. & Jackson, J.E. 1977, *Statistical Methods for Social Scientists*, Academic Press, New York.

Harrington, J.W. Jr 1989, *Trade in Services Between the U.S. and Canada: Status and Prospects*, Canada–United States Trade Center, Occasional Paper No. 2, Department of Geography, University of Buffalo.

Harris, C.S. 1983, *Small Business and Job Generation: A Changing Economy of Differing Methodologies?*, Business Microdata Project, Economic Studies Program, The Brookings Institution, Washington, DC, 25 February.

Harris, R.I.D. 1988, 'Technological change and regional development in the UK: Evidence from the SPRU database on innovations', *Regional Studies*, **22**(5), 361–74.

Harrison, B. & Kleuwer, J. 1989, 'Reassessing the Massachusetts miracle: Reindustrialization and balanced growth, or convergence to Manhattanization?', *Environment and Planning A*, **21**, 771–801.

Harvey, D. 1987, 'Flexible accumulation through urbanisation: Reflections on "post-modernism" in the American city', *Antipode*, **19**(3), 260–86.

Harvey, D. 1988, 'The geographical and geopolitical consequences of the transition from Fordist to flexible accumulation', in *America's New Market Geography: Nation, Region and Metropolis*, eds G. Sternlieb & J. Hughes, Center for Urban Policy Research, Rutgers State University, New Jersey.

Harvey, D. 1989, From managerialism to entrepreneurialism: The transformation of urban governance in late capitalism, Paper presented to the Vega Symposium, Stockholm, 24 April.

Hayek, F.A. 1945, 'The use of knowledge in society', *American Economic Review*, **35**, 520.

Hayes, R.H. & Wheelwright, S.C. 1979, 'Link manufacturing process and product life cycles', *Harvard Business Review*, **57**(1), 133–40.

Heiner, R. 1988, 'Imperfect decisions and routinized production implications for evolutionary modelling and inertial technical change', in *Technical Change and Economic Theory*, eds G. Dosi *et al.*, Frances Pinter, London.

Hemer, J. 1984, *Information Networks Designed to Support Innovation in the Less Favoured Regions of the Community: Final Report on the Case Study in Boden Wuerttenberg*, Report prepared for EC's Directorate General for Regional Policy, ISI Institute, Karlsruhe, FRG, **III**, Regional Reports, October.

Henderson, J.V. 1986, 'Efficiency of resource use and city size', *Journal of Urban Economics*, **19**, 47–70.

Hendricks, C. 1988, The rebirth of European railways: German high speed trackbound transportation systems, Paper presented to the Annual Meeting of IISI, Seoul, October.

Hensher, D.A., Brotchie, J.F. & Gunn. H. 1989, A methodology for investigating the passenger demand for high speed rail, Paper presented to Australian Transport Research Forum, Perth, 21 pp.

Hepworth, M.E. 1986, 'The geography of technological change in the information economy', *Regional Studies*, **20**(4), 407–24.

Hepworth, M.E. 1987a, 'Information technology as spatial systems', *Progress in Human Geography*, **11**, 157–80.

Hepworth, M.E. 1987b, 'The information city', *Cities*, August, 253–62.

Hepworth, M.E. 1988, *Planning for the Information City: The Challenge and Response*, Newcastle Studies of the Information Economy No. 6, Centre for Urban and Regional Studies, The University of Newcastle-Upon-Tyne.

Hepworth, M.E. 1989, 'Wheels and wires: Transport', *Town & Country Planning*, **58**(6).

Hepworth, M.E. & Dobilas, G.P. 1985, 'The information revolution and the city: Toronto in the eighties', *Urban Resources*, 3(1), Fall, 39–46.

Hepworth, M.E., Dominy G. & Graham, S. 1989, *Local Authorities and the Information Economy in Britain*, Newcastle Studies of the Information Economy No. 10, Centre for Urban and Regional Studies, University of Newcastle-upon-Tyne.

Hepworth, M.E. & Robins, K. 1988, 'Information versus the regions', *Intermedia*, 16(1), 40–4.

Herrigel, G. 1988, 'Industrial order and the politics of industrial change' in *Toward a Third Republic?*, ed. P. Katzenstein, Cornell University Press, Ithaca, New York.

Hirota, R. 1984, Present situation and effects of the Shinkansen, Paper presented to International Seminar on High-speed Trains, Paris, November, 15 pp.

Holly, B.P. 1987, 'Regulation, competition and technology: The restructuring of the U.S. commercial banking system', *Environment & Planning A*, 19, 635–52.

Holmes, J. 1986, 'The organization and locational structure of production subcontracting', in *Production, work, territory: The geographical anatomy of industrial capitalism*, eds A.J. Scott & M. Storper, Allen & Unwin, Boston, 80–106.

Horiuchi, Y. 1989, 'Shinkansen extensions at lower cost', *Railway Gazette International*, 145, 487–91.

Houee, M. 1986, 'The relations between high speed trains and the organization of regional transport services', *Journal of Advanced Transportation*, 20, 107–32.

Hourcade, J.C. (ed.) 1988, *Strategies Used by Energy-importing Developed Countries to Adapt to the Oil Shocks: Adjustment Behaviors of Consumer Countries'*, NEED No. 9, CIRED, Paris, September.

Howells, J. 1987, 'Developments in the location, technology and industrial organization of computer services: Some trends and research issues', *Regional Studies*, 21(6), 493–503.

Howells, J. 1988, *Economic, Technological and Locational Trends in European Services*, A report prepared for the Commission of the European Communities, FAST Programme, Avebury, Aldershot, Brookfield, Hong Kong, Singapore, Sydney.

Hymer, S. 1972, 'The multinational corporation and the law of uneven development', in *Economics and World Order: From the 1970's to the 1990's*, ed J.N. Bhagwati, MacMillan, New York.

Innis, H.A. 1950, *Empire and Communication*, Clarendon Press, Oxford.

Innis, H.A. 1951, *The Bias of Communication*, University of Toronto Press, Toronto.

Ishinomori Shotaro 1988, *Japan Inc.: An Introduction to Japanese Economics (The Comic Book)*, trans. B. Scheiner, University of California Press, Berkeley, Los Angeles.

ISTC 1989, *The Human Dimension of Competitiveness*, Industry, Science and Technology Canada, Ottawa.

ITAP 1983, *Making a Business of Information: A Survey of New Opportunities*, HMSO, London.

Jacobs, D. 1986, 'Breaking urban data bottlenecks with a private lightwave bypass', *Proceedings of the Tenth Annual International Fibre Optic Communications and Local Area Networks Exposition*, Information Gatekeepers Inc., Boston.

Janssen, B. & Machielse, C. 1987, *Logistics in Production and Transport*, TNO-INRO Paper, Delft, The Netherlands.

Janssen, B. & Van Hoogstraten, P. 1989, 'The "new infrastructure" and regional development', in *Regional Policy at the Crossroads: European Perspectives*, eds L. Albrechts, F. Moulaert, P. Roberts & E. Swyngedouw, Jessica Kingsley Publishers, London.

Jenks, L. 1971, *The Migration of British Capital to 1875*, Nelson, London.

Jennings, D.M., Landweber, L.H., Fuchs, I.H., Farber, D.J. & Adrion, W.R. 1986, 'Computer networking for scientists', *Science*, **231**, 943–50.

JETRO 1983, *Technopolises*, Japan External Trade Organization, Now in Japan No. 34, Tokyo.

JNR 1986, *Shinkansen*, International Department Report, Japanese National Railways, Tokyo.

Johanson, J. & Mattson, L. 1987,'Interorganizational relations in industrial systems: A network approach compared with the transactions cost approach', *International Studies of Management & Organization*, **XVII**(1), 34–48.

Johnston, R. & Lawrence, P. 1988, 'Beyond vertical integration – the rise of the value-adding partnership', *Harvard Business Review*, July–August, 94–101.

Journet, M. 1989, 'Link round Paris forges TGV network', *Railway Gazette International*, **145**, 471–3.

Kahn, R.E. 1987, 'Networks for advanced computing', *Scientific American*, **257**, 129–35.

Kamada, M. 1980, 'Achievements and future problems of the Shinkansen', in *The Shinkansen High-speed Network in Japan: Proceedings of an IIASA Conference, Luxenburg, 27–30 June 1977*, eds A. Straszak & R. Tuch, Pergamon, Oxford, 41–56.

Kamien, M.I. & Schwartz, N.L. 1982, *Market Structure and Innovation*, Cambridge University Press, Cambridge.

Kanayasu Iwao, 1987. 'Daiyonji zenkoku sogo kaihatsu keikaku', *Geographical Review of Japan*, **60**(B), 213–14.

Karunaratne, N.D. 1986, 'Analytics of information and empirics of the information economy', *The Information Society*, **4**, 313–31.

Kawashima, T. & Stohr, W. 1988, 'Decentralized technology policy: The case of Japan', *Environment & Planning A: Government & Policy*, **6**(4), 427–40.

Keen, P. 1986, *Competing in Time: Using Telecommunications for Competitive Advantage*, Ballinger, Cambridge, Mass.

Kehoe, L. 1989a, 'Minicomputer makers face a dilemma', *Financial Times*, 24 Nov.

Kehoe, L. 1989b, 'Uncertainties prevail', *Financial Times*, 24 Nov.

Kellerman, A. 1984, 'Telecommunications and the geography of metropolitan areas', *Progress in Human Geography*, **8**(2), 222–46.

Kenney, M. & Florida, R.L. 1987, *Beyond Mass Production: The Social Organization of Production and Innovation in Japan*, Technology, Innovation and Social Change Project Working Paper No. 6, Ohio State University, Columbus.

Kenney-Wallace, G.A. & Mustard, J.F. 1988, 'From paradox to paradigm: The evolution of science and technology policy in Canada', *Daedalus*, Fall, 191–214.

Kidder, R.M. 1988, *International Agenda for the 1990s*, Stanley Foundation, Muscatine, Iowa.

Kirton, P., Ellershaw, J. & Littlewood, M. 1988, 'Fast packet switching for integrated networks', *Telecommunications Journal of Australia*, **38**, 53–9.

Kitamura, K. 1987, 'Creating cities of the future, *Science and Technology in Japan*, April/June.

Klein, B. & Leffler, K. 1981, 'The role of market forces in assuring contractual performance', *Journal of Political Economy*, **89**(4), 615–41.

Ko Kheng Hwa 1988, 'Effective information strategies for the government service: The Singapore experience', in *Information Systems for Government and Business: Trends, Issues, Challenges*, ed. H. Sazanami, United Nations Centre for Regional Development, Nagoya, Japan, 505–16.

Kobayashi, K. 1986, *Computers and Communications: A Vision of C & C*, MIT Press, Cambridge, Mass.

Kobayashi, K. 1987, 'Implications of global integrated communications networks and services for future society', Proceedings of the Fifth World Telecommunications Forum, Part 1, International Telecommunications Union, Geneva, 109–15.

Kogane, Y. 1988, 'Long waves of economic growth', *Futures*, October, 532–48.

Kokudocho keikaku 1984, *Nihon 21 seiki he no tenbo: kokudo kukan no atarashi maraizo o gamete* (Observations of Japan in the Twenty-first Century – Our New Future Image of Land Space), Kokudocho keikaku, Tokyo, .

Kokudocho keikaku 1985, *21 seiki johoka to kokudocho – johoka no shindoganin to kokudo ni shaesu: inpakuto ni kansuru chosa* (Land and Informisation in the Twenty-first Century – Picture of Land Use, People and Progress in Information: Survey of Impacts), Kokudocho keikaku/Chosa kyoruhen, Tokyo.

Kometsky, G. 1987, *Essentials of Marketing High Technology*, Prentice Hall, New Jersey.

Koopmans, T.C. 1957, *Three Essays on the State of Economic Science*, McGraw-Hill, New York.

Koppelman, F.S. & Saloman, I. 1988, Teleshopping or going shopping: A dilemma for the indivual, Paper presented to Seminar on Information, Technology and the Meaning of Space, Frankfurt, 16–19 May.

Korte, W.B., Robinson, S. & Steinle, W.J. 1987, *Telework: Present Situation and Future Development of a New Form of Work Organisation*, North Holland, Amsterdam, New York, Oxford, Tokyo.

Kotz, D.M. 1987, 'Long waves and social structures of accumulation: A critique and reinterpretation', *Review of Radical Political Economics*, **19**(4), 16–38.

Kromenacher, R.J. 1984, *World-Traded Services: The Challenge for the Eighties*, Artech House, Destham, Mass.

Kuo, E.C.Y. 1987, 'Information technology development in Singapore', in *Toward an International Service and Information Economy: A New Challenge for the Third World*, ed. D.I. Riddle, Friederich Ebert Foundation, Frankfurt, West Germany, 105–18.

Kuttner, R. 1983, 'The declining middle', *Atlantic Monthly*, July, 60–72.

Laffont, J.-J. 1987, 'Towards a normative theory of incentive contracts between government and private firms', *The Economic Journal*, **97**, 17–31.

Lamb, A. 1986, 'International banking in London, 1975–85', *Bank of England Quarterly Bulletin*, **26**, 367–78.

Lamberton, D.M. 1987, 'The Australian information economy: A sectoral analysis', in *Challenges and Change: Australia's Information Society*, ed. T. Barr, Oxford University Press, Melbourne.

Lamberton, D.M. 1988, 'Secondary sector analysis: Methods and data requirements', in *The Cost of Thinking*, eds M. Jussawalla *et al.*, Ablex Publishing Corporation, Norwood.

Lamberton, D.M. 1989, Information society, Paper presented to ICTM Conference on International Telecommunications Futures, University of Nebraska, 5–7 June.

Langdale, J.V. 1984, 'Computerization in Singapore and Australia', *The Information Society*, **3**, 131–53.

Langdale, J.V. 1985, 'Electronic funds transfer and the internationalization of the banking and finance industry', *Geoforum*, **36**, 1–13.

Langdale, J.V. 1987, 'Telecommunications and electronic information services in Australia', in *The Spatial Impact of Technological Change*, eds J.F. Brotchie, P. Hall & P.W. Newton, Croom Helm, London, New York, Sydney, 89–103.

Langdale, J.V. 1988a, 'Telecommunications and the multi-function polis: International, urban and regional development implications', Paper presented to International Geographical Congress, Study Group 9, Sydney, August.

Langdale, J.V. 1988b, 'International telecommunications and trade in services: Policy perspectives', Paper presented to International Geographical Congress, Study Group 9, Sydney, August.

Lash, S. & Urry, J. 1987, *The End of Organized Capitalism*, University of Madison Press, Madison.

Laudon, K.C. 1987, 'Promise versus performance of cable', in *Wired Cities: Shaping the Future of Communications*, eds W.H. Dutton, J.G. Blumler, & K.L. Kraemer, G.K. Hall & Co., Boston, Mass., 27–40.

Lazak, D. 1987, 'Evolution of teleports and telematic cities', in *Information Network and Data Communication I*, ed. D. Khakhar, Elsevier, Amsterdam.

Lepage, H. 1978, *Tomorrow: Capitalism*, Open Court Publishing, La Salle, London.

Lesser, B. 1987, 'Technological change and regional development,' in *Still Living Together: Recent Trends and Future Directions in Canadian Regional Development*, eds W.J. Coffey & M. Polèse, Institute for Research on Public Policy, Montreal.

Leyshon, A., Daniels, P.W. & Thrift, N.J. 1987a, *Internationalization of Professional Producer Services: The Case of Large Accountancy Firms*, Working Papers on Producer Services No. 3, University of Bristol & University of Liverpool.

Leyshon, A., Daniels, P.W. & Thrift, N.J. 1987b, *Large Commercial Property Firms in the U.K.: The Operational Development and Spatial Expansion of General Practice Firms of Chartered Surveyors*, Working Papers on Producer Services No. 5, University of Bristol & University of Liverpool.

Lindbeck, A. 1989, *Science, Technology and Economic Growth*, Paper presented to OECD International Seminar, Paris, June.

Link, A.N. 1980, 'Firm size and efficient entrepreneurial activity: A reformulation of the Schumpeter hypothesis', *Journal of Political Economy*, **88**(4), 771–82.

Little, J.S. 1989, 'Exchange rates and structural change in U.S. manufacturing', *New England Economic Review*, March/April, 56–70.

Lucas, R.E. Jr 1988, 'On the mechanics of economic development', *Journal of Monetary Economics*, **11**, 3–42.

Machlup, F. 1962, *The Production and Distribution of Knowledge in the United States*, Princeton University Press, New Jersey.

Machlup, F. 1980–4, *Knowledge: Its Creation, Distribution and Economic Significance*, 3 vols, Princeton University Press, New Jersey.

Mahon, R. 1987, 'From Fordism to ?: New technology, labour markets and unions, *Economic and Industrial Democracy*, **8**(1), 5–60.

Maillat, D. 1984, 'Mobility channels: An instrument for analysing and regulating the local labour market', *International Labour Review*, **123**(3), 349–62.

Maillat, D. 1988, *SMEs, Innovation and Territorial Development*, Regional Science Asociation, European Summer Institute, Arco, Italy.

Maillat, D. & Perrin, J.-C. (in press), *Entreprises, Types d'Innovations et Développement des Milieux Locale: Les Variables Territoriales*, ERESA–Economica, Geneva, Paris.

Maillat, D. & Vasserot, J.-Y. 1986, 'Les milieux innovateurs, le cas de l'Arc Jurassien suisse', in *Milieux Innovators en Europe*, ed. P. Aydalot, GREMI, Paris, 361.

Maillat, D. & Vasserot, J.-Y. 1988, 'Economic and territorial conditions for indigenous revival in Europe's industrial regions', in *High Technology Industry and Innovative Enviroments*, eds P. Aydalot & D. Keeble, Routledge & Croom Helm, London, New York, 163–83.

Maillat, D., Crevoisier, O. & Vasserot, J.-Y. 1988, 'L'apport du milieu dans le processus d'innovation: le cas de l'Arc Jurassien suisse', *Colloque GREMI II*, GREMI, Ascona.

Malecki, E.G. & Nijkamp, P. 1988, 'Technology and regional development: Some thoughts on policy', *Environment & Planning C: Government Policy*, **6**, 383–99.

Manchester, P. 1989, 'A boon for programmers', *Financial Times*, 24 Nov.

Mandeville, T.D. 1985, 'Information flows between Australia and Japan', *Papers of the Regional Science Association*, **56**, 189-200.

Mandeville, T.D. 1987a, 'An international comparison', in *Challenges and Change: Australia's Information Society*, ed. T. Barr, Oxford University Press, Melbourne.

Mandeville, T.D. 1987b, *The Japanese Technopolis Concept: Its Relevance to and Implications for the Establishment of a Multi-function Polis in Australia*, unpublished discussion paper prepared for the Coordinator-General, Queensland, Information Research Unit, Department of Economics, University of Queensland, August.

Mandeville, T.D. 1988, 'A multi-function-polis for Australia', *Prometheus*, **6**(1), 94–106.

Mandeville, T.D. 1989, The Multi-function-polis – an information age institution, Paper presented to the Third International Workshop on Innovation, Technology Change and Spatial Impacts, Cambridge, UK, September.

Mandeville, T.D. & Lamberton, D.M. 1988, *The Multi-Function-Polis: Inventing an Institution. Vol. I: Basic Concept. Vol. II: Supporting Material*, Report prepared for The Director-General, Queensland Premier's Department, Information Research Unit, Department of Economics, University of Queensland, May.

Mansell, J. 1987, *Workplace Innovation in Canada*, Economic Council of Canada, Ottawa.

Mansell, R. 1986, 'The telecommunications bypass threat: Real or imagined?', *Journal of Economic Issues*, **20**(1).

Mansell, R. 1988, 'Telecommunication network-based services: Regulation and market structure in transition', *Telecommunications Policy*, **12**, 243–56.

Markides, C. & Berg, N. 1988, 'Manufacturing offshore is bad business' *Harvard Business Review*, September–October, 113–20.

Marks, G.A. 1988, 'University of Michigan', in *Campus Networking Strategies*, ed. C. Arms, EDUCOM Strategy Series on Information Technology, Digital Press, New York, 178–204.

Markus, G.B. 1979, *Analyzing Panel Data: Quantitative Applications in the Social Sciences*, vol. 18, Sage, Beverly Hills.

Markusen, A. 1985, *Profit Cycles, Oligopoly, and Regional Development*, MIT, Cambridge.

Markusen, J.R. 1986, *Intra-firm Service Trade by the Multinational Enterprise*, Series on Trade in Services, Institute for Research in Public Policy, Vancouver.

Markusen, J.R. 1989, 'Service trade by the multinational enterprise', in *Multinational Service Firms*, ed. P. Enderwick, Routledge, London, 35–60.

Marshall, J.N. & Bachtler, J. 1984, 'Spatial perspectives on technological changes in the banking sector of the United Kingdom', *Environment and Planning A*, **16**, 437–50.

Marshall, J.N., Wood, P., Daniels, P.W., McKinnon, A., Bachtler, J., Damesick, P., Thrift, N., Gillespie, A., Green, A. & Leyshon, A. 1988, *Services and Uneven Development*, Oxford University Press, London.

Martin, J. 1978, *The Wired Society*, Prentice-Hall, Englewood Cliffs, New Jersey.

Marx, K. 1967, *Capital: A Critique of Political Economy, vol. 1, The Process of Capitalist Production*, trans. from the 3rd German edn by S. Moore & E. Aveling, ed. F. Engels, International Publishers, New York.

Masuda, Y. 1985, 'Three great social revolutions: Agricultural, industrial, and information', *Prometheus*, **3**(2), 75–89.

Matteaccioli, A. & Peyrache, V. 1989, 'Milieux et réseaux innovateurs: Synthése sous l'angle de la complexité', *Cahiers du C3E*, **78**, 1–25.

McAuslan, P. 1988, 'Public law and public choice', *The Modern Law Review*, **51**(6), 681–705.

McClelland, M.C. 1976 edn, *The Achieving Society* (with new introduction), Irvington Publishing Inc., New York.

McCormack, G. 1989, 'And shall Jerusalem yet be built? Japan's "Multi-function Polis" Project and Australia', *ASAA Review*, **12**(3), 1–6.

McCurdy, T. 1988, *Employment Income and Occupational Effects of Computer-based Automation in Canada*, Economic Council of Canada Discussion Paper No. 340.

McHale, M.C. 1984, *The Feminist Model*, Center for Integrative Studies, State University of New York, Buffalo.

McKenna, R. 1989, *Who's Afraid of Big Blue*, Addison-Westey, Mass.

McKinsey & Company 1987, *Systems Technology and the U.S. Commercial Banking Industry*, McKinsey, New York.

McLuhan, M. 1964, 'Introduction', in *The Bias of Communication*, 2nd edn, ed. H.A. Innis, University of Toronto Press, Toronto.

Mehler, M. 1988, 'Mini-fabs reshape IC production', *Electronic Business*, 1 June.

Meier, R.L. 1961, *A Communications Theory of Urban Growth*, MIT Press, Cambridge, Mass.

Meier, R.L. 1966, *Science and Economic Development: New Patterns of Living*, 2nd edn, MIT Press, Cambridge, Mass.

Meier, R.L. 1985, 'High tech and urban settlement', in *The Future of Urban Form: The Impact of New Technology*, eds J. Brotchie, P.W. Newton, P. Hall & P. Nijkamp, Croom Helm & Nichols, London, Sydney, New York.

Meier, R.L. 1987, 'Thinking beyond post-industrial: The social perspectives,' in *The Spatial Impact of Technological Change*, eds J.F. Brotchie, P. Hall & P.W. Newton, Croom Helm & Nichols, London, New York, Sydney.

Meier, R.L. & Shen, Q. 1987, *Efficient, Ecologically Balanced Settlement on Estuaries: Shanghai*, Center for Environmental Design Research Working Paper, University of Claifornia, Berkeley.

Meier, R.L. & Shen, Q. 1989, *Planning and Designing for the Long Term in Coastal China: The Urban Ecosystems Approach*, Center for Environmental Design Research Working Paper, University of California, Berkeley.

Melody, W.H. 1987, Telecommunications: Implications for the structure of development, Paper presented to the 5th World Telecommunication Forum, International Telecommunication Union, Geneva, 19–27 October.

Menadue, J. 1988, MFP: Opportunities and pitfalls for Australia, Paper presented to the Multi-Function Polis Forum, Melbourne, Australia, 22 July.

Mensch, G.O. 1979, *Stalemate in Technology: Innovations Overcome the Depression*, Ballinger Publishing Company, Cambridge, Mass.

Meyer-Krahmer, F. 1985, 'Government promotion of the linkages between research institutions and industry in the Federal Republic of Germany', in *Financing Systems for Science and Technology*, United Nations, Selected Papers, Conclusions and Recommendations, International Seminar on Institutional Linkages in Technological Development, São Paulo, 25–28 November.

MFP Briefing 1989, Premier's Department, Brisbane, 30 March.

Mifsud, P. 1987, *Milieux Urbains et Développement Local*, CREUSET, Saint Etienne.

Miles, I. 1988, *Home Informatics: Information Technology and the Transformation of Everyday Life*, Frances Pinter, London.

Miles, I., Rush, H., Turner, K. & Bessant, J. 1989, *Information Horizons*, Edward Elgar, Aldershot.

Miles, R. & Snow, C. 1986, 'Organizations: New concepts for new forms' *California Management Review*, **XXVIII**(3), 62–73.

Miller, R. & Côté, M. 1987, *Growing the Next Silicon Valley: A Guide for Successful Regional Planning*, Lexington Books, Lexington.

Ministry of International Trade & Industry, 1987a, *A Multi-function Polis Scheme for the 21st Century: A Discussion Paper*, MFP Planning Committee, MITI, Tokyo, Japan, February.

Ministry of International Trade & Industry, 1987b, *A Multi-function Polis Scheme for the 21st Century: Basic Concept'*, MFP Planning Committee, MITI, Tokyo, Japan, September.

Ministry of International Trade & Industry, 1987c, *Multi-function Polis of the 21st Century: Reference Material'*, MFP Planning Committee, MITI, Tokyo, Japan, September.

Ministry of Posts & Telecommunications 1987, *1987 White Paper: Communications in Japan*, Ministry of Posts and Telecommunications, Tokyo, Japan.

Mitchell W. 1988, *Government As It Is*, Hobart Paperback 109, IEA.

Mitsubishi Electric Corporation 1985, *Technopolis: A Knowledge-oriented Future for Industrializing Countries*, Prepared by PADECO, Mitsubishi Electric, Tokyo.

Miyakawa, H. 1985, 'Present and future of new media in Japan', *Science and Technology in Japan*, **5**, 8–19.

Monck, C.S.P., Quintas, P.R., Porter, R.B. & Storey, D.J. 1988, *Science Parks and the Growth of High Technology Firms*, Croom Helm, London.

Morgan, K., Harbor, B., Hobday, M., von Tunzelmann, N. & Walker, W. 1989, *The GEC-Siemens Bid for Plessey: The Wider European Issues*, Centre for Information & Communication Technologies Working Paper No. 2, University of Sussex, January.

Morgan, K. & Mansell, R. (in press), 'The coming intelligent network: Regulatory regimes, innovation and the new telecommunication paradigm', in *Regulation, Innovation and Spatial Development*, ed. P. Cooke, Unwin Hyman, London.

Morgan, K. & Pitt, D. 1989, 'Coping with turbulence: Corporate strategy, regulatory politics and telematics in post-divestiture America', in *European Telecommunications Policy Research*, ed. N. Garnham, IOS, Amsterdam.

Morgan, K. & Webber, D. 1986, *Divergent Patterns: Political Strategies for Telecommunications in Britain, France and the Federal Republic of Germany*, Government & Industry Working Paper No. 6, University of Sussex.

Morris-Suzuki, T. 1988, Technopolises, teletopias and multifunction polises: Japanese regional planning in the information age, Paper presented to International Geographical Congress, Study Group 9, Sydney, August.

Mosco, V. 1988, 'Introduction: Information in the pay-per society', in *The Political Economy of Information*, eds V. Mosco & J. Wasko, University of Wisconsin Press, Wisconsin.

Moskoritz, D. & Mammon, D. 1985, 'Information technologies in government: Organizational and management issues, in *Managing New Technologies*, International City Managers Association.

Moss, M.L. 1986, 'Telecommunications and the future of cities', *Land Development Studies*, **3**(1), 33–44.

Moss, M.L. 1987a. 'Telecommunications and international financial centres', in *The Spatial Impact of Technological Change*, eds J.F. Brotchie, P. Hall & P.W. Newton, Croom Helm, London, New York, Sydney, 75–88.

Moss, M.L. 1987b, 'Urban development in a global economy', in *Telecommunications: A Strategic Perspective on Regional Economic and Business Development*, eds M. Estabrook and H. Lamarche, The Canadian Institute for Research on Regional Development, Ottawa.

Moss, M.L. 1988, 'Telecommunications: Shaping the future', in *America's New Market Geography: Nation, Region and Metropolis*, eds G. Sternlieb & J.W. Hughes, Rutgers State University, Centre for Urban Policy Research, New Jersey.

Moulaert, F., Martinelli, F. & Djellal, F. (in press), 'The functional and spatial division of labour of IT consultancy firms in Europe', in *Regulation, Innovation and Spatial Development*, ed. P. Cooke, Unwin Hyman, London.

Mowery, D. (ed.) 1988, *The Future of Technology and Work*, National Academy of Science, Washington.

Moyal, A. 1984, *Clear Across Australia. A History of Telecommunications*, Nelson, Melbourne.

Mueller, D. 1972, 'A life cycle theory of the firm', *Journal of Industrial Economics*, **20**(3), 199–219.

Mulgan, G.J. 1989, 'Costs and tariffs in ISDN and broadband networks: A case of whatever you can get away with?', in *European Telecommunications Policy Research*, ed. N. Garnham, IOS, Amsterdam.

Myrdal, G. 1957, *Economic Theory and Undeveloped Regions*, Methuen, London.

Naisbitt, J. 1982, *Megatrends*, Warner, New York.

Nakamura, H. & Ueda, T. 1989, The impacts of the Shinkansen on regional development, Paper presented to the Fifth World Conference on Transport Research, Yokohama, July, 16 pp.

National Advisory Board on Science and Technology 1988, *Report of the Industry Committee*, presented to the Prime Minister of Canada, Ottawa.

National Institute for Research Advancement 1988, *Agenda for Japan in the 1990s*, NIRA Research Output No. 1, Tokyo, Japan.

NBST (National Board for Science and Technology) 1987, Final Report to the Community Programmes Division, DG XVI, of the Commission of the European Communities (STRIDE Committee, Research and Technology Development Project), Dublin, Ireland, June.

NCB 1987, *Singapore: The Information Centre*, The National Computer Board, Science Park Drive, Singapore.

Nelson, R.C. 1988, 'Videoconferences on a micro', *Computer Decisions*, December, 76–7.

Nelson, R.R. & Winter, S.G 1977, In search of a useful theory of innovation, *Research Policy*, **6**, 36–76.

Nelson, R.R. & Winter, S.G. 1982, *An Evolutionary Theory of Economic Growth*, Harvard University Press, Cambridge, Mass.

Newman, W. & McFarland, C. 1988, 'Why ISDN?', *Telecommunications*, **22**(2), 34–45.

Newstead, A. 1989, 'Future information cities: Japan's vision', *Futures*, **21**, 263–76.

Newton, K. 1988, 'Factories for the future', in *Strategies for Industrially Emerging Regions in Canada: Proceedings of the 26th Annual Conference of the Canadian Research Management Association, St Andrews, New Brunswick, Canada, 18–21 September 1988*, ed. D. Abbott.

Newton, P.W. & Cavill, M. 1989, Computers, telecommunications and planning, Paper presented to the International Conference on Computers in Planning, Hong Kong, 22–24 August.

Newton, P.W. & O'Connor, K. 1987, 'The location of high technology industry: A spatial perspective', in *The Spatial Impact of Technological Change*, eds J.F. Brotchie, P. Hall & P.W. Newton, Croom Helm, London, New York, Sydney.

Newton, P.W., Taylor, M.A.P. & Sharpe, R. (eds) 1988, *Desktop Planning: Microcomputer Applications for Infrastructure and Services Planning and Development*, Hargreen Publishing Co., Melbourne & Edward Arnold, London.

Newton, P.W., Zwart, P.R. & Cavill, M. 1990, 'Towards real time spatial information systems', *Proceedings, URPIS 18*, Canberra, November.

Nijkamp, P. 1988, 'Informatics or oracles in regional planning', in *Informatics and Regional Development*, eds M. Giaoutzi & P. Nijkamp, Avebury, Aldershot, 23–41.

Nijkamp, P. & Giaoutzi, M. 1988, 'Information: A key force for spatial dynamics', in *Informatics and Regional Development*, eds M. Giaoutzi & P. Nijkamp, Avebury, Aldershot, 1–17.

Nishida, M. 1980, 'History of the Shinkansen', in *The Shinkansen High-speed Rail Network of Japan: Proceedings of an IIASA Conference, Luxenburg, 27–30 June 1977*, eds A. Straszak & R. Tuch, Pergamon, Oxford.

Nishioka, H. & Takeuchi, A. 1987, 'The development of high tech industry in Japan', in *The Development of High Technology Industries: An International Survey*, eds M.J. Breheny & R.W. McQuaid, Croom Helm, London, New York, Sydney.

Noam, E.M. 1986, *The Political Economy of ISDN: European Network Integration vs. American System Fragmentation*, New York, mimeo, quoted in Snow, M.S. 1988, 'Telecommunications literature: A critical review of the economic, technological and public policy issues', *Telecommunications Policy*, June, p.159.

Nobuyuki, K. 1986, 'Intelligent buildings rise in Tokyo', *Japan Quarterly*, **33**, 154–8.

Noël, A. 1987, 'Accumulation, regulation, and social change: An essay on French political economy', *International Organization*, **41**(2), 303–33.

Norton, R.D. & Rees, J. 1979, 'The product cycle and the spatial decentralization of American manufacturing', *Regional Studies*, **13**, 141–51.

Noyelle, T.J. 1986, *New Technologies and Services: Impacts on Cities and Jobs*, University of Maryland, Institute for Urban Studies, Washington DC.

Noyelle, T.J. 1987a, 'International trade and FDI in services: A review essay', *The CTC Reporter*, **23**, Spring, 55–8.

Noyelle, T.J. 1987b, Economic development: A look forward to the 1990s, Paper presented to the Conference on the Future of the Metropolitan Economy: New Challenges for Policy and Policy-oriented Research, TNO Research Center for Urban and Regional Planning, The Hague, 9–10 June.

Noyelle, T.J. & Dutka, A. 1987, *Business Services in World Markets: Accounting, Advertising, Law and Management Consulting*, Ballinger, Cambridge, Mass.

Noyelle, T.J. & Stanback, T. 1984, *The Economic Transformation of American Cities*, Rowman & Allanheld, Totowa.

Nusbaumer, J. 1987, *Services in the Global Market*, Keuver, Boston.

O'hUallachain, B. 1988, Agglomeration of services in American cities, Paper presented to the Association of American Geographers Annual Meeting, Pheonix, April.

Oakey, R. 1984, *High Technology Small Firms: Regional Development in Britain and the United States*, St. Martin's Press, New York & Frances Pinter, London.

Ochel, W. & Wegner, M. 1987, *Service Economies in Europe: Opportunities for Growth*, Frances Pinter, London.

Odle, M. & Armington, C. 1983, *Weighting the 1976–1980 USEEM Files for Dynamic Analysis of Employment Growth*, Business Microdata Project, Economic Studies Program, The Brookings Institution, Washington, DC, April.

OECD 1981a, *Information Activities, Electronics and Telecommunications Technologies*, Vol. 1, OECD, Paris.

OECD. 1981b, *Recent International Direct Investment Trends*, OECD, Paris.

OECD 1983, *International Trade in Services: Insurance*, OECD, Paris.

OECD 1984, *International Trade in Services: Banking*, OECD, Paris.

OECD 1985, *Venture Capital in Information Technology*, OECD, Paris.

OECD 1988a, *New Technologies in the 1990s: A Socioeconomic Strategy*, OECD, Paris.

OECD 1988b, *The Telecommunications Industry: The Challenges of Structural Change*, ICCP Series No. 14, OECD, Paris.

OECD 1988c, *New Telecommunication Services – Videotex Development Study*, ICCP Series No. 16, OECD, Paris.

OECD 1989a, *Government Policies and the Diffusion of Microelectronics*, OECD, Paris.

OECD 1989b, *Telecommunication Network-based Services: Policy Implications*, ICCP Series No. 18, OECD, Paris.

Olson, J.E. 1988, 'Customers, competition and compatibility: A new convergence shaping the Information Age', *International Journal of Technology Management*, 3(4).

Olson, M.H. 1987, 'Organizational barriers to telework', in *Telework: Present Situation and Future Development of a New Form of Work Organization*, eds W.B. Korte, S. Robinson & W.J. Steinle, North Holland, Amsterdam, New York, Oxford, Tokyo.

Onda Masahiko 1988, 'Tsukuba science city complex and Japanese strategy', in *Changing the Technopolis: Linking Technology, Commercialization and Economic Development*, eds R.W. Smilor, G. Kozmetsky & D.V. Gibson, Ballinger Publishing Co., Cambridge, Mass., 51–68.

PA Computers & Telecommunications 1986, *A Review of International Trade in Tradeable Information*, Department of Trade and Industry, London.

PA Consulting Group 1988, *Evolution of the United Kingdom Communications Infrastructure*, Report to the Department of Trade and Industry, HMSO, London.

Park, J. 1989, Standards: The desire to be able to interconnect with others, Paper presented to URPIS Conference, Perth.

Parker, E., Hudson, H., Dillman, D. & Roscoe, A. 1989, *Rural America in the Information Age: Telecommunications Policy for Rural Development*, The Aspen Institute & University Press of America.

Pearce, D. & Redclift, M. (eds) 1988, *Sustainable Development*, Special issue of *Futures*, Butterworths, London, December.

Pecqueur, B. 1987, 'Tissu économique local et systèmes industriels résiliaires', *Revue d'Économie Régionale et Urbaine*, **3**, 369–78.

Perez, C. 1985, 'Microelectronics, long waves and world structural change: New perspectives for developing countries', *World Development*, **13**(3), 441–63.

Perrin, J.-C. 1986, 'Technologies nouvelles et synergies locales', *Notes de Recherche du CER*, **67**.

Piore, M. J. & Sabel, C. 1984, *The Second Industrial Divide: Possibilities for Prosperity*, Basic Books, New York.

Pirie, M. 1988, *Privatisation: Theory, Practice and Choice*, The Adam Smith Institute, London.

Planque, B. 1983, *Innovation et Développement Régional*, Economica, Paris.

Planque, B. & Py, B. 1986, 'La dynamique de l'insertion des PME innovatrices dans leur envirnoment', *Notes de Recherche du CER*, **68**.

Plewis, I. 1985, *Analyzing Change: Measurement and Explanation Using Longitudinal Data*, John Wiley, Chichester.

Plunkett, S. 1989, 'Getting rid of paper work', *Today's Computers*, 21–22 June.

Pommelet, P. 1989, 'Roissy et Massy dans le Project Régional d'Aménagement', *Cahiers de l'Institut de l'Aménagement et d'Urbanisme de la Région d'Ile-de-France*, **89**, 27–31.

Porat, M. 1977, *The Information Economy: Definition and Measurement*, Special Publication 77–12(1), Office of Telecommunications, US Department of Commerce, Washington DC.

Potter, S. 1987, *On the Right Lines? The Limits of Technological Innovation*, Frances Pinter, London.

Powell, W. 1987, 'Hybrid organizational arrangements: New form or transitional development?', *California Management Review*, **XXX**(1), 67–87.

Powledge, T.M. 1989, 'Waiting for the national science network,' *AAAs Observer*, supp. to *Science*, 3 March, 1–6.

Price, K.A. 1986, *The Global Financial Village*, Banking World, London.

Price Waterhouse 1988, *Information Technology Review 1987/8*, Price Waterhouse, London.

Pyne, A. 1988, 'Future developments in electronic messaging', in *Electronic Message Systems 88: Proceedings of the International Conference, London, December 1988*, Online Publications, London, 23–32.

Quarterman, J.S. & Hoskins, J.C. 1986, 'Notable computer networks', *Communications of the ACM*, **29**, 932–71.

Queensland Premier's Department 1987a, *Multi-Function-Polis*, Draft discussion paper, Premier's Department, Brisbane, July.

Queensland Premier's Department 1987b, *Strategic Issues Related to Proposed Multi-Function-Polis Arrangements*, Premier's Department, Brisbane, November.

Queensland Premier's Department 1988a, *The Multi-Function-Polis of the 21st Century: A Queensland View*, Discussion paper, Premier's Department, Brisbane, February.

Queensland Premier's Department 1988b, *Opportunity Areas and Policy Issues in the Multi-Function-Polis*, Discussion paper, Premier's Department, Brisbane, March.

Quévit, M. & Bodson, S. 1988, 'L'entreprise innovatrice dans son environnement local: Le cas de la Région de Liège', *Colloque GREMI II*, GREMI, Ascona.

Quintas, P.R. 1987, Seminar presentation, Science Policy Research Unit, Sussex University. Seminar based on findings later published in Monck *et al.* 1988, *Science Parks and the Growth of High Technology Firms*, Croom Helm, London.

Raschbilder, H.G. & Wackers, M. 1987, 'Status of the maglev and linear drive technology program in the Federal Republic of Germany', in *Proceedings of the International Conference on Maglev & Linear Drives*, Institute of Electrical & Electronic Engineers, New York, 147–54.

Rasiah, R. 1988, 'The semi-conductor industry in Penang: Implications for the new international division of labour theories', *Journal of Contemporary Asia*, **18**(1), 24–46.

Rasiah, R. (forthcoming), 'Labour process in the electronic industry in Penang', *Journal of Contemporary Asia*.

Renner, M. 1989, 'Rethinking transportation', in *State of the World – 1989*, eds L.R. Brown *et al.*, Worldwatch Institute, Washington.

Rheingold, H. 1985, *Tools for Thought: The People and Ideas Behind the Next Computer Revolution*, Simon & Schuster, New York.

Rhodes, R.G. & Mulhall, B.E. 1981, *Magnetic Levitation for Rail Transport*, Clarendon Press, Oxford.

Rice, V. 1987, 'The upstart start-ups' *Electronic Business*, 15 August, 46–64.

Richardson, J.B. 1987, 'A sub-sectoral approach to services: Trade theory', in *The Emerging Service Economy*, ed. O. Gisrini, Pergamon, Oxford.

Richardson, J.B. 1988, Towards an agreement on trade in services, Paper presented to Conference on Services, Trade & Development, Geneva, May.

Richardson, J.J., Moon, J. & Webber, D. 1984, Information technology, employment and economic recovery: The role of the British, French and West German governments, Paper presented to the RIPA Conference on the Shifting State: Rules, Roles and Boundaries in the 1980s, University of Aston, UK, 14–15 September.

Rimmer, P.J. 1989a, 'Putting multi-function polis into context: MITI's search for a place in the sun?', *Australian Planner*, **27**(2), 15–21.

Rimmer, P.J. 1989b, 'Japanese communications developments and the Australian transport land use-system: The missing link', *Multidisciplinary Studies, Institution of Engineers, Australia*, **GE13**(2), 57–72.

Rimmer, P.J. 1989c, 'Urban change and the international economy: Japanese construction contractors and developers under three administrations', *Pacific Cities in the World Economy: Comparative Urban & Community Research*, **2**, 156–99.

Roberts, J. & Morrison, P. 1989, *Forecasting the Adoption of New High Technology Products*, Internal Paper, Telecom Australia, Strategic Analysis Group, Melbourne.

Roberts, M.M. 1988, 'Introduction', in *Campus Networking Strategies*, ed. C. Arms, EDUCOM Strategy Series on Information Technology, Digital Press, New York, 1–16.

Roberts, P. 1989, 'Making the ground rules for a hi-tech city', *Australian Financial Review*, 14 June.

Robinson, A. 1980, 'Giant corporations from tiny chips grow' *Science*, **208**, 480–4.

Robinson, S. 1986, 'Analysing the information economy: Tools and techniques', *Information Processing and Management*, **22**, 183–202.

Robson, B.T. 1986, 'Coming full circle: London versus the rest, 1890–1980', in *Regional Cities in the UK*, ed. G. Gordon, Harper & Row, London.

Rogers, T.J. 1988, 'Return to the microcosm', letter to the Editor, *Harvard Business Review*, July–August, 139–40.

Roobeek A.J.M. 1987, 'The crisis of Fordism and the rise of new technological paradigms', *Futures*, April, 14–27.

Rosenberg, N. & Frischtak, C.R. 1983, 'Long waves and economic growth: A critical appraisal', *The American Economic Review*, **73**(2), 146–57.

Ross, M.H. 1982, 'Fibre optic networks or communication satellites – alternatives?', in *International Telecommunications*, ed. K.L. Lancaster, Lexington, Toronto.

Rothenberg, N. 1982, *Inside the Black Box: New Technology and Economics*, University Press, New York.

Rothwell, P., Dodgson, M. & Lowe, S. 1988, *Technology Transfer Mechanisms: Part I The UK: Part II The USA, Japan, France, Germany and the European Community*, Report to the National Economic Development Office, SPRU, London, mimeo. Published in edited and abbreviated form by the National Economic Development Office 1989, as *Technology Transfer Mechanisms in the UK and Leading Competition Nations*, Innovation Working Party, NEDO, London.

Rothwell, R. 1989, 'Small firms, innovations and industrial change', *Small Business Economics*, **1**(1), 51–64.

Rothwell, R. & Beesley, M. 1987, *United Kingdom Research and Technology Development Policy: Some Regional Impacts*, Report to STRIDE Committee, Research and Technology Development Project, European Commission, Brussels, February.

Rothwell R. & Zegveld, W. 1981, *Industrial Innovation and Public Policy*, Frances Pinter, London.

Rothwell, R. & Zegveld, W. 1985, *Reindustrialization and Technology*, M.E. Sharpe Inc., Armonk, New York.

Rubin, M.R. 1988, 'The secondary information sector: Its meaning, measurement and importance', in *The Cost of Thinking*, eds M. Jussawalla *et al.*, Ablex, Norwood.

Rugman, A.M. 1981, *Inside the Multinationals: The Economics of Internal Markets*, Croom Helm, London.

Rummel, R.J. 1970, *Applied Factor Analysis*, Northwestern, Evanston.

Russell, J. 1986, *On Base Modernization*, Michigan Technology Deployment Service, Lansing, Michigan.

Sabel, C. 1989, 'Flexible specialisation and the reemergence of regional economies', in *Reversing Industrial Decline?*, eds P. Hirst & J. Zeitlin, St. Martin's Press, New York, 17–70.

Sabel, C. & Zeitlin, J. 1985, *Historical Alternatives to Mass Production: Politics, Markets and Technology in Nineteenth Century Industrialization*, Past and Present No. 109.

Sack, R. 1984, 'The societal conception of space', in *Geography Matters*, eds D. Massey & J. Allen, Cambridge University Press, Mass.

Sakamoto, N. 1988, 'The intelligent revolution comes to Japan,' *Japan Update*, Winter, 11–16.

Sakashita Yuko 1987, 'Satellite city', *Look Japan*, **14**(6), 26.

Salomon, I. 1985, 'Telecommunications and travel: Substitution or modified mobility?', *Journal of Transport Economics & Policy*, **19**(3), 219–35.

Salomon, I. 1986, 'Telecommunications and travel relationships: A review', *Transportation Research*, **20**(3), 223–38.

Salomon, I. 1988a, 'Transportation–telecommunication relationships and regional development', in *Informatics and Regional Development*, eds M. Giaoutzi & P. Nijkamp, Avebury, Aldershot, 90–102.

Salomon, I. 1988b, 'Geographical variations in telecommunications systems: The implications for location of activities', *Transportation*, **14**, 311–27.

Sanuki, T. 1980, 'The Shinkansen and the future image of Japan', in *The Shinkansen High-speed Network in Japan: Proceedings of an IIASA Conference, Luxenburg, 27–30 June 1977*, eds A. Straszak & R. Tuch, Pergamon, Oxford, 227–51.

Sapir, A. 1982, 'Trade in services: Policy issues for the eighties', *Columbia Journal of World Businesses*, Autumn, 77–83.

Sarson, R. 1989, 'Taking the credit with paperless trading', *The Guardian (London)*, 9 February, 31.

Sassen, S. 1988, *The Mobility of Labour and Capital*, Cambridge University Press, New York.

Sauvant, T. 1987, *International Trade in Services: The Politics of Transborder Data Flows*, Westview Press, Boulder.

Savelberg, F. & Vogelar, H. 1987, 'Determinants of northern high-speed railway', *Transportation*, **14**, 97–112.

Saxenian, A. 1980, *Silicon Chips and Spatial Structure*, Working Paper No. 345, Institute of Urban & Regional Development, University of California, Berkeley.

Saxenian, A. 1989a, 'The cheshire cat's grin: Innovation, regional development and the Cambridge case', *Economy and Society*, **18**(4).

Saxenian, A. 1989b, The political economy of industrial adaption in Silicon Valley, unpublished dissertation, Department of Political Science, Massachusetts Institute of Technology.

Scherer, F.M., Beckenstein, A., Kaufer, E. & Murphy, R.D. 1975, *The Economics of Multi-plant Operation: An International Comparisons Study*, Harvard University Press, Cambridge, Mass.

Schiller, D. 1985, 'The emerging global grid: Planning for what?', *Media, Culture and Society*, **7**, 105–25.

Schimank, H. & Scholz, L. 1987, 'Innovationdynamic der Deutschen Wirtschaft in der Achtzieger Jahren', in *IFO-Schnelldienst*, **1–2/87**, 20–8.

Schnaars, S.P. 1989, *Megamistakes. Forecasting and the Myth of Rapid Technological Change*, The Free Press, New York.

Schoenberger, E. 1987, 'Technological and organizational change in automobile production: Spatial implications', *Regional Studies*, **21**(3), 199–214.

Schott, J.J. 1989, 'US–Canada free trade: Implications for the GATT', *Economic Impact*, **66**, 43–9.

Schumpeter, J. 1911, *The Theory of Economic Development*, Harvard University Press, Cambridge, Mass.

Schumpeter, J. 1939, *Business Cycles*, McGraw-Hill, New York (reprinted by Porcupine Press, Philadelphia, 1982).

Schumpeter, J. 1942, *Capitalism, Socialism and Democracy*, Harper & Row, New York.

Schwamm, H. & Merciai, P. 1985, *The Multinationals and the Services*, Institute for Research & Information on Multinationals, Geneva.

Science Council of Canada 1989, *Enabling Technologies: Springboard to a Competitive Future*, Minister of Supply and Services, Ottawa.

Scott, A.J. 1983a, 'Industrial organization and the logic of intrametropolitan location: I. Theoretical considerations', *Economic Geography*, **59**(3), 233–50.

Scott, A.J. 1983b, 'Industrial organization and the logic of intrametropolitan location: II. A case study of the printed circuits industry in the Greater Los Angeles region', *Economic Geography*, **59**(4) 343–67.

Scott, A.J. 1986, 'Industrial organization and the location: Division of labour, the firm and spatial process', *Economic Geography*, **62**(3), 215–31.

Scott, A.J. 1988a, *Metropolis: From the Division of Labor to Urban Form*, University of California Press, Berkeley.

Scott, A.J. 1988b, *New Industrial Spaces*, Pion, London.

Scott, A.J. & Angel, D.P. 1987, 'The U.S. semiconductor industry: A locational analysis', *Environment & Planning A*, **19**, 875–912.

Scott, A.J. & Angel, D.P. 1988, 'The global assembly-operations of U.S. semiconductor firms: A geographic analysis', *Environment & Planning A*, **20**, 1047–67

Scott, A.J. & Storper, M. 1988, 'Flexible production systems and regional development: The rise of new industrial spaces in North America and western Europe', *International Journal of Urban & Regional Research*, **12**(2), 171–86.

Seisan kozoka 1988, *MFP koso ni tsuite*, Seisan kozoka (Industrial Structure Council), Tokyo.

Sellgren, J. 1987, 'Local economic development and local initiatives in the mid-1980s', *Local Government Studies*, November/December, 51–68.

Senn, L. & Bramanti, A. 1988, 'Le cas de Bergame', *Colloque GREM III*, GREMI, Ascona.

Siegel, B. 1987, *The Internationalization of Service Transactions: The Role of Foreign Direct Investment on International Trade in Services*, The Institute for Research on Public Policy, Series on Trade in Services, Victoria, British Columbia.

Siler, C. 1989, 'How to bypass your friendly phone company', *Forbes*, 21 August, p. 88.

Smilor, R.W., Kozmetsky, G. & Gibson, D.V. 1988, *Creating the Technopolis: Linking Technology Commercialization and Economic Development*, Ballinger, Cambridge, Mass.

SNCF 1986, *The French TGV System – Achievements to Date and Future Developments*, SNCF, Paris.

SNP 1988, *Switched Network Products Report 1988*, Telecom Australia, mimeo.

Solo, R. 1985, 'Across the industrial divide: A review article', *Journal of Economic Issues*, **1**, 829–36.

Sperling, D. 1988, *New Transportation Fuels: A Strategic Approach to Technological Change*, University of California Press, Berkeley.

Stanback, T. 1985, 'The changing fortunes of metropolitan economies', in *High Technology, Space and Society (Urban Affairs Annual Reviews, Vol. 28)*, ed. M Castells, Sage, Beverly Hills.

Staple, G.C. & Mullins, M. 1989, 'Telecom traffic statistics – MiTT matter', *Telecommunications Policy*, **13**(2), 105–28.

Starr, P. 1987, 'The limits of privatisation', *Proceedings of the Academy of Political Science*, **36**(3), 124–37.

The State of Small Business: A Report of the President 1984, US Government Printing Office, Washington, DC.

The State of Small Business: A Report of the President 1987, US Government Printing Office, Washington, DC.

Steindl, J. 1965, *Random Processes and the Growth of Firms: A Study of the Pareto Law*, Hafner Publishing Company, New York.

Steinle, W.J. 1988, 'Telematics and regional development in Europe: Theoretical considerations and empirical evidence', in *Informatics and Regional Development*, eds M. Giaoutzi & P. Nijkamp, Avebury, Aldershot, 72–89.

Stern, M. 1985, *Trade and Investment in Services: Canada/US Perspectives*, Ontario Economic Council, Toronto.

Stigler, G.J. 1961, 'The economics of information', *Journal of Political Economy*, **69**, 213–25.

Stigler, G.J. 1951, 'The division of labor is limited by the extent of the market', *Journal of Political Economy*, **59**(3), 185–93.

Stöhr, W. 1986, 'Territorial innovation complexes', in *Milieux Innovateurs en Europe*, ed. P. Aydalot, GREMI, Paris, 29–54.

Stoker, G. 1988, *The Politics of Local Government*, Macmillan, London.

Stonier, T. 1983, *The Wealth of Information. A Profile of the Post-industrial Economy*, Methuen, London.

Stonier, T., Jayaweera, N. & Robertson, J. 1989, *The New Economics of Information*, The New Economics Foundation, London.

Storper, M. 1985, 'Oligopoly and the product cycle: Essentialism in economic geography', *Economic Geography*, **61**(3), 260–82.

Storper, M. 1989, 'The transition to flexible specialization in the US film industry', *Cambridge Journal of Economics*, **13**, 273–305.

Storper, M. & Christopherson, S. 1987, 'Flexible specialisation and regional industrial agglomeration: The case of the US motion picture industry', *Annals of the Association of American Geographers*, **77**, 104–17.

Storper, M. & Scott, A.J. 1988, 'The geographical foundations and social regulation of flexible production complexes', in *Territory and Social Reproduction*, eds J. Wolch & M. Dear, Allen & Unwin, London.

Storper, M. & Walker, R.A. 1983, 'The theory of labour and the theory of location', *International Journal of Urban and Regional Research*, **7**, 1–41.

Stowsky, J. 1987, *The Weakest Link: Semiconductor Equipment, Linkages, and the Limits to International Trade*, Berkeley Roundtable on the International Economy (BRIE) Working Paper, University of Claifornia, Berkeley.

Sunman, H. 1986, *France and Her Technopoles*, CSP Economic Publications Ltd, Cotswold, Hoely Park, Cardiff, UK.

Sweeney, G.P. 1982, *Information and the Transformation of Society*, North Holland, Amsterdam.

Sweeney, G.P. 1985, *Study on Information Networks Designed to Support Technological Innovation in the Less-Favoured Regions of the Community*, Institute for Industrial Research and Standards, Dublin, April.

Swyngedouw, E.A. 1989, 'Perspectives on a "regulation approach" to spatial change and innovation: A case-study of the Hasselt/Genk metropolitan region', in *Urban Change and Innovation*, eds P. Nykamp & H.J. Ewers, Gower, Aldershot, London.

Takac, P. & Zinn, D. 1988, *Electronic Data Interchange in Australia: Markets, Opportunities and Developments*, RMIT Centre for Technology, Policy and Management, Melbourne.

Tanaka Kakuei 1973, *Building a New Japan: A Plan for Remodelling the Japanese Archipelago*, trans. Simul International of Nippon retto kaizo-ron, Simul Press, Tokyo, Japan.

Tatsuno, S. 1986, *The Technopolis Strategy: Japan, High Technology, and the Control of the 21st Century*, Prentice-Hall, New York.

Tatsuno, S. 1988, 'Building a Japanese technostate: MITI's technopolis program', in *Changing the Technopolis: Linking Technology*, eds R.W. Smilor, G. Kozmetsky & D.V. Gibson, *Commercialization and Economic Development*, Ballinger Publishing Co., Cambridge, Mass., 3–22.

Taylor, J. & Williams, H. 1988, Telematics and the local government mission, Paper presented to the Workshop on Local Government: Managing in an Uncertain Environment, European Group of Public Administration, Leuven, Belgium, September.

Teece, D.J. 1985, 'Multinational enterprise, internal governance and industrial organisation', *American Economic Review*, **75**(2), 233–8.

Teece, D.J. 1986, 'Profiting from technological innovation: Implications for integration, collaboration, licensing and public policy', *Research Policy*, **15**, 285–305.

Teece, D.J. 1987, 'Capturing value from technological innovation: Integration, strategic partnering, and licensing decisions', in *Technology and Global Industry*, eds B.B. Guile & H. Brooks, National Academy Press, Washington, DC.

Terasaka Akinobu, Wakabayashi Yoshiki, Nakabayashi Itsuki & Abe Kazutoski 1988, 'The transformation of regional systems in an information-oriented society', *Geographical Review of Japan*, **61**(B)(1), 159–73.

Thomas, G. & Miles, I. 1988, *New Interactive Services in the UK*, Report to the Leverhulme Trust, SPRU, mimeo (in press with Longmans, Harlow as *Telematics in Transition*, 1990).

Thomas, G. & Miles, I. 1989, 'Telecommunications services' in *Technology Strategy and the Firm*, ed. M Dodgson, Longman, London.

Thomas, J.N. 1987, 'Innovation et territoire', *Revue d'Économie Régionale et Urbaine*, 3, 379–419.

Thompson, W. 1975, 'Internal and external factors in the development of urban economies', in *Regional Policy: Readings in Theory and Applications*, eds J. Friedmann & W. Alonso, MIT Press, Cambridge, 201–20.

Thorgren, B. 1970, 'How do constant systems affect regional development?', *Environment & Planning A*, **2**, 409–27.

Thrift, N. 1987, 'The urban geography of international commercial capital', in *Global Restructuring and Territorial Development*, eds J. Henderson & M. Castells, Sage Publications, Beverley Hills.

Thrift, N., Leyshon, A. & Daniels, P. 1987, *Sexy Greedy: The New International Financial System, The City of London and the South East of England*, Working Paper on Producer Services No. 8, University of Liverpool, October.

Thwaites, A. 1982, 'Evidence of product innovation in the economic planning region of Great Britain', in *Technology: A Key Factor for Regional Development*, ed. D Maillat, Georgia Publishing Company, Saint-Saphoria.

Toda, T. 1987, 'The location of high-technology industry and the technopolis plan in Japan', in *The Spatial Impact of Technological Change*, eds J.F. Brotchie, P. Hall & P.W. Newton, Croom Helm, London, New York, Sydney.

Tolliday, S. & Zeitlin, J.L. (eds) 1987, *The Automobile Industry and its Workers: Between Fordism and Flexibility*, St. Martin's Press, New York.

Tsuchiya, M. 1988, 'Strategic use of information systems among Japanese private corporations', in *Information Systems for Government and Business: Trends, Issues, Challenges*, ed. H. Sazanami, United Nations Centre for Regional Development, Nagoya, Japan, 517–22.

Tullock, G. 1976, *The Vote Motive*, Hobart Paperback 9, IEA.

Tyler, G. 1988, 'Videoconferencing. New lease of life', *Communications Management*, 25–27 October.

United Nations Committee on Trade & Development (UNCTAD) 1989, *Trade and Development Report, 1988*, United Nations, New York.

United Nations 1983, *Salient Features and Trends in Foreign Direct Investment*, United Nations, New York.

US Congress, Office of Technology Assessment 1985, *Automation of America's Offices*, OTA-CIT-287, December, US Government Printing Office, Washington, DC.

US Department of Commerce 1988, *NTIA Telecom 2000*, National Telecommunications and Information Administration, October.

US Government 1983, *U.S. National Study on Trade in Services*, Office of the U.S. Trade Representative, Washington, DC.

Valentine, I.R. 1987, 'The X.400 interworking experience', in *Electronic Message Systems 87: Proceedings of the International Conference, London, November 1987*, Online Publications, London, 127–32.

van der Ryn, S. & Calthorpe, P. (eds) 1986, *Sustainable Communities: A New Design Synthesis for Cities, Suburbs and Towns*, Sierra Club Books, San Francisco.

Vernon, R. 1963, *Metropolis 1985*, Doubleday Anchor Books, Garden City, New York.

Vernon, R. 1966, 'International investment and international trade in the product cycle', *Quarterly Journal of Economics*, **80**(2), 190–207.

Vernon, R. 1979, 'The product cycle hypothesis in a new international environment', *Oxford Bulletin of Economics & Statistics*, **41**(4), 255–67.

Vervest, P.H.M. 1986, *Innovation in Electronic Mail: Towards Open Information Networks – Perspectives on Innovation Policy*, North Holland, Amsterdam.

VFT 1988, Concept Report, VFT Joint Venture, Canberra.

VFT 1989, Progress Report, VFT Joint Venture, Canberra.

Vickery, G. 1986, 'Technology transfer revisited: Recent trends and developments', *Prometheus*, **4**(1), 25–49.

Vitalari, N.P. & Venkatesh, A. 1987, 'In-home computing and information services: A twenty-year analysis of the technology and its impacts', *Telecommunications Policy*, March, 65–81.

von Hippel, E. 1986, 'Lead users: A source of novel product concepts', *Management Science*, **32**, 791–805.

Voros, G.L. 1989, 'Forecasting the future for facsimile', *Business Communications Review*, **19**(1), 44–6.

Walker, R. 1985, 'Technological determination and determinism: Industrial growth and location,' in *High Technology, Space and Society*, ed. M. Castells, Sage Publications, Beverly Hills, 226–64.

Walker, R.A. 1989, Regulation, flexible specialization, and capitalist development: The forces of production in the dynamics of industrial change, Paper presented to the International Symposium on Regulation, Innovation, and Spatial Development, University of Wales, Cardiff, UK, 13–15 September.

Webber, M.M. 1964, 'The urban place and nonplace urban realm, in *Explorations into Urban Structure*, eds M.M. Webber, J.W. Dyckman, D.L. Foley, A.Z. Guttenberg, W.L. Wheaton & C.B. Wurster, University of Pennsylvania Press, Philadelphia, 79–153.

Weber, A. 1909, *Theory of the Location of Industry*, trans. C.J. Friedrich, University of Chicago Press, Chicago.

Weber, A.F. 1969, *The Growth of Cities in the Nineteenth Century: A Study in Statistics*, Greenwood Press, New York.

Wheeler, J.O. & Mitchelson, R.L. 1989a, 'Information flows among major metropolitan areas in the United States', *Annals of the Association of American Geographers*, **79**(4), 523–43.

Wheeler, J.O. & Mitchelson, R.L. 1989b, 'Atlanta's role as an information center: Intermetropolitan spatial links', *Professional Geographer*, **41**(2), 181.

Whitehorn, C. 1989, 'The network comes to town', *Mercury* (The Magazine for Customers of Mercury Communications Ltd), Spring, 6–7.

Wild, J.P., Brotchie, J.F. & Nicolson, A.J. 1985, 'A high speed rail link – Sydney–Canberra–Melbourne', Proceedings of the Conference on Rail Engineering, Brisbane, Institute of Engineers, Australia, pp. 211–16.

Williams, H & Charles, D. 1986, *The Electronics Industry in North East England*, Report to Department of Trade and Industry (Regional Office).

Williams, K., Cutler, T., Williams, J. & Haslam, C. 1987, 'The end of mass production?', *Economy & Society*, **16**(3), 405–39.

Williamson, O.E. 1975, *Markets and Hierarchies: Analysis and Anti-Trust Implications*, The Free Press, New York.

Williamson, O.E. 1985, *The Economic Institutions of Capitalism*, The Free Press, New York.

Willinger, M. & Zuscovitch, E. 1988, 'Towards the economics of information intensive production systems: The case of advanced materials', in *Technical Change and Economic Theory*, eds G. Dosi *et al.*, Frances Pinter, London.

Wilson, R., Ashton, P. & Egan, T. 1980, *Innovation, Competition, and Government Policy in the Semiconductor Industry*, Heath, Lexington, Mass.

Wolfson, M. & Leckie, N. 1988, *The Distribution of Income Among Families and Workers 1967–1986*, Paper prepared for the Economic Council of Canada.

Zamanillo, D.G. 1985, 'Connection of facsimile terminals in an ISDN field trial environment', in *Data Communication in the ISDN Era*, ed. Y. Perry, Elsevier, Amsterdam.

Zorkoczy, P. 1984, *Information Technology*, Van Nostrand Reinhold, New York.

Zwart, P. 1989, *Fastpac and GIS/LIS Telecommunication Needs*, Internal Paper, Telecom Australia, Melbourne.

Zwart, P. & Newton, P.W. (in press), 'The next revolution', *Journal of the Urban and Regional Systems Association*, **2**.

INDEX